Love and Liberty

LOVE AND LIBERTY.

A THRILLING

NARRATIVE OF THE FRENCH REVOLUTION OF 1792.

BY

ALEXANDER DUMAS.

AUTHOR OF "THE COUNT OF MONTE CRISTO," "THE THREE GUARD-MEN," "TWENTY
YEARS AFTER," "BRAGELONNE, THE SON OF ATHOS," "THE CHEVALIER,"
"THE MEMOIRS OF A PHYSICIAN," "ADVENTURES OF A MARQUIS," "CAMILLE,
OR, THE FATE OF A COQUETTE," "FORTY FIVE GUARDSMEN," "LOUISE
LA VALLIERE," "COUNTESS OF CHARNY," "QUEEN'S NICKLACE,"
"THE IRON HAND," "THE IRON MASK," "ANDRE DE TAVERNEY,"
"EDMOND DANTES," "SIX YEARS LATER," ETC., ETC., ETC.

"MARCH ON! MARCH ON! OH CHILDREN OF THE LAND,
THE DAY, THE HOUR OF GLORY, IS AT HAND!"

PHILADELPHIA:
T. B. PETERSON & BROTHERS;
306 CHESTNUT STREET.

ALEXANDER DUMAS' GREAT WORKS.

COUNT OF MONTE CRISTO.	$1 50	*MEMOIRS OF A PHYSICIAN*	$1 00
THE IRON MASK	1 00	*THE QUEEN'S NECKLACE.* .	1 00
LOUISE LA VALLIERE	1 00	*SIX YEARS LATER*	1 00
ADVENTURES OF MARQUIS.	1 00	*COUNTESS DE CHARNY.* . ..	1 00
DIANA OF MERIDOR.	1 00	*ANDREE DE TAVERNEY* .	1 00
THE THREE GUARDSMEN....	75	*FORTY-FIVE GUARDSMEN* .	75
TWENTY YEARS AFTER . .	75	*THE IRON HAND..*	75
BRAGELONNE, SON OF ATHOS	75	*THE CHEVALIER.*	1 00
CAMILLE, CAMELIA LADY....	1 50	*THE CONSCRIPT*	1 50

Above are in paper cover, or in cloth, at $1.75 each.

EDMOND DANTES	75	*MAN WITH FIVE WIVES*	75
THE FALLEN ANGEL..	75	*THE TWIN LIEUTENANTS*	75
FELINA DE CHAMBURE	75	*ANNETTE, LADY OF PEARLS*	50
THE HORRORS OF PARIS ..	75	*MOHICANS OF PARIS* . .	50
SKETCHES IN FRANCE	75	*GEORGE; OR THE PLANTER*	
ISABEL OF BAVARIA .	75	*OF THE ISLE OF FRANCE*	50
THE CORSICAN BROTHERS	50	*THE MARRIAGE VERDICT...*	50
THE COUNT OF MORET.	50	*BURIED ALIVE..........* . .	25

CONTENTS.

Prologue.

A MAN OF THE PEOPLE.

(RENE BESSON)

CONTENTS. 21

LOVE AND LIBERTY.

Prologue.

CHAPTER I.

HOW M. DUMAS CAME TO WRITE THESE MEMOIRS.

Of all the remarkably interesting events connected with the French Revolution, perhaps the one most worthy of notice is the flight of Louis XVI, and his capture at Varennes.

At the time when I determined to take the trip of which I will give you some details, and which put me in possession of the memoirs I am about to publish—that is to say, about the 19th of June, 1856—I had read almost all that had been written concerning the above-mentioned flight.

I wish to start from Châlons, because from the fact of the King being recognized there, came the train of events which ended at Varennes on the evening of his arrest.

The capture of Louis at Varennes was the culminating point of royalty. For although it took seven hundred and four years to arrive at Varennes, it took but nineteen months to descend from Varennes to the Place de la Revolution.

It is not because the heads of three persons, who were in the carriage that took royalty to the precipice, fell on the scaffold, that we mark out the event as the greatest in the French Revolution, and, indeed, in the whole history of France. No! It is because the arrest of the King in

(23)

the little town of Varennes, unknown on the 22nd of June, and on the morrow fatally immortalized, was the source of the political convulsions which have since occurred.

My resolution to go to Varennes once taken, I started from Paris on the 19th of June, 1856, and on the 20th of the same month, at one o'clock next morning, I arrived at Châlons.

I was, as you know, in search of details actually seen by eye-witnesses. I soon discovered two old men who could give me the necessary information. One was a Monsieur Ricaise, at Châlons—one of the postilions who drove the King; the other, Monsieur Mathieu, notary, at St. Menehould, who had seen the horses changed at the moment that Drouet recognized the King.

But it was especially necessary to discover some one at Varennes who remembered some incidents connected with the affair; because at Varennes occurred the most dramatic part of the whole catastrophe

I first asked a keeper of the records whether he knew any one who had seen the King, and assisted to arrest him?

He mentioned Colonel Réné Besson.

I asked him to give me his address.

"I will do better," said he,—"I will take you to him."

At the very moment that we entered by the Rue de l'Horloge, that place where Louis XVI was arrested, which, singularly enough, has the shape of the axe of the guillotine, my guide put his hand on my shoulder.

"Eh!" said he; "here is the very man we want."

And he showed me, at the corner of the Place Latry and the Rue de la Basse, a fine old man, warming himself in the rays of the sun, and sitting in a large arm-chair before his door.

It was Colonel Réné Besson.

We drew near to him.

Imagining that we had some business with him, he arranged himself more comfortably in his chair, and waited an explanation.

"Ah, ah! is it you, Monsieur Leduc?" said he.

"Yes, Colonel, it is I; and in good company, too, as you may see," my companion replied.

"Colonel," I call on you in right of being the son of

one of your old companions in arms; for you took a part
in the Egyptian campaign, under General Desaix?"

"Yes, sir, I did," answered he.

'The fact of being the son of an old companion in
arms," I continued, "and of bearing the name of the conqueror of Murad Bey, induced me to take the liberty of
calling on you, and asking for information on certain points.
To commence. Were you at the battle of Valmy?"

"I was with my regiment six days before, on the 2nd of
September; and I just missed leaving my bones at La
Force, in trying to rescue a woman—a princess, I should
say."

"The Princess Lamballe?"

"Exactly so"

"At this period, I was living then, in the Rue Saint
Honoré with the carpenter, Duplay."

"You have seen Robespierre, then?"

"Just as I have you. It was I who made the table on
which he wrote the greater part of his speeches."

"And Danton?"

"Danton! It was he who enrolled me on the 2nd of
September. But I knew Danton, as you say, and Camilles
Desmoulins, Saint Just, and afterwards, later on, the Duke
D'Enghien, and even Marshal Ney."

"You have seen the Duke D'Enghien?"

"I was secretary to the Minister of War who sentenced
him."

"And also Marshal Ney?"

"It was he who made me lieutenant-colonel in the
retreat from Moscow."

"I will never leave you, Colonel; I will be your secretary, and we will write your memoirs."

"You are too late," said he, laughing; "my memoirs are
already three-fourths finished"

"What? Do you mean to say you have written——"

"Oh, simply to amuse myself: and there is my secretary.
Hush!"

At this moment the door opened, and a beautiful girl of
seventeen or eighteen came towards us.

"Is that your secretary?" I asked.

"Yes; Marie, my dear little granddaughter." Bow to
Monsieur. You ought to, after the sleepless nights you
have passed through thinking of him."

"I?" said the girl, blushing. "I do not know the gentleman!"

"But you know 'Monte Christo' and the 'Three Musketeers?'"

"Monsieur Dumas! Is it possible?" cried she.

"Yes, Monsieur Dumas. You see that you know him."

"Oh, sir, I am so glad to see you!"

"You will be my accomplice, then, against the Colonel?"

"Against my grandfather?"

"Yes. He has written some memoirs"

"I know that. It is I who write from his dictation."

"Ah! they are worth reading."

"Oh, grandpapa, Monsieur Dumas says that your memoirs are worth reading!"

"If he wishes to read them, I shall not hinder him," said the Colonel."

"Will you really permit me, sir?"

"If I refused you, I should be attaching too much importance to them."

"Colonel, I am like the gamin of Paris of Monsieur Vanderburch—I should like to embrace you'

"Embrace my secretary; that will give more pleasure to both of you."

I looked at Marie and she blushed as red as a cherry.

"Mademoiselle!" I said, imploringly.

She held up her cheeks to me.

I took her hands in mine, and looked at her intently.

"Has Mademoiselle," I asked the Colonel, "a page in your memoirs?"

"The last—a white page But Marie has something to tell me. What is it, my child?"

"That supper is ready, grandpapa'

"You hear. Have you an appetite?"

"Unfortunately, I have just dined."

"I should have liked to clink glasses with you."

"Will you allow me to breakfast with you to-morrow, instead? You see, I am taking a liberty with you already. Mademoiselle can give me the memoirs this evening. I will read them to-night, and return them to-morrow."

"What! read them to-night? How many pages are there, Marie?"

"Seven or eight hundred, grandfather," replied the young girl.

"Seven or eight hundred pages! If you will permit me, I will copy them"

Well, the Colonel allowed me to copy from his manuscript all that had reference to the arrest of the King at Varennes; and when he died, left me sole possessor of his memoirs.

Colonel Réné Besson has been gathered to his fathers three months since, at the good old age of eighty-seven. He died, on a beautiful sunlit afternoon, when the mellow tints of autumn were melting into the snowy wreaths of winter. Peace be with him.

Eight days after his death, I received the manuscript, with a letter from Marie, who has become one of the most charming girls I ever met with

The manuscript I now publish, is that of Colonel Réné de Besson; and I give it the title that was chosen by him.

(Signed)　　ALEXANDRE DUMAS.

A MAN OF THE PEOPLE.

(RENE BESSON.)

CHAPTER I.

CONCERNING HIS PARENTAGE AND EARLY YOUTH.

I was born in the village of Islettes, on the banks of a little river called the Biesme, in the Forest of Argonne, situated between St. Menehould and Clermont, on the 14th of July, in the year 1775.

I never had the happiness to experience a mother's love; she survived but a few days after my birth. My father, who was a poor carpenter, out-stayed her loss but five years

At five years of age, therefore, I was an orphan, without a friend in the world.

I am wrong and ungrateful to say that. I had one—my uncle, my mother's brother. who had the post of keeper in the Forest of Argonne. His wife, on my mother's death, supplied her place; and he, on the death of my father, found me bread.

My father died so poor, that all had to be sold to pay his little debts, with the exception of his box of carpenter's tools, which had been taken to Father Descharmes (that was my uncle's name), and placed out of sight in a little room belonging to me.

The Forest of Argonne was Government property, and was preserved for the pleasure of the nobles attendant on the Court; but that did not hinder the young people of the environs from coming secretly with the keepers, to enjoy a little sport with the deer and the hares.

There was one, who took part in these hunting parties, whom I knew well—Jean Baptiste Drouet, son of a post-master at St. Menehould; also William, a friend of his; and one Billaut, who afterwards took the name of his native place, and called himself Billaut Varennes.

All three were to acquire a certain celebrity in the middle of those revolutionary movements, still hidden in the future.

Certain young noblemen, by very special favor received privileges of game denied to the outer world.

Amongst the number of those young nobles, was M. de Dampierre, the Count de Mannes, and the Viscount de Malmy.

The former was at this time a man of about forty-five years, the latter not over twenty.

I select these out of the number, because they will play leading parts in the events I am about to describe.

Even when I was quite a child, I learned the difference that subsisted in their characters.

Every now and then, on hearing that a herd of wild boars had been seen in the forest, or that the snow-storm had driven out the wolves, a courier would arrive from Paris, and announce " The gentlemen of the Court."

Then it was that the fun took place.

If it were summer, a tent was pitched, in which the gentlemen took their meals.

If it were winter, they stopped at St Menehould, and

put up at the "Hotel de Metz," making a rendezvous with the keepers at daybreak at a likely spot for wild boars or wolves. When there, the dogs were unleashed, and the sport commenced.

When they went away, they would leave twenty or twenty-five louis to be divided among the keepers.

In general, these nobles of the Court were exceedingly polite towards the underlings. Twice the Prince de Conde and his son, the Duke D'Enghien came.

On such occasions, being, as it were, high holiday, I would follow the sportsmen. Once when the Duke D' Enghien lost his way, I put him right, and he offered me a louis. I refused it. (I was only nine years old)

He looked at me with astonishment, and asked my name,

"Réné Besson. I am the nephew of Father Descharmes," I replied.

"Good, my boy," said he; "I won't forget thee!"

Two years afterwards the Prince came back. I was then eleven, and thought that he must have lost all remembrance of me.

But he had not; and he came to me.

"Ah, art thou not Réné Besson?" he said. "Nephew of Father Descharmes?"

"Yes, Prince."

"Then here is something for thee," said he, giving me a gun. "And this is for thy uncle," he continued, handing me a folded paper.

This paper contained the appointment of my uncle to the vacant post of chief huntsman.

As for the gun, it was a beautiful weapon, and I have carefully kept it through my career, in memory of the unfortunate Prince who gave it.

In the meantime I was growing up. I had learned to read and write indifferently well; and whilst my uncle was busy in his vocation, I used to occupy myself with carpentry, a calling for which I evinced much aptitude and taste.

I was now twelve years of age. I knew every inch of the Forest of Argonne, and I was as good a shot as any of the keepers, and my sole ambition was to take my uncle's place when he resigned, which he intended to do in four or five years.

There was a place, however, left vacant by the resignation of a keeper, which I thought would just suit me for the time; and I determined to solicit the patronage of the Duke D'Enghien.

Time passed on, and we arrived at the opening of the year 1788.

For five years we had not seen M. Drouet, for, after a quarrel with his father, he had enlisted in the Queen's Dragoons.

One fine morning, however, we heard from his friend William that Father Drouet had become reconciled to him, and had resigned to him his situation of postmaster.

One day, we saw a dragoon stop in front of our house, get off his horse, fasten his bridle to a ring, and then come tramping up to the door.

"Well, Father Descharmes," said the soldier, "haven't you a glass of wine in the house for an old friend?"

My uncle looked at him amazed.

"Ah!" said I; "don't you recognize him, uncle? It is Monsieur Jean Baptiste."

"Well, I never—so it is!" cried my uncle, coming forward with outstretched hands.

But, stopping for a moment, he added, "I beg your pardon, Monsieur Drouet."

"Pardon for what?—for remembering a friend? The fault would have been to forget him. Come, shake hands Are not all Frenchmen brothers?"

"They are; but, at the same time, there are great and small."

"Good! but, in two or three years, I will say to you, 'There are neither great nor small. All are children of one mother, and all will have their rights before man, as before heaven."

"Ha! Is that the sort of schooling they give you in the Queen's Dragoons, Monsieur Jean Baptiste?"

"Not only in the Queen's Dragoons, but in all other regiments, old Nimrod."

My uncle took three glasses from the cupboard, filled two, and half-filled the other for me.

Drouet took up his glass.

"To the nation!" said he.

"What is that word?" inquired my uncle.

"It is a new one, which I hope will yet gain the rights

of the middle classes. That youngster there; what are you going to do with him?"

"Make him my successor."

Diouet shook his head

"My good old Descharmes!" said he, "you belong to the past. Better far an independent and honorable position for a man, than to wear a livery which, no matter how gay it is, puts you at the mercy of the first whipper-snapper that comes. I thought René was a carpenter?"

"So I am, Monsieur Jean Baptiste; but I only play at joiner work."

"Nay, look you here!" said my uncle, proud to be able to show some of my handiwork. "Here is a wardrobe the youngster has made."

Diouet went forward, and examined the construction in question with more interest than it deserved.

"Good—very good!" he said. "Go on as you are doing, my boy; and, believe me, it is far better to work for the public, than to be a game-keeper dependent on a prince, liable to be turned away should a wild boar make an unforseen bolt, or a wolf force the line of beaters."

"But," answered I, "you must know that I have a gun, Monsieur Jean Baptiste; and a gun, too, given me by the Duke D'Enghien."

And saying this, I showed him the cherished weapon, with as much pride as my uncle had displayed in exhibiting my efforts at wardrobe making.

"A pretty gun," he said, looking at it attentively; "and I see that it bears the royal mark. If you take my advice, you will not hesitate between the plane which your father left you, and a gun which a prince gave you. The carpenter's plane is the bread-winner that the philosopher of Geneva put into the hands of his favorite pupil; and ever since the day that 'Emile' appeared, the plane has been ennobled."

"What is 'Emile,' Monsieur Jean Baptiste?" I asked.

"It is the work of one who teaches that all men are citizens together, and that all citizens are brothers. Keep your gun, René, to preserve your country, but also keep your plane to preserve your independence. Be a carpenter to the people at large, my boy; but be no one's servant, not even if he be a prince. The first opportunity I have, I will send you 'Emile' to read."

So saying, and squeezing the hand of his old friend, M. Jean Baptiste remounted his horse. As I held his stirrup he lifted me gently to his saddle bow, and placed his hand on my head.

"Réné Besson," he said, with dignity, "in the name of that grand future of liberty, with which France is even now in travail, I baptize thee citizen."

Then relinquishing me, and striking his spurs into his horse, he disappeared down the forest.

Next day a messenger came from M. Jean Baptiste Drouet, who, faithful to his promise of the night before, sent me a little book, with these words written on the first page—

"To the Citizen Réné Besson, carpenter."

The little book in question was "Emile."

<hr>

CHAPTER II.

THE FIRST SEEDS OF A POLITICAL FAITH.

When I came to examine the book which M. Jean Baptiste had sent me, and the title of which was "Emile, or Education," I sought out the chapter which had direct reference to my own case.

In the course of my search I came across the following paragraph:—

"It is my positive desire that Emilie should learn a trade. An honest one, at least, you will perhaps say. What means that? Every calling useful to the public is an honest one, is it not? I don't wish particularly that he should be a carver and gilder, neither do I particularly care that he should be an actor, or a musician. Still, let him adopt any one of those professions, or others resembling them, that he may fancy. I do not wish to fetter his will in anything, only I would rather he was a shoemaker than a poet, and would much prefer him to earn his livelihood by paving-stones than by porcelain."

I read over and over again, the paragraph which opened up this train of thought; and at last, I understood it.

Let no one be astonished that my intelligence was so slow. Taken up as I was until I had reached at this time, my fourteenth year, with the usual jog-trot of rustic occupations, my mind had remained in a sort of twilight.

I continued my reading.

"The needle and the sword can never be wielded by the same hand. If I were a king, I would only permit the ell, the wand, and the shears, to women, and to maimed men, equally feeble with the weaker sex. I would forbid callings against health, but not those which are simply laborious, or even dangerous, for those demand at once both strength and courage. Everything considered, the trade which I should like a pupil of mine to adopt of himself would be that of a carpenter."

"Ah," said I, "what a good fellow this Monsieur Rosseau is! How I do like him!"

I tackled to my book again.

"Touching a carpenter's trade, it is a tidy calling: it is useful; you can follow it in the house; it requires both skill and industry; whilst the exercise of taste is not excluded from the articles it turns out."

So, then, I was precisely in the state recommended by the author of "Emile."

Not only that, but I did not even require to learn the trade he praised; I knew it already. I read on as follows:—

"Of all states and conditions of life, the most independent is that of a mechanic. A mechanic is dependent upon his work only; he is just so much free as an agricultural laborer is a slave; for the latter can only prepare the field, and leave the product thereof to fate. A foe—a powerful neighbor—a law-suit, can deprive him of his field, in fact, that very field can be made to vex him in a thousand different ways. But, if fate disturbs a mechanic, he gathers his tools together, and, carrying his sturdy arms with him, away he goes."

At this point, I looked at my own arms, already muscular and well-developed, and I swung them in the air with pride. Evidently the man was right who wrote those lines.

I uttered a cry of joy; and rushing into my little workshop, I hugged severally to my bosom my hammers, my planes, and my chisels. Then, strong with a new strength,

2

I felt irresistibly impelled to rush off at once, and thank
M. Jean Baptiste Drouet for lending me the precious book.
St. Menehould was exactly three miles away, and it was
only eleven o'clock in the morning. I could easily be home
again by five or six, and my good uncle would not make
himself uneasy at my absence. Besides, I was quite sure
that he would approve of my errand.

<hr>

CHAPTER III.

A STRANGER OF INFUENCE TURNS UP.

OUT I set at once, taking my book with me, to read on
the way; and so interesting did I find the adventures of
" Emile," that I found myself near my friend's house
actually without being aware of it.

In the distance I could see M. Jean Baptiste superintending some postilions, who were putting fresh horses to a
carriage. He was standing on the threshold of his door.

Running up in a state of great excitement, I cried out,
" Monsieur Jean Baptiste, it's I ! "

" Well," he said, laughing; " I am quite aware of the
fact. What do you want, my boy ? "

" What do I want ? Oh, I want to thank you, and to
tell you that I will never be a keeper. The only calling
worth following is that of a carpenter, and I mean to be
one, Monsieur Drouet."

The carriage went off.

" So you have been reading ' Emile ? ' " he asked, taking
me inside.

" Yes; up to here." And I showed him page 160 of the
work.

" Bravo ! " said Monsieur Drouet. " But it is not
enough to read; you must also understand."

" Of course, M Jean Baptiste," said I. " There are
many things that I cannot understand, but I always look
to you for an explanation."

" So you are come expressly for that ? "

" No, M. Jean Baptiste. Not expressly for that, but to

thank you for your kindness. After my father, who gave me life—after my aunt and my uncle, who have fed me, I owe more to you than to any other person in the world; for has not Rousseau himself said that every man is born twice—first, physically, then intellectually? And it is you who have successfully brought me through this second birth."

I must pass over that afternoon of familiar intercourse with my mentor and my friend. Suffice it to say, that my new-born resolutions were strengthened, my eyes still more widely opened to my own wants and requirements; and when I set out on my return, I felt that, indeed, a path had been tracked for me across the yet untrodden wilderness of life.

There are few landscapes so pretty in the middle of France as that which presents itself to the eye on arriving at the Forest of Argonne.

This struck me as it had never done before, and I paused involuntarily to gaze at the scene.

At this moment two travellers came towards me, followed by a carriage slowly toiling up the ascent.

One of these strangers particularly attracted my attention. He might be about fifty years of age, of no great stature, but wiry and strongly built. He had a noble head, and his weather-beaten face was lit by the glance of an eagle. Had not the scar of a sabre wound sufficiently indicated his profession, I could have told he was a soldier from the unmistakable way in which he wore his civilian's suit.

His companion, younger and stouter, was likewise a soldier; but evidently not of the same standing.

These two men halted a moment near me, less to look at the landscape than to continue an animated conversation, in which the elder sustained the principal part.

"Yes, my dear Thévenot," he said, "I will never give in on this point. If ever France is invaded by Montmedy and Verdun, it is here that we must meet the enemy; with 20,000 soldiers I'll engage to stop a foe 80,000 strong. The Forest of Argonne is the Thermopylæ of France."

"That is to say, General," replied the other, who looked like his aide-de-camp, "if the two or three roads through the forest could be defended as easily as this one; for it is quite evident that a couple of batteries with six guns each would make this defile impracticable."

"There are only two roads," returned the General; "the one we are now pursuing, leading to Islettes; and the other, the Grand Prés road. Both these routes conjoin at Verdun."

"I thought there was a third—namely, the Chéne-Populeux road."

"I don't think that road leads through the forest at all; but I will ask our driver."

The General did so.

The bumpkin only shook his head.

"I only know," he said, "the road I'm accustomed to travel, and that's not it. Beyond that, I can't tell you anything; but," he added, nodding towards me, "if you want to know all about this part of the country, why, there's the nephew of Father Descharmes, who knows it all blindfold. Hilloa, boy! come and speak to these gentlemen!"

I approached, cap in hand, for the look of the elder traveller inspired me with respect.

"Friend," said the General, seeing that I waited till he spoke to me; "we want to know where the Chéne-Populeux road leads from, and if it takes you through the forest, or round by the outskirts?"

"It leads from Stenay, monsieur, takes round by the forest, and opens upon Voneg, at the River Aisne."

"Ah, now we have it, Thévenot; but as, so far as I can remember, the Chéne-Populeux road is only a narrow defile, I still hold my original opinion"

"Will you get in now, gentlemen?" asked the postilion. "My horses are well breathed by this time."

"Thank you, my young friend," said the General, waving his hand towards me. But just as he had his foot on the step the distant sound of an alarm-bell, violently rung, came through the stillness.

"What is that?" cried the General.

"A fire at the village of Islettes," said I. "Look! you can see the smoke above the trees!"

And, without any further speculation, off I ran towards the village. The General called after me, but I did not stop to listen.

However, before I had gone a hundred yards, the carriage rattled past me at a gallop. The General, evidently moved by a humane motive, was hastening, like myself, towards the scene of the catastrophe, where I soon arrived.

All the village was astir, and I found the General and his companion had taken command of the rustics, just as they would of an army on the field of battle.

The fire had broken out in the workshop of a cart-wright. The fiery element had attacked an adjacent shed full of wood, and threatened to reduce the neighboring house to ashes.

Now, at Islettes, fire-engines were unknown, and I need scarcely say that handing along little buckets of water from the river was by no means an effectual remedy.

"We must cut off the fire!" shouted the General.

"But how?" returned the peasants.

"I want somebody," cried the General, "who will get up upon the roof of that shed, and cut away the principal support. The post will fall, and carry the roof with it."

"Oh, yes!" said a voice, "and the somebody in question will go down with the roof!"

"Very likely!" acquiesced the General, calmly; "but the fire will be smothered, and the rest of the village saved."

At that moment, a certain passage from "Emile" flashed across my mind.

"Give me an axe!" I cried. As I spoke, I saw one leaning against a house near which I was standing.

I laid down my "Emile" and a dictionary which M. Jean Baptiste had given me; seized the axe, and rushed into the house adjacent to the shed. Already its inmates were carrying out all their little property, expecting every instant that their cottage would be in flames.

Up the little wooden stairs I rushed, and scrambled out on the roof through a sort of trap-door.

It was my first experience upon roofs; but as I had been accustomed to climbing trees up to any height, a promenade on the thatch was only child's play.

Below, all was hushed in anxiety. I could only hear the peculiar billow-like sounds of the flames, and the fall of the burning fragments as they gave way under the fire.

Presently I found myself in a dense atmosphere of smoke

and sparks. I was nearly stifled; but I knew that all eyes and hearts were fixed upon me, and that gave me strength to succeed or to die, as it might be.

Supporting myself by the chimney, I commenced to cut away a hole round about the roof-tree.

I was strong of my age, and could wield with dexterity the axe—that instrument of my adopted calling; but though at every blow the upright beam trembled—on the other hand, the advancing flame seemed to increase in volume.

There was, in a word, a battle between me and the flame, and I felt proud to have an element for my foe. All at once, the gable-end fell in with a terrible crash; the other supports of the roof being weakened by my blows, gave way, and the roof itself fell, smothering, beneath the raging flames. I flung the axe away from me, and held on like grim death to my chimney. A whirlwind of smoke and fire blotted me from the crowd below, and, half suffocated as I was, I could still hear and understand their murmur of pain and anxiety.

The crisis was over. With one last effort I struggled to my trap-door, and in another moment—I know not how—found myself safe and sound in the open air.

Friendly arms embraced me, and looking up, I saw it was the General, who held in one hand my precious books. "My boy," he said, "you are brave, and you read Rousseau · therefore I do not offer you a reward. But you will be a true man, and I embrace you."

And again he pressed me in his arms.

By this time, my uncle, and, indeed, all the village, were at my side; and whilst I was receiving their congratulations, the General and his friend had departed. No one knew who they were.

This was an important day in my life; for I had learnt to understand what was conveyed in that most beautiful of all human words—self-devotion.

CHAPTER IV.

I EDUCATE MYSELF FOR CONTINGENCIES.

NEXT day I laid up for myself a course of study—physical and intellectual In the morning I read and studied my books; during the day I worked at my carpentry; towards evening I indulged in shooting, in gymnastics, and sports of that nature; and at night I again returned to my books. I improved every day.

About a week after the events of the last chapter, M. Drouet, and two friends came to my uncle's.

M Drouet and his friends shook me by the hand. He asked me how I was getting on, and I told him all, regretting at the same time that I had no money to buy books, or get instruction in Latin.

"No money!" said Jean Baptiste. "Who hinders you from making it?"

" Making it? " I answered. " But how? "

"With your plane, of course."

" But, Monsieur Drouet, I have no customers.

" I will find them for you."

" Where? "

" To begin with, the postmaster of St. Menehould, Jean Baptiste Drouet by name. The fact is, I require a quantity of carpentry work done in my house, and you must undertake it."

" I am not good enough workman for that, Monsieur Drouet "

" But if I find you good enough? "

" Then I would not like to take your money."

" Nonsense ! I must get somebody to do it, so that is settled. Now, about the Latin. I will find you a teacher —Monsieur Fortin, the Curé of Islettes."

" How will I pay him? "

" I don't think that he would take your money."

" But I take yours, Monsieur Drouet."

" Ah, that is different Government does not pay me to make wash-hand-stands but it does pay Abbé Fortin to instruct his flock morally and intellectually."

"I should like to offer him something."

"Exactly—not as a right, but as a graceful act of
courtesy; and as I know the Father Fortin does not
despise the good things of this life, you can shoot him a
hare occasionally, or knock him up a cupboard, to keep his
preserves in."

"A thousand thanks, Monsieur Jean!"

"Listen! I have it in my mind's eye that you will be
a soldier—at all events, the education necessary for an
officer will not be thrown away. For six francs a month,
Bertrand, of Islettes, the old soldier, will teach you fencing; and, for a trifle more, Mathieu, the land surveyor, at
Clermont, will show you how to draw a plan. As for
horsemanship, I will give you the run of my stable; so,
there you are, with your life-time all mapped out. Now,
let us to the forest."

At dinner that day, the conversation turned upon politics, and particularly on the unpopularity of Marie Antoinette, the Queen. All this was Greek to me, till M Jean
Baptiste explained the situation of affairs.

Marie Antoinette, it appeared, daughter of the Austrian,
Marie Therèse, and ancient enemy of France, had been
accepted by the French people as a harbinger of union and
of peace. Very different, however, had been her influence.

In a word, Marie Therèse hoped that Louis XVI would
some day aid her to get back the provinces wrested from
her by Prussia.

Until 1778, Marie Antoinette did not meddle with affairs
of state. Up to that time, Turgot was the ruling spirit;
but, at last, he had to succumb to that famous De Calone,
who used to reply thus to the demands of the Queen:
"Madame, if it is possible, it is already done; if it is impossible, it will be done."

Misrule went on. The King, despite his impoverished
treasury, bought St. Cloud; the Queen, whilst her people
were starving, purchased Rambouillet, and lavished millions
of francs which were not her own upon her immediate favorites. Scandal arose; and when scandal gets into everybody's mouth, it is worse than truth.

M. de Calone resigned. He could not make both ends
meet.

The next Prime Minister was Brienne, a Queen's favorite; and, when he fell, Paris was illuminated from the Bastille to the Cour de la Reine

M. de Necker reigned in his stead. He was a Genevese banker, and a financier of the first force; but even he failed to see a way out of the royal bankruptcy, and it was whispered that he was going to ask the nation what it thought of matters—France was to speak.

This was the great news at my uncle's dinner-table that day, and our three guests were very merry over it, and pledged fidelity to each other however these events might turn out.

And they kept their word.

CHAPTER V.

I BREAK WITH THE ARISTOCRACY.

NEXT morning I set out for St. Menehould, to see about M. Drouet's job. He told me what he wanted, and that he should require the new furniture I was to make him to be of good, well-seasoned oak. In order that I might set about it the more easily, he paid me one hundred francs in advance; and with this prodigious sum in my pocket, I went off to select the necessary timber, when whom should I meet but Bertrand. The old soldier informed me that M. Drouet had spoken to him about giving me fencing lessons, and I arranged with him, on the spot, when I was to take them. I fact, I began that very day.

I remember well how my hand trembled with pleasure, when I grasped the foil for the first time. At the end of an hour, I knew the five parades, and could disengage decently.

"That will do for to-day," cried my master, more tired than I was myself.

I recollected something.

"Monsieur Bertrand," said I; "I shall perhaps not be able to pay you till the end of the month."

"Oh, that's all settled. Monsieur Drouet has paid me a month in advance. He said that he owed you money."

I felt a glow of emotion at this new proof of my good friend's generosity.

As I was crossing a field on my way home, I met the surveyor, M. Mathieu. My good genius had preceded me there, too: the surveyor was quite ready to impart to me the mysteries of the chain and level.

Leaving him, I went home in great glee, took my gun, and sallied forth to slaughter partridges for my Latin master. I was fortunate enough to knock over a brace of birds and a hare, which I sent the same night to the Abbé Fortin.

Next day, as I was planing away with great zeal, the Abbé himself stood before me.

" Well, my boy, you 'have sent me some game, and you must now help me to eat it. Dinner at two, and I shall be glad to see your uncle, if he will come with you."

" Oh, Monsieur l'Abbé, it is too much honor!"

" At two o'clock, mind Marguerite, the housekeeper, does not like to be kept waiting."

So saying, the worthy Curé left me.

My uncle, I found, would not be at home till the evening, so, at the hour appointed, I found myself alone, tapping at the Abbé's door, and dressed out in all my Sunday splendor

The Curé opened it himself.

" Ah, monsieur, I am so sorry to trouble you ! "

" Trouble ? Nonsense ! Only Marguerite cannot be at the door and at her kitchen stove at the same time. Talking of which, she tells me we will not have dinner till three. Now, what do you say to a first Latin lesson, as my friend Drouet tells me that you wish to learn that language."

I was only too glad to acquiesce; and, before dinner was served, I understood that there were five declensions in the Roman tongue.

During the simple repast which followed, I surveyed the Abbé's furniture with a critical eye, and a mental resolve to do it all up for him again.

Then, after having arranged about my future hours with my kind preceptor, I returned home, one step further up the ladder of progress. That very evening, we were apprised of a visit of the Count de Dampierre, the Viscount de Malmy, and some other young nobles.

Hitherto, I had been in the habit of accompanying them, dressed in regular keeper's costume, but now I stuck steadily to my carpentry work.

"Holloa, Réné!" said M. de Dampierre; "don't you go with us to-day?"

"No, Monsieur le Comte," I replied; "I have a lesson in mathematics to-day."

"What?" he exclaimed, with surprise. "Do you study mathematics?"

"Yes, and history and Latin, also."

"And is all this necessary in our days for a game-keeper?"

"I am not going to be one."

"What then?"

"I mean to be a carpenter, like 'Emile.'"

"I don't know him."

"No? It is the 'Emile' of Monsieur Jean Jacques Rousseau that I mean; but if the nation wants me, I shall be a soldier."

"What do you mean by nation?"

"I mean our country—France."

"We call that the kingdom, do we not?"

"Yes, Monsieur le Comte; but some think it high time that we should call it a nation."

"Then the mathematics are to teach you military engi-neering?"

"Yes; every officer should know how to draw a plan."

"Officer! But before you can be an officer, you must be an aristocrat."

"At present, yes; but by the time I am ready, there may be changes in the system."

"You heard that, Maimy," said M. de Dampierre, turn-ing to the Viscount.

"Yes!" replied the other, shrugging his shoulders.

"And what do you think of it all?" asked M. de Dam-pierre.

"I think that the class to which he belongs are losing their heads altogether."

I planed away vigorously, and affected not to hear. By-and-bye they strolled off to the forest, laughing, whilst I got ready to go to M. Mathieu, for my first lesson in engineering.

CHAPTER VI.

THE NATION AND THE BASTILLE.—VERDICT FOR THE FORMER

At the end of the fifteenth day the Abbé Fortin had his furniture retouched, and when three months had expired I had finished the carpentry work for M Drouet.

The work was estimated at five hundred francs, the materials alone costing a hundred and twenty; so that I received three hundred and eighty, with the compliments of my two masters on the excellency of my workmanship.

Whilst I was still engaged on the completion of the order, M. Drouet advanced me five hundred francs, to enable me to buy the wood, and at the same time, to take my lessons in the use of implements of warfare, and purchase useful books.

The warrant expected from M. Necker, for the convocation of the Etats Généraux, had appeared. For the first time, a great nation, or a great kingdom, as M. Dampierre said, admitted all its members to political rights.

No sooner had the warrant appeared (which can be translated in these words:—" All will assemble to elect; all will write their grievances in the books given to them for that purpose ") than all France thrilled, as it were, with an electric shock, and the people leapt from darkness into light.

That cry, treasured up for two centuries, becomes stronger and stronger every day. They complain that the year 1788 was barren; that the winter was bitterly cold; that the famine in the following spring was terrible.

They went to the municipality of St. Menehould, to write in the books; and my capital penmanship procured me the office of secretary.

Afterwards, they went to election. MM. Drouet, Guillaume, and Billaud exercised enormous influence.

M. Dampierre was balloted with a poor parish priest. The priest prevailed over him.

The event deceived all. The Etats, which ought to have opened on the 27th of April, were adjourned to the 4th of May.

The Court was frightened, and delayed the matter as long as it could

All France had its eyes turned to Paris. Every hour brought forth unexpected events.

On the 5th of May, the opening of the Etats, in the procession from Versailles, the King was applauded, and the Queen hissed

On the 8th of May, the three classes were changed into two—the one formed of the third class, the other of the nobility and clergy.

On the 18th of June, the assembly hall was closed by order of the King

On the 22nd of June, the oath of Jeu-de-Pauvre was taken.

This oath was the declaration of war from the third Etat against the nobility and clergy. It was the first menace direct from the people against the throne.

All in a moment, these comparatively small events ceased, and a portentous calm intervened, so to speak, as if the minor combatants held their weapons to intently watch the issue of the combat between their superiors

On the 12th of July, M. Drouet started for Paris.

It was the day of the dismissal of Necker—it was the day when Camille Desmoulins, jumping on a table in a *café*, drew his sword, and crying, "To arms!" placed the leaf of a tree in his hat.

We had no news of M. Drouet up to the 15th

On the morning of the 15th, MM Dampierre and De Valmy went out hunting, to which sport were invited two or three of their friends from Clermont and Varennes; among others, a certain Chevalier de Courtemont, whom we shall come across later on.

It was evident that the hunt was but a secondary affair, and that the real object was to meet and hear the news from Paris.

M Dampierre had heard, on the 13th, that Paris was on fire, and the Court at Versailles guarded by German troops,—Benzenval commanding, under the old Marshal de Broglie.

The theatres were shut. The dismissal of Necker had, to a certain extent, paralyzed the public mind. Statues of him and of the Duke of Orleans were covered with crape, and paraded through the streets of Paris.

The procession, armed with sticks, swords, and pistols, after having passed through the streets Saint Martin and Saint Honoré, arrived at the Place Vendome.

There one division stopped, and having dispersed the people, destroyed the bust of the Prince and the Duke of Orleans, and put to death a French guard who disdained to fly.

That was not all.

M. de Bezenval had put a detatchment of Swiss and four pieces of cannon in battery on the Champs Elysées, the crowd retired to the Tuileries, and the Prince de Lambese, a German, charged upon them with his cavalry, inoffensive though they were, and was the first to enter, on horseback, the gardens of the Tuileries. A barricade stopped him. From the back of that barricade, stones and bottles were thrown at him. He perceived that a group of men were shutting the gate, to take him prisoner. He ordered a retreat, and, in flying, crushed one man under his steed, and severely wounded another with a blow from his sabre.

The crowd now entered the armorers' shops, and ransacked them.

The cannons were mounted on the Bastille, which was reinforced by another detachment of Swiss.

They knew nothing more on the night of the 13th, nor on the next day.

M. Dampierre ordered that if news came in the day, it was to be delivered to my uncle.

At four o'clock the sport finished, and they returned to the house A dinner, prepared as usual, awaited them.

The companions remained at table, visibly pre-occupied; the conversation was nothing but conjectures. They spoke in strong terms of the National Assembly. They wished to have been in the place of M. Brézé, or M. de Bezenval, of M de Lambese; they were sure that they could have done better than they did.

The Queen was too good, not to have commanded the Swiss to exterminate the wretches.

At six o'clock, M. Dampierre's servant brought a despatch. It was dated the morning of the 14th.

On the night of the 13th the people had forced the doors of the Invalides, and had taken thirty thousand muskets. They had also forced the doors of the Arsenal with sledgehammers, and had taken seven or eight tons of powder. That powder had been distributed under the lamp-lights. Each man bearing a musket received fifty cartridges

The Court had ordered all the foreign regiments, useful to royalty, to be at hand, if wanted.

M de Launay, the Governor of the Bastille, who knew his unpopularity, and upon whom they could count, because of that unpopularity, had pledged himself to blow the Bastille into the air, along with half Paris, before he would surrender.

This news the companions thought good, as it promised a desperate resistance.

On the other hand, who were the people who menaced royalty? Men ignorant of the use of fire-arms, undisciplined, and without leaders, who would retreat at the first cannon-shot, and fly at the first charge

How could that rabble hold out against practised soldiers, who feared not death, but disgrace?

On mastering the despatch, M Dampierre told each guest to fill his glass; then, lifting his own, " To the victory of the King, and the extermination of the rebels!" he cried. " Drink with me, gentlemen."

" To the victory of the King, and the extermination of the rebels!" cried all, with one voice.

But before they had time to put the glasses to their lips, a furious gallop, coming from the direction of Paris, was heard; and, shouting with joy, a horseman, with a tricolor in his hat, shot past like a whirlwind, crying to M. Dampierre and his friends these words—not less terrible than those that Belshazzar read, in letters of fire, on the wall,— " The Bastille is taken! Long live the people!"

The horseman was Jean Baptiste Drouet, who was riding at full speed to announce to his friends at Varennes the news of the victory that the people had obtained over their King.

This news which he proclaimed in every city and in every village that he passed, brightened his route with a flash vivid as lightning.

CHAPTER VII.

CONCERNING THE BASTILLE.

ALL France gave one cry of joy when the news arrived that the Bastille was taken.

All the world knew the Bastille—that prison which has given its name to others.

From one end of France to the other, all shook hands, congratulating each other on the event.

And, strange to say, the Bastille was taken by those who had never entered it—in fact, it was a place of imprisonment for nobles only.

One would have thought, from the fact of their attacking it, that it was a place which they themselves had to dread.

Ah! it was a horrible den. You were not dead there; but what was worse, you were forgotten.

Your father, wife, or brother dared not speak of you, for fear they should be sent there likewise.

Once there, you no longer had a name, but a number. You died, and they buried you under a false name.

No; the King did not deprive you of your head; he was too good for that; he only forgot you.

Instead of dying in a moment, you suffered unutterable tortures for perhaps thirty years.

In the reign of Louis XVI all the rigors of prisons were softened, with the exception of the Bastille, the discipline of which was harsher than ever. In former reigns they had barred the windows; but now they also stopped the promenades in the gardens.

It is true that Louis XVI did not actually do this himself but he suffered it to be done, which is all the same.

Louis XVI did not himself shut up the garden. No; it was De Launay, who was as unpopular as he well could be.

At the Bastille all bought the places that they occupied, from the Governor down to the gaolers. Every situation was worth having, except that of the prisoners.

The Governor had sixty thousand livres salary. He made a hundred and twenty thousand by his plunders.

We have already spoken of the garden of the Bastille

open to the prisoners It was but a little plot of ground, planted, as it were, upon a bastion

A gardener offered a hundred francs a year for it; and this scoundrel, who was wringing from the pitiful allowances of the prisoners the sum of a hundred and twenty thousand francs per annum, actually, for the sake of this paltry sum, deprived the poor wretches under his rule of the breath of air that made life supportable, of the sole gleam of life that intervened 'twixt them and the tomb.

He well knew that he would never survive the capture of the Bastille—this man of iron, who had a Bastille in place of a heart.

The Governor's hundred and thirty-five barrels of powder were placed in a vault, situated in the centre of the fortress. The Bastille blown into the air would astound Paris in its ascent, and utterly destroy it in its stupendous fall. This he knew When the prison was entered by the people, he clapped a torch to the touch-string. An Invalide seized his arms; two sous-officers crossed bayonets across his breast. He snatched a knife from his belt; they took it out of his hands.

Then he demanded to be allowed to march out with the honors of war.

This demand met with a positive refusal.

At last, he would be satisfied were he allowed to depart with life alone.

Two of the conquerors of the Bastille—Hullin and Elie —promised this in the name of all.

He begged them to conduct him to the Hotel de Ville, where he had some shadow of authority.

In the meantime, whilst the people were dashing themselves against the granite and the oak, and demolishing the two stone slaves that supported the clock, and breaking open the dungeons, with the intention of liberating the prisoners confined therein, Hullin and Elie took away De Launay, hiding him as much as possible by placing themselves in front of him

But when he arrived at the gates, the Governor was recognised He had no hat, Hullin, fearless of consequences, gave him his own

Turning into the Rue St. Antoine, one who had taken part in the combat, recognised the prisoner.

3

Farther on, came some who had not yet been engaged in the siege, and who, as a matter of course, were more blood-thirsty now that the danger was over. They wished to massacre the prisoners. De Launay remained alive through the protection of Hullin and Elie.

Elie, less powerful than Hullin, was carried away by the crowd, amongst whom he was lost sight of.

At the Arcade St. Jean, Hullin himself lost sight of De Launay, but by a superhuman effort he separated the crowd, and regained him. He dragged him to some adja-cent steps, but in the effort fell. Twice did he again raise himself, only to fall again. At the third time, De Launay had disappeared. He looked for him on all sides, and at last recognised his head fixed on the extremity of a pike, and borne above the crowd.

That head Hullin would have saved, had it been possible, at the risk of his own.

During this time, the mob had released the prisoners in the Bastille.

There were nine.

Two or three, on seeing the door open, cried out that the people had come to slay them, and prepared to defend them-selves with chairs, but the intruders cried out in a loud voice, " Free ! Free ! "

One could not understand it, and fell suffocating, pressing his heart with his two hands

Another stood speechless, with his eyes fixed on space ; a venerable man was he, with a white beard descending to his breast. They took him for a spectre.

The conquerors told him that he was free.

He understood them not.

" How is Louis the Fifteenth ? " asked he.

" He has been dead fifteen years."

" How long had he been in the Bastille ? " they asked him.

" I know nothing about it," he replied

" Who are you ? "

" I am the Elder-born of Space."

He was mad.

Under the staircase, in a sort of tomb, they found two skeletons. Who were they ? No one knew. The work-men took them away, and buried them in the Cemetery of St. Paul.

All the world wished to see the Bastille. They showed Latude's ladder, that immense work of patience and of genius.

For a month the old place was not emptied

They heard sighs. A report ran about that there were hidden dungeons known only to the Government, in which the unhappy prisoners were suffered to die of hunger

The architect of the city, Citizen Palloy, was ordered to pull down the old fortress. Of the best stones, he made eighty-six models of the Bastille, which he sent to eighty-six different departments.

With the others, he built the Pont de la Revolution on which the head of Louis XVI was exposed after execution.

CHAPTER VIII.

THE DUKE D'ENGHIEN'S LAST DAY'S SPORT.

For a long time, reports of hidden dungeons and forgotten prisoners agitated Paris. Paris had had a mountain on its breast, and could not accustom itself to the deliverance from it.

To pity succeeded fear. Had they really escaped from that calamity with which De Launay had threatened them? They reported that there were underground passages from the Bastille to Vincennes; and that in those passages the powder was concealed just under the Faubourg St. Antoine, which would one day blow up from one end to the other.

These fears had a good effect. They, for a time, dissipated the feeling of famine which was gradually creeping over Paris.

Foulon said, "The French have no bread; why should they not eat hay? My horses eat it"

True or not, he expiated this sneer with his life, and they carried his head about with a mouthful of hay stuffed between his teeth.

But, alas! it seemed that the French people had nothing to do but to eat what Foulon recommended.

From Paris, the fear of famine was dispersed among the provinces.

" Foulon," said all, " had predicted it."

They must mow all France.

All said that his ghost appeared to execute the menace.

Then report went about that bands of robbers had been seen mowing the green wheat.

The municipality of Soissons wrote to the Assembly a letter full of fears. " The robbers had cut," they said, "all the wheat for miles around, and were now marching on the city."

Soissons demanded help.

The Assembly sent a thousand men, who searched on all sides, twelve miles a-day. They could not find the robbers.

No matter, ten, twenty, a hundred people had seen them.

In the midst of this disputed news, other transpired which was but too true.

A certain lord having heard that De Launay had wished to blow up the Bastille, resolved, if it were in his power, to complete that which the Governor had been unable to do.

He announced that, in honor of the taking of the Bastille, he would give a grand entertainment, to which all were invited—workmen, artisans, tradesmen, countrymen, soldiers, women, old men, and children.

In this time of famine, when all lived on an ounce or two of bread per diem, a good dinner was a public service. Everybody—about 5,000 persons, that is to say—rushed to the fête. In the midst of it, an explosion was heard, and the surrounding plain was covered with dissevered limbs.

The gentleman, whose name was Mennay de Quincy, escaped to Switzerland, and avoided punishment.

Later on, he returned ; and, as he was a member of Parliament, he was arranged before it, and acquitted.

But the breach between the nobles and the people was now opened. The poor Count de Haus, who was incapable of committing such a crime, was accused of abetting M. de Quincy.

Some days afterwards, being at Neuville le Pont, he was insulted by the people, who proceeded to extremities ; and he had but just time to spring on his horse, and gallop off to a place of safety.

Fear had now seized upon us, as well as every one else

On the 18th of July, four days after the taking of the

Bastille. the Prince Condé, the Duke d'Enghien, M. Vaud-
revil. and M. de Broglie were announced.

Their arrival astonished my uncle. as it was not the hunting season, the wood being very thick, the shooting was
difficult

The Prince de Condé replied that he only wished to hunt
a stag. the King having commanded him, in the possibility
of a war, to examine into the condition of the defences of
Verdun.

The courier was ordered to procure horses from Clermont,
and to command the two carriages punctually at five
o'clock

So, taking this view of the matter, there was nothing extraordinary in it at all.

The Princes, mindful of the sport they had had. were determined to enjoy another day of it, although it was not
the proper season , but they could surely do as they liked.

The Duke d Enghien commanded me to accompany
them

I said good-bye to my books for the day, took the gun
which the Duke had given me, and followed them.

The Prince was then eighteen years of age—not much
older than I was. It was probably on account of the sim-
ilarity of our ages, that I was favored by so much of his notice.

I remarked that, though courteous as usual, he was profoundly sorrowful

He asked me what progress I was making in my education.

I told him. When I mentioned M. Drouet, he asked if
he were not the postmaster at St Menehould.

On my response in the affirmative, " A hot Republican,
if I mistake not ?" he said.

I replied that, through him, this part of the country had
been apprized of the capture of the Bastille.

He asked me some questions about the general disposition of the country—as much of the nobles as of the lower
classes.

I told him that the love of the people for their King was
great, and that they equally hated the nobles, which was
true

He covered his face with his handkerchief, and sighed.

I looked at him with astonishment.

"Pardon me, Duke," said I; "but I heard the Prince de Condé say that he was going to inspect the fortifications of Verdun, in case of war."

He looked at me to see what I was driving at.

"Excuse my question, Duke," said I, "but do you think it probable that we shall have war?"

"Very probable," said he, looking at me in his turn. "But why that question?"

"Because, in that event, your Grace, I shall not have lost my time."

"What would you do if there were war?"

"If France be menaced, every one capable of bearing a musket should fly to its defence."

He looked at my gun. It was the one which he had given me.

"So you can not only carry a gun, but you know how to use it."

"In fact, your Grace," said I, laughing, "thanks to your noble gift, I am such a capital shot, that if I had a Prussian or an Austrian at the end of it, I fancy they would pass an uncomfortable quarter of an hour."

"You think so?"

"I am certain of it A Prussian or an Austrian would be bigger than that pigeon you see there"

And I pointed to one perched about three hundred paces off, on the dry branch of a tree.

"You are mad," said the Prince. "That bird is three times out of range."

"Certainly, your Grace, for shot; but not for ball?"

"Your gun is loaded, then, with ball?"

"Yes, your Grace; I seldom use anything else."

"What are you doing, Henri?" the Prince de Condé said, as he appeared in view.

"Nothing, father," replied the Duke; "I am only saying a few words to this boy here."

He then bade me farewell, saying that he hoped I would always "think of him kindly" And waving his hand, he resumed his seat by his father's side, and disappeared

I stood almost heart-broken on the spot where the Prince addressed his last words to me.

One would have thought that I had a presentiment of the awful circumstances under which I should meet him again.

All the towns had organized national guards. after the example of Paris Chalons had set the example: St Mene-hould had followed it M Drouet was captain He came to ask Bertrand to be his lieutenant, and to see how many men he could recruit at Islettes

It was the report of bandits having been seen about which induced them to organize the National Guard

In eight days, all France was armed Each day the National Assembly gave audiences to ten couriers. It had at its disposal a million of men

Drouet and Bertrand took a stroll in the village of Is-lettes

They enrolled twenty men.

The keepers of the Forest of Argonne enlisted themselves and formed that part of the brigade of which Father Des-charmes was chief

I wished to be one of M. Bertrand's detachment, conse-quently in M. Drouet's company

He accompanied me as far as Father Descharmes' cottage, and asked me about the visit of the evening before.

He also asked if the Princes had not returned.

" No; because they have gone to Verdun," said I.

" Why did they not send to hire their horses from my place ?"

" Because they preferred to have them from Clermont "

" Hum !" said M. Jean Baptiste. " Do you know who they were who accompanied the Duke d'Enghien and the Prince de Condé ?"

" I heard them mention M. Vandreul and M Broglie "

" Exactly," said he. " René. they come not to inspect Verdun They have abandoned the King, and quitted France. They have gone to intrigue with strangers."

Then I remembered the sadness of the Duke d Enghien ; and I called to mind his peculiar look when I said that an Austrian or Prussian were easier to shoot than a pigeon. I also remembered his last words before leaving—" I hope that you will always think of me with kindness."

Poor Prince ! He had left France, and that was the cause of his sorrow.

" Would that all would follow his example," murmured M. Drouet, " from the first to the last ! But," continued he, grinding his teeth, " I fancy that if the King or Queen were to try that move, they would not escape so easily."

CHAPTER IX.

I GO TO MAKE CAPTIVES AND AM TAKEN CAPTIVE MYSELF.

Our National Guard was at first a curious sight

The first rank were armed with guns; the second with scythes; the third with clubs, and so on.

Later on, the armorers made some pikes for those who had no guns.

But however the guard was armed, there is no doubt but that it was filled with enthusiasm

Not a man, had he received the order, would have hesitated to march on Paris.

What was most remarkable, with regard to this corps, was the manner in which the battalions seemed, as it were, to spring from the earth. Liberty was as yet quite young; and yet she had only to strike with her foot on the ground, to raise this deadly harvest of men.

It was in the sainted year of 1789 that all France became soldiers. After the 14th July, every Frenchman was born with teeth ready to bite a cartridge.

Villages and towns joined in one compact; and that was, to mutually help each other when necessary.

One day, we saw arrive, by way of Clermont, the people of Verdun; and, by way of Paris, the people of St. Mene hould.

They had heard that a band of robbers had issued from the Forest of Argonne, set fire to Islettes, and plundered the village.

A hundred men from Clermont, under the command of M. Matthieu, and two hundred from St Menehould, under M. Drouet, had therefore set out, to render what assistance they might in the extermination of the brigands, of whom they had as yet not seen a trace.

They made merry, therefore, instead of fighting, and in the place of the rattle of musketry, was heard the more peaceful song

Eight days afterwards a man passed on horseback, going from Clermont to St. Menehould, and crying out, "The brigands are marching on Varennes! Help! help!"

The man disappeared from view—none knew him No matter, all leaped up, the drum beat the rappel; fifty men put themselves under the direction of Bertrand, and, without inquiring the number of the enemy, marched to Varennes Needless to say I was one of them.

From the height of the hill of Neuvilly we saw a great cloud of dust, about half a league ahead of us

They were the men of Clermont who, having started some half an hour before us, were about half a league ahead

At that sight, all elevated their hats on the ends of their muskets or pikes, and shouted " Vive la nation'"

That cry had almost completely taken the place of " Vive le Roi' '

We arrived at Varennes, which we expected to find in flames, with the streets running blood From the height of the hill, which descends to the Rue des Religieuses, we had a good view of the town.

All was quiet

The people of Clermont, when they first arrived were taken for the brigands, whom they were expecting every moment

When they recognised them, there was a general embracing, and crying ' Vive la nation'"

Then we arrived, in our turn; and two hours afterwards, the men of Montfalcon, De Bousance, and De Vouziez. The latter had marched eight leagues in five hours.

They bivouacked in the Place de Latry, and the Place de Grand Monarque

They then laid out tables for a public repast, where, after an ancient custom, each one chose his companions, and found his own dinner.

I had one visit to pay in Varennes—a place to which I seldom came, and where I only knew two persons, M Guillaume and M. Billaud

I remembered me of one of the two master workmen who had priced my carpentry work for M Drouet, and who said that if I had no work to do, and would accept it of him, he could always find me plenty.

His name was Father Gerbaut

I asked his address He lived in the Rue de la Basse Cour. The houses were not numbered at that period. On the left, descending to the Place Latry, next door to a large grocer's, his house was situated

I called. He was out; but expected home every moment.

I was received by his daughter, a charming girl, a little younger than myself—that is to say, about sixteen or seventeen years of age.

She asked me to wait till her father returned, or to give her my name if I feared becoming weary of staying with her.

Of course, I rejected with scorn the idea that any one could become wearied in the presence of one so gracious and charming.

It was the first time in my life that I had ever addressed a compliment to a female.

Indeed, it was the first time that I had been in conversation with a girl at all.

Up to this time, I had scarcely given women a moment's consideration.

Directly I told my name to the young girl, her face, which had before been amiable, brightened into a look of friendship.

"I know you," said she; "you worked for M. Diouet; my father has mentioned you to his workmen, more than once, as an example to be followed. Do stay; he will be glad to see you."

On looking around me, I perceived a harpsichord.

"You are a musician, I perceive, mademoiselle."

"Oh. Monsieur René, you must not call me that. The organist of St. Ugengoult has given me a few lessons, and, as he says I have some voice, I practise singing to amuse myself."

"Mademoiselle," said I, "can you believe that I have never heard the sound of a harpsichord, or any song, but that of the washerwomen, as they beat their linen? Will you sing something for me as well as yourself, and I shall be completely happy?"

"With the greatest pleasure," she replied.

And rising up, she crossed over to the harpsichord; and, after a simple prelude, she sang—

> "How sad to me the day
> When thou art far away!"

Every one knows that pretty romance, the "Devin de Village."

But it had never seemed so charming to me as when issuing from the lips of my pretty songstress.

Mademoiselle Gerbaut had sang very simply, but with that coquetry so natural to women. Her face was variable; and as she sang without accompaniment, leaning slightly back in her chair, her half-closed eyes gave a somewhat sentimental expression to the rest of her face. Her mouth was beautifully formed, she spoke almost without any perceptible movement of the lips, and you saw, at the first glance, that what she said was neither artificial nor constrained.

I was delighted with her. I said nothing, but my looks spoke more than words could have done.

"Mademoiselle," said I, not being able, in my enthusiasm, to think of any thing else, "have you read 'Emile?'"

"No, monsieur," she replied, "but my mother has read it, and that is why I am named Sophie."

"You are named Sophie!" cried I, seizing her hand, and pressing it to my heart, "now I am completely happy!"

She looked at me with an astonished smile.

"And why are you so happy because my name is Sophie?" said she.

"Because now I can look upon you as a sister more than a stranger. Oh, Sophie—dear Sophie!"

Sophie regarded me with a more astonished expression of face than ever; and I know not what she might have said, had not M. Gerbaut made his appearance at that moment.

"Ah! is that you, René?" said he; "you are, indeed, welcome. I asked the news from your friends on the Place there, and when they told me that you were at Varennes, I knew you would not go without calling to see me."

'Yes, M. Gerbaut," I answered, going up to him, and shaking his hand; "but I did not expect to find what I have found."

"And, pray, what have you found?"

"Mademoiselle Sophie, who has been kind enough to sing me an air from the 'Devin de Village' de M. Rousseau.'"

"Ah, indeed! She did not require much persuasion, did she?"

"Only great men, or great fools, require to be asked twice," said Sophie, laughing; "and as I am not a genius or a——"

Here she paused, while a sweet smile played over her lips.

"Fool," continued M. Gerbaut, "you sang to him."

"Did I do wrong, father?"

"Certainly not. As long as you sing to your equals, and without affectation, well and good. You know what I mean?"

Sophie bent her eyes, blushing.

"We must change our quarters, I think," said Father Gerbaut, half smiling, half serious.

"Wherefore?" said I, breaking into the conversation.

"Because we are just opposite to the 'Hotel de Bras d'Or,' where many handsome young gentlemen put up, and who are fond of music as a vehicle for making love.'

"Oh, father!" murmured Sophie; "say not so!"

"What would you have?" cried M. Gerbaut "They are no friends of mine who would bring trouble into peaceful families. When I understood that the princes and great lords had left the country, I had hoped that these gentlemen would have gone in their train. But no; they stay to make love to our wives and daughters, and to conspire against the nation. But this is not the time to speak of that. This is a *fête* day for Varennes. I must pay a visit to the cellar and larder. After dinner we will have a dance. Will you be Sophie's partner?" said M. Gerbaut to me.

"I should be only too happy," cried I; "but perhaps Mdle. Sophie does not think a young apprentice worthy of offering her his arm?"

"Oh, M. Réné!" said the young girl; "you listen to my father, and then do me a grievous wrong, without any foundation for it."

Sophie and myself bounded down the staircase, and in a moment found ourselves under a bright sun in the street, as I could not help thinking, like two butterflies emerged from a chrysalis state

Whilst I had been waiting at M. Gerbaut's, and whilst

I had been listening to Sophie's song, the streets of Varennes had undergone a great change.

The city was holding high holiday, with which, however, was mingled a certain degree of solemnity.

All the houses were hung with tapestry; and outside the doors tables were laid, covered with flowers, at which the inhabitants of the houses were seated, eating, waited upon by their servants, if they had any, if not, by themselves.

As if they wished that the dead should participate in the joy of the living, garlands of green boughs, intermingled with flowers, were suspended from the gates of the cemetery, which stretched from the church to the side of the Rue de l'Horloge. In the middle of the Place was erected a scaffolding, filled with amateur musicians, who wished to promote a dance after dinner. On the front of this temple of Terpsichore was written "Vive le Roi! Vive la nation!" Underneath this, in large letters, was inscribed the word "Fraternité!"

It was, in fact a brotherly rejoicing. Those who there met for the first time were members of one great family, which had existed for centuries, only it ignored the tie which bound one to the other.

But common danger had caused to meet the two ends of the thread, and in their union they found force.

After passing the houses leading to the Place Latry, we arrived at the open space in front of the Rue de l'Horloge, and entered into the midst of the crowd.

There seemed to be collected all the inhabitants of the High Town.

In each street the tables were arranged on the right and left side of the houses; a space in the middle being left for the promenaders. The Rue des Religieuses, which runs down from the foot of the hill, made a most perfect and picturesque view.

We got mixed up with a lot of other persons, when all of a sudden a crowd of horsemen—young gentlemen, apparently—appeared on the crest of the hill, and, putting their horses at full gallop, dashed into the Rue des Religieuses. There was a general cry of "Each one for himself!" and we turned to fly; but as we had been in front before, we now naturally found ourselves in the rear.

Thinking but of Sophie, I wished to put her under one

of the tables, to be out of the way of danger; but curious to relate, she did not seem to know the peril she was in, and would not stir till it was too late; and I had just time to clasp her in my arms, and throw myself in front of her.

I had scarcely accomplished this, than, on turning round, I discovered myself face to face with a horseman, whose steed was perfectly unmanageable, and turned round and round, threatening us with his hoofs as he did so

I had but one hope, and that was to preserve Sophie. I caught hold of the horse's bridle, the cavalier raised his whip, the horse gave a plunge, and, whether through accident or intention, the blow, instead of falling on the horse, struck me on the shoulder.

The shame of being struck, more than the pain of the blow, caused the blood to rise to my head. I seized the horseman by his waist, lifted him from the saddle, the horse bolting away at the moment, upsetting a woman and two or three children in its wild career, and fell with him on the pavement; but, being the more vigorous, I was the uppermost, and soon had him at my mercy, with my knee on his breast.

It was only when his hat fell from his head, that I recognised who my adversary was.

" M de Malmy!" cried I.

And taking my knee from his breast, and releasing his arms, I stood a little on one side.

" Ah, wretch!" cried he regaining his whip. " Do you know what is the penalty for laying hands on a gentleman?"

" M. le Viscount!" cried Sophie, pale with terror, placing herself, at the same time, between us.

He smiled a grim smile, grinding his teeth as he did so.

" I am determined, mademoiselle. Had he been a gentleman, I would chastise him with a sword; but as he is not, I shall punish him with this whip."

He raised it.

I looked for something with which to defend myself. At that moment, a man sprang over one of the tables, seized the Marquis with one hand, and possessed himself of the whip with the other.

" Monsieur," said he, " whips were made for horses and dogs. René Besson is a man."

"A man?" repeated the Viscount, furiously.

"Yes, a man; and one whom you may not insult."

"Who are you?" asked the Viscount.

"You know me very well M. de Malmy, but as you ask, I will tell you. I am Jean Baptiste Drouet, postmaster at St Menehould. I am not of noble birth, I know full well, but for six years have I served my country as a soldier and that is better than a gentleman who spends his life in eating, drinking, and hunting. This I say for the benefit of you and your friends, and if you want me, you know where to find me."

Saying these words, Drouet pushed De Malmy aside, and turned to confront two or three other young gentlemen, who, having dismounted, had come to join in the quarrel.

"When we change horses at your post-house, M. Drouet," said one of these young men, "we do not generally approach, but send our domestics to bear our orders to you."

"I would much rather deal with your servants than with you, M. de Courtement. They, at least, have not sold their wives or daughters in the Parc au Cerfs."

The young noble took this as a sarcasm on his birth, with regard to which infamous reports had been bruited about.

He had a hunting-knife in his belt, and suddenly drew it, maddened with anger.

But before the knife could do any mischief Drouet drew a pistol from his pocket, and presented it full in the face of the Chevalier.

"Monsieur," said he, "I could shoot you like I would a wild beast; and two hundred people would bear witness that you offered the first insult; but the time has not yet come when all shall have their dues. So go your way in peace, and let the matter stand as it is."

"Oh, without doubt, that proceeding would suit you wonderfully well," said M. de Malmy; "but, for the sake of an example, I must proceed otherwise."

Raising his whip, he advanced on M. Drouet, who making a spring to one side jumped on a table, and cried out, in a powerful tone of voice, "Help! To my assistance, men of St Menehould!"

A hundred voices responded to the cry; a crowd rushed

to where we were; and in a moment, the five or six gentle-men were completely in our power.

Each had seized the arms that came nearest to hand—one a pike, another a musket; thus showing by their alac-rity, their wish to be of service to their commander They were informed of the origin of the dispute, and wished nothing better than to fan up the embers of the old quarrel between the nobles and the people.

The young gentlemen saw that it was useless to attempt resistance

"Murder us!" cried the Viscount; "even as your friends at Paris have murdered De Launay, Foulon, and Berthier."

"Our friends, as you call them, in Paris, disgraced them-selves by laying hands on men who were scarcely good enough to die by the hands of the common executioner. But what would you have ? The people have cried for jus-tice, and it has been denied them. Is it, then, wonderful that they should take the law in their own hands when the opportunity presented ? But as for you, gentlemen, as you are not gaolers, like De Launay, or extortioners, like Fou-lon and Berthier, you have not merited death, but simply a little lesson, which I shall have great pleasure in giving you."

"Give a lesson to us?" cried the young men, mad with rage.

"Yes; but it shall not be harsh or spiteful. This is a day of brotherly fraternity. Are you our brothers ? Will you share in our *fête?* Forget the hard words that have passed between us ; or, if you cannot, put them down to the account of that goddess who is aptly called Discord. The tables await you. Sit down among us, and we will give you the place of honor; and the first one who forgets to pay the respect which is due to you, shall be chased from the midst of us, as one unworthy of participating in our reunion. Do you agree with me?" cried Drouet to all who were around

"Yes! yes!" replied all, with one voice, with the excep-tion of the young nobles, who still continued silent.

"What if we refuse?" at last said one of them

"If you refuse," said Drouet, "go to the 'Bras d'Or,' or the 'Grand Monarque;' eat and drink as you like—you are free; but disturb not our enjoyment. Am I not right, my friends?" continued Drouet, for the second time addressing the crowd.

The applause was as loud as before.

"And if we do not promise to leave you in quiet enjoyment of your *fête*—what then?" asked another of the young nobles.

"As, by that act, you will prove that you are not good citizens, and that you are desirous of breaking the public peace, we shall ask you to leave the town quietly; and, if you refuse, we will expel you by force."

"Bravo! bravo!" cried all.

M. de Malmy interrogated his companions with his eyes; and as he saw the same expression in all theirs, "Messieurs," said he, "I regret that, in the name of my friend and myself, I must refuse the great honor that you offer us I regret, also, that we cannot pledge our word not to interrupt the *fête*, as we are not sufficient philosophers to avoid breaking our promise; so—as we have no further business to detain us in town—we ask your permission to make our most respectful adieu, and to go and seek our pleasure elsewhere."

"As you wish, M le Viscount," said M. Drouet. "You are free to go." Then, assuming the tone of command which sat so well on him, he said, "Allow these gentlemen to pass, and preserve complete silence; the one who passes a remark, will have to answer for it to me."

Not a sound could be heard.

In the midst of this oppressive silence, the young nobles remounted their horses, and returned by the way that they had arrived.

No word was spoken, no movement made; but the people followed the little party with their eyes until they finally disappeared from view on turning into the road leading to Clermont.

Then a voice was heard, calm, but commanding in its tones It was Drouet's.

"Lieutenant Bertrand," said he, "place sentinels at the gates and see that the young nobles do not re-enter the town, during the continuance of the *fête*."

Then, turning to the crowd, "Am I not right, my friends?" said he.

4

"Vive M. Drouet! Vive la nation!" cried the people, with one voice.

A few cries of "Down with the nobles!" were heard, but they had no response. In fact, Drouet turned to whence those cries proceeded, and made a gesture of disapprobation.

The *fête* then continued as happily as if nothing had happened

---

CHAPTER X.

TOUCHING MADEMOISELLE SOPHIE.

I HAVE said how much my encounter with De Malmy seemed to affect my companion, but that might have been accounted for in three ways. First, her fear for herself; second, her fear for me; and lastly, perhaps, her fear for my adversary.

I had not forgotten what Father Gerbaut had said with regard to his daughter's looking higher than her position warranted, and to the attention which she drew from the young gentlemen who put up at the "Bras d'Or," some of whom were, no doubt, those with whom we had been in contest.

I had naturally followed, with my eyes, the little caval-cade, until it finally disappeared.

On withdrawing my looks from it, I perceived that Sophie was half fainting. I offered her my arm, which she took, trembling at the same time all over.

"Oh, M. René," said she, "I was so frightened! How glad I am that it ended as it did!"

For whom was she frightened? and for whose sake was she so glad that all was over?

Was it for our sakes, or for that of the young lords?

I did not like to ask her.

M. Drouet walked along the Place with us. We passed under the arch, and entered the Rue de la Basse. Cour Billaud lived some distance away, and Guillaume almost in the country; so those three young men went to the "Hotel du Bras d'Or," and although the brothers Leblanc wished to give them a dinner for nothing, they insisted on paying for everything that they had.

The table at which they dined was on the other side of the street, just opposite to ours.

The clock of St. Gengoult gave the signal for dinner.

The two first toasts proposed were "The King!" and "The nation!" They then drank another "To the health of those who, believing them to be in danger, had flown to their succor."

Sophie eat but little, in spite of my remonstrances. Now and then, her father broke out into violent abuse against the young nobles, and I saw the tears trembling on her eyelashes every time that he did so.

We crossed the bridge thrown over the River Aire. Two streams of promenaders were continually passing—the one set mounting up, the other coming down. The Place du Grand Monarque was splendidly illuminated. The tables were not in any one's way, being, for the most part, piled in front of the door of the church.

The Place du Grand Monarque being smoother and better paved than the Place Latry and, besides, not having the dispiriting influence of a cemetery, was chosen for the ball room.

The signal for the dance was given by a joyous peal from the church bells, to which violins and clarionets replied, and a quadrille was speedily formed

My partner took my arm for the second dance, but suddenly complaining of illness, she implored me to take her home.

I was not an experienced dancer, but under Sophie's tuition I got on so well, that I tried all I could to dissuade her from retiring ; but she said, with a sad smile, "Do not ask me to remain, René," and so I was obliged to comply with her request.

I gave her my arm, and we retraced our steps to the house.

M Gerbaut had heard all about the fracas in the Rue des Religieuses, and was very well pleased that we had given the young gentlemen a lesson.

Sophie, who had her arm in mine, heard all that he said to me, with downcast eyes, and gave no sign of approbation or otherwise, but I felt her shudder under her father's words.

As I was leaving, "Mademoiselle," said I, " I.go back to-morrow, with my friends, probably before you awake ; so permit me to say good-bye this evening, and to tell you before M. Gerbaut, what pleasure I feel in having made your acquaintance."

" And I, M. Réné," said she, "like you as a friend, and am well disposed to love you as a brother."

" Very well, my children," said Father Gerbaut, "embrace each other and say good-bye."

Sophie turned to me both cheeks, which I kissed with a feeling of ineffable pleasure.

She then retired to her own room ; I followed her with my eyes to the door, when she turned, and gave me a parting glance, and a parting smile.

" She is a good girl, after all," said her father.

" A good girl, M. Gerbaut ? Say, rather, an angel ! "

" Angels are not so common as all that, my boy. But," continued he, leading me along the corridor, and opening a door, " here is your room, not only for to-night, but for ever, if you will enter into my service. You shall have board and lodging, and twenty-five crowns a month. Do you hear me ? "

I shook him by the hand, and thanked him for his kindness. He then wished me to come down stairs again, to drink a glass to the health of the nation. But I pleaded fatigue, and want of sleep, and entered my chamber.

The real reason why I did not comply with his offer, was that I wished to be alone.

I shut the door, for I was afraid that any one might come and look for me. But there was no fear of that Every one was so busy enjoying himself, that they had no time to think of aught else.

I threw myself on the bed, and thought of Sophie.

M. Drouet had given me a sincere liking for intellectual existence, but Sophie awakened in me another kind of existence, that of love ; and I felt, for the first time, that indescribable, but pleasurable sensation, which predicts the dawning of that passion.

A new future opened before me. This was the scene. A happy, though, perhaps, a humble home, with a careful and a beloved wife. I could see myself, at set of sun, walking by the river's side, her heart beating against mine.

I could fancy delaying under the tall trees, to hear the blackbird's song. In a word, this dream of the future was that twofold life which, till then, had never engaged my boyish thoughts. Now, I seemed to have taken one step into this fairyland; and, although I trembled still, I would fain go on.

What, then, prevented me, I asked myself, from making this dream a reality? Why did I not at once close with M. Gerbaut's offer? It was because my heart misgave me. I thought of Sophie's evident leaning towards men of a higher class; I reflected that, to her, I must be a mere boy. And I groaned in spirit that I was not half-a-dozen years older.

At daybreak, the reveillé was beaten. My comrade had passed the night on the Place and in the streets, dancing and drinking. I jumped from my couch, and, having hastily dressed myself, crept on tip-toe to the door of Sophie's chamber, wishing to say adieu, even if only through the key-hole.

I had trodden as lightly as possible, scarcely hearing my own footsteps; and how great was my astonishment on seeing the door open a little way, and a hand put out.

It was easy to see, through the crevice from which the hand was protruded, that Sophie had not retired to rest at all; or, if she had, that she had not undressed herself.

I seized the hand, and pressed it to my lips.

She withdrew it, leaving, at the same time, a little billet in mine, and quickly closed the door.

I could scarcely believe my eyes. I approached a window, and, by the light of early dawn, read these words:—

"I have no friends, Réné. Be one to me. I am very unhappy!"

I pressed, with one hand, the billet to my heart, and, with the other extended towards her chamber, I swore to accept and prove myself worthy of the friendship so mysteriously offered.

Then, perceiving that all was quiet in her room, I went down stairs, took my gun, and, throwing one parting glance at her window, passed into the street.

The curtain drew back, giving me a glimpse of her face.

She nodded, throwing me a sad smile, and the curtain was replaced before the window.

Small as the time was that I had for observation, I could not help thinking that her eyes were reddened with weeping.

There was nothing wonderful in that.   Had she not told me, in her letter, that she was very unhappy ?

There was a mystery, which, no doubt, thought I, time will clear up.

I walked rapidly down the street, in the direction of the Place, knowing that, if I did not make a vigorous effort, I should never be able to tear myself away from the vicinity of the house.

The men of Clermont, D'Islettes, and St. Menehould—in fact, all who followed the same route—were collected in one group.   They drank one last toast, shook hands for the last time, and separated.

Father Gerbaut conducted us as far as the top of the Hill des Religieuses, and there renewed the offers that he had previously made to me.

I reached Father Descharmes' cottage, and, for the first time, found it lonely, and my room wretched.

On the morrow, I recommenced my usual routine of life ; and though I had the same wish to make progress in my studies, still there was a dreary blank in my heart, which they could not fill.

CHAPTER XI.

WHAT " BROTHERHOOD " MEANT.

I HAVE told you all that took place up to this time.

My life continued the same as ever, with the exception of a dreary feeling about the heart.

The events that took place in Paris had no direct effect upon me.   I heard them as one might hear the echo of a distant thunder-clap.

In this way we heard of the abolition of titles, on the 1st of August ; of the suppression of tithes ; of the recognition of religious liberty; of the orgie of the gardes du corps; of the insult offered to the national cockade; of the days of the 5th and 6th of October; of the return of the King and Queen to Paris; of the plots and intrigues of the Court; of the prosecution of Bezenval and Favras; and of the publication of the Red Book by the assembly.

The Red Book revealed all

The King, who had, on the 12th of February, sworn friendship to the Constitution, not only was in direct correspondence with the exiles, but went to Trèves, a military post, where his stables were situated, and which was in charge of Prince Lambese, the very man who had charged on the people in the garden of the Tuileries, on the 12th of July, and wounded an old man with his sabre, and trodden the helpless under foot.

The same kind of thing went on at Versailles. The King had a Minister of Foreign Affairs; uniforms were made for the gardes du corps, and sent to Trèves; horses were bought in England for the accommodation of the King's household; and the only grumble that Louis XVI made, when he paid the bills, was, that, at least, they might have bought the horses in France

The Comte D'Artois, the Prince Condé, and the other exiles, received enormous pensions.

They had not then been able to find what became of the sixty millions

But now the Red Book pointed out where they had gone.

If, up to this moment, there had been any hesitation on the minds of the people, that hesitation now disappeared.

They knew where was their enemy

The enemy was the exiles, and their ally, the King, who pensioned them.

This was the reason why the Assembly struck a decisive blow, and put up for sale, at one time, ecclesiastical benefices to the tune of four hundred millions. Paris alone bought two hundred millions' worth.

All the municipalities followed that example. They bought a great number, and then sold them, one by one. In a word, they wished to expropriate the clergy, and they did hesitate to do it.

There is something miraculous in this, and which does not appear in the history of any other country.

And that is, the spontaneous organization of France by itself. The Assembly was only a secretary. France did the deed; the Assembly registered it.

Before that, the division of old France into provinces was abolished; the boundaries had been already changed; there were no longer Provençals, Bretons, Alsaciens, Picards, or French.

The Champ de Mars was Mount Tabor, transfigured by the sun of June.

Valence gave, on the 29th of November, 1789, the example of the first federation; and each strove to follow the example given by the zealous Dauphin, our vanguard against the great enemy, the Savoyard King.

From anterior ages, the eldest man has always presided, whether noble or not. His age makes his right—his white locks his crown.

Rouen searched for an old Chevalier of Malta, eighty-five years of age, to preside at its federation.

In St. Andeol, there were two old men, respectively ninety-three and ninety-four years of age, the one a noble, and the other a plebeian—the one a colonel, the other a laborer. These two embraced at the altar, and the spectators embraced each other, crying, "There is no longer an aristocracy, no longer a working-class—there are only Frenchmen!"

At Lous le Lauheur, a citizen, whose name is forgotten, gave this toast:—

"To all men, equally to our enemies: let us swear to love and protect them."

Open the book of royalty, and see if you can find a sentiment equal to that inscribed on the first page of the book of the people.

From all places, provincial and isolated, one cry arose:—"To Paris! To Paris! To Paris!"

As this cry burst from the throat of France, Royalists and Jacobins trembled. The Jacobins said, "The King, with his smile, and the Queen, with her white lips, will fascinate the credulous people from the provinces, and will cause them to turn against us, and the revolution will be at an end."

The Royalists said, "To bring these provincials, already ripe for tumult, to Paris, the centre of agitation, is but bringing oil to feed the lamp of revolution. Who can say what will be the effect of this immense concourse, and what fearful events may come to pass through the incursions of two hundred and fifty thousand souls, from all quarters of France, into Paris?"

But the impulse was given, and the movement could not be stayed.

France wished, with that powerful will which nothing could arrest, to know itself.

The corporation of Paris demanded of the Assembly the general federation.

The Assembly, pretending to accord to their wish, named the 14th of July, the anniversary of the taking of the Bastille.

The news was propagated among all the provinces of the kingdom; but as they feared so great an assemblage in Paris, and wished to put all possible obstacles in their way, all expenses were put down to the charge of the localities.

All our department clubbed together I was comparatively rich, having in my possession three or four hundred crowns, gained by my own labor, and saved by my own economy.

Father Descharmes had offered to give me what sum I wanted; but I refused to accept anything.

For some time, the poor old man had been declining in health. He had served princes all his life, and now missed them. One thing greatly perplexed him, and that was, whether France had the right to act as it was acting?

They had offered him a deputyship to the federation; but he shook his head, saying, "I am too old; Réné will go in my place."

Afterwards, he had a long conversation with M. Drouet, in the course of which he gave him some papers, which he sorted with care, put in his portfolio, and took to St. Menehould

On the eve of departure, a carriage drove up to the door of my uncle's cottage; and, to my astonishment, I saw Sophie and her father alight from it.

I rushed out with a cry of joy, but suddenly stopped myself

What would Sophie—what would her father think?

Father Gerbaut smiled. Sophie made a step in advance, and gave me her hand.

"Well, how is old Nimrod getting on?" said Father Gerbaut to my uncle, who had just come out of his room.

"As well as can be expected at my age, M. Gerbaut. It is necessary for the violet to blossom in spring, and the beech-tree to put forth its buds in May. He is just sixteen and a-half years old. When I was at that age, I already had a sweetheart."

I felt myself blushing to the very tips of my ears.

"Ah! I never had but one love. But where are you going to in this fashion?" asked my uncle; "for I cannot think that you came all this way on purpose to pay me a visit."

"No, my old friend; though I am delighted to see you. I am on my way to St. Menehould, to put a few little affairs of mine in order. I have been appointed a member of the Federation, and I do not know how long we may be compelled to stay in Paris."

"What a pity that you have not got a third seat in your carriage. I also have business at St. Menehould, and I would have asked you to give me a lift."   •

"Good!" said M. Gerbaut; "all can be arranged. Sophie does not much care to go to St. Menehould. Do you, Sophie?"

"I only care to go, so as to be with you, father."

"Well, then, stay here with Réné. You can stroll, in the wood, like two lovers, and we, like two old fogies as we are, will go and look after our affairs. If Réné were a young nobleman, I should not place so much trust in him; but he is a good lad, a clever workman, and an honest man, and as I would trust him with a purse, so will I trust him with my child."

I looked joyfully at Sophie, but she showed neither pleasure nor sorrow; she seemed to be exactly of her father's opinion, that we might be trusted together.

M. Gerbaut and Father Descharmes got into the vehicle, and drove off in the direction of the village of Islettes.

CHAPTER XII.

WHAT PASSED IN THE FOREST.

FOR some time I followed the carriage with my eyes, for I feared to look at Sophie, as I could not help thinking that the expression of her face would decide my future happiness or misery.

After a time I made up my mind; I turned round.

Sophie had a smile on her lips, but it seemed as if the rest of her face was overshadowed with sadness.

I offered her my arm, which she took.

"What would you like to do?" I asked her. "Would you rather stay here, or take a stroll in the wood?"

"Take me under the shadow of yon great trees, M. René. In my little chamber at Varennes I stifle for want of air."

"It is singular, Mdlle Sophie, that I always believed that you preferred the town to the country."

"I prefer nothing. I live, that is all."

She heaved a sigh.

The conversation fell.

I threw a side glance at Sophie. She appeared fatigued and in pain.

"You look pale," said I; "and although you do not prefer the country to the town, I fancy it does you more good"

She shrugged her shoulders, by way of reply.

"Perhaps," said she.

I turned towards my uncle's cottage, all covered with ivy and creepers, surrounded by flowers and shadowed by the branches of chestnuts and beech-trees.

It was beautiful, seen half in light and half in shadow. A cat was sleeping comfortably on the window-sill; two dogs were playing in front of the door; and a black-headed linnet was singing in its cage.

It was a beautiful picture of contented country life.

"Look, Mdlle Sophie," said I drawing her attention to the scene. "Would a little place like that, with a man who had the honor of being beloved by you, suffice for your ambition?"

"Who told you that I had ambition, Réné?"

"I ask you, do you think that you could be happy under those circumstances?"

She looked at me.

"You see, then, that I am now miserable?"

"You told me so in a letter, when I was staying at Varennes, eight months ago."

"And have you not forgotten what I wrote to you so long as eight months ago?"

I drew a little portfolio from my pocket, and out of it I took a little scrap of paper, on which was written, in her hand—

"I have no friend, Réné; will you be one? I am very unhappy."

"If the paper is a little crumpled," said I, "it is because a day has never passed without my reading it."

"Then how is it that I have never seen you since that morning, Réné?"

"For what purpose? Since you wrote to me you cannot have doubted me."

"You have a good heart, Réné, and I did not wish to see you to get that opinion from you."

"That is well. If you had had need of me, you had but to write, and I should have been with you in a moment. At first, day after day, I hoped for a letter. Oh, if I had received one!—had it been only the one word 'Come!'— with what joy would I have flown to your side! But such happiness was not for me. Days, weeks, months passed away, and I remained alone with my sorrow, without ever being called away to offer you a consolation."

She looked at me with an expression of affectionate tenderness.

"Ah, Réné, I should have liked to have seen you; but not hearing from you, I thought that you had forgotten me."

"Oh, Mdlle. Sophie!" I cried; "I am not sufficiently happy or unhappy for that."

"In truth, my dear Réné," said she, trying to smile, "you have quite the air of a hero of romance."

"As I have never read a romance, I scarcely know what that is."

"A hero of romance, Réné," said Sophie, smiling at the

experimental lesson in literature she was trying to give me, "is a man who loves without hope."

"That is good. Then am I a hero of romance. By the bye, what are these heroes supposed to do?"

"Everything impossible, in order to touch the heart of the woman they vainly love."

"Then I am ready to do so; but, if commanded by you, I should know not impossibility."

"Do not put your life in danger, Réné," said Sophie. "Sighing for that would not benefit either of us."

Now it was her turn to stop, and. having turned the corner of the road, she pointed out to me my uncle's house under a different aspect, but still how beautiful!

"You just now asked me, Réné, if that house, in company with a man whom I loved, would not satisfy my ambition? Well, Réné, in my turn, I adjure you, in the name of that friendship that I have avowed towards you, wish for nothing more than that calm and peaceful existence that Providence has placed in your way. Follow the example of your uncle, who, for eighty years, has lived in peace with himself and with all mankind, without seeking to better his condition, and without ever wishing for a larger house, or a greater extent of land. In fact, this forest before us—is it not his? Do not its trees give him shelter? Do not the birds which inhabit it sing for his gratification. and do not the animals that make it their home serve for his food? In name, it belongs to the King; but, in reality, it is his. Réné, find a woman who loves you; that, I am sure, will not be difficult. My father tells me that you are one of the best carpenters that he knows. Ask the consent of your uncle—he will not refuse it; and live, as he has done, on the little spot where the happiest years of your life have passed away."

In my turn, I shook my head.

"You will not?" said Sophie. "What, then, do you intend to do?"

"Mademoiselle Sophie," said I, "I purpose being a man."

"Has not your uncle been also a man, Réné?"

"Yes; but a man useless to his country. The times in which he lived, and the times in which we live, are different. The tranquillity which existed in his generation is not permitted in this."

"You are ambitious, Réné?" asked Sophie.

"It is not ambition, mademoiselle; it is obedience to the designs of heaven. There are times when every man, great or small, carries his mission in himself. What, then? He must keep that mission till it is fulfilled. Who knows but that even I, insignificant as I am, have one? You have already drawn me from the crowd of my equals, because you condescended to take my arm. It was not all that I could have wished. Oh, Sophie, I ask you, here, under the shelter of these great trees, the most sacred temple that I know of, will you promise to be mine? Will you give me all the love that you can, and the happiest day of my life will be that on which I can prove my devotion to you! Oh, Sophie, give me hope!"

"I believe you, Réné; in fact, from the first moment I saw you, I never doubted you. Ah! why were you not always with me, to support me with your arm when I stumbled, and with your heart when I doubted? I have called on you many times, Réné"

"Can this be true, Mademoiselle Sophie?" cried I, filled with joy.

"Yes," said she, "but do not misunderstand me. I do not love you. I never shall love you, Réné," continued she, looking me full in the face. "I feel instinctively that I have need of your friendship. Why I should implore it, how it can be useful to me, I know not; but still I feel sure I shall have recourse to it some day; and if you are away from me, Réné, on that day, whose help shall I implore? If you are near to me, I can rely on you; can I not? Again I say to you, as I wrote once before, I am truly unhappy."

She took her arm from mine, hid her face in her hand, and I could see by the heaving of her bosom that she was weeping.

"Mademoiselle Sophie!" said I.

"Leave me, my friend—leave me. I do not like to weep before you, and I feel that I must weep."

And, with one hand, she made me a sign to go.

I obeyed.

She sat down by the side of a little brook, which fell into the Brésme, and taking off her hat, which she placed by her side, began to pluck flowers, and throw them into the water.

Sixty years have passed since that day, and I fancy that I can still see the poor child with her golden hair floating in the breeze, the tears coursing down her cheeks, throwing the flowers into the current of the Biésme, which would carry them to the Aisne, the Aisne to the Oise, the Oise to the Seine, and the Seine to the sea.

After about an hour had passed, she got up silently, came towards me, and smilingly took my arm.

We retraced our steps to my uncle's house.

We had scarcely arrived, when we heard the sound of wheels. It was Father Gerbaut's carriage.

Sophie, who had not spoken one word all the way home, seized my hand.

"Réné," she said, "do not forget that you have given me your word, I trust you."

"Mademoiselle Sophie," said I, pressing her hand to my heart, "one call alone can be stronger than yours—that of my country."

M. Gerbaut stayed about an hour to rest his horse, and then, with Sophie, mounted into his vehicle

The poor girl waved her hand. Father Gerbaut cried "Farewell!" and the carriage disappeared behind a clump of trees, which hid the road to Meuvilly.

I returned to where Sophie had been sitting down: I picked up the flowers she had let fall, and placed them in my little portfolio, together with the letter which she had written to me at Varennes, and in which she had poured forth all her soul.

<hr />

CHAPTER XIII.

THE PEOPLE IN COUNCIL.

ON the morrow, the ninth of July, '90, we were *en route* at daybreak, drums beating in front of us, to assist in the celebration of the grand fête of the general federation

Father Descharmes embraced me, with an expression of sorrow which wounded me to the heart

"Perhaps you youngsters are in the right," said he, "and

we old men are in the wrong. But what will you, my child. One cannot give up in two days the creed of sixty years."

"I know not what may come of all this, but I hope that my eyes will be closed in death before it does come."

"But uncle," said I, "although it would be a great treat to me to go to Paris and see the fête, still, if you wish it, I will not go."

"No, my boy, go; and heaven grant that I may live to see your return, and that we may meet again in this world."

I embraced him as I wept, for I loved him dearly.

Had he not fed and clothed me and brought me up, and watched the infant become, under his roof a man?

"Bring my arm-chair to the door," said he; "I do not wish to lose the last glimpse of the setting sun."

I obeyed. Leaning on my shoulder he reached the door, and sitting down in the chair, took my hand, and kissed me, saying "Go!"

I departed, returning in time to see this good old servitor of royalty die. With kingcraft he suffered, and with its death he died.

When I lost sight of him, it seemed as if I had left him for ever, and I felt half inclined to return at once, never to leave him; but the temptation of seeing Paris was too much for me, and in another moment we were in sight of the houses of Islettes.

A surprise awaited me there.

The inhabitants, not wishing to be separated from their Curé, had put him into a little carriage drawn by a horse, and the good priest, his eyes overflowing with tears, was bidding farewell to Mademoiselle Marguerite, who wept on the steps in front of the door of the Presbytery.

In those days, a journey of forty leagues was no small matter, and the poor girl believed that the good Abbé Fortin had departed for ever.

We continued our route, the drums beating, and the carriage rolling ahead of us. Some of our party pressed on in front, to form an escort of honor for the worthy priest

We found M Drouet awaiting us at the head of the deputation, on the Place of St. Menehould.

Amongst the deputation, was an old soldier of the Seven Years War, who had served under Marshal Saxe, and who was present at the battle of Fontenoy; and a sailor, who was in active service at the time of the birth of the Bailli de Suffren. Both, living ruins of an ancient regime, wished to witness the dawn of a new era

M Drouet had placed a carriage at their service, but they would not use it. It therefore proceeded empty in the midst of the *cortége*, in the front rank of which the two veterans marched with heads erect—a benediction, as it were, bestowed by the dead era on the age which was just about to dawn.

All the high roads of France were filled with processions like ours, all hastening to one great focus—Paris.

Never since the Crusade had so great a number, of their own will, bent their steps in one direction.

All along the road, deputations came to greet the travellers.

They offered hospitality to the old men and priests. It was impossible to provide for all, so the main body bivouacked in the open air.

Great fires were lighted, at which every one prepared his simple meal. There was no lack of wine in a country which particularly cultivated grapes.

On the morrow, at daybreak, all started at beat of drum. When the noise of the drum ceased, all joined in the chorus of the *Ça ira* of '90, which has nothing in common with the menacing and bloodthirsty *Ça ira* of '93.

This song kept up the energies of those men on the march, who were toiling along under a hot July sun, to the end of the journey. It supported those laborers who were making the arena, so to speak, where great deeds were to be done.

We have said that it was with an unwilling heart that the Assembly decreed the federation—that it was with an unwilling heart that the city had sent its workmen to the Champ de Mars, to prepare for that great and solemn reunion The time approached—the work did not proceed. What happened?

All Paris rose, and proceeded to the Champ de Mars carrying various implements of labor — one a pickaxe another a shovel, and so on.

And not only did the people—not only did the *bourgeosie* do this, but old men and children, lords and laborers, ladies

5

of rank and women of shame, actors and actresses, priests and soldiers,—all joined in the work, which did not even close when night fell like a shroud over the city of Paris.

The invalids, who could not work on account of their being maimed, held the torches, to lighten them at their labors.

Begun in the morning of the 9th of July, this stupendous work was completed in the night of the 13th, two hours before sunrise.

We arrived on the 12th, in the evening.

Paris was crowded; but, strange to say, the hotel keepers and letters of lodgings, instead of raising their prices, lowered them considerably. This spoke well for the disposition of Paris towards us.

Truly this was not the federation of France, but the fraternal greeting of the world.

A Prussian Baron—Jean Baptiste de Clootz, better known by the name of Anacharsis—presented himself before the National Assembly with twenty men of different nations—Russians, Poles, men of the north, men of the west, men of the east, and men of the south,—all habited in the costume of their country. He came to ask permission for them to appear at the federation of the Champ de Mars, as they wished to represent the federation of the world.

Later on, this same Anacharsis Clootz wished to give twelve thousand francs, to make war against royalty.

One may imagine my astonishment on finding myself in Paris, on the Boulevards, gazing at the ruins of the Bastille.

Drouet pointed it out to me, afterwards, the patriotic workmen on the Champ de Mars. I rushed to join them; and, seizing a spade, was speedily hard at work.

My fellow-workman appeared to be an artizan of about fifty years of age. He gave orders to a boy about my age, who was close at hand.

On seeing the ardor with which I worked, he asked me who I was, and whence I came.

I told him that my name was Réné Besson; that I came from the new department of the Meuse; and that I was apprenticed to a carpenter, by trade.

When he heard this, he held out his hand, a smile illuminating his austere visage.

"Take that, boy," said he. "If you are an apprentice, I am a master; and here are two lads, about your age, who live with me, to learn their trade If you have nothing better to do, come and sup with me to-night—you shall be made welcome."

I shook hands with him, and accepted his kind offer. The French, at the dawn of the Revolution, were a nation of brothers

As the clock struck five, we threw down our tools, gave ourselves a wash in the Seine; after which we crossed over to the other side of the river, and entered the Rue St. Honoré.

The master and I had walked side by side all the way, the two apprentices following behind.

He asked me some questions about our department, what political opinions we had, and whether I knew any one in Paris.

I answered all his questions with becoming modesty.

My companion stopped at the commencement of the Rue St. Honoré, on the left-hand side, opposite a church, which I discovered later on to be the Church of Assumption.

"We have arrived," said he; "I will go first, to show you the way."

He passed down a passage, at the extremity of which I perceived a light

I involuntarily raised my head, and read on the façade of the house these three words:

"Duplay. Master Carpenter."

I entered—the apprentices followed me.

CHAPTER XIV.

MY NEW PARISIAN FRIENDS.

THE carpenter, Duplay, in contact with whom fortune had brought me, had, at that period—that is to say, on the 12th of July, 1790,—the celebrity of having given shelter to a notorious revolutionist, which celebrity afterwards was attached to his name, his family, and his house.

He was a good patriot, and attended constantly at the Jacobin Club which was held in the neighborhood, and where almost all his evenings were passed, applauding the speeches of a little advocate of Arras, who, though ridiculed in the National Assembly, was appreciated in the Rue St. Honoré. The name of this little advocate was Robespierre.

When we arrived, we found the table laid for supper, through the forethought of his two daughters, Estelle and Cornelie. Their old grandmother was seated in an armchair, and Madame Duplay was in the kitchen, devoting all her attention to the forthcoming meal.

I was introduced to the two young ladies, both very charming girls. Estelle was a blonde, with beautiful blue eyes, and a figure wonderfully symmetrical, and flexible as a reed.

Cornelie was a brunette, with eyes black as sloes, and a stately and majestic contour.

Estelle dropped her eyes, as she curtseyed.

Cornelie smiled, and looked me full in the face.

Neither, however, paid much attention to me after the first salutation. I was younger than the youngest of them —that is to say, in their eyes, almost a child.

As to the apprentices, one appeared to be about eighteen, and the other a month or two older than I.

The elder was called Jacques Dinant. I don't know what has since become of him. The other was Félicien Herda, afterwards a celebrity in the Revolution.

This latter was a young man—fair, of a light complexion —a regular child of Paris—irritable, and as nervous as a woman. The nickname which his comrades gave him, as his irritability was always dragging him into controversy, and as he used always to say " No " to every theory, was " Citizen Veto."

Need I say that the veto was the prerogative of the King, and that it was through his wrong use of this privilege on two occasions that he alienated his people.

Madame Duplay appeared from the kitchen, with the first course. I was presented to her; but she paid even less attention to me than her two daughters had done.

She was about thirty-eight or forty years of age, and

must, at one time, have been beautiful, but with those coarse and too matured charms common to the lower orders of the people

She shared all the patriotic opinions of her husband, and was, like him, an ardent admirer of Robespierre

There was a discussion during supper concerning the relative merits of the Jacobin leaders, in which the apprentices took part as equals of their master

I fancied, somehow, that Félicien Herda regarded me with an evil eye. As the stranger, I had the seat of honor next to Mademoiselle Cornelie, and I think he must have looked upon it as an encroachment on his privileges.

Although well read in antiquity, I was profoundly ignorant of modern politics, and this gained me the pity of M. Duplay.

I knew the name of the famous Club of Jacobins, where Monsieur passed his patriotic evenings. but of all else I was ignorant.

From that bed of aristocratic Jacobins of '89, one could not foretell the springing up of the terrible and popular Jacobins of '93

Robespierre alone appeared, but he began to assume that pale and impassible visage which was never forgotten, if once seen

Duplay promised to take me to the Jacobins, and to show me him who was known among them by the title of an " honest man "

Robespierre had, as yet, but on two occasions spoken; and he had obtained the name of the " Timon of public affairs."

I know not if it was the view of Robespierre, whom I saw that night for the first time, that engraved the words on my mind, but I know this—that, in sixty years, I have not forgotten one word of his biography, or one lineament of his face.

I feel that I could draw his portrait now, as life-like as when he appeared first to me, on the platform, preparing to address us, and, from that time to the end, I was his most devoted admirer.

Robespierre was born in 1758, in that old, sombre, ecclesiastical and judicial town of Arras, capital of Artois, a province of France only 150 years, and where may yet be seen the ruins of the immense palace of its King-Bishop.

His father, an advocate of the council of the province, lived in Rue de Rapporteur. The young Maximilian was born there, that name being given him in honor of the last conqueror of the city.

Notwithstanding his hard work, the advocate was poor; but a wife, older than himself, helped to alleviate their poverty. She died. He thought the burden too heavy to bear alone, so, one morning, he decamped, and was no more seen in Arras.

They spoke of suicide, but nothing was proved.

The house was shut up, the four children abandoned. The eldest, Maximilian, was eleven; after him, came his brother, whom they called "young Robespierre;" after him, two sisters, one of whom, called Charlotte de Robespierre, has left some rare and curious memoirs. The other sister died three or four years after the disappearance of her father.

What with the death of his mother, and the absence of his father, there was enough to render the boy serious and unhappy. The friends who assisted the family asked the powerful Abbé of St. Vaast, who possessed a third of the town, and who had the disposal of many bursarships at the college of Louis-le-Grand, to give one to young Maximilian The charitable Abbé complied with their desire.

He started alone for Paris, with a letter of recommendation to a prebendary, who died almost at the same time as the young bursar entered the college.

It was in that ancient building that the young pupil grew pale, sickly, and envenomed, like a flower deprived of the sun; away from home, away from his friends, separated from all who loved him, and from all who could have brought a glow to his cheeks, or imparted happiness to his withered soul.

It was there that he met Camille Desmoulins, an ecclesiastical bursar like himself, and Danton, a paying pupil.

The sole friendship of his boyhood was formed with these two. How lightly that friendship weighed in the balance we know, when he believed that the moment had come to sacrifice it on the shrine of his country.

Two things militated against the firm continuance of this friendship; the one, the gaiety of Camille Desmoulins; and the other, the immorality of Danton, who paid no attention to the reproaches of his fellow-student.

Robespierre paid for his bursarship with laurel crowns. He left with the reputation of being a sound scholar—a reputation which gained him few friends and little honor. He afterwards studied with a procureur, entitled himself to practise. and returned to Arras a middling lawyer. but a stern politician, and having learnt to smile with the lips while the heart was filled with gall.

His younger brother took his place at college, while Maximilian, through the kindness of the Abbé de St. Vaast, was nominated a member of the criminal tribunal.

One of the first cases that he had to judge was that of an assassin. The crime was not only patent, but avowed. It fell to Robespierre to pronounce sentence of death.

The next day he sent in his resignation, not wishing to be put to a like test again.

That is how it was that he became an advocate. His philanthropy made him the defender, in place of the condemner of men. Duplay pretended to know. from certain sources. that Robespierre had never undertaken to defend a cause that was not just, but even were it just. he had to uphold it against all. He examined the cause of the peasants who brought a complaint against the Bishop of Arras, found it just, pleaded against his benefactor, and gained the day

This rectitude, although it had no material influence on his fortunes, increased greatly his reputation. The province sent him to the Etats Généraux, where he had for his adversaries all the nobility and clergy of his native State.

For adversaries — we say too much The priest and nobles thought too little of him to regard him in such a light.

This contempt, which had followed Maximilian to college, pursued him with greater violence now that he had attained a seat in the National Assembly.

He was poor and they knew it. They ridiculed his poverty; he thought it an honor. Having nothing, receiving nothing, but his salary as a member of the Assembly, a third of which went to his sister, he still lived When the Assembly put on mourning for the death of Franklin, Robespierre, too poor to purchase a suit of black, borrowed a coat for four francs, which, being too long or him, excited, throughout the time of mourning, the irrepressible mirth of the Assembly. The only consolation left him among all this ridicule was, that no one doubted his honesty.

"Had I not confidence," said he, in one of his speeches, "I should be one of the most wretched men in the world."

Yet, notwithstanding this, the man was not popular. Some few, indeed, through a species of instinct, saw that he was capable of great things, and among these were Duplay, his wife, and his two daughters.

All these details were given me during supper with the persistence of conviction. It was, therefore, with the liveliest satisfaction that I hailed M. Duplay's offer to take me to the Jacobins' Club, and looked forward with curiosity to see him whom they called *honest*, and afterwards stamped *incorruptible*.

CHAPTER XV.

I GO TO THE JACOBINS' CLUB.

AT nine o'clock, we left the house, and walked up the Rue St. Honoré towards the Palais Royal.

A current of people pointed the way, stopping at the little door of the Jacobin convent, which exists to this day.

I knew not that this was the place where the aristocratic and literary assembly held their meetings until told so by Duplay.

The entry was as difficult as that of a sanctuary. By special favor, as chief carpenter to the Duke of Orleans, Duplay had a card of admission.

At the door, Cornelie, Estelle, and the two apprentices left us, plunging down a staircase veritably built in the thickness of the wall.

I asked M. Duplay where they were going. He told me that there was, under the church, a smaller hall—a sort of crypt—where the workmen and their wives held a club—the workmen attending in the day, their wives at night. They there explained to each other the constitution.

Two ushers kept guard on each side of the door.

One, small and fat, with a bass voice, was the famous

singer, Lais, whom the *habitués* of the Opera applauded up to 1825.

The other, a handsome young man with wavy hair, undistigured by powder, and a generally aristocratic air, was a pupil of Madame de Genlis, the son of the Duke of Orleans, the Duke of Chartres, the conqueror of Jemappes, and the future King of France.

By his side was his young brother, the Duke of Montpensier, for whom, with great trouble, he had obtained admittance, notwithstanding his extreme youth.

On entering, at sight of the orator, who occupied the tribune, I cried out, "Ah! there is M. Robespierre."

In fact, after the portrait M. Duplay had given me, it was impossible not to recognize him. The impression he produced upon me was profound.

Yes, it was he, although his face had not yet assumed the grim and fantastic appearance that it did later on. There he was with that primly-brushed olive-colored coat, and that waistcoat of snowy whiteness, with his hair powdered, and thrown back from his brow, the skin of which, in its hideous wrinkles, reminded one of the parchment on a death's head.

It was that wrinkled face, sullen and acute; that eye, with its tawny yellow pupil, which shot between its retracted lids a glance replete with malice, that seemed to wound aught it fell upon; it was that mouth, broad and stern, with its compressed lips, it was that voice, harsh in all its notes, and resembling the laugh of a hyena, or the scream of a jackal; it was the whole figure of the man, quivering with a nervous spasm, which caused his fingers to be continually drumming on the ledge of the rostrum, like a pianist on the keys of a spinnet, it was, in short, the revolution incarnate with his implacable good faith, his freshness of blood, his mind determined, bloodthirsty, and cruel.

As we entered, he finished his speech, and descended amid shouts of applause.

I followed him with my eyes, in spite of myself, into the midst of the crowd, through which, small and thin as he was, he easily passed. Not a hand but was stretched out to grasp his, not a voice that did not address him. One man, dressed in black, stopped him, as he passed the desk, and said one word to him. He started, his face expressed hatred and disgust, and he passed on without replying.

" Who was that sombre-looking man who spoke to M. de Robespierre ? " said I, to M. Duplay.

He smiled.

" It is a customer of mine, to whose intervention with the Duke of Orleans I owe the right of coming here. His name is M. de Laclos, and he has written a very bad book."

" What book ? " asked I.

" ' Les Liaisons Dangereuses.' "

" Well, what then ? Speak lower."

" He is the man of the Duke of Orleans ; he it was who, in the Cour des Fontaines, under the shadow of the Palais Royal, published *Le Journal des Amis de la Constitution.* Robespierre hates him on account of his fame, but he is all-powerful here. It is he who disposes of the purse of the Prince. Hush! M. de Sillery, the husband of Madame de Genlis, is listening to us."

All this was Hebrew to me. I asked who M. de Sillery and Madame de Genlis were.

" Ah ! of course," said he ; " I forgot that you had only just arrived in Paris, from the depths of some impenetrable forest, and of course know not the names of those who are around us."

" I fancy that I know the name of M. de Sillery. If I do not deceive myself, he has been sent by the nobility of Champagne."

" Good, my boy, good ! "

" But it is the man," continued I, " that I do not know."

" Well, I will tell you all about the man. We begin to know names, as well as men. Charles Alexis Brulart is a marquis, like Lafayette, but having, like him, renounced his title, on the night of the 4th of August, he calls himself Sillery, as I call myself Duplay. As to his courage, it cannot be doubted. At twenty years of age, he assisted in the campaign of the Indies, and gained his rank at the point of the sword."

" What rank did he gain ? " asked I.

" Captain in the navy."

" But he wears the uniform of a colonel of grenadiers."

" Yes. He has left the navy for the army ; he is the accredited agent of the Duke of Orleans. In his youth, he was called Comte de Genlis; that, as I have told you, is the name of his wife. She has acquired a double, and doubtful, celebrity, as the friend of the Duke of Orleans, whose children she has educated, and as a writer, in which occupation she is at present engaged."

"But what does M. de Sillery say to all this?" asked I. Duplay lifted his brows.

"No wonder M. Robespierre is not his friend!"

"One cannot be friendly with Robespierre and the Duke of Orleans at the same time," said Duplay, shaking his head. "But patience!" All eyes are turned towards a man who enters. One felt, at first sight, without knowing him, that he was some great personage.

An immense forest of hair; a head resembling, for size and marked outline, a lion's or a bull's, indicated a ruler of the multitude. I had not time to ask Duplay who he was, for every mouth murmured the word "Mirabeau!—Mirabeau!"

"Ah!" cried Duplay; "there is the hurricane that brings us news. Draw near to him, that you may say, when you return home, that you have not only seen and heard Mirabeau, but that you have touched him."

We approached; but, of a truth, it was necessary to approach in order to hear.

All the audience collected round him.

I looked for M. de Robespierre, to see if he pressed round like the others.

He was isolated, alone, leaning against the rostrum, with a disdainful air, watching the men following the idol of popularity, like a shower of leaves after an autumn storm.

He knew that the crowd never drew near him, incorruptible; but it rushed after Mirabeau, the corrupted; and, at the same time, he both envied and blamed him.

The debate of the National Assembly had been stormy. There were a few nobles there, who witnessed, with profound grief, that union of all the parties of France.

Mirabeau had been insulted in the rostrum. A gentleman, M. Dambly, had threatened him with his walking-stick. Mirabeau stopped his speech, drew his tablets from his pocket, and demanded M. Dambly's address.

He cried it out from one end of the hall to the other.

"Very good!" said Mirabeau; "you are the one hundred and fiftieth person who has insulted me, and with whom I will fight when I have the time. Until your turn has come, hold your peace. I ask the President to make you pass your word to that effect."

Mirabeau related the story with incredible irony. All laughed—all said he was in the right.

"And Lameth?" asked several members.

"Which?—Alexander or Charles?"

"Charles"

"Oh, that is another matter! After practising with the rapier for two days, he could not decide upon anything; and, at the close of the Assembly, M. de Castrie cried out that he was a coward. They went out, and fought, and Lameth received a rapier thrust in his arm."

"Is it true that the sword was poisoned?" asked one voice.

"I know not that; but I do know that they are preparing to raze M. de Castrie's house to the ground."

This news was greeted with a shout of laughter.

At this moment, an eager voice was heard, urging the debate. Robespierre was on the forum.

He began to speak in the midst of the noise. As far as I could judge, he spoke for union; but the noise and excitement were so great, that it was almost impossible to hear what he said

But, accustomed to noise and interruptions, Robespierre continued, with that indefatigable perseverance, and that indomitable stubbornness which made his greatness, and, finally, his triumph.

Robespierre had spoken for ten minutes, and would, probably, have eventually succeeded in gaining silence, had not all attention been distracted from him by another arrival.

This was one of the heroes of the duel which Mirabeau had spoken of—Charles Lameth. He carried his right arm in a sling; but, with that exception, looked and walked wonderfully well.

All crowded round him, as they had done round Mirabeau, but with a different sentiment.

Charles Lameth was the friend of all the intelligent

young men who composed the majority of the Jacobin Club

Duplay pointed out to me, successively, Laharpe; the poet. Chenier, the painter. David, the tragedian, Talma, Audrien, Ledaine, Larive, Vernet, Chamfort—all men of intellect Then I returned to the rostrum. Completely abandoned, Robespierre had descended, after throwing upon that gathering of life, hope, and activity, a glance that seemed to presage evil to come.

No one knew that he had ascended the rostrum; all were equally ignorant of his descent Perhaps I was the only one who noticed the look of malignant hatred with which he regarded that knot of literary and scientific men, who had utterly disregarded—whether wilfully or not—himself and his discourse.

Presently, Duplay took my arm, and led me out of the hall.

"Return in a year," he said, "and your eyes will be opened There will be fewer plumes, fewer epaulets, less embroidery, but more men."

CHAPTER XVI.

PARIS BEFORE THE REVOLUTION.

I WISHED to go to the Rue Grange Batélière, where M. Drouet lived, and where he had appointed a rendezvous at the "Hotel des Postes;" but M. Duplay insisting that I should partake of the hospitality of a bed, as I had already done of the table, I felt that I could not well refuse.

It was arranged that I should share Félicien's room, in which they made me up a bed. On the morrow, at day-break, I should be at liberty to seek out M. Drouet, after my hair had been arranged according to the new fashion.

As that was an operation which must be performed sooner or later, on entering the house I seized upon a pair of scissors, handed them to Mademoiselle Cornelie, and asked her to perform on me the same feat that Delilah performed on Samson—viz, to cut off my flowing locks.

The sacrifice was consummated amid the laughter of the two girls.

One person alone did not join in the merriment thus provoked, and that person was he whose room I was going to share for the night. It was evident to me that he loved Cornelie, and was jealous of me—absurd idea; but the first stage of jealousy is absurdity.

The operation was over; they led me to a mirror to see if I were satisfied with the change worked in my personal appearance. At the first glance I felt inclined to laugh myself; I was more than clipped—I was almost shorn.

My ridiculous appearance restored Félicién to good humor with Mademoiselle Cornelie; and, as the servant appeared to announce that the room was prepared, he asked me to follow him, and he would show the way.

The first things that I remarked on entering the room were a pair of fencing foils, and a couple of masks to protect the face. I thought these rather strange ornaments for the bed-chamber of an apprenticed carpenter.

"Do you know what those are for?" asked he with a braggart air.

"Yes," replied I.

"Can you use them?"

"Not particularly well at present; but another month or two in the Salle d'Armes will improve me, I hope."

"To-morrow," said he, "if you like, we will have a bout."

"I am not sure whether I shall be able to. I fear that M. Drouet will be anxious about me."

"Will you have a bout now?" said he.

"Certainly," I replied, "if you wish it; but we have plenty of time before us. I shall not leave Paris without returning to thank M. Duplay, and then we shall have a better opportunity."

These evasive answers made Félicién think that I was not particularly anxious to cross foils with him; so he commenced a recital of his prowess and so, kindly lulled me to sleep.

I awoke, as usual, at daybreak, and slipping quietly out of bed, I dressed myself with as little noise as possible, so as not to awaken Félicién, and when ready, I left the room, and descended into the court.

All of M. Duplay's household were asleep, but the door was left open, so that I did not waste an instant.

The clock of the Church of Assumption sounded the half-after four o'clock as I left the house. I was utterly incapable of finding my way about Paris, in which I had arrived only the evening before; but the solemnity to be observed on the morrow had early drawn crowds abroad, so the streets were pretty full notwithstanding the untimely hour.

I asked my nearest route, they pointed out to me the Boulevards. Arrived there, I had only to follow that by no means despicable portion of my body, my nose, and, in a very short time, I discovered the Rue Grange Batêlère. Ten minutes after, I entered the "Hotel des Postes," and discovered, to my great joy, that M. Drouet was within.

I rushed to his chamber, and opened the door gently. He was not only awake, but on his feet.

"Ah! there you are!" said he, after having looked at me for an instant without having recognised me, on account of the disappearance of my hair. "Where have you been, you vagabond? I have been in a nice state of mind, I can assure you. It appears that you have been taken in a trap, like a fox, and been compelled to leave your tail behind you."

But you also have acquiesced in the mode."

"Yes; but not with the same enthusiasm as you. You have been foolish enough to cross the Pont Neuf, my boy."

Not knowing what happened on the Pont Neuf, I could not appreciate M. Drouet's pleasantry.

I told him all that had happened—from my meeting with the carpenter, on the Champ de Mars, to my visit to the Jacobin Club.

"Very good," said Drouet. "You passed last night among the aristocracy—you shall pass this among the *canaille*"

"Shall we spend the night together?" cried I, joyously.

"Yes; I will take you to the Cordeliers, where you will meet neither dukes, nor princes, nor marquises, but three citizens, whom you tell me you have often thought of—to wit, Marat, Danton, and Camille Desmoulins; in the meantime, we will take a stroll round Paris."

"What I wish most to see, M. Drouet, is the Bastille."

"You mean to say, the place where it stood?"

" Yes."

" Come along, then ; we will breakfast at the first restaurant we find. and then, hey ! for the Place de la Bastille."

M. Drouet knew Paris very well, having been there about twenty times.

We were not long before we arrived at a wall, on which was written, in large letters :—

" Here was the Bastille."

Why did the germs of the Revolution suffocate themselves under those dismal arches? Why, in 1300, did they discourse the holy gospel? Why, during the captivity of King John, did the Provost of Paris, Etienne Marcel, making himself a dictator, establish a popular club there, equal to that of the eighteenth century? Why were the Cordeliers, especially, of all the minor orders of St. Francis, republican in their tendencies—so much so, that, three centuries before Barbeuf and Prudhomme, they had dreamt the abolition of the rights of property ?

The 13th of July was Vesuvius, with its fire-ejecting crater, threatening to destroy Naples, and overturn the world.

To-day, all has ended in smoke—with, perhaps, a few cinders as a memorial.

CHAPTER XVII.

I ATTEND A MEETING AT THE CORDELIERS.

WE were engulfed, so to speak, M. Drouet and I, in the cave of the Cordeliers.

The hall was deep and broad, and lighted with smoky lamps ; a cloud formed by their smoke, and the breath of the audience, floated over our heads, and seemed to weigh heavily upon our chests.

There were no cards of admission—any one might come who liked ; the consequence was that the hall was crowded to excess, and every one ran a chance of suffocation. At the end of a minute, by means of vigorous pressure, we managed to force a passage into the body of the hall.

At first, we were obliged to keep our eyes shut, on account of the smoky atmosphere; but when we got accustomed to it, we could see objects, as it were, through a dense fog

I raised myself up on tiptoe, to see the popular man, *par excellence* All cried out, " Vive Lafayette ! "

We passed the Tuileries, and the door of the clock-tower, and gained a bridge. A sort of sympathy drew us to the Champ de Mars.

There was the same amount of bustle as on the day before A hundred thousand workmen were throwing up the earth, and forming a valley between two hills

The work progressed as if under the wave of an enchanter's rod There was no doubt but that all would be ready for the morrow, so that in seven days the gigantic undertaking would have been completed The middle of the place was entirely clear Here they erected the altar of the country, and in front of the Ecole Militaire, built up seats for the King and the Assembly.

At the end of a wooden bridge thrown over the river, near Chaillot, they erected a triumphal arch.

It was impossible not to become maddened amid this confusion We could resist no longer, but seizing the nearest implements that lay nearest at hand, we, with a shout of " Vive la nation ! " set ourselves to work with the rest.

At six o'clock we ceased, heated with our exertions. We were hungry. It was useless to look for a restaurant.

At eight o'clock we left the Champ de Mars, and passing through the Boulevards des Invalides, and the Rue Plumet, we shaped our course to the Cordeliers.

An immense crowd of people—some fifty or sixty thousand, perhaps—filled the place and the adjacent streets.

Those who had been unable to find lodgings had encamped there, or on the Boulevards.

Being anxious to see historical localities, I asked M. Drouet to take me to the Hotel de Ville. We went up to the Rue St Antoine, M. Drouet showing me the steps on which they had slain De Launay, the lantern on which they had hung Foulon, and the corner of the quay where they had killed Flesselles.

Everywhere—on the boulevards, in the places, in the churches, on the bridges—all was gaiety; every one was shaking hands with everybody; strangers in a moment
6

became old friends A shout of "Vive le Roi!" surrounded you with friends—a shout of "Vive la nation!" with
brothers.

After dinner, we proceeded to the Jacobin Club. It was
crowded, like all the rest—if possible, more so.

"Look, look!" said M. Jean Baptiste, the moment it
was possible to see.

"Look! Where?" said I.

"There—on the President's chair, between two candles!
Do you see any one?"

"Oh, M. Drouet!" said I, trembling.

"Well, what do you say?" asked he.

"I say that it is not a man whom you point out to me."

"What is he, then?"

"A monster!"

"Good! Look at him for some length of time, and you
will get accustomed to his face, all hideous as it is."

That man was M. Danton.

He rang the bell, and shook with a fury that seemed to
animate all he did.

In a moment all was silence.

His mouth, like the top of a cyclops, opened, and a voice,
which could have thundered down the noise had it continued, pronounced these words, "It is Marat's turn to
speak!"

Let us say a word or two about Marat before we proceed
any further.

Marat was born in 1744, at Neuchatêl. He was, at the
period of which I speak, forty-six years of age. His
mother, nervous and romantic, was ambitious enough to try
and make her son a second Rousseau. His father, a Prot-
estant clergyman, well read and hard-working, taught his
son the elements of science, and all the other branches of
knowledge that he was acquainted with, so that the young
man resembled a dictionary full of errors, and without even
method or form.

His grandfather nicknamed him Mara—the "t" is an
addition of his father's, or his own. He had been a teacher
of languages in England, and understood English pretty
well. He also dabbled a little in physiology and chemistry,
but in a slight degree. In '89 he became veterinary surgeon to the Comte D'Artois.

On the 14th of July, the day of the taking the Bastille, he found himself on the Pont Neuf, and escaping being crushed to death by a detachment of hussars. Marat ordered them, in the name of the people, to throw down their arms —so he said, at least, but no one believed it

Marat was not brave. He hid himself all day for the flight He said that the satellites of Lafayette and De Bailly were looking for him, whereas, in fact, they never thought of him. In the evening, he crept out like a beast of prey; his eye, yellow as that of an owl, seemed better adapted for seeing in the dark than in the daylight He lived, creeping from hiding-place to hiding-place, never seeing the light of day, and writing continually, imparting to his compositions all the bitterness and acerbity of his forced mode of life. From time to time he would exalt and provoke himself to blood. They say that blood was his ordinary drink—that he imbibed it when he was thirsty. His physician shook his head, and said, "Marat writes red." His friends the journalists lifted him up to laugh at him. They called him the divine Marat. The people took a leaf out of their book, and called him a god. Let Marat do what he liked, the people applauded. Marat did more than lead them—he gave them room for amusement.

Amid the murmur of applause which greeted him— applause which had been, in conjunction with silence, denied to Robespierre the evening before Danton, opening the door of the rostrum, said, "It is Marat's turn to speak!"

Scarcely had the words been pronounced, when Marat was seen mounting the steps leading to the rostrum, in which he appeared, with a lurid smile on his coarse mouth, seeming to embody, at one and the same time, three distinct genera: the man, the frog, and the serpent.

That *Thing*, dressed in almost rags, with dishevelled hair, squinting eyes, broad nose, and hideous appearance, was *the Friend of the People!* They had concluded by giving Marat the name of his journal

At last, his hideous head appearing over the ledge of the rostrum, radiant with pride, and held, as it were, defiantly back to hide a neck covered with ulcers, all cried out, "Speak, Marat, speak!"

"Yes," replied Marat, with a deep voice, "I am going to."

All was hushed, as if by magic. Danton covered his face with his hands, and listened with a smile of scorn, while a young man placed himself in front of the rostrum, his arms crossed over his breast, in the attitude of a gladiator, defying his enemy.

"Look—look!" said Drouet.

"At whom? Marat? I can see him."

"No, no! that young man in front of the rostrum."

"Who is he?"

"Camille Desmoulins, the man of the thirteenth of July; the man of the Café de Foy; the man of the green cockade!"

"Silence! silence!" cried out several voices.

Marat, hearing a whisper, had turned his evil eyes on us.

We became as still as mice.

"Great treason!" cried Marat; "but that is not wonderful—they would not follow my advice; and I tell you that until the heads of some of the National Assembly ornament pikestaffs, things will go wrong. Do as I tell you, and the Constitution will be perfect."

"Why—why—why—don't you send a mod-mod-model to the Assembly?" said the young man, in front of the rostrum, with a terrible and painful stutter in his speech.

"I am framing it," said Marat, "while you make love, Camille, I think."

"Dream, you mean!" said the same satirical voice.

"Silence! silence!" cried the audience.

"Yes; I am preparing a scheme for our Constitution."

"Tell—tell it us, great—great legislator!" said Camille, totally disregarding the cries for silence.

"I say that the form of government should be monarchical," continued Marat; "that Monarchy is the guiding-star of France, and that the person of the King should be sacred, only to be approached through the medium of his ministers."

"Ah, aristocrat!" cried Camille.

"M. Danton," cried Marat, furiously, "it is my turn to speak and I demand silence!"

"Silence! silence!" again cried the crowd.

"Citizen Camille," said Danton, in a voice as satirical as that of the man whom he reproved, "I call you to order!"

"Then ask the speaker," said the imperturbable Camille, "to give us part of his plans for the legislation."

"Firstly," cried Marat, I demand that the blasphemer's tongue be cut out!"

"Well, cut my to-to-to-tongue out! I blas-blas-blaspheme! I say Marat is a fool!"

And, suiting the action to the words, he protruded his tongue at Marat, and made a grimace

Some of the audience could not avoid laughing.

Marat was mad with rage.

"I again say," said he. "in my project for our Constitution, that the city is burdened with two hundred thousand poor people. I argue the right of the poor to share"

"Good!" said Camille. "We are ready; let us plun-plun-plunder!"

"Yes, plunder!" cried Marat, rapidly becoming more and more excited. "When one has nothing, he has a right to take the superfluities of the rich—rather than starve, he has the right to take and devour their palpitating flesh! Let man commit what outrage he likes on his fellow-men—it is no worse than a wolf killing a sheep!"

"Marat has asked for me to be called to order: I ask that he may be called to reason."

"Why should I have pity on men?" yelled Marat. "Firstly, pity is only a folly, acquired in society In nature, neither man nor inferior animals know pity. Does Bailly, who tracks me, or Lafayette, who hunts me down, or the National Guards, who seek to slay me, know pity?"

"Who prevents your eating them?" said Camille.

"No, no!" said Marat, sneering at Camille in his turn. "No, I will not eat them; I will leave Lafayette to the women, and will cry unto them, 'Make him an Abelard!' I will leave Bailly to the people, and will cry unto them, 'Hang him, as you have hanged Foulon, as you have hanged Flesselles!' I will ask for the heads of the National Guards—I will ask for the heads of the aristocrats—I will ask, not for six hundred heads as I did yesterday, but for nineteen thousand four hundred!"

"Make it twen-twenty thousand, round numbers!"

The admirers of Marat chafed. Marat's mouth shut, his eyes darted fire, his head was drawn back, he looked as if he could have swallowed his adversary at one mouthful.

The friends of Camille, Frérone, and Danton, the ene-mies·of Marat, took the part of Camille Desmouslins.

They would have come to blows, despite Danton's contin-uously ringing the bell for order, and his terrible voice sounding far above the din, and crying, "Silence! silence!"

I passed with M. Drouet to the side of Camille Desmou-lins, for whom I felt a sympathy as strong as my hatred of Marat. The attention of all, however, was now drawn to the entrance of a new personage, on whom all eyes were fixed.

CHAPTER XVIII.

THE FEMALE ELEMENT IN POLITICS.

THIS new comer was a woman.

But a strange one, having a good deal of the masculine in her composition—a perfect amazon—one might say a virago.

She was habited in a long dress of red stuff, surmounted by a cape; she wore a plumed hat, and a large sword at her side.

I touched M. Drouet's arm.

"Oh!" said I; "who is that?"

"I am no wiser at present than yourself," said he; "unless it is—yes, it is the famous Théroigne de Méri-court."

I had once or twice heard the name of the heroine of the 5th and 8th of October—the impetuous Liégoise, beauti-ful, but terrible; who, at Versailles, with a smile and soft voice, had ordered the regiments of Flanders to lay down their arms. An unhappy affection—the treason of an unfaithful one, had thrust her out from woman's life. She had embraced the cause of the Revolution with transport. It was her last love. The unhappy woman was whipped by the Royalists in the Garden of the Tuileries, became insane, and died in Bicetre, or Charenton, I forget which, after twenty years of agony.

But at present she was young, pretty, proud, if not happy. Alas! her misplaced love had seared her heart.

Her entrance was great.

"There is the Queen of Sheba!" cried Camille Desmoulins, stammering more than ever.

Then, turning to Danton, "Rise up, Solomon," said he; "and go and receive her Majesty!"

She stood boldly in front of Danton, put her hands on the hilt of her sabre, and said, "If thou art Solomon, build the temple. We have space enough on the site of the Bastille, or better on the Field of the Federation. I will head the subscription."

She took a gold chain from off her neck, and threw it to Danton.

"I ask to speak," said a tall, fair man, with a strong German accent; "to support the proposition of the Citizen Théroigne."

"Citizen Anacharsis Clootz will address the meeting," said Danton. "Place to the orator of the human race."

The Prussian Baron mounted the rostrum.

"Look!" said Drouet; "there is a republican who has a hundred thousand crowns a year, and yet they say that only the bootless and stockingless are revolutionists."

"Yes," said he, with a soft smile and quiet voice, which contrasted with the harshness of the former speaker; "yes, I second the motion of Citizen Théroigne. The temple should be built in Paris. Why was Paris built at an equal distance between the Pole and the Equator, if not to be the centre of attraction for all men? At Paris will one day assemble the Etats Généraux of all the world. You are laughing, Camille, you eternal grinner. The day is not so distant as you suppose. Oh, that the Tower of London may fall as did the Bastille! Oh, that a second Cromwell may rise from insignificance into power, and the tyrant of a day will be seen no more! When the tricolor of liberty floats, not over England and France alone, but over all the world, there will then no longer be provinces, soldiers, and vessels of war; here will be a people, and better than that, a family. It will then be as easy to go from Paris to Pekin as from Bordeaux to Strasbourg; the shores of the ocean will be brought together by a bridge of ships; and the East and the West will embrace on the Champ de la Fédération. Rome was the queen of nations by force of arms; Paris will be the same by dint of peace. Think not that this is mere

imagination, oh, my brothers! No, the more I think over
the matter, the more sure am I that I am right, and the
more I believe in the possibility of one great and united
nation. Oh, listen to the voice of reason, may patriotism
warm your hearts to build up a temple which will hold
all the representatives of the human race. Then ten
thousand men will suffice to represent the universe!"

"Bravo! bravo!" cried all from all sides.

"There are plenty of heads to chop off here and there,"
said Marat.

"Ye-ye-yes," stammered Camille Desmoulins; "six
hundred yes-yes-yesterday, ninteen thousand four hun-hun-
dred to-day; and if a to-morrow arrives, there will be fif-
fif-fifty thousand."

"Anacharsis," cried Danton, "you err, but on the side
of a good and generous heart."

The terrible man looked at him with a soft smile, and he
continued. 'Men will be what they ought to be, when
one can say, 'The world is my country, the world is mine;'
but till then, there are more proscriptions, more banish-
ments, more exiles. Nature is one; why is not society
one?' They are divided forces, which strike one another
when nations are driven against each other by the breath
of hatred, and, like clouds, they strike and are scattered.
Tyrants, we wish not that, and the proof is that we demand
not your death. Kill yourselves, slay each other. Descend,
O kings, from your thrones, and we will give you your
choice 'twixt misery and a scaffold. Usurpers of sover-
eignty! Balthazars of modern times! is it possible that
you see not on your palace walls, amid the glare of your
thousand lamps, the shouts of your revelries, and the crash
of your song, the writing, not in fire, but in your people's
blood, *Mene, Mene! Tekel Upharsin?* Lay down your
sceptres and your crowns, and head a revolution which
delivers kings from the grasp of kings, and the people from
the rivalry of the people."

"A-a-amen," stammered Camille Desmoulins. "Ana-
Anacharsis wishes to carry me away by the hair of my
head, as the angel did Habakkuk."

"Long live Camille Desmoulins!" said Théroigne, while
the friends of the true son of Voltaire tendered him their
hands. "If ever I have love, it shall be for you, I promise
you. By the bye, you are fond of Sieyès?"

"Yes, truly." replied Theroigne "Between you and me, he is the only one who gives me the idea of a man"

"What am I, then?" said Danton

"What are you?" said Theroigne, scanning him from head to foot. "You are only a fool."

"Well re-re-replied" said Camille, "that is what I call taking the bull by the horns."

"In the meantime," cried Marat. "you are losing sight of the public safety. I speak to you of a great treason, and you will not listen. Lafayette"

"Ah, good!" said Camille "Go on Marat!""

"Lafayette has caused to be made in the Faubourg St Antoine ten thousand snuff-boxes all of which are embellished with his portrait as General of the National Guard. Lafayette aspires to the dictatorship"

"Of tobacco merchants?" queried Camille Desmoulins

Marat's yellow skin assumed a green tinge, and perspired with rage.

"He has some scheme beneath that" continued he, "so I pray all good citizens in whose hands these snuff-boxes may fall, to destroy them."

"In order to discover the names of his accomplices?" asked Camille.

"There are many of them. I told you that twenty thousand pieces of cord would suffice, but bring thirty or forty thousand, and you will not have enough"

The applause drowned the voice of Marat, but eventually their breath failed them, and they could hear Camille Desmoulins, who, like a swimmer who had dived, again remounted to the surface

"Always tragic, friend Ma-Marat—always tragic! hyper-tragic, in fact"

"And these cords," continued Marat— "take care, Camille Desmoulins, that one of them is not first tried on you"

"In that case," replied the incorrigible railer "I have a chance if they take me, of growing ugly. You have—"

Here the laughter broke out irresistibly, and as it was from Camille's side, he may be fairly said to have gained the victory.

Marat descended, furiously shaking his fist

"Return to thy cave, night-bird! Go back to thy hole,

hyena! Sneak into thy nest, viper!" murmured Danton, with a look of ineffable disdain. But Danton's murmurs were like thunder; every one heard them.

When Marat left, all joined in brotherly communion, his presence having alone restrained them hitherto.

M Jean Baptiste knew Danton, and went to shake hands with him, and to compliment Camille Desmoulins

I could not turn my eyes from the face of the ex-advocate, that terrible blind man whom Providence had given to guide the revolution.

I shall have occasion to speak again of him, and to show what sensibility of heart was hidden beneath that rough exterior.

We left the club at midnight, and returned to the "Hotel des Postes," Rue Grange Batéliére.

At daybreak on the morrow we had to be under arms.

CHAPTER XIX.

THE FIELD OF THE FEDERATION.

I COULD not sleep all night

I had seen so much since my arrival, and had been in company with so many great men—Mirabeau, Robespierre, Lameth, Laclos, Chemier, Talma, David, Laharpe, Danton, Marat, Desmoulins, Anacharsis Clootz, and Herbert—that their names continued to ring in my soul like an alarm bell.

And through them all passed the beautiful amazon in her red robe; and that seemed so strange to me, coming as I had for the first time from the Forest of Argonne, and feeling, as it were, in another world, or else in a state of furious delirium.

I arose at daybreak. Alas! the morning was dark and rainy-looking; thick black clouds were chasing each other over the sky once so pure and brilliant, but now changing its opinions, and becoming aristocratic.

I awoke M. Drouet. I was astonished that any one could sleep on the night heralding in such a day. He jumped up and dressed himself. We took our guns, and descended.

We soon joined our friends of St. Menehould and Islettes, formed rank, and marched to the Champ de Mars.

At the door of Sainte Honoré, we met the orator of the human race, who had passed the night at the Cordeliers.

He had with him a body of men, Poles, Russians, Turks, Persians, all in their national costumes. He took them to the federation of France before he took them to the federation of the world.

We marched by the river's side, and soon arrived at the Champ de Mars.

A hundred and sixty thousand people were seated on the slopes, a hundred and fifty thousand on the plain itself, and yet there was sufficient space left to accommodate fifty thousand of the National Guard.

A second amphitheatre in a semi-circle formed in the space between Chaillot and Passy accommodated more than a hundred thousand people.

Anacharsis Clootz was right. This looked well for a federation of the world.

We crossed the river by the wooden bridge thrown over it at Chaillot, and passing under the Arc de Triomphe, entered the Champ de Mars, and arranged ourselves in front of the altar of the country. The honors were for the provincial National Guard.

We were removed only a hundred paces from the raised seats destined for the King, the Queen, and the National Assembly.

All in a moment it began to rain. It was now eight o'clock, and as the King and Queen were not expected till ten, there was plenty of time to get both wet and cold. Some of the National Guards began to dance a farandole to keep the warmth in them; the example was contagious, the muskets were stacked, and each man choosing a partner from among the female spectators, the extraordinary spectacle of two thousand people dancing at one time commenced.

At half-past ten the cannon announced the arrival of the King, and the drum recalled each man to his post. The female dancers were re-conducted to their friends, and the guard presented arms.

The carriages of the King, Queen, and other dignitaries

of the realm came at a foot pace. They stopped at the raised benches; the King, descending first, gave his hand to the Queen, and they took their respective places, accompanied by the Assembly.

Now, not only had the day, but the moment arrived.

Stationed close to the benches, of which we had an excellent view, I had been awaiting with impatience the arrival of the King and Queen, of whose personal appearance I had formed my own ideas, which I am bound to say were very far from the truth

The King was not sufficiently kingly. The Queen was too much a queen.

While the King was bowing to the people, and seating himself in the midst of the cries of "Vive le Roi!" M. de Talleyrand, the lame bishop, the Mephistopheles to another Faust, whose name was Napoleon, proceeded, attended by two hundred priests, to the altar of the country. All wore tri-colored sashes.

The regimental bands strike up, but are scarcely heard. But forty pieces of cannon, discharged at the same time, command silence.

The taking of the oath followed.

Three hundred thousand hands are uplifted at one and the same time on the Champ de Mars. The rest of France was joined in spirit to those who swore in the name of all.

They had hoped that the King would descend from his seat, mount the altar, and there, holding up his hand, swear in the sight of all his people.

They were mistaken. The King swore from his seat, placed in the shadow—in fact, almost hidden. The idea that struck the hearts of all, was that the King swore with regret, and without intending to keep the oath that he had taken.

This was the oath that all knew beforehand, but which few could hear, thanks to the fashion in which the King spoke ·—

"I, King of the French, swear to the nation to employ all the power which has been delegated to me by constitutional law, in maintaining the constitution and executing the laws"

Ah, King, King! it is with greater heart and better faith that your people have sworn.

The Queen did not swear, she sat in a reserved seat, with the Dauphin and the princesses. On hearing the King's voice trembling and hesitating she smiled, a singular light gleaming in her eyes the while.

M. Drouet, as well as myself, remarked that smile, and he frowned.

"Ah M. Drouet," said I. "I like not that smile! And I never could have believed that that beautiful Queen could have smiled in such a fashion.

' The Queen's smile matters little," replied M. Drouet. "The King has sworn—that is the great point. The oath is registered at this moment in the hearts of twenty-five millions of Frenchmen. It will be worse for him if the oath be not kept."

*   *   *   *   *   *   *

Every time that I have been to Paris since that day, I have paid a visit to the Champ de Mars, the only monument left of the Revolution.

The last time I made the pilgrimage was in 1853. I had come to buy the History of the French Revolution, by Michelet.

I seated myself on a hillock, and much in the same way as M. Chateaubriand on the ruins of Sparta cried out in a loud voice, three times. " Leonidas! Leonidas! Leonidas!'" I read aloud the following lines of the eloquent historian, which chimed in so well with my own thoughts —

"The Champ de Mars is the sole monument left of the Revolution. The Empire has the Arc de Triomphe. Royalty has its Louvre and its Invalides. The feudal Church of 1200 has its throne in Notre Dame.

"But the Revolution has alone for its monument an empty space.

"This monument is sand, and desert as the plains of Arabia. A mound to the right, a mound to the left, like those which the Gauls erected in memory of their fallen heroes.

"Though the plain be dry, and the grass be withered, still a day will come when it shall be again clothed in green.

"For mingled with this earth is the sweat of the brow of those who on a sacred day raised these hills—on a day when, awakened by the cannon of the Bastille, France poured in from the north and south—on a day when three millions as one man swore eternal peace.

"Ah! poor Revolution, so confiding in the first blush of thy youth, thou hast invited the world to love and peace.

"Oh, my enemies! said'st thou, there are no longer enemies.

"Thou heldest out thine hand to all—thou hast offered the cup to drink to the peace of nations, but they would not."

CHAPTER XX.

I GO BACK AGAIN.

WE arranged to leave Paris on the following morning.

It was three hours after noontide when the ceremony was over. I made a rendezvous with M Drouet for five o'clock at the "Hotel des Postes," and left him to give my thanks and bid adieu to Maître Duplay and his family.

All the household had been to the fête of the federation.

I met the group, consisting of M. and Madame Duplay, the two daughters, and the two apprentices, at the top of the Rue St Honoré.

I went up to and saluted them.

They, too, had remarked the hesitation with which the King took the oath, and were, in consequence, sorrowful.

We entered the house; the dinner awaited us; Duplay invited me to join them; I assented.

During the meal, Félicién, sure of his superiority over me as a fencer, spoke of the promise I had made to try a bout with him; and asked me, if, after dinner, I was prepared to stand by our agreement, and give M. Duplay and his daughters, the pleasure of witnessing our prowess. I replied that if it would please my worthy hosts, I should only be too happy to make such a slight return for their kindness and hospitality towards me.

Dinner finished, we passed into the workshop, Félicién evidently expecting an easy victory over me, and speaking much as a master would to a pupil.

M Duplay and the young ladies being seated, we each took our mask and foil

"Be easy." said Félicién, in a whisper intended to be heard; "I will not hurt you."

"Thanks!" replied I, "for I shall probably be at your mercy"

"Would you like to begin?" asked Félicién.

"As you please," said I.

We placed ourselves on guard

At the first pass, I saw that Félicién tried to touch me; which, between strangers, lacks courtesy.

However, I appeared not to notice it, and contented myself by parrying his thrust.

Now came my turn

I made four or five passes only; but they were sufficient to show me that, though Félicién was a tolerable fencer, he had no chance with me.

I had paid great attention to the instructions given me, as I wished to make rapid progress; while Bertrand being an able master, and I his sole scholar, he was enabled to devote all his attention to me.

Félicién, also, after the first few passes, perceived my superiority over him.

I allowed him to make five or six thrusts at me, simply contenting myself with parrying them.

Once he grazed the wristband of my shirt, but he did not dare say "Touched!"

I saw the blood mount to his face.

"My dear Félicién," said I, "I have been three hours under arms, and am fatigued. If you will allow me, I should like to put an end to our combat. The ladies, I am sure, will accept my excuse."

"They may, but I will not," said he. "I know full well, by the strength of your parries, that your arm is not fatigued. Say that you believe yourself to be a better fencer than I am, and that you are generous enough not to pursue your advantage."

"Then you wish to continue?"

"Certainly. If you are the better man, I will take the lesson, as an obedient scholar should"

"You hear the promise that M. Félicién makes," said I, turning to M. Duplay; "and you are witness that I continue solely on that agreement?"

"Yes, yes!" cried all the spectators, especially the two girls, who seemed to me to wish the pride of the apprentice lowered.

I saluted Félicién with my foil.

"I await you," said I; "take care of my ripostas, which are very rapidly delivered."

"We will see," said Félicién, dealing me a thrust which I had only just time to parry.

But, at last, I touched, almost imperceptibly, his breast with the button of my foil.

He bounded backwards; and while neither of us cried "*Touched?*" yet all the spectators saw that it was so.

He again rushed on me, his teeth set, his lips pale.

He crossed my foil, and passed *one, two*. But in retreat, his foil caught my guard, and snapped off, about two inches from the button.

But he continued to fight, as if he knew not that his weapon was broken. So I took the first opportunity that offered, and, twisting his blade out of his hand, sent it flying across the room.

"Pardon me," said I, "for disarming you; I know that it is not etiquette; but neither is it etiquette to fence with a buttonless foil. You might have dangerously wounded me, and been unhappy yourself ever afterwards."

Then, taking off my mask, I hung it on the wall, and placed my foil by the side of it.

Félicién saw plainly that I did not wish to continue the combat; and, without taking off his mask, he stalked out of the room.

"Ah!" cried M. Duplay; "you have read him a good lesson, and I must say that he deserved it. Now then, say good-bye to the ladies, and let us be off to the Rue Grange Batélière, where you will introduce me to M. Drouet. I need not tell you that if I hear of your coming to Paris without paying me a visit, I shall be your bitter enemy for life."

I bade the two girls good-bye, and we set out.

As I expected, Félicién was awaiting us in the court.

The moment he saw me come out with M. Duplay, who evidently only came with me to prevent a quarrel, Félicién began to divest himself of his upper garments; but M. Duplay cried out, "Come here, you young vagabond!— I tell you, come here!"

Félicién approached unwillingly.

"Give your hand to my young friend here—he has a right to it."

"Has what ?" asked Félicién.

"Nothing," I hastened to reply. "M. Duplay believes that you knew your foil to be unbuttoned, but I have told him 'no!' Come; shake hands, and be friends."

I held out my hand.

Félicién took it with rather a bad grace.

"There," said M. Duplay; "you have said adieu! We go our way—you can go yours."

And he dismissed him with a wave of his hand.

We went our way.

"You see, I was right in coming out with you," said M. Duplay. "The little scoundrel was waiting there to pick a quarrel with you. He would not be a bad carpenter if he would work, but he thinks the trade beneath him. He loves, and is jealous of Cornélie. One can easily see that, but he is eighteen months younger than she. I don't think that Cornélie is very fond of him; but you have given a lesson to M. Veto, and you have done well."

I did not reply, as I agreed in every respect with M. Duplay.

As the clock struck five, we arrived at the Rue Grange Batélière. We found M. Drouet punctual. I introduced M. Duplay, whom he already knew through my speaking of him.

We spent the evening fraternising with the Parisians.

We each of us received a medal in commemoration of the occasion.

At five o'clock in the morning, the drum beat the recall. We formed ranks, and set out for the Barrier Pantin. Meaux was fixed upon as our first halting-place.

Four days after our departure from Paris, we arrived at Menehould about three hours after mid-day. We had, on an average, marched about twelve leagues a day.

M. Drouet wished me to dine with him, but I knew that my uncle would be uneasy if I returned not with the others; and, somehow or other, I had a presentiment that I must hasten, if I wished to see him alive.

I was a quick walker. I ran down the slope of the mountain, and traversed the village at a quick trot.

7

On passing the priest's house, I saw Mademoiselle Marguerite in the doorway. When she saw me, she came forward.

I feared what she was going to ask; so I at once said, "M. le Cure is in capital health, and will be here in an hour. What news of my uncle?"

"Good, my dear René—good; but you have mentioned to him your arrival?"

"No, I have not. Why should I?"

"Well, he told me that you would arrive at half-past seven this evening; and he said, 'Thank heaven, I shall be able to see and bless him before I die!'"

"He said that? Well, I must hurry on, for I have no time to lose."

On leaving the village, and turning the first angle of the forest, one could see the cottage of Father Descharmes.

I turned the corner in a moment.

Father Descharmes was at the door, seated in his armchair, in the same place I had left him, enjoying the rays of the setting sun.

I waved my hat on the end of my musket. I thought that he feebly waved his hand in return.

I ran quicker than ever; and the nearer I came the more his face brightened up.

When I was not more than ten paces distant, he lifted himself from the chair, and, raising his eyes to heaven, he said "I knew well that I should see my child again. 'Now let Thy servant depart in peace, according to Thy word.'"

I heard these words, and threw myself on my knees.

"Bless me, oh, my uncle!" I cried.

My voice was choked with sobs, for I saw that I had arrived just in time to receive his last breath.

I felt the old man's hands placed upon my forehead, and I fancied that I heard his voice murmuring feebly a prayer.

When the prayer was finished, he cried, "Oh, heaven, receive my spirit!"

I felt his hand slowly slipping from my brow.

I stayed a moment immovable, and then, taking his hands in mine, I raised myself gently, and looked at him.

He had fallen backwards, his head resting on his breast, and his eyes and mouth open.

But the mouth no longer had breath, and the light had departed from the eyes.

He was dead!

CHAPTER XXI.

I EXCHANGE MY GUN FOR THE PLANE.

I WILL not exaggerate my grief; I will simply say that I loved my uncle as a father, and my sorrow for his loss was full and sincere.

In my absence, the two keepers—the one named Flobert, and the other. Lafeuille—had taken it in turns to minister to his little wants.

When he died, Flobert was in the house. I called, and he came to me.

The name of Drouet filled my heart, and rested on my lips.

At that moment a postchaise passed, going in the direction of St. Menehould I ran after the postilion, my eyes filled with tears.

"Tell M. Jean Baptiste," cried I to him, "that my uncle died at the moment of my arrival."

"Is it possible? Poor Deschannes! I spoke to him yesterday! He was seated in his easy-chair, in the doorway, and he told me that he expected you this evening."

He then drove on.

"You will not forget to tell M. Drouet, will you?" I repeated.

"Certainly not. Do not be afraid, M. Réné; I shall not forget it."

I had such confidence in M. Drouet, that I did not think it necessary to ask him to come. I had only to tell him my sorrow, and I knew that he would come

As I expected, two hours after, I heard the gallop of a horse. I rushed to the door, and M. Drouet was there.

He had met M. Fortin as he was coming in the same carriage which had taken him to the Federation. He had pressed on his steed; he had seen Marguerite in passing;

and in all probability the good priest would be there in an hour, with his housekeeper, to say the prayers for the dead by the bedside of Father Descharmes.

M. Drouet wished to lead me away; but, smiling, in the midst of my tears, "What would my poor uncle say of me on high," I said, "if any other hand than mine performed the last sad offices for the dead?"

"Do you feel yourself strong enough for it?" asked M. Drouet.

"Is it not my duty?"

"Without doubt. But one cannot always do one's duty."

"I hope that heaven will always give me strength enough to perform mine."

"Breathe that prayer night and morning, and it will be of more benefit than all the prayers printed in the Church Service."

The burial was to take place at four o'clock in the Cemetery of Islettes. After it was over, he proposed that I should go with him to St. Menehould, to pass the night, and in the following morning with a notary, who would arrange the deceased man's papers &c., &c.

In the afternoon, at four o'clock, my uncle's corpse, accompanied by the whole village of Islettes, followed by me, his sole relative, and by Drouet, Billard, Guillaume, Mathieu, and Bertrand, his friends, was placed in its last resting-place, accompanied by the blessings of the Abbé Fortin, and all those who knew his upright and irreproachable life.

The funeral over, M. Drouet put the key of the cottage in his own pocket. Then we mounted into M. Drouet's cabriolet, and drove off to to St. Menehould.

In the evening, M. Drouet went to seek the notary, who promised to run over the following day, after breakfast, to open the will, and make an inventory. On the morrow, at mid-day, in the presence of MM. Fortin, Drouet, Bertrand, and Mathieu, the will was opened.

It appointed me his sole heir, and at the same time indicated a cupboard in which would be found, in a bag, two hundred and sixty louis d'or, which comprised his whole fortune.

It also charged me to give all the little things he had collected, and which were of no use to me, to the poor of the village of Islettes; also to give all the implements of the chase, with the exception of those which pleased me, to his old friends, Flobert and Lafeuille

On no account was anything to be sold.

As I was under age, M. Drouet, by my uncle's wish, became my guardian.

As a matter of course, I immediately handed over to him the two hundred and sixty louis which my uncle had left me, telling him to keep them till I came of age.

All being thus arranged, I placed on a wheelbarrow, which Bertrand lent me, all my carpentry tools, my compasses, my plane, and so on.

Two hours after, I arrived at M. Gerbaut's. On my entrance, I found the whole family at supper.

" M Gerbaut," said I, " you offered me, if at any time I desired to work under a master, an apprenticeship—are you inclined to stand by your agreement ? "

" Thanks, my boy, for having thought first of me. But sit down and eat ; it will be time enough to think of work to-morrow."

"Sit down by my side, my friend," said Sophie, with a sweet smile, holding out her hand.

She drew her chair a little nearer to her father's, and I accepted the place thus offered.

CHAPTER XXII.

MY NEW LIFE UNDER SOPHIE'S FATHER.

THE changes made by death excepted, there is this strange and touching peculiarity of country life, that, whilst kingdoms are rent, hedgerows, and fields, and rustics, apparently remain ever the same.

Nearly a year had passed since I last set foot in Father Gerbaut's house, and on entering I found everything the same as when I had last left it; the covers laid in the same places, on the same table, and for the same number of persons. Not only were material affairs the same, but the affections remained unaltered. Sophie had said, " Come, my brother," and I came. She gave me her hand, and said, " Brother, you are welcome ! "

And yet a great agitation prevailed over the whole surface of France; all the ancient names of the provinces had been changed. France ·was divided into eighty-three departments. One part of Champagne had taken the names of the Department of the Meuse; the part neighboring was now the Department of the Marne. The little River Biesme, which served as a line of demarcation between Germany and France, and, likewise, between Champagne and Clermontois, fixed the limit of the two departments. Les Islettes, Clermont, and Varennes were in the Department of the Meuse.

Municipalities were constituted under the name of corporations; M. Gerbaut was nominated municipal councillor, and our neighbor, M. Sauce, grocer, procureur of the corporation.

I say our neighbor, because the two houses were separated only by a lane.

The two families frequently visited each other. M. Gerbaut and M. Sauce, with their blushing honors thick upon them, were patriots.

Madame Sauce was a fine woman, but coarse and vulgar. a veritable dealer in candles, butter, and sugar; rather given to serving short measure, but otherwise incapable of committing a fraud. The mother of M. Sauce, an old lady of sixty-three or sixty-four years, was a Royalist. The children, the eldest of whom was only twelve, were incapable of having an opinion.

We shall see presently what Sophie's opinions were.

Opposite us was the tavern of the " Bras d'Or," belonging to the brothers Leblanc. Interest made them play a little comedy. As they had the patronage both of the patriotic young men in the town, and the Royalist young nobles from the vicinity, the one brother was a patriot, and the other a Royalist. The elder cried " Vive la nation " with the young tradesmen, while the younger shouted " Vive le Roi " with the noblesse.

In the midst of all this, a national decree was propagated, which caused some uneasiness in the province.

" It was the civil constitution of the clergy.

It created an episcopal chair in each department.

It ordered the election of bishops and priests to be conducted after the fashion of the primitive church: that is to say, that they were to be elected by a majority of votes; all the salaries of the clergy were to be paid from the King's treasury; perquisites were abolished.

The clergy were desired to take an oath to maintain that constitution; those who would not, were compelled to resign their benefices in favor of those who would

If, after being dismissed, they attempted to renew their functions, they were prosecuted as disturbers of the public peace.

From this arose the troubles in the Church, and the division between the constitutional priests and those who refused to take the oath.

If one looks back on that great epoch, and on the two remarkable years of '89 and '90, one cannot fail to be astonished. Can any one explain the precautions taken by nature, that the men and the events should arrive at the same time for that awful result which followed?

In 1762, M de Choiseul suppressed the order of the Jesuits; that is to say, deprived the Church of its wisest and most powerful supporters.

Afterwards, in the years '68, '69, and 70, the Revolution produced Chateaubriand, Bonaparte, Hoch, Marceau, Joubert, Cuvier, Saint Martin, Saint Simon, Lesneur, Les Cheniers, Geoffrey Saint Hilaire, Bichat, Lamancourt, all of whom, in 1792, where in the bloom of life and genius.

Whence came those births sublime and terrible, produced in the space of three or four years? Whence came that burst of genius prepared twenty-four or twenty-five years before to second political eruption? Whence came that body of superior men who closed the eighteenth and opened the nineteenth century? Whence came that phalanx more than human, and who raised the hand to swear to the constitution before the altar of their country?

Let us forget the death of Mirabeau, the last upholder of the monarchy, whom heaven struck in an unexpected manner, at the moment he forsook the cause of the people; and who, in dying, counselled the flight of the king—a flight which, had it succeeded, would have saved the life of his Majesty, but successful or unsuccessful, must inevitably have brought the monarchy to the ground.

All knew not the cause of that reason or corruption on
the part of Mirabeau ; whether it was that his aristocratic
instincts, kept under for a time by his father's severity, had
sprung into light on contact with royalty, or not, seemed
to be doubtful.

The Queen was a great enchantress. She was a Circe,
fatal to those who stopped not their ears, to avoid listening
to the blandishments of her sweet voice. She had the fatal
gift, which Mary Stuart possessed, of leading all her friends
to death.

The end of Mirabeau was announced in the provinces
almost at the same time as his illness,   .

It was on the 20th of March that the news of his illness
was bruited about in Paris. It appeared that on the 27th,
two days previous, being at his house at Argenteuil, he was
seized with a violent cholic, accompanied with almost unen-
durable agony.   He sent for his friend and physician,
the famous Cabanis, and distinctly refused to see any
other. This was wrong, perhaps , a hospital surgeon or a
practised physician might have saved him

As soon as the news was received, the crowd pressed to
the door of the sick man's house.

Barnave, his enemy, almost his rival, who would have
died, slain by the Queen, for an interview like that which
Mirabeau had had with her, came to see him conducting a
deputation of Jacobins.

The priest came, and would not be denied. This was
exactly what Mirabeau feared—the influence of priests upon
his dying volition.

They refused admission to the sick man's chamber, saying
that Mirabeau wished only to see his friend M. Talleyrand,
to whom, he said, he could confess, without any great fear
of virtuous indignation.

For some months he had been suffering, he believed, from
the effects of poison. Administered by whom ? He would
have been puzzled to tell that himself All the world, except the parties interested, knew about his interview with
the Queen at St Cloud, in the month of May, 1790.
Whether his malady was natural, or the effects of a crime,
he took no measures whatever to arrest its progress.

Vigorous of body, perhaps more vigorous in imagination,
he had passed the night of the 15th of March in an orgie,

th component parts of which were women and flowers, perhaps the only two things that he loved. He used money simply to gratify his tastes in these respects.

On the morning of the 2nd of April after a night of agony, which inspired the famous prophecy "I carry with me the mourning of monarchy its remains will be the prey of factions.' —awakened from the bosom of grief, if one can use the term, by a cannon shot, he cried.

He summoned his valet, was shaved, washed and perfumed all over his body After his last toilette was completed opening his window to admit the young April sun, which was brightening the first blossoms on the trees, he murmured, smiling, "Oh, sun if thou art not God himself, thou art his cousin german'

Afterwards, his last insupportable suffering seized him. He could not speak but snatched a pen, and wrote plainly the one word *Dormir*—" Sleep,

Did he ask for death like Hamlet, or only for opium to soothe his passage from one world into the other?

At about half-past eight, he moved, lifted his eyes to heaven, and heaved a sigh It was his last!

In the evening, the theatres were closed, as if some great national calamity had occurred

The mask was taken from that immobile face, from that powerful head which Camille Desmoulins called a magazine of ideas exploded by death. His placid brow expressed the serenity of his soul, and his face bore no trace of either grief or remorse.

There is no doubt but that Mirabeau, when he promised the Queen all his support, fully intended to keep that promise, not only as a gentleman but as a citizen.

The funeral ceremony took place on the 4th of April: four hundred thousand persons followed in the procession. Two instruments were heard for the first time on that occasion, filling the breasts of the spectators with their vibrating notes, they were the trombone and the tom-tom.

At eight in the evening, he was placed in the temporary tomb provided for him in the Pantheon

We say temporary, because his body remained there only three years

It was removed at the time when the Convention having slain the Jacobins, and slain itself having no more living to slay, determined to dishonor the dead.

It was ordered that the corpse of Honoré Riquette de Mirabeau, traitor to the people. traitor to his country, and sold to royalty, should be removed from the Pantheon.

The order was executed, and the corpse of Mirabeau was thrown into the criminals' cemetery, at Clamart.

It is there that he now sleeps the sleep of hope, waiting the day when France, an indulgent—nay, let us rather say an impartial mother, will give him, not a Pantheon, but a tomb; not a temple, but a *mausoleum*.

CHAPTER XXIII.

THE ARRIVAL OF THE DRAGOONS.

DURING the ten months that I stayed with M. Gerbaut, my life was monotonous in the extreme.

As I was an excellent workman, he gave me, as well as board and lodging, a salary of thirty francs a month, and often gave me to understand that he wished that I were a few years older, that he might give me his daughter in marriage, and surrender to me his business. But the fact was, I was a year younger than Sophie.

But it was not that only which rendered a union impossible between us; it was that invincible sorrow, denoting a passion hidden in the depths of her heart.

My opinion was, that the young man for whom she entertained this hidden feeling was the Viscount de Malmy.

Sophie gave me all that she had promised—sisterly love. It was impossible to be kinder or more affectionate to me than she was. On Sunday, I invariably took her out for a walk, and she never would accept any other arm than mine; but this friendship did not induce her to confide to me the cause of the sorrow which I could plainly see was preying upon her constitution.

Sometimes the young nobles came, and, as I have told you, put up at the Brothers Leblanc.

On those days, Sophie always found a pretext for not going out with me, taking care that the pretext was plausible.

She shut herself up in her chamber, the window of which was exactly opposite the window of the "Bras d'Or," and stayed there the whole time that the young nobles were at Varennes.

More than once, under these circumstances, I had half a mind to get up in the night, and see if the darkness hid any mystery with regard to Sophie and the Viscount, but I always had strength enough to resist the temptation. I thought to myself I had no right to surprise any of her secrets, which, notwithstanding our friendship, she had not thought fit to confide in me.

One night, whilst passing along the corridor, I fancied I heard two voices in Sophie's room; but instead of stopping to listen, I felt ashamed of the action which jealousy prompted me to commit, and I determined, nothwithstanding the pangs I suffered, that Sophie should have no reason to suppose that I suspected anything.

My grief, undoubtedly, was great; but my pity for her was greater, and I felt that strong as my anguish was, she was preparing for herself an after day of sorrow and remorse.

From the 1st to the 15th of June, the visits of M. Malmy and M. Dampierre were more frequent than usual.

An instinctive hatred made me keep aloof from M. de Malmy; but the Count, in memory of Father Descharmes, never met me without speaking.

But, for the most part, they did not come as far as the Rue de la Basse Cour. M de Malmy alone, and his friend the Viscount de Courtemont, went to the "Bras d'Or;" the Count de Haus stayed on the top of the Hill des Religieuses with one of his friends, an old Chevalier of St. Louis, named the Baron de Prétontaine.

On the 20th of June, about three o'clock in the afternoon, M. Jean Baptiste arrived.

In the course of the ten months since I had last been at Varennes, he had paid two or three visits to his friends Billaud and Gillaume, and had never failed to come and see me, and to invite me to take breakfast with him, as the case might be

This time he had a more mysterious air than usual; he engaged a private room at the Brothers Leblanc, ordered dinner for four, and asked his two friends to come and join us immediately at the "Bras d'Or."

For some time the horizon had been lowering.

It was evident that there was some counterplot hatching.

On the 1st of March we had heard of the affair of the Gentlemen of the Dagger.

On the 20th of April, we had heard that the King, intending to go to St. Cloud, had been stopped by the people, and was afraid to leave the Tuileries.

We knew, vaguely, what was going on in Italy. The Count D'Artois was at Mantua with the Emperor Leopold, asking for an invasion of France. The King did not ask that invasion, but D'Artois knew well that he would be glad of it. A year before, everybody saw, from the letter from the Count de Provence to M. de Favras, how little place the King held in the calculations of his brothers

The young King of Sweden, Gustavus, after having been the enemy of Catharine, conquered by her, became her friend, and at the same time her agent, and was at Aix, in Savoy, publicly offering his sword to the King; while the Count de Fersen, an intimate of the Queen's, was carrying on a correspondence with M de Bouillé.

People said that for the last three months the Queen had caused to be made a trousseau for herself and children.

They said, likewise, that she had caused to be made a magnificent travelling outfit, sufficient for at least an absence of six months

Her friend, M de Fersen, they said, was superintending the construction of an English chaise, capable of holding from ten to twelve persons.

All these rumors tended to one end, and caused the two last appearances of M Drouet at Varennes.

His post-house was situated on one of the short cuts to the frontier, and by the road many nobles had emigrated, as if to point out the proper route for the King.

A new event had taken place, which had appeared to M Drouet of sufficient importance to warrant a consultation with his friends

This was the event I speak of.

On the 20th of June, in the morning, a detachment of hussars, with brown dolmans (some said that they were a part of De Lauzun's regiment, others that they were a part of Esterhazy's), had entered St. Menehould by the Clermont road.

At that time, when the troops were billeted on the tradespeople, the authorities were generally informed of their arrival two or three days in advance.

In this case, the authorities had received no advice.

M Drouet had spoken to the officer commanding the detachment This officer, whom he remembered to have seen two months before passing between St Menehould, Chalons, and Varennes, was called M. Goguelet

Recognised by M. Drouet, this officer had no hesitation in chatting with him He said he had been sent with his forty men to form an escort for a treasure.

While M. Jean Baptiste was talking with him. a messenger arrived from the municipality, asking the reason of his coming unannounced and unexpected.

"Don't trouble yourself about nothing," replied the officer, "myself and my men will sleep here; but as we set off in a hurry on a particular service, we are utterly without rations. We will pay all our expenses. so as not to be a burden on the tradespeople. To-morrow, at daybreak, we start for Pont-de-Somme-Vesles."

The messenger took this response to the authorities; but they, not being satisfied with it, sent him back with a request that M. Gogulet would step up to the Mayor's house.

He accordingly went there, M Drouet following.

When asked the reason of his march, the officer exhibited an order from M de Bouillé, commanding him to be at Pont-de-Somme-Vesles on the 21st of June, to take charge of, and escort some treasure which was there, to St Menehould, where he was to surrender his trust to Colonel Dandoin, of the First Regiment of Dragoons

They then asked where were M Dandoin's dragoons.

"He follows me,' he replied; and will arrive here to-morrow morning"

The interrogatory was not pushed any farther; but M Drouet was not satisfied, so he had run over to Varennes, to inform his companions of the event, and to hold a consultation with them

Just as he had finished his tale, the younger brother Leblanc entered

He had come from Stenay.

"Do you wish to see some beautiful horses, M. Jean Baptiste?" asked he.

"I should like nothing better," replied Drouet, "especially if they are for sale, as I want a remount."

"I don't think that they are for sale; but what is astonishing is that they are harnessed in relays."

"Where are they?"

"At the 'Grand Monarque,' with Father Gautier."

M. Jean Baptiste looked at us.

"It is well, Victor," he said; "I will go there after dinner. Have you any other news?"

"No; there is a movement going on among the troops at Stenay, but there is nothing astonishing in that. I should not be surprised if we received an announcement of their arrival here to-morrow."

"Nor I," said Drouet.

We finished dinner, and entered into the Rue de la Basse Cour, crossed the bridge, and arrived at the "Grand Monarque," where we found six horses being carefully attended to by the two grooms.

"Those are fine horses. Whose are they, my friend?"

"My master's!" insolently replied one of the grooms.

"The name of your master is a secret, I suppose?" queried M. Drouet.

"That depends upon who asks me."

M. Guillaume frowned.

"This is an insolent scoundrel," said he, "who merits being taught how lackeys should speak to men?"

"Will you teach me?" asked the groom.

"Why not?" asked Guillaume, going a step nearer to him.

M. Jean Baptiste stopped him by taking hold of his arm.

"My dear Guillaume," said he, "don't put yourself out; perhaps this good man is forbidden to speak, and has come like M. Goguelet, for the treasure."

"Do you know M. Goguelet, and why we are here?"

"You are here for the treasure which the hussars are bringing from Pont-de-Somme-Vesles, to hand over to the dragoons who were awaiting them at St. Menehould."

"If you are one of us, monsieur," said the groom, touching his hat, "I have no reason to refuse telling you to whom the horses belong. They are the property of the Duke of Choiseul."

"You have said well," said Drouet, laughing; "and we were going to quarrel with one of our friends."

" If you are a friend, monsieur, you might tell me whom you are, as I have told you about the horses ? "

" You are right I have no motive for concealing my name. I am Jean Baptiste Drouet, postmaster at St Mene-hould."

" As you have said. you are *probably* one of us."

At this moment, Father Gautier stepped out from the kitchen door.

M. Drouet thought he had better say no more to the groom, for fear of exciting suspicion

" Ah, ha ' Father Gautier," said he ; " your kitchen appears to be in full blow."

The fires in fact, were at their highest.

" It is so, M Drouet; but the astonishing part of it is, that I do not know for whom the cooking is going on."

" You don't know for whom ? "

" No. I received on the 14th, an order from the military commandant to prepare a dinner for five o'clock, and it is now the 24th, and no one has arrived to eat it ; but as it is a written command, I am not afraid, for eaten or not, the dinners are always paid for."

M. Drouet again looked at us.

" Perhaps they are some great lords about to emigrate," said M Jean Baptiste.

" And who take away our money," replied Father Gautier.

" In any case, they will leave you a little of theirs. Six or eight dinners, at how much a head ? "

" Three crowns, not including the wine."

" And for how many people ? "

" Eight or ten ; the number was not definitely arranged."

" Father Gautier," said M. Drouet, " you will yet die rich."

He then shook hands with him, smiling.

We left the house, and soon found ourselves in the street.

" My friend," said M Drouet, " without doubt, something extraordinary is about to take place I shall return to Saint Menehould without losing a moment. Guillaume will go with me When you get home, watch day and night. Sleep with one eye open, and hold yourselves in readiness for whatever may happen "

We returned quickly to the " Bras d'Or ," M. Drouet

saddled his horse with his own hands. M. Guillaume borrowed one of the elder of the Leblancs, and they both set
off for St. Menehould at a sharp trot, recommending us
both to keep our eyes and ears well open.

CHAPTER XXIV.

THE NIGHT OF THE 21st OF AUGUST, 1791.

ONE can easily understand that it was late when we
sought our respective couches, and that we rose early the
next morning, having kept one eye open all the time that
we slept.

When I say we, of course I speak of M. Billaud and the
elder Leblanc, whom M. Drouet had taken into his confidence.

About eleven in the morning we heard that a detachment
of hussars had been seen on the road from Stenay.

I left my work, giving a few words of explanation to
M Gerbaut and Mdlle. Sophie. They partook of the general agitation which pervaded the town, or rather the air
which seemed tremendous with coming events.

Mdlle. Sophie was very much excited, especially when I
announced the approach of the hussars. Two days previously, MM. Malmy and Courtemont had arrived at Varennes.

I crossed the bridge and entered the Grand Place on one
side, at the same moment as the hussars entered it at the
other.

They stopped a moment on the Place, spoke to the groom,
who had arrived the evening before with the relays, which,
by superior orders, they had stabled in the old Convent of
the Cordeliers.

They were commanded by a tall officer of effeminate
appearance, and blonde complexion. He spoke French with
a very strong German accent. His name was M. de Rok-
rey.

He put up in the Place, not at an hotel, but with a
tradesman of the town, to whom he bore a letter of recommendation.

Behind me a great number of the inhabitants of the High Town were descending and forming themselves in groups with those of the Low Town.

About one o'clock, two young officers arrived by the same route, and stopped to speak with him who commanded the detachment.

One of them approached me, and asked if I knew the whereabouts of Neuvilly.

I told him it was half-way between Clermont and Varennes, and pointed out the direction to take.

"Can you tell me, sir," said he, "the cause of the agitation of the people?"

"The movements of the troops about the city for the last two days. It is reported that they are to form a convoy for a treasure, and the inhabitants are curious."

The two officers looked at each other

"Can one get to Neuvilly," asked one of the two, "without passing through the town?"

"Impossible!" replied I. "A canal of great width intersects the road; and even if your horses could swim across they would not be able to mount the opposite bank."

The officer turned round to his friend.

"What will you do? It appears that the relays must pass through the town."

"We have plenty of time," replied his friend; "the courier will precede the carriage two hours."

The two officers thanked me for my information, and proceeded to the " Hotel du Grand Monarque," in the court of which they dismounted, having thrown the bridles of their horses to the stable boys in attendance.

It was evident that the persons expected would arrive from the opposite side of the city—that is to say, the side on which Paris lies.

It was, therefore, but lost time to stay in the Low Town.

I walked up to the High Town, crossed the bridge, and returned to M Gerbaut's just as they were sitting down to dinner Notwithstanding the stifling heat, the Place de Latray was crowded.

During dinner, Father Gerbaut lost himself in vain conjectures as to what was going on Sophie, on the contrary, said not a word, scarcely lifted her eyes from her plate, and ate little or nothing.

8

Not being authorized by M. Drouet to tell what I knew, I also held my peace.

In the mean time, in order that the reader may fully understand what was about to take place, it is necessary for me to describe the scene of action.

Varennes, as I before told you, is divided into two parts, the High Town and the Low Town. The High Town was called the Château.

On coming from Clermont, you enter Varennes by a straight road, which, for more than two leagues, has not a single curve in it, with the exception of where it enters Neuvilly.

All of a sudden as you approach those scattered houses which always foretell a city, the road takes a sudden turn to the right, and falls, as it were, into the midst of the city by the Rue des Réligieuses.

This descent ends at the Place de Latry.

That Place is, or rather was at the time of which I am writing, entirely blocked for two thirds of its length by the Church of St. Gengoulf, the side of which touched the right side of the Place (I speak of the right side with reference to Paris), and the façades of which overlooked a cemetery, which, stretching from the side of the Rue de l'Horloge, left a passage of about thirty yards open to the sky.

Another passage, intended for carriages, was formed, but on account of an arch stretching over it, it was impossible for vehicles loaded too high to pass underneath.

Emerging from under that arch, one stood facing, five or six paces off, the Rue de la Basse Cour. On entering, you could see on the right of him the "Hotel du Bras d'Or."

A little further on to the left stood the house of M. Sauce, Procureur de la Commune.

I have already said that his house was only separated from M. Gerbaut's by a passage.

The Rue de la Basse Cour descends rapidly to a little Place, where it joins the Rue Neuve and the Rue St. John.

A little running stream of rather deep but clear water, over a pebbly bottom, intersects the Place. A bridge, narrower than the one you would find there to-day, joins the two parts of the town—that is to say, the High and Low Town. The bridge crossed, and the corner of the "Grand Monarque" rounded, you find yourself in the Grand Place.

It was on that Place that the hussars were stationed
before they took up their lodgings in the old Convent of
the Cordeliers, and it was at the "Grand Monarque,"
which bore the effigy of Louis XVI, that the relays stopped; also the two officers whom I have since discovered
were M. de Bouillé, the younger, and M de Raigecourt,
and where, for eight days, they had prepared dinner for an
imaginary traveller who was always expected, and who
never came.

This being all explained, the reader will be able the
better to understand the various scenes of the drama, which
will, in due time, be laid before him

Tired of seeing nothing fresh, though the day had been
passed in excitement, at the moment the clock struck eight
I quitted the house of M Gerbaut. My intention was to
walk along the road leading to Neuvilly, and if I saw
nothing, to return home, go to bed, and patiently await the
morrow.

Many houses had their windows open, and were lighted
up

The "Hotel du Bras d'Or" was one of these.

Some young townsmen were playing at billiards on the
first floor. They were MM. Coquilard, Justin, Georges,
and Soucin. Two travellers staying at the hotel by chance
were playing with them. These were M. Thevenin, of
Islettes, and M Delion, of Montfaucon.

I passed under the arch, and entered the Place; two or
three houses alone were lighted up.

The crowd had dispersed; not a light was burning in the
Rue des Religieuses, with the exception of two lanterns,
which only made the darkness in the street visible.

I walked up the street, and stopped on the summit,
whence I could see the whole town.

All seemed to sleep The Low Town betrayed, especially
on the Place, no more life.

I saw torches waving in the direction of the "Grand
Monarque."

I was occupied in watching them, when I fancied that I
heard the gallop of a horse.

I laid myself down with my ear to the ground.

The noise was now more distinct, on account, no doubt,
of the horse having passed from the earth on to the stones.

I jumped up, convinced that a horseman was approaching.

And not only that, I fancied that I heard in the distance the rumble of the wheels of a carriage.

The event expected all day, and watched for by night, was about to happen.

I hid myself in the angle of the wall.

The gallop approached rapidly.

Presently I distinguished, in the midst of the road, a horseman.

When the straggling houses came in view, the horseman stopped indecisively.

It was evident that he knew not whether to stop or continue his route.

For the moment, I thought of showing myself, and offering to guide them; but, on second thoughts, I considered it the least likely mode by which to gain information.

I therefore stayed where I was, doubly hidden by the night and the wall.

The horseman dismounted, passed the bridle of his horse over his arm, and walked on a few paces, knocking at the doors of the different houses to see if they would open.

At last he knocked at No. 4. That opened.

It was the property of a small householder, called Jourdan.

" Who are you, and what do you want ? " asked a voice.

" Pardon, monsieur," returned the courier: " but is this Varennes ? "

" Did you wake me up to ask me such a question as that ? You are laughing at me ! "

" Excuse me, monsieur, but I am a stranger here, and wish to know if I have really arrived at Varennes."

" You have, monsieur. If you have come for beds, find them, and leave me to my sleep. Good night ! "

" Your pardon, monsieur," said the courier ; " I came not here to sleep, but am in advance of a carriage which expects relays at Varennes."

" I am sorry for you ; but it is no use expecting relays at Varennes, for we do not possess a post-house."

" I know that, monsieur."

" Why did you ask me, then ? "

A woman's voice was heard.

"Come to bed, Martin," said she. "You ought to see that he is only making fun of you."

"You hear—my wife calls me!"

He tried to close the door, but the unknown stopped him by placing his arm in the aperture.

"Ha, monsieur!" said the tradesman; "what does this mean? Do you wish to do me an injury?"

"Do not be frightened, I only wish to ask you a question."

"You have asked me ten already."

"I know that I am at Varennes, thanks to you; I know that there is no post-house, but I knew that before. Having been so kind as to answer those questions, perhaps you will not object to one more?"

"How? Did not you tell me that you were preceding a carriage to Varennes?"

"No doubt; but you have not allowed me to continue. A relay ought to be ready opposite the first houses of Neuvilly; I wished to ask—have you seen that relay?"

"Oh, that is another thing; you should have begun to speak in that manner!"

"Have you seen them?"

"The relay?"

"Yes, the relay."

"No, monsieur, I have not."

"You must tell me all that you know, at once," cried the impatient courier.

"I have told you about the relay, but you did not ask me till just now."

The same woman's voice was again heard, crying out afresh. "Make him go, husband," she said; "he is only making a fool of you—he is doing it for a wager."

"You hear, sir," said the man; "my wife says you are doing it for a wager."

"Nothing of the kind, I assure you, monsieur. Thank you for your information; you can now shut your door, and reseek your wife."

The tradesman slammed his door in a rage.

"Shall I wait here?" soliloquised the unknown.

He was not long kept waiting. During the dialogue on the door-step, the carriage was rapidly drawing nigh; not only did he hear the wheels, but the neighing of the horses.

The courier, placing himself in the midst of the road, awaited its arrival.

<hr />

CHAPTER XXV.

THE TRAGEDY OF ROYALTY BEGINS.

SCARCELY five minutes had passed, when I began to distinguish a black phantom; and soon after I saw the sparks flying from under the horses' hoofs.

As the mass approached, I saw that it was composed of two carriages.

The first was an ordinary cabriolet; the second, an immense travelling carriage.

On seeing the road blocked by one man, on foot, holding a horse by the bridle, the postilion cracked his whip, and shouted to the horses to go on.

But the unknown, in an imperative voice, cried out "Stop!" lifting his hand at the same time. "I wish to speak to the travellers in the second carriage!"

"Oh, Valory!" cried a voice from the first; "is anything wrong?"

"No, madame; only a slight mistake."

Then approaching the second carriage, "Pardon," said he; "we have arrived at Varennes, and there is no relay."

"How!—no relay? What is the reason of it?" replied a female voice.

"I know not; but I am very nervous about it."

"Wake up, monsieur," said the same voice, with an impatient gesture. "Do you not hear what M. Valory says?"

"What does he say?" replied a masculine voice.

"He says that we are at Varennes, and that there are no relays."

"Has he asked?"

"For a quarter of an hour I knocked; for another quarter, I talked, I asked, and commanded fruitlessly."

"Let us get out," said the masculine voice, "and take a look about for ourselves."

The door opened.

"No," said the female voice; "let me get down; I will manage it,"—and she leaped nimbly to the earth.

"Madame—madame!" said the voice of a child; "let me get out with you"

"No, Louis," said the lady; "stay in the carriage with your papa; I shall come back in a moment. Give me your arm, M de Valory"

The courier approached, respectfully, his hat in his hand, and offered his arm to the lady who asked it.

"Here," said she; "just here is a door opening."

But as she spoke the words, though in the slightest degree open, it was shut again

M. de Valory jumped forward, and, at the risk of cutting his hand, seized the door on his side, and pulled it violently backward.

The door yielded to the force used, and showed a man of fifty or fifty-five years, holding a candle in his hand. He was attired in a dressing-gown, and had his naked feet thrust into slippers.

This was the same M Préfontaine whom I have already spoken of, and with whom M. Dampierre stayed when he came to Varennes.

"What do you want, Monsieur?" asked the astonished old Chevalier; "and why do you break open my door?"

"Monsieur," replied the courier, "we do not know Varennes; we are *en route* for Stenay. Will you be kind enough to point out the road we ought to follow?"

"If I render you this service, perhaps I shall be compromised!"

"You, I am sure, will never refuse to render a service to a lady who is in danger."

"Monsieur," said the old gentleman, "the lady who is behind you is not simply a woman." Then lowering his voice, he said, "It is the Queen!"

M. de Valory tried to deny it; but the Queen, taking him by the arm, "Lose no time in discussion," she said; "tell the King alone that we are discovered"

At this moment, two other young gentlemen, dressed as couriers, jumped down from the box of the chaise.

"Sire," said M Valory, "the Queen desires me to tell you that she is recognised."

"By whom?" asked the King.

"By an old man, of courteous manners, who, though a little timid, has the air of a gentleman."

"Ask him to come and speak to me," said the King.

M. Valory transmitted the invitation to the gentleman.

He went to the carriage, showing signs of great apprehension.

The Queen followed him; her face, made visible by the light of the candle which he held, expressed supreme disdain.

"Your name, sir?" asked the King.

"De Préfontaine," replied the interrogated, hesitatingly.

"Who are you?"

"Major of cavalry, sire, and Chevalier of the Military Order of St. Louis."

"In your double capacity as major of cavalry, and Chevalier of the Order of St. Louis, you have twice sworn fealty to your King It is, therefore, your duty to aid me in the difficulty in which I find myself."

The Major murmured some words; the Queen stamped her foot with impatience.

"Ah, sire!" said she; "see you not that the Major is afraid."

The King looked as if he had not heard her remark.

"Monsieur," continued he, "have you heard that a detachment of hussars, and relays of horses, await a treasure which must pass through Varennes?"

"Yes, sire," replied M. de Préfontaine.

"Where are the hussars? Where are the horses?"

"In the Low Town, sire."

"And the officers?"

"At the 'Hotel du Grand Monarque.'"

"Monsieur, I thank you," said the King. "You can return to your house; no one has seen you—no one has heard you; therefore, no harm can happen to you."

The Major took the hint, and retired, after having made a profound obeisance.

"Messieurs," said the King, addressing the two young gentlemen who had dismounted from the box-seat, "take your places. You, M de Valory, jump on your horse, and gallop on to the 'Grand Monarque.' You hear that our escort is there."

The two young gentlemen took their places, and M. de Valory vaulted into his saddle

The King and Queen re-entered the carriage, the door of which was shut by one of the postilions.

"Postilions!" cried all three gentlemen, with one voice, "to the 'Hotel du Grand Monarque'"

The men whipped up their horses; but at the same instant, a man, covered with dust, on a horse flecked with foam, seemed to spring from the ground, and rushing diagonally across the road, cried out, in a voice of thunder, "Stop, postilions! You drive the King!"

I uttered a cry of astonishment, for I recognized the voice of M Drouet.

The postilions who had hitherto been lashing their horses, stopped, as if stricken by a cannon-shot.

The Queen felt, without doubt, that it was a moment for decisive action.

"Order them! Command them!" she cried, to the King.

The King put his head out of the carriage window.

"Who are you, sir," said he, "that you dare to give orders here?"

"A simple citizen, sire," replied M Drouet; "but," continued he, raising himself in his stirrups, and stretching out his arm, "I speak in the name of the nation and of the law. Postilions! not a step farther, on your lives!"

"Postilions!" cried the King. "to the 'Grand Monarque!' It is I who command you'"

"To the 'Grand Monarque!'" cried the three gentlemen.

"Postilions!" cried M. Drouet, "you know me well, and are accustomed to obey me. I am Jean Baptiste Drouet, postmaster at St Menehould."

M. de Valory saw the indecision of the postilions—ten men stopped by one. He saw that it was necessary to slay that one, and, drawing his *couteau de chasse*, he went at him.

In a moment, I jumped out of my hiding-place, and seized the bridle of his horse.

The horse, being frightened, reared, and threw its rider.

M. Drouet recognised me.

"Ah! is it you, René?" he exclaimed. Follow me!"

Sticking his spurs into his horse, he seemed to sink into the ground, so quickly did he disappear down the declivity of the Rue des Réligieuses.

"Here I am! Here I am, M. Drouet!" cried I, following quickly behind him.

M. Drouet dashed down the Rue des Réligieuses, crossed, like a flash of lightning the Place Latry, plunged under the arch, and reappeared in a moment on the other side, in front of the "Hotel Bras d'Or," running up against another cavalier as he did so.

"Is it thou, Drouet?" said the cavalier.

"Is it thou, Guillaume?" cried Drouet.

"Yes!" "Yes!" each replied simultaneously.

Both dismounted, that they might pass under the entrance of the inn.

In the meantime, the billiard-players, hearing a noise, rushed to the window, to see what it meant.

"Be on your guard!" cried M. Drouet. "The King, with his family, are trying to escape! They are travelling in two carriages Wake up M. Sauce!—cry ' Fire! fire!' Guillaume and I will guard the bridge."

At this moment, I arrived, and dashed against the door of the Procureur de la Commune, crying as loud as I could, "Fire! fire!" as M. Drouet had recommended.

In the meantime, he and Guillaume had disappeared down the Rue Neuve.

At the end of the bridge, they encountered a cart filled with furniture.

"Whose cart is that?" cried M. Drouet.

"Mine." replied the driver.

"Ah, is it yours, Regnier?" said Guillaume. "You, I know, are a good patriot. Turn your cart across the bridge; it will stop the passage of the king."

"The King?"

"Yes; the King He wishes to get to the Place of the ' Grand Monarque,' where the hussars await him."

"I have seen them," said Guillaume.

"And I also," said Regnier.

"Now to work," said the two young men.

"Yes; to work!" replied the proprietor of the furniture.

And all three with their united efforts, managed to upset the cart across the bridge.

When the operation was finished, they listened.

They heard the rumble of the carriages, which descended the Rue des Réligieuses at full speed, at the same time the cry of " Fire ! fire !" burst upon their ears.

I will now tell you what occurred on the high road, after M. Drouet and I left the two carriages, as well as I can from the description given me afterwards by M. de Préfontaine, who, though he had closed his door, took good care to open his window, and, therefore, saw and heard all that passed.

M de Valory, when he fell, did not abandon his hold on the bridle of his horse, and as he tumbled on soft ground, he escaped with a few bruises.

He was, therefore, soon again mounted, and, threatening the postilions with his raised whip, he cried, " Well, wretches, have you understood ?"

" Certainly ; and have you ?"

" What ?"

" That which M. Drouet said. He told us not to go any farther "

" You dare to quote M. Drouet, when the King commands !"

" Get rid of the three scoundrels !" said one of the young gentlemen on the box, " and let us drive the carriage ourselves "

" Gentlemen !" cried the Queen, who saw that there was going to be bloodshed.

Then to the postilions—" Gentlemen," she said, in her softest voice, " I do not order, I entreat. Fifty louis to each one of you, if you drive us safely to the ' Grand Monarque ' "

Frightened of the swords of the gentlemen, and melted by the entreaty of the Queen, the postilions set off at a gallop

But they had lost ten minutes, and these ten minutes M. Drouet had turned to profit

They dashed on, but were obliged to avoid the arch, for fear of breaking their heads, so they turned round the church, and began to descend the Rue Basse Cour.

But before they could execute that manoeuvre, their course was suddenly arrested.

The cabriolet, as we have said, preceded the chaise ; but

scarcely had it turned out of the Place, when the bridles of the horses were seized by two men. These were the elder Leblanc, and M Thevenin, of Islettes.

That first carriage contained but two maids of honor to the Queen—Mesdames Brunier and De Neuville.

"Messieurs! messieurs!" cried they; "what is your will ? "

At this moment, a man advanced towards the cabriolet. He was the Procureur de la Commune, M Sauce, who, awakened from his sleep had sallied out, determined to do his duty.

"Excuse me, ladies," said he, " but, without doubt, you have passports ?"

" They are with the people in the other carriage," replied Madame de Neuville.

The cabriolet having stopped, the chaise was forced to do likewise; thus it was completely blockaded MM. Drouet, Guillaume, and Regnier, having finished barricading the bridge, rushed to the spot. There were four persons, armed with guns—namely, our four billiard-players, Coquillard, Justin, Soncin, and Dehon , a fifth had arrived—namely, Billaud, who had heard the noise; and a sixth, M Bellay, opened his door, and seemed not less ardent than the others

All at once, I felt my arm grasped by a trembling hand, and the voice of Sophie whispered in my ear " For the love of me, René, do not meddle in this matter ! "

If M. Drouet had required my assistance, I am afraid that he would have triumphed over Sophie; but he did not, as he was incurring no present danger ; so I stood silent, motionless at the corner of the street, with Sophie on my arm.

M. Gerbaut's window opened, and we heard him ask what was the matter.

All the windows and doors in the street opened one after the other, the cries of " Fire ! fire !" having alarmed all, and made them anxious to see what was the matter.

During this time, M. Sauce had been approaching the chaise ; and as if he knew not who the travellers were—" Who are you ? "

"I am the Baroness de Korff," replied Madame de Tourzel, governess of the Dauphin.

" Where are you going ? "

" To Frankfort, with my two children, my two sisters, my steward, and my two female attendants. The latter are in the first carriage."

" Madame,' said Sauce, " you are going the wrong way to Frankfort—but that is not the question. Have you a passport ? "

Madame de Tourzel drew the passport from her pocket, and presented it to the Procureur de la Commune.

The passport was correct. It was, in fact, that of Madame de Korff, which M. de Fersen had given to the Queen.

M. Sauce took the passport, which the false Baroness handed him ; and, by the light of a lantern which an officious bystander offered him, began to reconnoitre the King.

The king, no doubt, wounded by the mark of disrespect, tried to make some resistance.

" Who are you, sir ? " asked he of the magistrate. " What is your rank ? Are you only a National Guard ? "

" I am Procureur de la Commune," replied M. Sauce.

The King, whether dumbfounded by the force of these words, or conceiving that the response was sufficient, made no further objections.

The procureur threw his eyes over the passport, and addressing, not the King, but the false Baroness de Korff,— " Madame," said he, " it is too late to viser a passport to-night ; and, on the other hand, it is my duty to detain you ! "

The Queen interposed.

" Why so, sir ? " she demanded in an imperative manner.

" Because, did I permit you to continue your route, I should be running a risk, on account of the reports that are flying about "

" Pray, sir, to what reports do you allude ? "

" The report of the flight of the King and his family," replied Sauce, fixedly regarding the King.

The travellers were aghast. The Queen drew back into the shadow of the carriage.

All this time, the passport was being examined, in a public room in the ' Grand Monarque,' by the light of two candles. A member of the council remarked that the passport was correct, since it had been signed by the King and the Minister for Foreign Affairs.

"Yes," remarked Drouet, who had arrived with Guillaume and Regnier during the discussion, "but it is not signed by the President of the National Assembly!"

"How?" said a voice. "Why should it be signed by him?"

"Certainly, it should be," said Drouet, "considering that France is a nation—considering that it has appointed deputies to maintain its rights. The true King of France is he who sat on a seat as lofty as the King's at the Champ de Mars—not only the veritable, but the more than King!"

All were silent. No one could oppose such logic as that. That great social question, which had disturbed France for seven hundred years,—"Is there in France an authority superior to the King's?" was settled in the public room of an inn in a little town on the borders of the Forest of Argonne.

Drouet walked straight to the carriage. In all popular movements he took the lead, and, therefore, the responsibility.

"Madame," said he, addressing the Queen, and not Madame Tourzel, "if you are really Madame de Korff— that is to say, a Swiss, and consequently a stranger—how is it that you have sufficient influence to command a military escort consisting of a detachment of dragoons at St. Menehould, and another at Clermont; also a first detachment of hussars at Pont-de-Somme-Vesles, and a second at Varennes?"

To end a fatiguing discussion, and one in which M. Drouet feared that the Procureur, an honest man enough, but not equal to any great situation, would eventually yield, he put his hand into the carriage as a support for the Queen, and said, "Will you be so kind, madame, as to descend?"

To tell the truth, the Procureur was most dreadfully embarrassed.

Encouraged by M. Drouet's invitation to the Queen, and hearing the tocsin begin to ring, he, however, approached the door—from which he had been turned to make place for M. Drouet—with great humility, his hat in his hand.

"The Municipal Council is deliberating," said he, "whether it would be advisable to allow you to continue your route; but a report, wrong or otherwise, has been spread about that it is the King and his august family whom we have the honor of receiving in our walls I beg you, therefore, to accept the shelter of my house, in all amity, until such time as the council shall have finished their deliberation. Against our will the tocsin has been sounded The concourse of the inhabitants of the city is increased by the entry of the country people ; and, perhaps, the King—if, in truth, I have the honor of addressing a King—may be exposed to insults which we should be unable to prevent, and which would fill us with unmitigated grief!"

It was no use his resisting. The Low Town was evidently ignorant of what was passing in the High Town. No succor arrived, or, indeed, appeared likely to arrive. The three young gentlemen dressed as couriers had no other arms than their *couteaux de chasse*, and could not undertake to fight with thirty men armed with guns. The tocsin still vibrated in the air, and found an echo in every heart.

The King set the example, and alighted.

I then had a good view of him, and my astonishment at seeing a king in such a costume was great.

He wore a drab gray coat, a satin waistcoat, and a pair of gray trousers, gray stockings, shoes with buckles, and a three cornered hat.

In descending, he knocked his head against the top of the door, and his hat fell off. His hair was in tresses on the top of his head, and was fixed there with an ivory comb.

In a word, his costume corresponded with the title of a steward, which he bore in the passport of Madame Korff.

I picked up the hat, and handed it to him

The Queen descended next, and after her, Madame Royale and the Dauphin, who was disguised as a little girl ; then came Madame Elizabeth, and, last, Madame de Tourzel.

Sauce had opened wide the door of his shop, and passed all sorts of compliments on the King whom he persisted in calling "your Majesty," though the King equally persisted that his name was M Durand

The Queen had not the courage to support this humiliating assumption.

" Well, then," said she, " if monsieur is your King, and I your Queen, treat us with the respect that our rank demands."

At these words, the King was ashamed, and said, " Very well, I am your King ; there is your Queen, and there are our children."

Though vulgar enough in his royal dress, the King lost altogether what little dignity he had under the costume of a steward.

Besides, always unfortunate, a grocer's shop, with its sur- roundings, was not the most romantic spot in which to utter those royal words :—

" Placed in the capital, in the midst of swords and bay- onets, I came to seek in the country, in the midst of my faithful subjects, the liberty and peace that were denied me in Paris."

Then, opening his arms, he pressed poor M. Sauce, par- alyzed with the honor, to his breast.

At the moment that the King embraced M. Sauce, a thunder of horses' hoofs was heard coming in an unexpected direction—that is to say, from the Place Latry.

The King believed that it was assistance, but the patriots smelt danger; and M. Drouet cried out, " Take the King up to the first floor ! "

Sauce asked the King to follow him, and he did so, with- out making any difficulty.

Scarcely was the door of the chamber on the ground-floor shut, when they heard a tumult at the head of the Rue de la Basse Cour, by the side of the Place Latry.

Many voices cried out " The King ! the King ! "

One voice alone replied, " If it is the King you want, you will have him dead ! "

Recognizing Drouet's voice, and thinking perhaps he might want me, I crept to his side.

At the moment that I opened a passage to him they were parleying; but M. Drouet and his friends parleyed with muskets in their hands, and the officers of hussars with their sabres on their wrists.

Between the two officers of hussars I recognised M. de Malmy on horseback, and covered with dust, like them.

It appeared as if he had guided them.

CHAPTER XXVI.

WHAT HAPPENED AT PARIS BEFORE THE DEPARTURE.

My story would be incomplete did I not follow the royal family in their flight from the moment that they left the Palace of Tuileries, till their appearance at the top of the Rue des Réligieuses; and did I not tell you through what circumstances M. Drouet was led to make his appearance in time to change the face of events, and to give that terrible blow to the throne of the Bourbons which occasioned Louis XVI not only the loss of his crown, but of his head.

I have already told you that Mirabeau, on his death-bed, asserted that the King's only hope rested in flight now that he was deprived of his assistance.

From that moment, Louis XVI had but one idea—to leave Paris—to leave France—to fly to a foreign land.

We have mentioned the date of April, 1791.

This is what happened on that date.

The King had wished to go to St Cloud; that was on the Easter Monday.

The King, the Queen, the bishops, the servants, filled the carriages in which they were to make the short travel of two leagues; but the people prevented the King from leaving the Tuileries.

The King insisted,; the tocsin of Saint Roch began to sound an alarm.

He leaned back in his carriage; thousands of voices cried, "No, no! He is going to fly!"

"I love you too well to leave you!" said the King.

"We, also, love you!" replied the spectators, with one voice; "but you alone!"

The Queen, shut out from the love of France, wept and stamped; but, for all that, was obliged to re-enter the Tuileries.

The King was a prisoner, there was no doubt about it; but it is permitted to a prisoner to escape.

From this moment the King prepared for flight.

Two other parties were as desirous as the King that he should leave France.

9

The one, the Royalist party, because the King, once free, would be able to re-enter France with a foreign army; the other, the Republican party, because they could not form a republic, without cutting his head off.

Therefore, one will perceive that they who arrested the King belonged to a third party—the Constitution.

His decision taken, the King began to put it into execution.

The Queen was the mainspring of the plot; the princesses of the house of Austria have been invariably evil genii to the Kings of France—Marie de Medicis, Anne of Austria, Marie Antoinette, and Marie Louise.

The King might have fled alone, and that was the idea that first occurred to him; in which case he would have travelled on horseback.

But, during the terrible night of the 5th of October, the Queen became so frightened, that she made the King swear never to leave France without her and their children.

It was then resolved that they should all, King, Queen, and children, fly together.

That doubled, trebled, and quadrupled the difficulty, and made escape almost an impossibility.

The Queen undertook the deception.

The Queen had more interest than the King in leaving France. Hear you that cry of the 18th of April, 1791, which interpreted the feelings of a nation, and which said, "We, also, sire! We love you, *but you alone!*"

In January, 1791, the flight was resolved upon.

In February, the King wrote to M. de Bouillé:—

"I have overtures to make to you on the part of M. Mirabeau. The Count de Lamark will be our intermediate."

He added:—

"Although these people are not very estimable, still I have paid M. Mirabeau a good sum of money. I think that he will be useful."

M. de Bouillé replied:—

"Cover with gold the defection of Mirabeau. He is an accomplished scoundrel, who will repair, through cupidity, the evil that he has worked through vengeance; but defy Lafayette, enthusiastic, chimerical, capable, perhaps, of being the chief of a party, but incapable of supporting a monarchy."

Remark that De Bouillé was the cousin of Lafayette. He was not, as one can see, blinded by the relationship

About the end of April, the King wrote again to M. de Bouillé.

"I go out almost incessantly in my carriage with all my family—a carriage made expressly to hold all."

M. de Bouillé replied :—

"In the place of that berlin expressly made, and which will naturally draw attention, it will be more prudent for your Majesty to use two English coaches"

The coaches mentioned were the post-chaises in common use at that period.

The counsel was good, but the Queen combated the idea. She did not wish to be separated from the King, and did not wish the children to be separated from herself.

M. de Bouillé continued :—

"Have with you in your perilous journey a man with the head of a Solon, and the arm of a Hercules—one who can plan and execute. I can point such a man out to you. He is the Marquis d'Agout, Major of the French Guards."

The King adopted this counsel. We will see, later on, how it was that M d'Agout did not arrive at Varennes.

The King, in a third letter, asked M. de Bouillé to establish relays from Chalons to Montmedy, his intention being to avoid Rheims, where he had been consecrated, and might be recognized, and pass through Varennes.

M de Bouillé replied, that in passing through Rheims, the carriage blinds could be drawn down; but that he was sorry that the King persisted in using that noticeable berlin; that at two points on the road to Varennes there were no post-horses, so it would be necessary to send some; and, lastly, that as there were no soldiers on that route, it would be necessary to order up some detachments, which might excite suspicion.

The King persisted in going the Varennes route.

He sent a million in assignats to M. de Bouillé, to defray whatever expenses there might be with regard to troops, &c., &c., and asked him to send an experienced officer to reconnoitre the road to Varennes.

M. de Bouille could not but obey so positive a command.

He sent. on the 10th of June, M. Goguelot to reconnoitre —a mission fitted only for a courageous and intelligent officer.

M. Goguelot was both.

On the appointed day the detachment set out.

One might have seen a train of artillery of six pieces setting out for Montmedy, the Royal Germans taking the Stenay route, a squadron of hussars going towards Dun, and another towards Varennes; and at the same time, fifty detached men under the command of M. de Choiseul, pushed on for Pont-de-Somne-Vesles, where the King would meet them as first post.

Afterwards, at St. Menehould, he would have found a detachment of dragoons, under the command of M. Dandouins.

At Clermont he would have found another detachment, under the command of M. de Damas.

He would have found the relays and a detachment of hussars, under the command of MM. Bouillé, *fils*, and De Raigecourt, at Varennes, and at Stenay he would have found M. Stenay in person.

All being arranged, the King wrote to De Bouillé, fixing the day for the 19th of the June following.

CHAPTER XXVII.

HOW THEY SET OUT.

THIS was the third or fourth time that the date of departure had been altered.

They had determined to depart on the 11th, but having refused to take Madame de Rochereul, *femme de chambre* to the Dauphin, and mistress of M. de Gouvion, aide-de-camp to Lafayette, and who was now on duty till the 12th, they thought that it was imprudent to depart on that day.

On the 13th of June, the Austrians began to advance on the French frontier, and to occupy posts two leagues from Montmedy.

The departure was postponed until the 15th following.

On the evening of the 15th, the King set out with the royal family, in a plain carriage, the berlin awaiting them at Bondy.

If the King did not arrive at Bondy at two o'clock, it was arranged that it should be taken for granted that he had been stopped at the Tuileries or at the barrier.

In that case, it was arranged that the person in charge of the berlin should set out alone, and not stop till he arrived at Ponte-de-Somme-Vesles; and when there, that he should inform M. de Choiseul that the project had failed.

M. de Choiseul would then tell M. Dandouins, M. de Damas, M. de Bouillé, and each would provide for their own safety.

M. de Bouillé received these new instructions, and arranged accordingly.

M. de Choiseul set out at the same time for Paris.

At Paris, M. de Choiseul awaited the orders of the King, and started twelve hours in advance

The men and horses belonging to M. de Choiseul would stay at Varennes from the 18th.

On the 19th, fresh and renovated, they would pass through Varennes, and put up at a farm, half way between Varennes and Neuvilly. One must call to mind that there was no post at Varennes.

On the arrival of the King, they would take the place of the post-horses from Clermont, and conduct the royal family to Dun.

On his return, M. de Choiseul, who, as we said, preceded the King by twelve hours, would take command of the forty hussars at Pont-de-Somme-Vesles. At Pont-de-Somme-Vesles he would await the King, and would escort him to St. Menehould. At St. Menehould the hussars would give place to the dragoons, and be left to block the road.

After the King, no one would be allowed to pass.

After twenty-four hours the road would be left clear, for by that time the King would be beyond the frontier.

M. de Choiseul had orders signed by the King, authorizing him to demand the needful number of men. Six hundred louis d'or were distributed by him to the soldiers.

On the 14th of June, M de Bouillé, who was in Hungary, received a letter from the King.

The departure is postponed for twenty-four hours. Whence came this new delay?

We will tell you: the reason was a serious one.

The King did not receive his quarterly income until the 20th; and being economical, he did not wish to lose it.

This reason, good as it was, made M de Bouillé despair.

In fact it made it necessary to give fresh orders all along the line. Instead of two days, the relays would have to wait three; the same with the troops.

On the 20th of June, M de Bouillé advanced to Stenay, where he found the Royal Germans.

We have already seen that, on the same day, the hussars arrived at St. Menehould, announcing the arrival of the dragoons.

We know, through M. Drouet, what a sensation their unexpected appearance created.

We have seen another hussar detachment arrive at Varennes, causing little less sensation than their brothers-in-arms did at St. Menehould.

Let us now turn our attention to Paris, and see what was going on these last few days.

We have already said that the Queen managed the diplomacy. She diplomatised wonderfully.

Firstly, she had used the white horses which drew the funeral car of M. Voltaire.

Secondly, on the 19th, she took a stroll with the Dauphin on the outer boulevards.

Thirdly, on the 20th, she said to M. Montmorin, Minister of Foreign Affairs, "Have you seen Madame Elizabeth? She causes me pain. I wished her to accompany me in the procession of the Fête Dieu, and she refuses me."

On the same day, meeting a commander of the National Guard, "Well, monsieur," said she, laughing, "do they still speak of the flight of the King from Paris?"

"No, Madame," replied the commander; they are too well convinced of the King's love for the Constitution and for his people."

"They are right," replied the Queen.

On the 17th, M. Moustier, ex-garde du corps, had been accosted by an unknown whilst he was walking in the Tuileries

The unknown had invited him to follow him in the name of the King.

M Moustier had obeyed. Ten minutes afterwards he was in the presence of the King.

Louis XVI saluted him by name.

The garde du corps, astonished, bowed.

"I know you, monsieur," said the King, "and feel assured that I can count upon you; that is why I am now addressing you."

"Whatever your wishes may be, I hope I shall prove myself worthy of your confidence, sire"

"Think you that I can count equally well on your two friends, De Valory and De Malden ? "

"I am assured of it, sire "

"Well, tell them to have made vests of chamois leather, trousers of hide, jack-boots, and velvet caps."

The choice of chamois leather was most imprudent, as it was the color of the Prince de Conde, when he emigrated.

M. de Moustier was then asked to walk every evening on the Pont Royal. There, a confidential servant, who knew him by sight, would bring him the last orders of. the King.

On the evening of the 19th, M. Moustier received the following order —

"M. de Moustier and his companions are desired to be in the court of the Chateau to-morrow, at nine o'clock in the evening; they will then learn what is required of them."

Now, about the passport. We know that the Queen travelled under the name of the Baroness de Korff. The two children were the Dauphin and Madame Royal; the intendant was the King; and the two *femmes-de-chambre* Mesdames de Neuville and Brunier.

That did not comprise, it is true, Madame Elizabeth, or M. d'Agout, whom M. de Bouillé had recommended the King to take with him, but they were obliged to trust something to chance

On the morning of the 20th, M. Moustier presented his two companions to the King.

M. Malden was to take the name of Jean, M. de Moustier the name ot Melchior, and M. Valory the name of François. As for M. de Choiseul, he awaited the orders of the King at his house, Rue d'Artois, on the 20th. Up to three o'clock, he had heard nothing, and he ought to start twelve hours in advance of the King. He began to despair, when a servant entered to say that a messenger had arrived from the Queen.

He ordered the messenger to be shown up.

The fellow entered. He had a great hat thrust over his eyes, and was wrapped in an immense cloak.

It was the Queen's hairdresser, the famous Léonard, who has left his memoirs to posterity. He was a personage of the utmost importance.

"What, Léonard! It was not you whom I expected; but, since you are come, make yourself at home."

"It is not my fault if I have kept you waiting, M. le Comte ; but it is but ten minutes since I left the Queen to come here."

"And she has told you nothing, given you no message?" cried the Count, astonished.

"She told me to take all her diamonds, and bring you this letter."

" Well, well—give it me !"

M. de Choiseul read the letter.

It was long, and full of instructions. It announced that they would leave punctually to the moment.

As to the Comte de Choiseul, it commanded him to set out that instant, begging him to take Leonard with him, who, continued Marie Antoinette, had orders to obey him as he would herself.

M. de Choiseul read aloud that recommendation to Léonard, who made a lowly obeisance.

He then burnt the letter.

At this moment one of the Comte's servant entered.

" The carriage awaits M le Comte," said he.

" Come, my dear Leonard—come !" said the young gentleman.

" Why should I come ?" cried the stupefied hairdresser.

" Why should you ? Are you not to obey me as you would the Queen ? Come! I command you !"

" But her Majesty's diamonds ? "

"You will bring them with you."

"Where?"

"Where we are going."

"But where are we going?"

"A few leagues from here. where we have to fulfil a most particular and important mission."

"Impossible, M. le Comte!" cried Leonard, drawing himself back with affright.

"Leonard, you forget that her Majesty said that you were to obey me as you would herself."

He then assisted the despairing hairdresser to mount into the cabriolet, and lashed the horse into full speed in the direction of the Petite Vilette.

At the same hour that M. de Choiseul passed the barrier the three guards were admitted to the presence of the King, and then shut up in an ante-chamber.

At ten o'clock M. de Lafayette was announced.

He was attended by MM. de Gouvin and De Romeuf, his aides-de-camp.

Madame de Rochereul. his mistress, had told him that the flight was arranged for the same night.

The Queen and Madame Elizabeth had gone in the evening, without an escort, to promenade in the Bois de Boulogne.

M. de Lafayette, with the exquisite politeness which was one of his characteristics, asked the Queen if she had enjoyed her stroll; and added, "Your Majesty was wrong to stay out so late."

"Why so, sir?" asked the Queen.

"Because the evening fog might do you an injury."

"What! a fog in the middle of June?" said she. "In truth, unless I manufactured one on purpose to hide our flight, which people talk so much about, I do not know where I should find one."

"The fact is, madame," replied the General, "people not only talk about your flight, but I have received information that it will take place this evening."

"Ah!" said the Queen; "I engage that it is M. de Gouvion who has given you that good news."

"Why I, madame?" said the young officer, blushing.

"I do not know," replied the Queen, "except that, perhaps. you hear a great deal more than is true at the cha-

teau. Wait! Here is M. Romeuf, who hears no news; I
am sure he will contradict the rumor."

"There is no great credit in doing that, madame," said
the young man, "when the King has given his word to
the Assembly not to leave Paris."

At ten o'clock, General Lafayette and his aides-de-camp
retired.

When they were gone, the Queen and Madame Elizabeth
summoned their domestics to perform the necessary offices
of their toilettes, and at eleven, as was their custom, they
retired for the night.

The doors shut, each commenced to dress.

The Queen and Madame Elizabeth assisted each other.
They had some plain dresses, and hats, with hoods, to hide
the face.

They had scarcely finished their disguise, when the King
entered, in his costume of intendant.

For the last eight days, the King's valet, Hue, had been
in the habit of going out in the costume the King now
wore, and by the same door the King intended to depart
from. This was done in order to accustom the sentinel to
a man dressed in gray

On arriving, he released the three guards from their
hiding-place.

Madame Royale was ready, but the Dauphin was not.
He had been awakened from his first sleep; and so, for the
sake of disguise, it had been arranged to dress him like a
girl. He made all sorts of objections to the humiliating
costume.

He asked, "If he were intended to act in a comedy?"
They replied "Yes." And as he liked comedies, he allowed them to finish his toilette.

The gardes du corps received their last instructions.

They were to travel as far as Bondy on M. de Fersen's
horses; after that they were to take post.

They had calculated that, if they went at a moderate rate,
they would be at Châlons in twelve or fourteen hours.
They approached the door, and listened. All was silent.

Let us see with what difficulties they encompassed themselves.

Firstly, against M. de Bouillé's advice, who proposed two
English diligencies, the Queen had had made two enormous
berlins, in which she might put her trunks, boxes and bags.

Then, in place of having a courier in simple livery, there were three gardes du corps, in the livery of the Prince de Condé.

Then, in place of choosing three men who knew the route, they chose three who had never travelled that way before.

Then, in place of hiding the King, who was supposed to be Madame de Korff's steward, in the other carriage, he was placed face to face and knee to knee, with his pretended mistress, in the principal conveyance.

Then, in place of having the carriages drawn by two, or even four, horses, they must needs have six, not remembering that the King alone is allowed to have that number

Then, in place of arming the gardes du corps to the teeth, they give them small hunting-knives for use, and locked up the pistols and other implements of warfare in the trunk, covered with red, bordered with gold, the same as the King used at Cherbourg

Then, in place of taking M. d'Agout, that resolute man who knew the route, and whom M de Bouillé had recommended, they take Madame Tourzel, the children's governess, who claimed the place by etiquette that D'Agout would have won by devotion.

Taking all in all, every precaution was taken.

Quos vult perdere Jupiter prius dementat.

CHAPTER XXVIII.

THE ROAD.

In a moment, the clock struck eleven.

Every stroke penetrated the hearts of the fugitives, and caused them to tremble.

They went out, one by one. But how were they able to make a passage to the court, you will ask? This is how it was.

Madame de Rochereul, whose duties had finished on the 12th, occupied a little chamber which opened into another, which had not been used for six months.

The empty apartment was M. Villequier's, first gentleman of the bed-chamber. It was empty because M. Villequier had emigrated.

That apartment, situate on the ground floor, had a door opening into the Cour des Princes.

On one side, the chamber of Madame de Rochereul opened both into one belonging to M. Villequier and Madame Royale

On the 11th, the moment that Madame Rochereul quitted the chateau, the King and Queen visited her apartment.

Under the pretext of enlarging Madame Royale's suite of rooms, the Queen kept these apartments, and said that the *femme-de-chambre* of the Dauphin could share those of Madame de Chimnau, maid of honor.

When in the apartment of M. Villequier, the King demanded the key of M. Renard, inspector of buildings. It was sent to him on the 13th of June.

Numerous as were the sentinels, they had neglected to place one at the door of that chamber, which had been unoccupied for the space of three months At eleven o'clock in the evening, the services in the chateau being finished, the sentinels were accustomed to witness the departure of a great number of people at one time.

So that once in the apartment of M. Villequier, and as the clock struck eleven, they had every chance of escaping unobserved.

It was M. de Fersen's business to smuggle the royal family out of Paris, unobserved.

He was waiting with a fiacre, disguised as a coachman, at the Wicket de l'Echelle ; thence he was to take the fugitives to the barrier at Clichy, where the berlin was in waiting, under the charge of an Englishman, Mr. Crawford.

The three gardes du corps were to follow, in another fiacre.

The two *femmes-de-chambre*, Madame Brunier and Madame de Neuville, went on foot to the Pont Royal, where they found a two-horsed carriage stationed, in which they started for Claye, where they were to await the Queen.

Madame Elizabeth stepped out first, with Madame Royale ; then came Madame de Tourzel, and the Dauphin, accompanied by one of the gardes du corps.

The two parties were separated one from the other by about twenty paces.

One of the sentinels crossed the road, and on seeing the first party, stopped them

"Oh, aunt!" cried Madame Royale; "we are lost! That man recognises us!"

Madame Elizabeth made no reply, but continued to advance.

Madame Royale was deceived. They were not recognised—or, if they were, it was by a friend

The sentinel turned his back on them, and allowed them to pass

At the expiration of five minutes, Madame de Tourzel, the two princesses, and the Dauphin were in the carriage, which was awaiting them at the corner of the Rue de l'Echelle.

M. de Fersen was so well disguised, that the princesses did not recognize him. It was he who knew them He leapt from his box, opened the door, and assisted them in.

At the moment that M de Fersen shut the door, an empty fiacre passed by. Seeing a brother cabman stopping, he stopped likewise, and began to enter into a conversation about the times.

M. de Fersen. a man of ready wit, sustained the conversation wonderfully, and. drawing a snuff-box from his pocket, offered his friend a pinch

He plunged his fingers deep into the box, took a long and voluptuous snuff, and drove on.

At this moment the King. followed by his garde du corps, came out in his turn, his hands in his pockets, and swaggering like a well-to-do tradesman.

He was followed by the second garde.

During his passage, one of the buckles of his shoes slipped off. The King did not care to stop for such a trifling matter as that, but the garde who came after him picked it up.

M de Fersen got in front of the King.

"And the Queen, sire?" asked he.

"The Queen follows us," replied the King.

He then got into the carriage in his turn.

They awaited the Queen.

Half an hour passed, and she did not arrive.

What detained her?

The Queen was lost. She maintained that the Wicket de l'Echelle was to the right. The third garde, not knowing Paris well, yielded to the Queen's certainty, though he fancied that it was to the left.

They therefore left by the wicket at the water's side; got confused on the quays; crossed the bridge; walked down the Rue du Bac, where the Queen was forced to acknowledge her error, as they had completely lost their way.

The garde was compelled to inquire the way to the Wicket de l'Echelle. They had to cross the Place de Carrousel a second time. Under the arch, they found themselves face to face with some lacqueys, carrying torches, and escorting a carriage which was approaching at a trot. The Queen had just time to turn her face to the wall, in order to avoid being recognised.

She had recognised Lafayette.

The garde came to the front, in order to the more effectually screen her.

But she struck the wheels of the carriage with the little cane that ladies carried at that period, saying, "Go to, gaoler!—I am out of thy power."

This is but a tradition; the garde says, on the contrary, that the Queen was so frightened, that she dropped his arm and fled, but that he ran after her, took her by the hand, and drew her back.

They crossed the Carrousel at full speed, passed the Wicket de l'Echelle, and at last saw the carriage which was awaiting them.

M. de Fersen assisted the Queen into the vehicle, and she sank into her seat by the side of the King, trembling with fear.

M. de Fersen had stopped a voiture, for the accommodation of the three gardes du corps.

They jumped into it, telling the driver to follow the other vehicle.

M. de Fersen, who knew not Paris much better than the garde du corps, who had followed the Queen, fearing to get lost in the streets, went to Faubourg St. Honoré, along the length of the Tuileries.

Thence, he soon found his way to the barrière of Clichy.

A few paces before the house of Mr. Crawford, the gardes

du corps got down, paid and dismissed their vehicle, and took their places behind the other.

The travelling berlin was ready when they arrived.

The change was effected.

M. de Fersen overturned his carriage in a ditch, then mounted on the box of the berlin. One of his men mounted a horse, and conducted them to Daumont.

They took at least an hour to arrive at Bondy.

All progressed capitally.

At Bondy, they found the two *femmes-de-chambre*, who were to have awaited them at Claye.

It appeared that they came in a cabriolet, expecting to find at Bondy a post-chaise, but there were none, so they had struck a bargain with the postmaster for a cabriolet, the price of which was a thousand francs.

The driver of the other cabriolet was brushing down his horse previously to returning to Paris.

At this place, M. de Fersen was to leave their Majesties.

He kissed the King's hand, in order that he might be able to kiss the Queen's.

M. de Fersen would rejoin them in Austria.

He returned to Paris, to acquaint himself with what was going on; he would then start for Brussels.

Man proposes, God disposes.

The Queen, two years later, was executed in the Place de la Revolution; and M. de Fersen perished at Stockholm, where he was slain in a riot, stricken to death by blows from umbrellas, administered by drunken women.

But, mercifully, the future was not known to them. They parted full of hope.

M. de Valory borrowed a post-horse, and galloped on in advance, to command the relays.

M. de Malden and De Moustier took their seats on the box of the berlin, which set off at the full speed of which six vigorous horses were capable.

The cabriolet came on in the rear.

M. de Fersen followed with his eyes the carriage, rapidly disappearing in the distance, and when it had entirely disappeared, he got into his own carriage, and returned to Paris.

He had on his costume as coachman; and much did it astonish the driver of the cabriolet to see a coachman kissing the hands of the King, disguised as a domestic.

It is true that M. de Fersen had only kissed the King's hands in order to be able to go through the same ceremony with regard to the Queen.

That was another imprudence added to those which we have already mentioned.

All went well as far as Montmirail, where the traces of the royal carriage snapped asunder.

It was necessary to stop. They thus lost two hours—the days were long; the night of the 20th of June is the shortest in the year.

Then they came to a hill. The King insisted on their walking up; thus they lost another half-hour.

Half-past four sounded from the cathedral as the berlin entered Chalons, and stopped at the post-house, then situated at the end of the Rue St. Jacques.

M. de Vallory approached the carriage.

" All goes well, Francis," said the Queen to him. "It seems to me that, if there had been an intention of stopping us, it would have been put into execution before now."

In speaking to M. de Valory, the Queen disclosed her countenance.

The King likewise imprudently showed himself.

The postmaster, Oudes, recognized him; one of the spectators, whom curiosity had drawn to the spot, at once knew that it was the King.

The postmaster saw the above-mentioned spectator disappear, and consequently feared some evil to the King.

" Sire," said he, in a whisper, "for heaven's sake do not expose yourself, or you are lost!" Then, speaking to the postilions, " How now, idlers!" cried he. "Is this the way that you treat well-to-do travellers who pay thirty sous ? "

And he himself, to set an example to the postilions, put his shoulder to the work.

The horses were put to, and the carriage was in readiness speedily.

" Off you go!" cried the postmaster.

The first postilion wished to raise his horses into a gallop. They both fell, but gained their feet again on the application of the whip. They wished to upset the carriage. The two horses under the guidance of the second postilion fell in their turn.

They drew the postilion from under the horse he had been riding, with the loss of one of his boots.

The horses picked themselves up, the postilion regained his boot, and, putting it on, he remounted his saddle.

Off goes the carriage.

The travelers breathe again.

But as the postmaster had warned them of danger, in place of riding in front, M. de Valory took up his position by the side of the carriage.

The fact of the horses having fallen one after the other, without any apparent reason, seemed to the Queen a presage of evil to come.

As yet, however, they had escaped the consequence of recognition.

The man who witnessed the arrival of the berlin had ran to the Mayor's house; but that official was a Royalist. However, the witness swore that he recognised the King and the other members of the royal family; so the Mayor, driven into his last entrenchment, was forced to proceed forthwith to the Rue St. Jacques, but, happily, when he arrived there, he found that the carriage had started some five minutes before.

Passing through the gates of the city, and noticing the ardor with which the postilion urged on their steeds, the Queen, and Madame Elizabeth gave vent each to the same cry:—"We are saved!"

But at that very moment a man, arisen, as it were, suddenly from the very bosom of the earth, passed on horseback to the door of the carriage, and said, "Your measures are badly taken! You will be stopped!"

It was never known who this man was.

By good luck, they were distant only four leagues from Pont-de-Somme-Vesles, where M. de Choiseul was awaiting them with his forty hussars.

Perhaps they should have sent M. de Valory to the rear, in order to prevent this.

But the last warning had increased the Queen's terrors, and she would not part with one of her defenders.

They incited the postilions to greater speed.

The four leagues were accomplished in an hour.

They arrived at Pont-de-Somme-Vesles, a little hamlet, consisting of two or three houses. They pierced with their

10

eyes the wood which overshadowed the farm to the left; and
the trees which indicated the windings of the river on the
right, formed, as it were, a curtain of green to hide the
modest streamlet from the curious eye, but still no De
Choiseul, no De Goguelot, no forty hussars were to be seen.

On seeing that the place was desolate, the Queen uttered
the words " We are lost ! "

In the meantime, let us explain why the hussars were not
at their post.

At eleven o'clock M. de Choiseul, still accompanied by
Léonard, in tears, who knew not where they were taking
him, and who believed himself to be the victim of some un-
justifiable violence, arrived at Pont-de-Somme-Vesles.

The hussars, as yet, were not at their posts; all around
was tranquil.

He alighted at the post-house, his example being followed
by Léonard, who had the diamonds still concealed in his
bosom, and asked for a private chamber in which to don his
uniform.

Leonard watched him ; his cup of misery was filled to the
brim.

Now that M. de Choiseul had, as he believed, nothing to
fear, he found time to pity him.

" My dear Leonard ! " said he, " it is time that you knew
the whole truth."

" How the truth ? Do I not, then, already know the
truth ? "

" You know a portion. It is now my duty to tell you the
rest. You are devoted to your customers, are you not, my
dear Léonard ? "

" In life and death, M. le Comte."

" Well, in two hours they will be here—in two hours they
will be saved."

The hot tears coursed down poor Leonard's cheeks, but
this time they were tears of joy.

" In two hours ? " cried he, at last.   " Are you sure of
it ? "

" Yes ; they were to have left the Tuileries at eleven or
half-past, in the evening ; they were to arrive at Chalons at
mid-day ; and an hour, or, at most, an hour and a-half, is
sufficient to cover the four leagues from Chalons to this
place. They will be here in an hour at the latest. I am

awaiting a detachment of hussars, which should arrive here under the command of M. Goguelot."

Hearing a rumbling sound, M. de Choiseul put his head out of the window.

" Ah, there they are, coming from the direction of Cilloy!"

And, in fact, the hussars were, at the moment, on the point of entering the village.

"Come on !—all is well !" said M. de Choiseul.

And he waved his hat, making signs out of the window.

A horseman approached at a gallop.

M. de Choiseul went down stairs to meet him.

The two gentlemen met in the high road.

The horseman, who was M Goguelot, gave M. de Choiseul a packet from M. de Bouillé. This packet contained six blank signatures, and a copy of the order which had been given by the King to every officer of the army whatsoever his grade, commanding them in all things to obey M. de Choiseul.

The hussars rode up. M. de Choiseul ordered them to picket their horses, and caused rations of bread and wine to be served out to them.

The news which M Goguelot brought was bad. All along his route, everybody had been in a state of expectation. The reports of the King's flight, which had been disseminated about for more than a year, had spread from Paris to the provinces; and the sight of the different bodies of men arriving at Dun, Varennes, Clermont, and St. Menehould, had awakened suspicion The tocsin had been sounded in a village by the side of the road.

M. de Choiseul had ordered dinner for M. de Goguelot and himself.

The two young men drew up to the table, leaving the detachment under the command of M. de Boudet.

At the expiration of half an hour, M. de Choiseul fancied that he heard a noise outside the door.

He went out.

The peasants from the neighboring villages had begun to crowd round the soldiers.

Whence came these peasants, in a country which was almost a desert?

It was surmised that some days before the inhabitants of

a tract of land, near Pont-de-Somme-Vesles, belonging to Madame d'Eblœuf, had refused the payment of irredeemable rights, on the strength of which they had been threatened with military law.

But the federation of 1790 had made France one great family; and the peasants of the villages had promised the tenants of Madame d'Elbœuf to use their arms if any soldiers showed themselves in the vicinity.

As we know, forty had arrived.

On seeing them Madame d'Elbœuf's tenants believed that they had come with hostile intentions against them; so they sent messages to all the neighboring villages, imploring them to keep their promise.

Those situate nearest arrived first, and that is how M. de Choiseul, on arising from table, found a turbulent throng of peasants surrounding the hussars.

He believed that curiosity alone had drawn them thither, and, without paying any further attention to them, gained the most elevated part of the road, which runs in a straight line through the plain of Châlons to St. Menehould.

A little further on than could be seen with the naked eye was the village itself.

An hour slipped away.

Two hours, three hours, four hours, followed in the track of the first.

The fugitives ought to have arrived in one hour at Pont-de-Somme-Vesles; and the time they had lost on the road made it half-past four, as we have said, before they arrived at Châlons.

M. de Choiseul was anxious.

Léonard was in despair.

About three o'clock, the numbers of peasants increased; their intentions became more hostile, and the tocsin began to sound.

The hussars were, perhaps, more unpopular than any other corps in the army, on account of their supposed plundering propensities. The peasants provoked them by all sorts of insults and menaces, and sang under their very noses—

> " The hussars are forlorn,
>   And we laugh them to scorn."

Presently better informed people came up, and spread a report that the hussars had come, not to injure Madame d'Elboeuf's tenants, but to escort the King and Queen.

This was also a very serious matter

At about half-past four, M. de Choiseul and his hussars were so completely hemmed in, that the three officers counselled together as to what was best to be done.

They agreed unanimously that it was impossible that they could hold out much longer

The number of peasants was augmented to about three hundred, many of whom were armed.

If, by ill luck, the King and Queen arrived at this critical juncture, forty men, supposing that each killed his adversary, would be insufficient to protect them.

M de Choiseul re-read his orders —

"Manage in such a manner that the King's carriage shall continue its progress without interruption."

But his presence and that of the forty men became an obstacle instead of a support.

There was no doubt about it. Their best plan was to depart.

But a pretext must be found. .

M de Choiseul, in the midst of some five or six hundred gaping peasants who surrounded him, summoned the postmaster.

"Monsieur," said he, "we are here for the purpose of escorting a treasure, but this treasure does not arrive. Do you know if any gold has been this last day or so to Metz?"

"This morning," replied the postmaster, "the diligence brought a hundred thousand crowns, and was escorted by two gendarmes"

If the postmaster had been prompted, he could not have spoken better.

"It was Robin and me who escorted it," cried a gendarme, hidden among the crowd.

Then M. de Choiseul, turning to M. Goguelot, said, "Monsieur, the Ministry have preferred the ordinary mode of carriage. As a hundred thousand crowns have passed through here this morning, our further presence here is unnecessary. Trumpeter, sound boot and saddle, and we will be off."

The trumpeter obeyed.

In a second, the hussars, who wished nothing better than to be off, were mounted.

" Gentlemen of the hussars, march.   Form by fours, and proceed at a foot pace."

And he and his forty men left Pont-de-Somme-Vesles at five punctually by his watch.

The detachment was to have fallen upon Varennes.   He took the by-road in order to avoid St. Menehould, but lost his way above Mofficouit.

The little troop hesitated for a moment, when a horseman coming from Neuville saw the perplexity of M. de Choiseul, and finding that he was a Royalist and a gentleman, asked if he could be of any assistance to him.

" Indeed you can," replied M. de Choiseul. " You can conduct us to Varennes by the Chalade."

" Follow me, then," cried the gentleman.

And he placed himself at the head of the hussars.

This gentleman was no other than M. de Malmy, and that is how it was that I met him on the Place Latry, between two officers whom I knew not—namely, M. de Choiseul and M. Goguelot.

CHAPTER XXIX.

STILL IN FLIGHT.

THERE was therefore, no escort awaiting the King at Pont-de-Somme-Vesles when he arrived there.

But if there was no escort, there were likewise no peasants. The road was clear; the King therefore changed horses without an obstacle, and started for St Menehould.

At St. Menehould, M. Dandoins awaited the King's arrival with as much impatience as M. de Choiseul and M. Goguelot had; and about midday he set out with his lieutenant on the road to Châlons, in the hopes of seeing some sign of his arrival.

This road is one long descent from St. Menehould to Châlons.   They cast their eyes for a length of two leagues on a straight line, traced, as it were, by a pencil, between two rows of trees, with uncultivated green patches of country around them

Nothing was visible on the road

M. Dandoins and his lieutenant returned to St. Mene-hould.

Two hours afterward they again strolled along that same road.

To get to the barracks situated at the bottom of the Faubourg Fleurion, it was necessary to pass right through the town.

They returned, as on the former occasion, without having seen anything.

These in-comings and out-goings excited the attention of a population already alarmed. They perceived that the two officers had the appearance of being restless and uneasy.

To the queries put them on the subject, they replied that they were awaiting a treasure which apparently was delayed, and that this delay gave rise to uneasiness.

About seven o'clock in the evening, a courier, dressed in a chamois-leather vest, arrived, drew up at the post-house, and commanded horses for two carriages.

The postmaster was Jean Baptiste Drouet.

M. de Dandoins approached M. de Valory.

"Monsieur," said he, in a whisper, "you are preceding the King's carriage, are you not?"

"Yes, monsieur," replied the courier; "and let me add, that I am astonished to see you and your men in police-men's hats."

"We did not know the exact hour of the King's arrival. Our presence annoys the people; demonstrations of the most menacing character with regard to us have been made, and they have tried to entice away my men"

"Silence," said M de Valory; "they hear what we are saying Rejoin your men, sir, and try to keep them to their duty."

MM. de Valory and de Dandoins then separated

At the same moment the crackings of a whip were heard, and the two carriages crossed the Place de l'Hotel de Ville.

They drew up in front of the post-house.

One can easily recognise the house, then built about three years, and which bears upon its face the date 1788.

Scarcely had the carriage stopped, when crowds of people surrounded them.

One of the lookers-on asked M. Malden, who was descending from the box, "Who are the travellers who journey in this style?"

"Madame the Baronne de Korff," replied de Malden.

"What! another of the exiles who are sucking at the vitals of France?" murmured the spectator, discontentedly.

"No; this lady is a Russian, and, consequently, a stranger."

During this, M. de Dandoins, his policeman's hat in his hand, approached the carriage-door, before which he stood, respectfully.

"Sir officer," said the King, "how is it that I found no one at Pont-de-Somme-Vesles?"

"I was asking myself, sire, how it was that you arrived without escort."

The sight of a commander of dragoons talking with the deepest respect to a sort of *valet de chambre*, seated in the front seat of the carriage, redoubled the astonishment of the people, and began to change that astonishment rapidly into suspicion.

Still, the King took no precaution to hide himself.

At this moment, M. Drouet came out from the door of his house, and seeing the man who was talking to the commander of the dragoons, he cried, "Just heavens—the King!"

He had much the same expression of face as he had at the federation, and his general appearance was such that he was not easily disguised.

A municipal officer was there; his name was Farcy.

Drouet touched him on the elbow.

"Do you recognize that man?" said he, pointing to the King.

"Yes," replied the other. "It is the King."

"Call together the municipal council."

Then, running to the door of the house, "Guillaume, Guillaume!" he cried.

Guillaume, who was within, ran out to him. Drouet pointed out to him the King.

"That is he whom we have been expecting," said he.

Meanwhile M. Farey had run to the municipality, and there made his report.

Drouet followed after him, and likewise entered the municipal council chamber.

Scarcely had he turned the corner of the street, than the carriages, which had been relayed in the twinkling of an eye, started off at a sharp trot.

A somewhat strange event accompanied their departure.

Behind the carriage a sous-officer of dragoons, whom we have seen speaking to the King, notwithstanding his inferior rank, pushed on at a gallop, firing, as he did so, a pistol in the air.

Without doubt, it was a signal; but the citizens took it as a sign for hostilities, especially as, on hearing it, the dragoons rushed to their horses.

At this pistol-shot, cries were heard. A man who was threshing in a barn on the left-hand side of the road, a little above the small bridge thrown over the Aisne, left the barn, and tried to stop the sous-officer with his flail.

The officer drew his sabre, cut the flail in half, and passed on.

During this time the municipal council had decided that some one should run after the royal carriages, and stop them.

"But who will do it?" asked the Mayor.

"I will," replied M. Drouet.

Other young men offered to accompany him; but he had not at the post-house more than one horse of his own, with the exception of a little pony, which was for his friend Guillaume, on which he could count as well as he could on himself. Two other citizens seized horses, and determining not to leave them, set out with them, or, at least, behind them.

They started, amid shouts of encouragement from the whole town.

Two hours after, the two citizens returned on their paltry hacks. They had not been able to keep up the pace.

But M. Jean Baptiste Drouet, bearer of *A Warrant from the Municipality to arrest the King*, and Citizen Guillaume, continued the chase.

I underline the warrant given by the municipality for

the arrest of the King. because I have never seen mention
made of it by any historian, and because, having seen the
warrant in M. Drouet's hand, I can speak positively with
regard to the existence of the paper.

I wish you to understand why I lay so much stress on
the fact of the existence of a warrant. It is because M.
Jean Baptiste Drouet, sent by the municipality of St.
Menehould to arrest the King and the royal family, is not
the isolated fanatic, obeying a regicidal impulse, as the
Royalist journals and histories would have it, but a citizen
of unblemished character, who fulfilled but his duty in
obeying the commands of the magistrates of his country.

But to return to our tale.

The royal carriage started, and MM. Drouet and Guillaume in pursuit. M. Dandoins ordered his dragoons to
mount, and follow.

But the order was more easily given than executed.

The pistol-shot fired by the sous-officer had found an
echo in the hearts—or, rather, the imaginations of—of
those who heard it. The National Guard armed themselves
with their double-barrelled guns. A tumultuous and noisy
mob gathered in front of the post-house—that is to say, on
the very road that the dragoons would be obliged to follow,
in order to come up with the royal carriages

M. Dandoins was about to spring into his saddle, when
the municipal council commanded him to surrender on the
spot at the Hotel de Ville.

He did so, and was then ordered to give his name and to
show his orders.

"I am named Dandoins," replied he. "I am a Chevalier
of St. Louis, a captain in the 1st Regiment of Dragoon
Guards, and there are the orders which I have received."

Suiting the action to the word, he placed on the table the
following order —

"On behalf of the King, I, François Claude Amour de
Bouillé, lieutenant-general of the King's armies, &c. The
captain of the 1st Regiment of Dragoons is ordered to
march, with forty men of his regiment, on the 19th, from
Clermont to St. Menehould, where, on the 20th and 21st,
he will await a convoy of money, which will be escorted by
a detachment of the 6th Regiment of Hussars from Pont-

de-Somme-Vesles, on the Châlons road The dragoons and their horses will be lodged equally among the hotel-keepers. The captain will be reimbursed for all expenses incurred for the provender for the horses, and each dragoon will receive increased pay in place of his rations.

"DE BOUILLE.

"Metz, 14th June, 1791."

At this moment the cries of the people mounted to the chamber in which the council were assembled, interrogating M. Dandoins. These cries demanded that the dragoons should be disarmed.

"You hear, captain?" said the Mayor "It is needful, in order to tranquillize the people, that your men lay down their arms. Go down, and order them to do so."

"I will do so, if you will give me a written authority," replied M. Dandoins.

The order was given, and at the command of M Dandoins the arms of the dragoons, and the accoutrements of the horses, were carried into the Hotel de Ville.

At the moment M. Dandoins and his lieutenant M. La Cour, reappeared at the door of the Hotel de Ville opening on the Place, the exasperation of the multitude reached a culminating point. Every voice cried, "He is a traitor! He knew all! He has imposed upon the municipality!"

They conducted the two officers to the town prison.

Let us now follow the royal carriages, and, as a matter of course, MM. Gillaume and Drouet, their pursuers.

They had seen them start at full gallop by the Clermont route.

At eight o'clock a courier arrived from M. de Choiseul.

This courier was poor Léonard, with his cabriolet

He came to tell M Damas that he had left M. de Choiseul at Pont-de-Somme-Vesles, at half-past four, and that up to that time no courier had arrived

Léonard told him also the danger that M Gorguelot, M Boudet, and their forty hussars, had incurred.

M Damas ran no less risk. The same excitement prevailed everywhere The sight of his soldiers had provoked murmurs. The hour for retreat approached, and he knew that it would be difficult to keep the men under arms, and the horses saddled, during the whole night, so manifest had the hostile demonstrations become.

In this interval the cracking of postilions' whips announced from afar the arrival of the carriages.

M. Bouillé's orders were to mount half an hour after the passage of the carriages, and to fall back upon Montmedy, in passing by Varennes.

M. de Damas rushed to the door, told the King what orders he had received from de Bouillé, and asked him what his orders were

"Let the carriages pass without making any remark," replied the King, "and follow with your dragoons."

During this time, incredible as it may appear, a discussion arose between the person charged with the payment of the postillion and the postmaster

It is a double post from St Menehould to Varennes. They did not wish to pay more than single. Ten minutes were lost in this squabble, which estranged the people, who were helping

At last, the carriages set off.

They could have been half a league distant when Drouet arrived

Above Islettes, he and Guillaume separated, Guillaume took the short cut by the wood, and thus gained a league; while Drouet followed the road, striving to arrive at Clermont before the King or, if he could not succeed in that, at any rate to catch him up at Varennes.

On the other hand, thanks to the advantage which the short cut gave him, Guillaume was sure to arrive at Varennes before the King

If the King took the Châlons route, Drouet would arrive at Verdun before him.

Drouet arrived at Châlons, not in time to arrest the King, but in time to prevent the dragoons from following him.

M. de Damas's dragoons were on horseback. M. de Damas ordered them to march four deep, with their swords drawn in their hand; but they stood motionless, thrusting their swords into their scabbards

At this moment, the municipal officers appeared. They commanded M. de Damas to order his men back to their barracks, as the hour for retreat had passed away.

During this time, Drouet had changed his horse and started off at a gallop.

M. de Damas who had not yet lost all hope of taking off his men, doubted to what end M. Drouet had set off. He called a dragoon, on whose fidelity he knew that he could depend, ordered him to catch up Drouet, stop him from following that road, and, if he resisted, to slay him.

The name of the dragoon was Legrche.

Without making any objection, with the passive obedience of a soldier—perhaps with the warm devotion of a Royalist,—he darted off in pursuit of Drouet.

Scarcely had he started, when, as you have already been told the council commanded M. de Damas to withdraw his men into barracks.

But instead of obeying, like M. Dardenis, M. de Damas drew his sword, struck his spurs into the belly of his horse, dashed into the midst of the crowd, and cried, "All who love me, follow!"

Three men alone replied to this appeal, and dashed after M. Damas, at a gallop, down the hill of Clermont.

Drouet was three-quarters of a league in advance of them, but he was pursued by a brave, determined, and well-mounted man.

Only on leaving Clermont the road splits—one part going to Verdun the other to Varennes.

It was not probable that the King would go to Varennes, where he had no relays: if that route had been indicated, it was simply to throw pursuers off the scent.

Anyhow, Guillaume would be at Varennes; and as he was a native of that place, he would have plenty of influence.

Drouet galloped, therefore, along the road to Verdun.

Scarcely had he gone two hundred yards, when he met a postilion, who was leading some horses.

"Have you seen a large berlin and a cabriolet going past, one with six horses and the other with three?"

"No, M. Drouet," replied the postilion.

The King had therefore gone to Varennes.

Drouet got on the road to Varennes by cutting across the country after having leapt a ditch.

This error, in all probability, saved him.

The dragoon, Lagache—who knew that the King had gone to Varennes, and not to Verdun and who saw Drouet take the road to Verdun,—did not think it worth while to pursue him much longer; and when he saw him change his route, it was too late—he was a good half-hour in advance of him.

In the midst of all this, the King, continuing his route, had left M. Dandoins and his dragoons behind him, at St. Menehould, and M. de Damas and his at Clermont.

The one and the other ought to be pushing on behind him; and in all probability there was nothing to fear in the localities through which he was now travelling.

This reflection brought tranquillity to the travellers, who, between Neuvilly and Varennes, find oblivion in sleep.

We have seen how M. Valory, not finding relays at his post, had thought fit to await the illustrious travellers, in order to consult with them.

We have seen the Queen descend from the berlin, take the arm of M. Valory, and interrogate M. Préfontaine.

We have seen M. Préfontaine advance, trembling, to the door of the King's carriage, answer his interrogatories, return to his house, shut his door, and afterwards open his window.

We have seen M. Drouet appear like a phantom from the midst of the shadow, forbidding the postilions to proceed, and rushing through the Rue des Religieuses on to the Place de Latry.

We have seen the royal berlin stopped, and the occupants forced to descend, and accept the hospitality of M Sauce, who ushered into a chamber on the first floor of his house the King, the Queen, Madame Elizabeth, Madame de Tourzel, Madame Royale, and the young Dauphin. The windows of this chamber were separated from the windows of mine by a passage, some seven or eight feet in breadth only.

We have also heard the noise at the top of the Rue Basse Cour, which was made by the arrival of the forty hussars of M. Goguelot and M de Choiseul, in the midst of whom I recognised M. de Malmy, who had, without doubt, served as their guide.

We can, therefore—a light being thrown on the past,—resume the thread of our story, without fear of complication or confusion.

CHAPTER XXX.

WHAT HAPPENED IN THE GROCER'S LITTLE SHOP.

At the end of some minutes, during which they had been parleying, M Goguelot and M. de Choiseul contrived to get admitted to the King.

M. Sauce, who, after he had conducted his guests to the chamber in which they were confined, had descended to get the key, remounted the stairs, followed by M. Goguelot and M. de Choiseul.

On seeing M Goguelot, the King joyously clapped his hands, for he was the only person that he knew whom he had as yet seen. He was, without doubt, the precursor of assistance.

Behind M. Goguelot, he recognised M. de Choiseul.

Other footsteps were heard on the staircase—they were those of M. de Damas

The three officers, as soon as they entered, bent looks of inqui around them.

This is what they saw on entering, and what I saw from my window.

A narrow room, in the midst of which was a cask, which served as a table; on that table was placed some paper and some glasses. In a corner stood the King and Queen; by the window were Madame Elizabeth and Madame Royale; in the background, the Dauphin, overcome with fatigue, was sleeping on a bed, at the foot of which was Madame de Tourzel; at 'the door were stationed the two *femmes de chambre*—Madame de Neuville and Madame de Brunier, acting as sentinels—or, rather, two women armed with forks.

The first word that the King uttered was, "Well, gentlemen, when do we start?"

"When it pleases your Majesty."

"Give your commands, sire," said M de Choiseul. "I have with me forty hussars; but lose no time. We must act before the citizens have an opportunity of bribing my men "

"Well, gentlemen, descend, and clear the way; but mind, no violence."

The young men went down.

The moment that M. de Goguelot had his hand on the street door, the National Guard summoned the hussars to dismount.

"Hussars," cried M. de Goguelot, "remain in your saddles."

"Wherefore?" queried the officer commanding the National Guard

"To protect the King," replied M. de Goguelot.

"Good!" returned the officers; "we can take care of him without you."

A hundred voices at the same time cried, "Yes, yes, yes! Make the hussars dismount! It is is our business, and not the business of strangers, to protect the King! Dismount, hussars—dismount!"

M. de Damas slipped through the crowd, and rejoined the three or four men who had been faithful to him.

M. de Goguelot exchanged signals with M. de Malmy, and in company with M de Choiseul again ascended to the King's chamber. Both addressed the Queen, as they knew that it was her head that planned.

"Madame," said M. de Goguelot, "it is no use thinking of proceeding in the carriages; but there is a way of safety."

"What?"

"Will you mount a horse, and set out with the King? He will take charge of the Dauphin. The bridge is barricaded, but at the bottom of the Rue Jean the river is fordable. With our forty hussars we will pass In any case, make a quick reselution. Our hussars are already drinking with the people; in another quarter of an hour they will be brothers."

The Queen drew back; that iron heart failed her at that critical moment. She again became a woman; she feared a struggle, a skirmish—perhaps a bullet.

"Speak to the King, messieurs," said she; "it is he who should decide on this plan; it is he who should command, it is for me but to follow."

She then added, timidly, "After all, it cannot be long before M. de Bouillé arrives.

The gardes du corps were there ready to attempt anything.

M. de Valory said, in his and the name of all his comrades, " Her Majesty knows that she can command. We are ready to die for her."

M. de Goguelot and M. de Choiseul chimed in.

" M. de Damas is below,'' said M. de Choiseul ; " he told us to tell your Majesty that he had but three or four dragoons, but that he could count on their fidelity as on his own."

" Let us set out, sire—let us set out, since the Queen places herself in your hands."

If the King replied yes, there was still hope.

" Messieurs,'' asked the King, " can you promise me that in the struggle which must take place as a consequence of our departure, no ball will strike the Queen, my sister, or my children ? "

A sigh passed the lips of the King's defenders. They felt him giving way in their hands.

" Let us reason coolly," said the King. " The municipal council do not refuse to let me go. The annoyance is, that we are compelled to spend the night here ; but before daybreak, M. de Bouillé will be acquainted with the situation in which we are. He is at Stenay. Stenay is but eight leagues from here ; two hours will take one there, and another two suffice to bring back a message. M. de Bouillé cannot fail to be here in the morning, then shall we depart without danger or violence."

As he uttered these words, without announcing themselves, or asking the permission of the King to be admitted, the municipal council entered the room.

The decision that they had arrived at was brief and precise.

The people strongly objected to the King's continuing his route, and had resolved to send a courier to the National Assembly to know its sentiments.

In fact, a citizen of Varennes, an M. Maugin, surgeon by profession, had started at full speed for Paris.

M. de Goguelot saw that there was not an instant to lose ; he dashed from the house, and found M. de Malmy at the door.

" Monsieur," he said, " you live here, therefore you know this part of the country. A man, come what will, must set out for Stenay to advise M. de Bouillé of the pre-

11

dicament in which the King is placed, and return with a
sufficient force to rescue him "

"I will go myself," said M. de Malmy.

And sticking his spurs into his horse, he set off at a
gallop.

At M. Gerbaut's door, he saw a file of National Guards,
who commanded him to stop.

"All very well," replied M. de Malmy ; "but I intend
to go on."

"Not you, more than another !" cried an officer, seizing
his horse by the bridle.

"If you advance another step," said M. Roland, the
commander of the National Guard, cocking a pistol, "I
will shoot you."

M. de Malmy, without reply, spurred his horse right on
to him.

M. Roland fired off the pistol so close that the flame
blinded M. de Malmy's horse, at the same time as the bullet passed through the fleshy part of the horseman's arm.

The frightened animal reared, and fell back upon his
master.

From the chamber where I was engaged in watching the
King, I heard the pistol-shot, the fall of the horse and
man, and the scream of a woman.

I recognised the voice of Mdlle. Sophie. I dashed down
stairs, and arrived in time to see her throw herself on the
breathless, and, as she thought, dead body of M. de Malmy.

"Réné, Réné !" she cried. "Help me—oh, help me !"

I rushed out of the house, took M. de Malmy in my
arms, and, at the moment when he tried to stand, I took
him into the house, and laid him on M. Gerbaut's bed.

"He is dead—he is dead ! They have killed him, the
wretches !" cried the unhappy and despairing girl, who was
covered with the blood which had flowed from his wound.

At this moment, M. de Malmy opened his eyes.

"He is not dead, Mdlle. Sophie," cried I.

"Oh !" said she.

And she threw herself prostrate on the bed.

"Leave me—leave me !" said M. de Malmy. making an
effort to lift himself up. "I must go and seek M de Bouillè."

Pain and weakness compelled him to fall back again.

"In the name of heaven, stay there, Alphonse!" cried Mdlle. Sophie. "Do not move, or you will uselessly throw away your life. You owe me somewhat; grant me that favor."

"I must," said the young man. "I think that my leg is broken."

"Réné, Réné! I pray, I implore you, my friend—my brother—run for a surgeon!"

"Immediately!" said I, dashing out into the street.

But it was impossible to move.

The crowd had become something fearful.

"Hussars!" cried M. de Goguelot, "are you for the King or the nation?"

They all replied, "For the nation!"

"The others?"

"For the King—for the King!" they cried out, in German.

"Do you hear them?" said M. Drouet. "They are strangers—they are Germans—that is to say, enemies."

"No, sir," cried the officer; "it is a Frenchman, who, in good French, says to you, "Make way, in the name of the King!'"

"And I reply to you, in better French, if your hussars do not lay down their arms, we will fire on them, and not one shall leave Varennes alive. Soldiers, present arms—and, gunners, to your pieces!"

Then, stepping two paces forward, he said to M. Goguelot, "Take care, sir. I have sighted you with my gun."

"Vive la nation!" cried the hussars, as they saw the musket-barrels pointed at them, with the matches burning brightly in the obscurity, and the two little pieces of cannon placed in battery at the bottom of the Rue St. Jean.

At this moment, several National Guards sprang upon M. Goguelot's horse, snatched the rider from the saddle, and dashed him head-foremost into the road, where he lay for a moment or so, completely stunned.

They treated M. Damas and M. de Choiseul, who appeared on the doorstep at that moment, in the same fashion.

In the midst of this struggle, I set out for the Place Latry, by way of the Rue l'Horloge. When I got there, I found that M. Maugin had started for Paris, by wish of the municipality, at full speed.

I ran to the house of another doctor of less skill than M. Maugin—a M. Saulnier—and brought him to the Rue de la Basse Cour, where the hussars were drinking and fraternizing with the National Guard.

M. de Malmy was wounded in the shoulder by a ball which had traversed the deltoid muscles. His leg was not broken, but his knee was badly sprained.

Mdlle. Gerbaut, who feared that the condition of the wounded man would not be improved by his remaining on the ground floor in direct communication with the street, begged us to carry M. de Malmy into a chamber where the surgeon could pay, without inconvenience, all the cares necessary to a man in his condition.

I assisted M. Saulnier—a sufficiently difficult job—to carry a man who could use neither his left arm nor his right leg. Afterwards, as I saw that my presence was not welcome to Mdlle. Sophie, and as I felt no particular interest in the wounded man, I retired, so as not to lose a single scene of the drama which was being played out before my eyes, and which was nothing less than a duel between a King and a nation.

CHAPTER XXXI.

THE RETURN OF ROYALTY IN ARREST.

In the midst of the tumult which was produced by the disarming of M. de Choiseul and M de Damas, and the cries of "Vive la nation!" shouted out by the hussars, to the great delight of the people, M de Goguelot, profiting by a moment of inattention on the part of his guards, rushed up-stairs, and, all bleeding as he was, entered the chamber of the King.

His head had been cut open by the fall, but he did not feel the wound.

The appearance of the chamber had changed. It had become a prison

Marie Antoinette, who was in reality the strength and life of the family, was overwhelmed. She had heard the cries, the shots, and she saw M. de Goguelot return all covered with blood.

The King, standing upright, prayed M. Sauce, the grocer, to assist them; as if he had the power, even had he wished to do so.

The Queen, seated on a stool between two packages of candles, likewise implored his assistance.

But with brutal and petty selfishness, he replied, "I should like to be able to serve you, certainly; but if you think of the King, I think of M. Sauce."

The Queen turned aside, shedding tears of rage.

She had never been so humbled before.

The day began to dawn

The crowd filled the street, the Place de la Rue Neuve, and the Place Latry.

All the citizens cried from their windows, "To Paris—to Paris—to Paris with the King!"

Alas! to show himself—he was to appear no longer, as on the 6th of October, on the balcony of the marble court, but at the windows of a grocer's house.

The King had fallen into a state of torpor.

The cries redoubled.

Five or six people had seen, or rather had caught a glimpse, of the King; the others wished to inspect him thoroughly.

At that period, when it took a diligence six or seven days to go to Paris, to have seen the King was a thing to talk about. Each one had formed an imaginary portrait of him for him or herself

Therefore the astonishment was intense when Louis the Sixteenth showed himself with swollen eyes, and proved to that multitude a thing which they did not before believe—namely, that a king may be fat, pale, bloated—with dull eyes, hanging lips, a bad peruke, and a gray suit of clothes.

The crowd believed that they were being deceived, and growled accordingly.

Afterwards, when they knew that it was the King, "Oh, heavens!" said they. "Poor man!"

Pity having once seized them, their hearts opened, and they began to shed tears.

"Long live the King!" cried the crowd.

If Louis XVI had profited by that moment—if he had prayed that concourse of people to help him and his children,—perhaps they would have passed him and the royal family over the barricaded bridge, and delivered them into the hands of the hussars.

He took no advantage of that pity and sorrow.

An example was given of the commiseration which the royal family inspired.

Sauce had an aged mother—a woman of some eighty years of age. She was born in the reign of Louis XIV, and was a Royalist. She entered the chamber; and seeing the King and Queen bowed down with sorrow, and the children sleeping on the bed, which had never been destined for such a mournful honor, she fell on her knees beside it, repeated a prayer, and, turning towards the Queen, "Madame," said she, "will you allow me to kiss the hands of the two innocents?"

The Queen bowed her head, in token of assent.

The good woman kissed their hands, and left the room, sobbing, as if her heart would break.

The Queen was the only one who did not sleep.

The King, who had need, whatever his preoccupation of mind might be, to eat and sleep well, having neither ate nor slept to his satisfaction, was distracted.

About half-past six, M. Deslon was announced.

M. Deslon had arrived from Dun with about a hundred men.

He had found the Rue de l'Hospital barricaded; had held a parley; and demanding admission to the presence of the King, was accorded permission to visit him.

He informed them how, at the sound of the tocsin, he had hurried on; and that M. de Bouillé, warned by his son and M. de Raigecourt, would, without doubt, arrive in a short time.

The King, however, seemed as if he did not hear him.

Three times M. Deslon repeated the same thing, and rather impatiently the last time.

"Sire," said he, "do you not hear me?"

"What do you wish, monsieur?" said the King, as if starting from a reverie.

"I ask your commands for M. de Bouillé, sire!"

"I have no more commands to give, monsieur—I am a prisoner.'"

"But, at least, sir—"

"That he does what he can for me."

M. Deslon retired, without being able to obtain another answer.

In fact, the King was indeed a prisoner.

The tocsin had completed its dismal task. Every village had sent its contingent. Four or five thousand men encumbered the streets of Varennes.

About seven in the morning. two men arriving by the Clermont road. and bestriding horses flecked with foam, pushed their way through the multitude

The shouts of the people announced something new to the King.

Soon the door opened, and admitted an officer of the National Guard.

It was the same Rayon, who, whilst snatching a moment's rest at Châlons, sent on an express to St. Menehould.

He entered the royal chamber fatigued, excited, almost mad, without a cravat, and with his hair unpowdered

"Ah, sire," said he, in a hoarse voice—"our wives, our children ! They slaughter them at Paris, sire ; you will not go much further. The interest of the State—"

And he fell, almost fainting, into an arm-chair.

"Well, sir," said the Queen, taking his hand, and showing him the Dauphin and Madame Royale sleeping on the bed, "am I not a mother too ?"

"In short, sir," said the King, "what have you to announce to me ?"

"Sire, a decree of the Assembly."

"Where is it ?"

"My comrade has it."

"Your comrade ?"

The officer made a sign to open the door.

One of the gardes du corps opened it, and they saw M. de Romeuf leaning against the window of the ante-chamber, and weeping.

He came forward, with downcast eyes.

The Queen started at sight of him.

It was the same young man who had accompanied M Lafayette in the visit he had paid the King just a quarter of an hour before he started

"Ah, monsieur ! is it you ?" said the Queen. "I could never have believed it."

It was she who should have blushed before him, and she tried to make him blush.

M. de Romeuf held in his hands the decree of the Assembly

The King snatched it from him, cast his eyes over it, and cried, " There is no longer a King in France!"

The Queen took it in her turn, read it, and returned it to the King.

The King re-read it, and then placed it on the bed where his children slept.

" No—no!" cried the Queen, exasperated, furious, mad with hate and anger; " I do not wish that infamous paper to defile my children."

" Madame," at last said Romeuf, " you have just reproached me for being charged with this mission. Is it not better that I should have undertaken the task than one who would have borne witness with regard to transports of passion?"

There was, in fact, at this action of the Queen's, a terrible murmur among the spectators.

The Queen had crumpled up the decree, and dashed it on the floor.

M. de Choiseul, who had regained his liberty, and who, at the moment, entered the chamber, accompanied by two messengers, picked up the decree, and placed it on the table.

The Queen appreciated his intention, and thanked him with a look.

" At least, sir," said she, addressing M. de Romeuf, " I hope that you will do all you can for M. de Choiseul, M. de Damas, and M de Goguelot when we are gone."

In fact, the Queen well understood that go she must.

It was seven o'clock in the morning, and M. de Bouillé had not put in an appearance.

The peasants of the villages round Varennes continued to pour into the town, armed with guns, pitchforks, and scythes, and each cried louder than the other, " To Paris! to Paris!"

The carriage was in readiness

The King made the most of each little obstacle, counting each moment, awaiting Bouillé

At last, it was necessary to make a move.

The King rose first.

The Queen followed his example.

One of her women—whether naturally, or whether as an artifice, to gain time—fainted.

"They may cut me into pieces if they will," said the Queen, "but I will not leave without one who has the misfortune to be my friend"

"As you will—stay if you like," said a man of the people, "At any rate, I will take the Dauphin"

He took the royal child in his arms, and stepped towards the door.

The Queen seized the Dauphin from him, and descended the stairs, blushing

All the family were filled with poignant anxiety. On arriving in the street. Madame Elizabeth perceived that half of the Queen's hair had turned gray; the other half was to grow gray at the Conciergerie in a second night of agony, which was not, perhaps, more terrible than that which we have recounted.

They got into the carriage; the three gardes du corps mounted on the box.

M de Goguelot, in the hope of bringing succor, had found means of escaping through the little passage situate at the back of the house of M. Sauce.

M. de Choiseul and M de Damas were conducted to the city prison, where M. de Romeuf caused himself to be imprisoned with them, for the sake of protecting them more efficiently.

At last, after having exhausted every possible means of delay, the carriage started, escorted by the National Guard, under the command of M. Signemont, by the hussars of M. de Choiseul, which had been sent to protect his flight, and by more than four thousand citizens of Varennes and its suburbs, armed with guns, pitchforks, and scythes.

The carriage of the King did not, as some historians say, pass the house of the grocer, Sauce; that was the historical limit of the fatal journey

The moment that the carriage moved, I felt great doubt —or, rather, great remorse

The catastrophe of the arrest of the King had brought in its train an event which, though I have but mentioned it in the place it occupied relatively to that arrest, influenced in a strange manner the whole of my life.

One can readily understand that I speak of M. de Malmy's wound ; of the impression that that wound produced on Mdlle. Sophie. and of the involuntary avowal that, on her part, she had made to me.

I had a deep affection for Sophie. This affection, more than fraternal, had a spice of jealousy in it ; although I must do the poor girl the justice to say that from the moment that she perceived my nascent love, she had done all she could to nip it in the bud, by telling me that she could never be anything more than·a sister to me. I always had the suspicion—I will not say that my rival, for there was no real rivalry, was M. de Malmy.

This time I could no longer doubt it, and I felt it impossible to remain under the same roof with him. Not only because Sophie loved him and he loved Sophie, but because I knew that he was the origin of all the misery and unhappiness that was gradually wearing her away.

As soon as I saw the King ready to set out, and the carriage about to move on to Paris, I bade adieu to M. Gerbaut, without telling him that I did not think of returning to Varennes, and started off without having the courage to see Sophie, whom however, I unexpectedly found in my road, barring up the corridor.

" What, Mdlle. Sophie ! "

She threw herself, weeping, on to my neck.

" Each one has his destiny, my good René," said she. "Mine is to suffer. I shall accomplish it."

" Shall I always be your brother ? " asked I, weeping myself.

" Ah, yes ! And if ever I have need of you, I will show you that I am your sister, by coming to you for assistance."

" Heaven guard you, Mdlle. Sophie," cried I, withdrawing myself from her embrace.

" And you, also—heaven bless you, René ! "

And I heard the sobs which followed these words even as far as the door which opened into the street.

I took my place at the door of the King's carriage, making a signal to MM. Drouet and Guillaume, who were on horseback, with the intention of preceding the carriages, in order to make way for, and protect them.

What was M. de Bouillé doing at this time ? We will tell you in the following chapter.

CHAPTER XXXII.

WHAT M DE BOUILLE DID IN THE MEANTIME.

M. DE BOUILLE was at Dun. where he had passed the night in a state of mortal disquietude.

It was the advanced post of his watch.

At three o'clock, having received no news, he proceeded to Stenay.

At Stenay he was in the centre of his forces, and was able to act with greater facility, having at his disposal a great number of men.

From four to five o'clock he was successively joined by M. de Rohrig, M de Raigecourt, and by his son.

He then knew all

But M. de Bouillé could but little depend on his men. He was surrounded by hostile villagers, as he called them—that is to say, patriotic. He was menaced by Metz, by Verdun, and by Stenay. It was his fear of Stenay that had caused him to quit Dun.

The Royal German was the sole regiment on which he could depend. It was necessary to keep up their loyalty.

M. de Bouillé and his son Louis sat themselves to the work body and soul.

A bottle of wine and a louis per man settled the affair.

But it took two hours to arm and set out.

At last, he started; but at seven o'clock, just at the time when the King got into the carriage.

In two hours he covered the eight leagues which separated him from Varennes

On the road he met a hussar.

" Well ? "

" The King is arrested."

" We know it. What then ? "

" He has just set out from Varennes."

" Where goes he ? "

" To Paris "

Bouillé did not give himself time to reply.

He dashed his spurs into the flanks of his horse.

His regiment followed him.

Varennes saw the regiment descend " like a waterspout amongst its vines," to quote the language of the *proces verbal*.

When he arrived at the Place du Grand Monarque, the King had started more than an hour.

He acted so as to lose no time. The Rue de l'Hopital was barricaded; the bridge was barricaded. They made a detour round the town; they crossed the river by the ford at the Boucheries, in order to take up a favorable position on the Clermont road, to attack the escort.

The order was given, and the manœuvre accomplished.

The river was crossed.

A hundred steps more, and they would be on the road.

But the Moulin Canal was on their way—six feet deep, and impossible to ford.

It was necessary to stop and march back.

For an instant, they held the idea of fording the river at St. Gengoult, taking the Rue St. Jean, passing through Varennes and falling on the rear of the escort.

But the dragoons were fatigued; the horses rebelled at every step It would be necessary to fight a way through Varennes, and to fight to get to the King.

They said that the garrison of Verdun were on the march, with some cannon.

Then courage failed them. They felt that all was lost.

M. de Bouillè, weeping with rage, dashed his sword into its sheath, and ordered a retreat.

The inhabitants of the high town saw him and his men standing there for an hour, unable to make up their minds to return.

Eventually he and his men took the route to Dun, and disappeared in the distance.

The King continued his way—*the way of the Cross.*

After the arrest of M. Dandoins and his lieutenant, an officer of the National Guard, Citizen Legay, had established under the trees at the angle of the Rue de la Post au Bois and the Rue du Marais a post of National Guards, picked men, and all ordered to fire on any one entering or leaving the city at a gallop, without responding to the challenge of the sentinels

Some minutes after these orders had been given, a

report was circulated that the hussars of Pont-de-Somme-Vesles had gone round the town, and that Drouet and Guillaume ran a great risk of falling into their hands.

M. Legay then asked for two volunteers to go with him on the road, and pick up what information they could with regard to Drouet and Guillaume.

Two gendarmes, Collet and Pointe, offered themselves, and all three set out on their voyage of discovery.

On the road they met the two citizens of St. Menehould, who had started on sorry hacks, and been unable to keep up the chase. They learnt from them that no accident had happened to the two messengers. Anxious to be the bearers of this good news, they put their horses to the gallop, and, forgetting the orders given by Legay, omitted to answer the challenge of the sentinels in ambuscade.

The sentinels fired. Two of the horsemen fell; one dead, and the other wounded.

Legay received five or six shots in the arm and hand.

The same day that the King repassed St. Menehould, the slain gendarme was buried.

The King, on arriving, found the church hung with black, and the whole town prepared to follow the body to its last home.

<hr />

CHAPTER XXXIII.

AN OLD ACQUAINTANCE TURNS UP.

NOTHING important passed between Varennes and St. Menehould. The illustrious prisoners, starting at every new noise, lost in a measure, as they approached the latter town, every hope of succor.

The first thing they encountered was a sort of rebuke from the dead. Of course, I allude to the interment of the man shot in the evening by the sentinels.

The royal carriages stopped in order to allow the funeral procession to pass. Two kings found themselves face to face with each other—a living majesty and the King of Death. The living King recognised the power of King Death, and bowed down before him.

St. Menehould was crowded. The National Guard poured in from all points, those from Châlons coming in public
or private vehicles. In fact, the affluence of people was
such that they feared a lack of provisions.

In the midst of all these people coming and going, I recognised, mounted on a little pony, M. Dampierre, our old
chasseur of the Forest of Argonne. He knew me, and
came to me, trying to force the line of guards on duty at
the side of the gates.

It was I who repulsed him, because he did not count on
my resistance.

"Pardon, M. le Comte," said I; "you cannot pass!"

"Why can I not pass?" asked he.

"Because it is ordered that none shall be allowed to approach the King's carriage."

"Who gave that order?"

"Our Captain, M. Drouet."

"A revolutionist!"

"Possibly so, M. le Comte; but he is our commander, and
we are bound to obey him."

"Is it forbidden to cry 'Vive le Roi?'"

"No, M. le Comte; we are all Royalists."

M. de Dampierre lifted his hat as high as his length of
arm would permit him, raised himself in his stirrups, and
cried "Vive le Roi!"

The King put his head out of the window, and without
any expression of gratitude or remembrance, bowed to him.

M. de Dampierre retreated out of the crowd with trouble,
being obliged to make his horse go backwards. I remember him as well as if the events occurred but yesterday.
He wore gray trousers, long riding boots, a white waistcoat,
a three-cornered hat, trimmed with gold lace. As usual
with him, he carried, slung over his shoulder, a little single-
barrelled gun.

I lost sight of him. I fancied that he took the direction
of the Rue de l'Abreuvoir.

During this time, the Mayor and members of the municipality had advanced as far as the bridge of the Aisne, situate at the extremity of the Porte au Bois, to meet the
royal family.

A municipal officer then took occasion to speak, and to
tell the King what alarms his flight had caused in France.

Louis XVI was contented to reply, with an ill-tempered air, " I never intended to leave my kingdom."

The crowd was so great that we took half an hour to go five-hundred yards.

About half-past eleven, the King mounted the steps of the Hotel de Ville, his garments covered with dust, and his face altered and careworn.

The Queen dressed in black. She had changed her robe at M. Sauce's, and held the Dauphin by the hand.

Louis XVI and his children were hungry.

As for the Queen, in the same manner, as she cared not to sleep, she now seemed to care not to eat

A breakfast had been prepared through the forethought of the municipal council, but as they were a long time serving it, a gendarme named Lapointe brought some cherries in his hat for Madame Royale.

The royal family had likewise need of rest.

The Mayor, M. Dupuis de Dammartin, offered them hospitality; they accepted it; only M Dupuis de Dammartin observed to the King that it would be just as well if the Queen and the Dauphin showed themselves to the people.

The King made no difficulty He showed himself first. Afterwards the Queen appeared in her turn. holding the Dauphin in her arms. The window of the Hotel de Ville —the only one which had a balcony—was so narrow that the King and Queen could not both show themselves at the same time.

A municipal officer then announced to the people that the King, being fatigued, intended to honor the citizens of St. Menehould by sleeping within their walls.

The carriages had already been taken to the stables, and the news of a halt for twenty-four hours was not less agreeable to us, who had been marching seven or eight leagues under a burning sun, than it was to the royal family. when the National Guards from the adjacent towns and villages, who filled the hotels and cafés. rushed into the place, crying "Aristocrats! Traitors!" and saying that the royal family were far too near the frontier to be allowed to halt

In consequence, they ordered the immediate departure of the King and his family

The King, having informed himself of the cause of the tumult, said, with his usual impassibility, " Very well; let us go."

The Queen then re-appeared on the balcony holding her son by the hand. She pointed out the National Guards to him, saying some words in a whisper.

An inhabitant of St. Menehould, who was at an adjoining window, assured me that the following were the words that she spoke. " Do you see those blue toads ? It is they who wish us to set out ! "

It is needless to say that the National Guards wore the blue uniform.

As the royal family crossed the hall of the Hotel de Ville, into which opened the door of the chapel, where the prisoners had heard mass, the Queen perceiving the captives, distributed among them five louis—the King ten.

At two o'clock the carriages started for Châlons. From the time that the King had been recognised he took the place of honor in the vehicle.

MM. de Malden, de Moustier, and de Valory, sat on the box, but they were not strapped to it as some people have said.

Not a single shout for the King, except that which Dampierre uttered, as we have before mentioned, was used at either his arrival or departure. The only shouts raised were " Vive la nation ! " " Vivent les patriotes ! "

About nine or ten in the morning the Comte de Hans arrived at St. Menehould, exasperated by the news of the arrest of the King.

Many persons had heard him say, " The King is arrested ! We are all lost ! But the King shall know that he still has some faithful subjects ! "

I have said that, after speaking to me, I had seen him go round to the side of the horse-pond.

As the royal carriage passed, he presented arms to the august prisoners, after the fashion of a sentinel.

The King recognised him, pointed him out to the Queen, and returned his salute.

M. Dampierre then put his horse to a gallop, and disappeared at the Rue de l'Abreuvoir so as to get in advance of the King's carriage, stopped in the most public part of the town, at the corner of the Rue de l'Abreuvoir, and presented arms afresh.

The King saluted him a third time.

Then pushing his horse through the crowd on the side where I was, he approached the carriage.

It was going at this time up the Fleurion at a foot-pace.

"Sire," said he, "you see before you one of your most faithful servants. My name is Duval de Dampierre, Comte de Hans. I have married a lady of the House of Legur, a relative of the minister of that name, and a niece of M. d'Allonville."

"All these names are known to me," replied the King; "and I am touched at the proof of fidelity which you give me."

This whispered conversation, after the pretence of the Comte in presenting arms to the King on his road, was a direct provocation to that crowd who were taking him who had wished to escape back to Paris.

In the meantime the Comte had been gently pushed on one side, and darting off, he disappeared in the distance.

The head of the procession reached the end of the town, and arrived at the decline of Dammartin la Planchette.

As they left the city, M. de Dampierre reappeared, and followed their route, keeping himself on the other side of the hedge and ditch. He wished, by some means, to get on to the top of the King's carriage, from whence he could hold communication with the royal party inside. These signs, as they could easily understand them, excited defiance.

They believed that in the few words exchanged at the door of the carriage, a project for a rescue had been broached; they closed round the carriage, and the words "Be on the alert!" circulated through the ranks of the National Guards.

M. de Dampierre tried to approach the carriage once again, and was repulsed, not only with murmurs, but with menaces, the guards crossing their muskets across the door to prevent his holding any communication with the King.

This almost insolent persistence on his part had exasperated even the most temperate.

Seeing that his efforts were useless, M. de Dampierre resolved to finish with an act of bravado.

Having accomplished two-thirds of the descent, at a spot called La Grevières, M. de Dampierre called out a second time "Vive le Roi!" fired off his gun in the air, and plunging his rowels into his steed, darted off at a gallop.

A wood was situated about half a league from the road. They believed that some troops were in ambuscade there,

12

and that the discharge of the gun was a preconcerted signal for them.

Five or six horsemen dashed off in pursuit of M de Dampierre ; ten or twelve shots were fired at him at the same time, but none of the bullets touched him.

M. de Dampierre, still at a gallop, waved his arm in a triumphant manner in the air.

I rushed off like the others, though on foot, not to capture M. de Dampierre—heaven forbid!—but, on the contrary, to help him if needful.

M. de Dampierre had already galloped more than five hundred yards, and he had almost escaped from his pursuers, when his horse, in leaping a ditch, stumbled, and fell.

But, with the aid of the bit and bridle, he managed to raise him up again, and once more set off at a gallop. His gun was left in the ditch.

At this moment a solitary gun was discharged.

It was fired by a peasant, mounted on a horse belonging to one of the hussars, which he had captured the evening before.

It was easy to see that M. de Dampierre was wounded. He fell backwards on the croup of his horse, which reared.

Then, in a moment, with the rapidity of lightning, on the little bridge of St. Catherine, by the borders of the ditch, the waters of which pass under the bridge, a horrible scene took place, which I saw in all its dreadful details, but was unable to oppose.

The peasant who had fired the shot, followed by about forty men, caught up the Comte de Haus, dealt him a blow with his sabre, and then unhorsed him. I saw no more. I heard the report of about twenty guns, into the suffocating smoke of which I dashed.

They were firing at M. de. Dampierre.

I arrived too late. Had I reached the mob sooner, it would have been to have died with him, for I could not have saved him.

His body was riddled with bullets, and gashed with bayonets; his face, scratched by the peasants' hob-nailed boots, was unrecognisable.

His watch was dashed to pieces by a ball which had penetrated his fob.

There was nothing to be done. I threw my gun over

my shoulder, and, with tears in my eyes and sweat on my brow, I rejoined my rank.

The royal berlin continued its route slowly and sorrowfully under a sweltering sun, along that unbending route which crosses like a pencil line that sorrowful portion of France called the Paltry Land.

CHAPTER XXXIV.

THE CRITICS CRITICISED.

NOT only does it seem to me sufficient to relate what I have seen; I desire also, as an eye-witness, to rectify history and to combat, on sure grounds, the mistake of historians.

In order to give a slight idea of the intense excitement of Republican France against the King, and more particularly against the Queen, I quote the following letter, the original of which was sent by the citizens of Counien to the municipal officers of Varennes:—

"27th of June, 2nd year of Liberty.

" GENTLEMEN,—

" Allow the patriotic women of the State, who have the honor of being members of the Club of the Society of the Friends of the Constitution, to present to you their best congratulations at the capture in your city of the execrable traitors, Citizen and Citizeness Capet, whose traitorous machinations have so long tried to crush freedom in France. Our only prayer is that both may speedily be humiliated. Vive la France ! Vive la Liberté ! A bas les Captes !

" For the Citizenesses of Counien,

(Signed) " CITOYENNE MARIE BENOIT.

" To the Municipal Officers of Varennes."

After this specimen of the feeling of the women of France can it be wondered that the fate of the King and Queen seemed assured. Either they must die, or France must sink lower than ever. This, of course, was only my opinion; but events have proved whether I was right or wrong.

CHAPTER XXXV.

IS LOVE ETERNAL?

THE route from St. Menehould to Châlons is long and fatiguing—nine apparently never-ending leagues, traversing flat and arid plains under a leaden sky, with a sun darting his 'scorching rays with reflected lustre on the musket barrels and sword blades

The royal family arrived at Châlons fatigued, dispirited and worn out, at ten in the evening.

Half the original followers of the royal escort had thrown themselves down under hedges and in ditches, unable any longer to proceed.

But the actual escort was as strong on arriving at Châlons as when leaving St. Menehould, since it was recruited by the National Guard of every village through which it passed; and the villages were pretty thickly scattered on the right and left of that road.

The authorities, of whom the Mayor took the lead, conducted the prisoners to the gate of the Dauphin. I use the word prisoners advisedly, as the royal family were in fact, at that time, prisoners of the nation.

Strange coincidence!—the gate through which they passed was the triumphal arch raised by the French people in commemoration of the entry of Madame the Dauphine into France.

It still bore the inscription, " *May it stand eternal, like our love.*"

The arch, in fact, still stood, but the love which prompted it had fallen away.

At Châlons, especially, opinion changes.

The bluffness of the national party was lessened. The old town where Attila lost himself, and which now preserved its trade only in the wines of Champagne, was inhabited by Royalists of the better class, and by poor gentlemen. These good people were sorely vexed to see their unhappy King in such doleful plight.

They expected his arrival; consequently a great supper was prepared

The King and Queen partook of the meal in public, as they did at Varennes. A sort of royal drawing-room was held. The ladies bore with them immense bouquets. The Queen was positively overwhelmed with flowers.

They determined to start on the morrow, feeling an increase of confidence on account of the reception they had met with.

Before they set out out, mass was celebrated at ten o'clock by M. Charber, perpetual-curate of Notre Dame. The King was present, accompanied by the Queen and the royal family; but hardly had the solemn service commenced, before a disturbance was made.

It was the National Guard of Rheims, who wished the King to set out at once. The time spent in mass appeared to them wasted, as they had come solely to gloat over the downfall of monarchy, and the ruin of their King. They broke open, therefore, the doors of the chapel, despite the resistance offered to them by the National Guard.

The King and Queen were advised to show themselves at the balcony. They did so; but the sight of their august persons exasperated, in place of calming, the turbulence of the excited populace, who shouted for the royal family to leave their city, and actually drew the carriages to the door, harnessed the horses, and did, in fact, all they could do to accelerate the departure of the King.

The King appeared again at the balcony, and pronounced the following words :—

"Since you oblige me to leave you, I go!"

Although this was a reproach more than anything else, it satisfied the people.

At eleven exactly, the royal family re-entered their carriage, and put themselves *en route*.

The heat was dreadfully oppressive. Their journey was made, as it were, through a blast furnace, and their eyes were incessantly tormented by a penetrating dust.

I happened to know the situation of a cool spring. I approached the royal carriage, and demanded respectfully of her Majesty the Queen if she desired a glass of fresh water, as we were near to some of a most excellent quality.

"Thank you," replied the Queen.

"Oh, do have some, mamma—do have some! I am so thirsty!" said the Dauphin.

"I wish it not; but give me some for my children," said the Queen.

Madame de Tourzal handed me a silver cup.

"Fill this up for me, also," said Madame Elizabeth.

She handed me another cup.

In fancy, after a lapse of sixty years, I can still see her angelic face—still hear that charming voice, whose entreaties were more than commands.

I leant my gun against the trunk of a tree, rushed to the fountain, and brought back the two cups filled with the sparkling water, which, through my rapidity, had not had time to lose its freshness.

The Dauphin and Madame Royale shared one cup between them.

Madame Elizabeth, after offering the other cup to the Queen, who refused it, drank it herself.

"Oh, what delicious water it is," cried the Dauphin. "Why does the world drink aught else?"

"Because they have drinks they like better," replied the King.

"My son thanks you, sir," said the Queen.

"I also thank you," said Madame Elizabeth, with her sweet smile.

I seized my gun, which had been left at the foot of a tree.

"I saw you once run after M. de Dampierre," said the Queen. "With what intention?"

"With the hope of saving him, if possible, madame."

"You have the same opinions, then, as M. de Dampierre," said the Queen.

"I agree with him in the respect which he feels towards your enemies."

"Do you know that you give an ambiguous answer, young man?" said the King.

"Yes, sire," I replied.

"Ha, ha!" said he.

Then to the Queen: "The minds of these people are poisoned against us, from their very childhood."

"Oh, papa!" cried the Dauphin, "what a beautiful gun he has!"

I was the person referred to. To the Queen and Madame Elizabeth I was "monsieur," but to the Dauphin I was simply "he."

The King looked at my gun.

"It is," said he, "a gun manufactured at Versailles. Where did you procure it?"

"The Duc d'Enghien gave it to me, sire."

"Yes," said the King, "the Condes have all the benefits on this side,—'the department of the Meuse,' as they call it."

Then looking towards me· "Have you ever served princes?"

"Sire," said I, smiling, "is it necessary to have served princes in order to receive a present from them?"

The Queen bent her regards upon the King.

"Strange!" said she.

I retreated a pace.

The King beckoned me, but not knowing how to address me, he said, "My young friend, you say that the Duc d'Enghien gave you that gun?"

"Yes, sire. I understand," said I, "that the King wishes to know upon what occasion this gun was presented to me. I was the nephew of a park-keeper of the Forest of Argonne, whose name was Father Descharmes. The Duc de Condé and the Duc d'Enghien often hunted in this forest. The Duc d'Enghien took a fancy to me, and gave me this gun."

The King, for a moment, appeared buried in thought.

"Your uncle is still alive?" he then asked.

"Sire, he is dead?"

"Why do you not solicit his place?"

"Because, sire, the keepers wear livery. I am a free man."

"Children suck in republican ideas, even with their mothers' milk!" murmured the King.

He then threw himself back in his carriage.

I know not if the King spoke again; but the carriage at the moment stopped; and, perchance, with it stopped something of importance.

We had arrived at Port Bassion.

Suddenly was heard a cry: "The commissaires! the commissaires!"

At this moment, a man on horseback dashed up to the door of the King's carriage. The King put out his head, to see what had caused the halt.

"Sire," said the horseman, "here are three deputies, who wish to direct the return of your Majesty."

"Aha!" said the King, "Can you tell me the names of these estimable gentlemen?"

"Their names, sire, are Citizens Latour-Maubourg, Barnave, and Pétion."

The three deputies represented the three different parties of the Assembly. Latour-Maubourg was Royalist, Barnave was Constitutional, Pétion was Republican.

The crowd respectfully drew back. Three men approached the royal carriage, stopped at the door, and saluted the King, who returned their inclination.

One of them held in his hand a paper, which he read in a loud voice. It was the decree of the National Assembly.

The man who read it was Pétion.

This decree ordered them to proceed to the King, not only to ensure his safety, but also as a mark of respect due to royalty, as represented in the persons of Louis XVI and Marie Antoinette.

The King knew that M. Latour-Maubourg was a Royalist.

He therefore desired that, as two deputies had to sit in the carriage with him, he would name the two. The Queen expressed the same desire.

M. Latour-Maubourg replied, in a whisper:—

"I accepted the sad mission which introduces me to your Majesty only in the hopes of being of some service to you. Your Majesty can, then, count upon me as a faithful follower. But I have not the power of Barnave, who exercises an enormous influence over the Assembly. He is vain as an advocate, and will be flattered by having a seat in the carriage of the King. It is, therefore, needful that he should occupy a place, and that the Queen should take the opportunity of improving his acquaintance. I, therefore, beg your Majesties to excuse my surrendering my seat."

The Queen bowed her head. She wished to again assume her womanly properties, and to seduce Barnave, as she had Mirabeau. To be sure, it was humiliating, but, at the same time, it was a distraction.

Strange contradiction! It was the King who had most repugnance to Barnave's occupying a seat in the royal carriage. Barnave, a little Dauphinois advocate, pride upon his face, his nose perked up in the air, and his *tout ensemble* proclaiming insufferable conceit, took his place. Pétion likewise, his rosy cheeks glowing with satisfaction, disposed of himself to his perfect content.

Barnave and Pétion, therefore, as we have said, entered the royal carriage.

Madame de Tourzel had resigned her place, and entered, with M Latour-Maubourg, the carriage set apart for the attendants.

Pétion at once proclaimed his discourtesy by claiming, as representative of the National Assembly, a seat with his face to the horses. The King and Queen made a sign to Madame Elizabeth, who at once changed places with him.

At last, all inside the royal carriage were satisfactorily arranged On the back seat were the King, Pétion, the Queen, and on the front, Madame Elizabeth, face to face with Pétion, Madame Royale and the Dauphin face to face and knee to knee with the Queen, who was opposite, also, to Barnave

At the first glance the Queen fancied that Barnave was dry, cold, and wicked.

Barnave had hoped to take the place of Mirabeau at the Assembly. He had succeeded in part; could not the Queen confer the rest ?

Why not ?

Had she not, at St Cloud, given a secret interview to Mirabeau ? Why should not he, Barnave, be accorded a similar favor

But then, public rumor spread abroad that one of the three gentlemen on the box of the carriage, " M. Fersen," was the accepted lover of the Queen

Strange thing ! As I have told you the good self-opinion of Barnave, he was yet jealous of M de Fersen.

With the admirable shrewdness of women, the Queen discovered this before a quarter of an hour had elapsed.

She managed to get the three guards, named respectively MM de Malden, de Valory, and de Moustier.

No Fersen !

Barnave breathed, smiled, and became positively charming.

Barnave was young, handsome, polished, of fascinating manners, and felt great commiseration for the unfortunate royal party.

In place of the Queen seducing Barnave, Barnave almost seduced the Queen.

CHAPTER XXXVI.

BARNAVE AND PETION.

ONE naturally asks how I became acquainted with all this.

I have already said that, on leaving Varennes, I had taken a place on the back of the carriage of the King. Happily, I had managed to retain my position, despite the heat, the fatigue, and the dust. Twice only. for a few minutes, had I quitted my location; firstly, to try and assist M. de Dampierre, and, secondly, to procure the water for Madame Elizabeth and the Dauphin Both times, on my return, I recovered my place. The glass windows of the berlin were let down on account of the heat, and the royal family, not speaking in very low voices, I managed to hear pretty well all that was said.

This explanation given, I will continue my story, with the history of the rudeness of Pétion, and the courtesy of Barnave

There was placed between Madame Elizabeth and Madame Royale, a bottle of lemonade and a glass. Pétion was thirsty, and felt inclined to drink. He took the glass, and handed it to Madame Elizabeth, who took up the lemonade, and filled it.

" Enough ! " said Pétion, lifting his glass as he would have done at a cabaret.

The Queen's eyes flashed with anger.

The Dauphin, with the impatience of a youngster, shifted in his seat; Pétion seized him, and imprisoned him between his legs.

The Queen said nothing, but again darted a look of menace at Pétion; who, remembering that it might be politic to gain the favor of the King, caressed the Dauphin's white locks with apparent affection.

The Dauphin made a grimace expressive of grief.

The Queen snatched him from Pétion's legs

Barnave, smiling, immediately opened his arms to him.

The boy seemed willing, and was, therefore, soon installed on Barnave's knees.

His instinct shewed him that he would find in Barnave a protector.

Playing with a button on the coat of the representative, he discovered that a device was inscribed upon it, and, after many efforts, succeeded in reading it.

The device was, " Live free, or die."

The Queen sighed, and regarded Barnave, her eyes filled with tears.

Barnave's heart smote him

This was his position He followed his own individual romance, in the midst of a royal and terrible history, when suddenly a noise was heard some paces behind the royal carriage.

The cries and tumult drew Barnave from the magic circle which surrounded him.

A venerable ecclesiastic approached the carriage, much in the same manner as M de Dampierre had done, and uplifted his hands and blessed the royal martyr.

The mob, unsatiated by one murder, rushed upon the priest, and drew him away, to slaughter him in the ditch by the roadside.

I was on the opposite side of the carriage to where this affair was taking place.

" M. Barnave, M. Barnave ! " cried I ; " help, help ! "

At the same moment, M. Barnave, putting his head out of the window, saw what was taking place

He placed the Dauphin in the arms of his aunt, and opened the carriage door with such violence and rapidity, that he almost fell out ; in fact, he would have fallen, had not Madame Elizabeth caught and retained him by his coat-tails.

" Oh, Frenchmen ! " cried he ; " ye are a nation of brave men—would ye become a horde of assassins ? "

At this eloquent appeal, the people let go the priest, who escaped, protected by the outspread arms and eloquent gestures of Barnave.

The door was again shut, Barnave retook his place, and the Queen said to him, " I thank you, M. Barnave."

He bowed his head.

Before the arrival of the commissaires, the King had eaten alone with his family; but now, after consulting the Queen, he invited them to share his repast.

Pétion accepted the invitation; Latour-Maubourg and Barnave declined.

Barnave insisted, however, on waiting on the royal family; but the Queen made him a sign, and he yielded.

I was one of the guard at the door of the dining-room.

In the evening, MM. Drouet and Guillaume set out at full speed, to inform the Assembly of what had taken place.

Drouet came to bid me good-bye.

"M. Drouet," said I to him, "you know me, as I am your pupil. I take the greatest interest in that which is going on. It will be something to talk about for the rest of my life. Give the order, before you leave, to have me always placed close to their Majesties. The fatigue will be nothing, and I wish to see all that goes on."

"Be it as you wish," said he, without making the least objection.

That was the reason why I had been appointed one of the guards that day at the door of the dining-room.

This is what happened at Dormans.

After dinner, the three commissaires went into the neighboring room—that is to say, the one at which I mounted guard.

"Citizens," said Barnave to them, "we are commissaires of the National Assembly, and not the executioners of the royal family; and to make them proceed under this burning sun is simply to conduct them to the scaffold."

"Good!" said Pétion. "What has happened to them has been brought on by their own follies."

"Still they are no less King and Queen," replied M. de Latour-Maubourg.

"If affairs keep progressing as they do now, it is extremely probable that they will not long even have that title to console them."

"Quite right," said Barnave. "But still I think that, as long as they retain the titles of King and Queen, they ought to be treated as such."

"I have no objection," said Pétion, in an indifferent tone. "Do as you like, most loyal gentlemen."

Saying these words, he left the room

Barnave and M de Latour-Maubourg, being alone, decided that the royal carriage should be accompanied only by a cavalry escort, so that it might proceed at a trot, and on the third evening arrive at Meaux

At that moment, they relieved guard. I ran to the postmaster at Dormans, who was a friend of M Drouet's, and with whom we had lodged on our way to the federation, and prayed him to lend me a horse, to go as far as Meaux, where the royal family would halt, to pass the night in repose.

In these critical times, paternal feeling elevated itself. The postmaster had seen M. Drouet the evening before, who had announced to him my arrival to-day. He would not let me hire the steed—he gave it to me.

They arrived at Meaux about six in the evening.

The King again invited the commissaries to sup with him, as he had before invited them to dine. Pétion accepted the invitation, M. de Latour-Maubourg and Barnave refused it.

But the Queen, with charming grace, turning towards Barnave, said, " Pray accept it, M. Barnave, as, after the meal, I shall have need of you."

Barnave bowed, the King signed to M. de Latour-Maubourg and the two took their places at the royal table.

They were located in the palace of the Bishop of Meaux, a melancholy-looking place enough, with its dark oak staircase and mysterious and dusty passages.

I was on guard at the garden gate.

After dinner, the Queen, who, as she had said to Barnave, had need of him, took his arm, and mounted the staircase to the apartments above, under pretext of seeing a chamber once occupied by Bossuet.

As for the King, he descended into the gardens with Pétion. Pétion it was who desired the *tête-à-tête.*

Pétion, who, apart from his folly, was a good man, and had a good heart, had formed an idea of escape for the King. It was, to allow the three body-guards to go, so that they might disguise themselves as National Guards, and so facilitate their entrance into Paris.

But, extraordinary to relate, the King could not understand this idea of Pétion's; and not wishing to be under an obligation to Petion, and having the absurd suspicion that he wished to assassinate the guards, he refused.

And yet, on the day when he could have caused Lafayette to be proclaimed Mayor of Paris, he nominated Pétion.

It was because the Queen hated Lafayette more than the King detested Pétion.

As for the Queen, no one knows what passed between her and Barnave, except through the account which she afterwards gave to Madame Campan.

The impression which the young representative produced on the Queen may be summed up in those words.

"If ever power returns into our hands, the pardon of Barnave is assured in our hearts."

The Queen was ready to pardon Barnave for his rebellion; France did not pardon him for his weakness.

The unhappy orator paid with his head for the few moments of happiness he spent with this second Marie Stuart.

Perchance he had the same honor as Mirabeau, of kissing her hand.

CHAPTER XXXVII.

PARIS.

Day dawned.

It was the 25th of June. They returned to Paris after five days' absence.

Five days! What terrible events had come to pass in the space of five days!

As they approached Paris, Barnave retook his seat at the back.

No longer was it a seat of honor, but the place of danger.

If a fanatic should fire on the King, which was, indeed, probable; if on the Queen, which was more than probable;—Barnave was there, to arrest with his own body the fell bullet aimed at loyalty.

M. Mathieu Damas had been charged by Lafayette, Royalist though he was, to protect their entry.

This able strategist had drawn from all parties in order to diminish the danger. He confided the guarding of the carriage to the grenadiers, whose tall hats hid entirely the doors; a line of horse grenadiers formed a second ring.

As for the three guards whom Louis XVI had not wished to go, two grenadiers, with their muskets bayoneted, sat a little behind the box-seat, ready to suppress any attempt at rescue or flight.

The heat was tremendous. The carriage, the nearer it approached Paris, appeared to be entering the mouth of a furnace.

The Queen, whom nothing hitherto had conquered, was beaten by the heat. Twice or thrice she cried, " I suffocate !"

At Bourget, the King asked for wine.

Broken down by fatigue, Madame Elizabeth slept.

The change of places had brought Pétion close by her. The face of the future Mayor of Paris had a remarkable expression of joy. The Queen, who cared not for sleeping herself, shook her by the arm in order to awaken her.

"Let her alone," cried Pétion. "Nature must take its course."

They passed the barrier, and entered into the midst of a moving and agitated people.

From time to time the crowd gave a tremendous yell. The King, trying to show *sang-froid*, began, apparently, to read.

"Suppose one were to applaud the King !"

" He shall be scourged ! "

"Suppose one were to insult him ? "

" He shall be hanged ! "

The crowd kept pace with the carriage.

Mathieu Damas, commanding the escort, did not wish to enter Paris by the Faubourg St. Martin. He was nearer the Faubourg St. Antoine, of terrible memory, on account of the attack and seizure of the Bastille.

He asked himself if he had a human barrier strong enough to protect the royal family from the crowd who had virtually sentenced them to death. He went round Paris by the external Boulevards, and entered it by the Champ Elysées and the Place Louis XV.

On the Place Louis XV stood, at that period, the statue of the monarch whose name the place bore.

They had bandaged the eyes of the statue with a hand-kerchief.

This allusion, though ignored by the King, still disquiet-ed him.

"Why this bandage on the eyes of my predecessor?" in-quired the King.

"To show the blindness of the monarchy, sire," replied Pétion.

In the progress from the Champs Elysées to the Place Louis XV, the barrier of grenadiers was often broken.

Then the Queen saw appear at the windows hideous faces, expressive of satisfaction and revenge.

What caused those devils to turn away and bow?

It was a kiss which the Dauphin sent them, and a bow from his sister; those white-winged angels hovering over the royal family.

Lafayette, with his etat major, passed by the Queen.

As soon as she perceived them, she cried out, "M Lafayette, above all things save my three body-guards; their crime has been but to obey me."

The same cry was uttered by her at Versailles on the 6th of October Their danger was really great.

The carriages passed through the gate of the Tuileries, which was vainly endeavored to be shut after them. They proceeded along the grand promenade of the garden, and halted only at the end of the great terrace which stretched along the front of the palace.

It was there that the crowd, greater than ever, awaited them. It was impossible to go farther; they must get out of their carriage.

The Assembly was not present, but it had sent twenty deputies.

Lafayette cleared a pathway from the terrace to the pal-ace door. He constructed an iron arch with the muskets and bayonets of the National Guard.

"M. Barnave," again cried the Queen, "I ask you to protect my three guards."

The children first descended, and entered the palace with-out opposition. It was then the turn of the three guards, for whom the Queen had asked protection from M. Lafayette and M. Barnave.

Then there came a terrible outcry.

I had left my horse at the top of the Champs Elysées, and marched with the grenadiers on foot. At first, they tried to turn me out, but the King said, "Let him alone; he is a friend."

They did leave me alone. M. Pétion gave me a side glance, M. Barnave smiled.

The King and Queen looked to see what would happen to the three guards, the King gazed with his usual apathy, the Queen with intense interest.

The sabres and pikes of the National Guard waved over them as they shouted, "Death to the traitors!"

All of a sudden, I saw a stream of blood running down M. de Malden's cheek.

Being in the circle, I drew him, with a vigorous effort, towards me, crying, "Peace! peace! I am the friend of M. Drouet."

Five hundred voices shouted, "Long live Drouet! Long live Guillaume!'"

I drew M. de Malden under the arch of the Grand Pavilion, but he would proceed no farther until assured of the safety of the King and Queen.

During this time, in the midst of the most terrible murmurs, they saved M. de Valory and M. de Moustier.

Like M. de Malden, M. de Valory was wounded; but also like M. de Malden, his wound was but slight.

At this moment, the Queen cried, in a suffocating voice, "Help! help!"

In getting out of the carriage, she found herself in the arms of two men, who regarded her with looks of mortal enmity, and at the same time held her fast.

These two men were M. de Aguillon and M. de Noailles. The Queen seemed likely to faint with terror. Both said to her, "Fear nothing, madame; we protect you."

At the peril of their lives, they conducted her to her room. There she was seized with agony. She called the Dauphin—she looked for the Dauphin, but no Dauphin was there.

Madame Royale took her by the hand and led her into the bed-room, and pointed out to her the Dauphin, who, overcome with fatigue, slept.

She could not believe, after the threats she had heard,

13

that the whole of the royal family could re-enter their palace safe and sound.

I returned to the carriage, where still remained Madame Elizabeth and the King.

Barnave thought that it would not be too much for him and Pétion to safeguard the King.

"Some one," cried he—"some one to offer Madame Elizabeth an arm."

Madame Elizabeth descended from the carriage with her usual angelic calmness.

"Monsieur," said she to me, "will you give me your arm?"

I was frightened out of my wits.

"Oh, madame," said I; "this dress?"

"The dress that you wear is far better than a royal robe. And besides," continued she, "I have watched you: you are a young man of a good heart."

I threw my gun over my shoulder, and took my hat in my hand.

"Madame," said I, "if you desire one ready to die for you—to throw down his life in your behalf, your choice could not fall on one better than myself."

They saw Madame Elizabeth take the arm of a simple National Guard, and they clapped their hands.

Arrived at the foot of the staircase, I wished to retire.

"My brother?" said she, trying to see.

I looked back.

"He is coming," said I, "between M. Barnave and M. Pétion."

I then bowed to Madame Elizabeth a second time.

"Will you not return to see us, sir?" asked Madame Elizabeth.

"I fear, madame, that I shall not again have the opportunity of being of service to you."

"Perhaps so, but you have been; and, whatever people may say, we are a family that never forget."

At this moment the King arrived.

"Thank you, gentlemen; thank you," said he to Barnave and Pétion. "I need not say to you that if you like to come up-stairs——"

"Sire," replied Barnave, "your Majesty and her Majesty the Queen are at present in safety. We must go to render an account of our mission to the Assembly."

They bowed to the King, and retired.

I did the same; that is to say, I bowed, but as I was retiring, Madame Elizabeth, pointing me out to the King, said, " My brother, this young man " "

She evidently, in her noble heart, did not wish me to go without some recompense.

" 'Tis true," said the King; " I forgot that he was your *protegé*."

" Say, rather, that I am his *protegé*."

He took me by the collar of my coat.

" Look here, young man; unhappy as we are, can we do nothing to help you " "

I felt wounded that the King should think that I required to be paid for what I had done.

" Sire," replied I, " if you make a promise to the nation, keep it; and, as a citizen, you will have done all for me that I can ask."

" You see, sister," said the King. " he is a savage "

" What is your name, sir ? " asked Madame Elizabeth.

" Réné Besson."

" Whence come you ? "

" From the Forest of Argonne."

" I told you he was a savage," said the King. " What else could you expect ? "

" What trade are you ? "

" A carpenter."

" My brother, you know the fable of the Lion and the Rat," said Madame Elizabeth.

" My friend," said the King. " you see that I must enter my house. If you have need of me, ask for Cléry, my *valet-de-chambre*."

" Sire," replied I, " a man who has an occupation has need of no one, much less of a King."

The King shrugged his shoulders, and mounted the staircase. Madame Elizabeth stayed behind.

" But, on the other hand, my friend," said she, " suppose that we have need of you ? "

" Ah, madame," cried I, " that is another affair ! "

" In that case, M. Réné Besson, ask for Cléry."

She followed her brother, whilst I stood there motionless,

regarding that angel who knew how to recompense one in asking.

On the morrow, the journalist, Prudhomme, wrote :—

"Certain good patriots, in whom the sentiment of loyalty has not extinguished that of compassion, appear uneasy concerning the moral and physical state of Louis XVI and his family, after a journey so fatiguing in all respects as that from St. Menehould.

"Let them reassure themselves. Our friend, on entering his apartments, on his return, felt no more fatigue than if he had been indulging in the pleasures of the chase.

"He ate his chicken as usual, and the next day played after dinner with his son.

"As for the mother, she took a bath on her arrival. Her first request was for boots; she having remarked with sorrow, that hers had been destroyed by travelling. She acted with hauteur to the officers picked out especially to guard her, and said that it was ridiculous and indecent to have the door of her bath-room and bed-chamber left open."

We quote these four paragraphs to show to what an extent party spirit can blind men.

The Citizen Prudhomme, who, after having written "The Revolutions of Paris in '91," was to write "The Crimes of the Revolution of '98," wrongfully describes four incidents :—"That the King ate a fowl, and that he played with his son; that the Queen had a bath, and shut her door when taking it."

It is always so. There can never be a revolution without a Prudhomme : first, to glorify them : and then to grossly insult.

CHAPTER XXXVIII.

I RESUME MY ORIGINAL PROFESSION.

It was nine o'clock in the evening. I went to look after my horse, which I had left in a house by the barrier. They gave it back to me as promised, and I retook it to the stables, always using the name of M. Drouet. I took a receipt for it, and at ten o'clock I entered the Rue St. Honoré.

I found all the family at table, as, on account of the day's excitement, the supper, which usually was partaken of at eight o'clock, to-night was delayed till ten.

They raised a cry of joy when they saw me. Maitre Duplay, who had been with the National Guard of the Quartier St. Honoré, fancied that he saw me at the door of the royal carriage, by the side of the grenadiers, but the thing appeared so improbable, that he had told it to his family more as a delusion than a fact.

Scarcely was I recognised, than the two girls immediately made a space for me between them.

This was the more easy, as the elder apprentice was absent, leaving only the one enamoured of Mdlle. Cornélie, Félicien Herda.

I did not want much pressing to sit down; I was literally dying of hunger and thirst. The young girls wished to ask me questions; but M. Duplay excused me until I had both eaten and drank.

In a few minutes, I rejoined the supper eaters, and set myself to gratify the public curiosity.

It was necessary for me to recount everything, omitting no details, from the moment when M. Drouet appeared to the King as a vision, on the top of the Hill des Religieuses, to the moment when the carriage started from the house of the grocer, Sauce, and, lastly, to their arrival at the gate of the Tuileries.

It can be easily understood with what avidity my tale was devoured, especially by the women. At that period, the women took a great interest in the Revolution. Madame Duplay, Mdlle. Cornélie, and Mdlle. Estelle made me repeat the same details over and over again; and, though they had a sigh for Madame Elizabeth, the Queen was ever an Austrian—that is to say, an enemy.

It was now eleven o'clock. Duplay, bursting with the news which I brought him, resolved to go to the Jacobin Club. There was no doubt but that, in consequence of the great events taking place, the club would, despite the late hour, be holding a sitting.

He asked me if I would like to accompany him; but,

indefatigable though I was, I asked his permission to retire to repose.

They gave me Dmuont's chamber, which was vacant, on account of its owner having left the shop some eight days previously. The ladies undertook to arrange the bed draperies, and perform all the little offices which come so gratefully from a woman's tender hand and kind heart. Félicién commenced by scowling at me; but when he perceived that upon Estelle, by tacit consent, fell the greater share of the labor on my account, his brow gradually relaxed.

Duplay set out for his club. They then informed me that my chamber was ready. It was the first time for four nights that I had slept in a bed, so you may imagine that I stood upon no ceremony. I made a hurried bow to all, rushed up to my room; and, on arriving there, blessed Madame Duplay for the quantity of water and towels that she had left me—as it required plenty of both to rid me of that accursed dust of Champagne, with which I seemed to be perfectly coated.

I jumped into bed, and, in a second, fell into the most profound sleep.

On the next morning, I was awakened by M. Duplay, after a most persistent shaking, which, in my sleep, I attributed to other causes.

"Ah!" said he; "when you sleep you do sleep, and no mistake, you drowsy provincials."

"Bah!" said I. "It is you, then, who have been trying to awaken me?"

"Yes; and who tried last night, but could not succeed."

"What did you wish of me?"

"Citizen Réné Besson, I fancied that you would excuse the breach of hospitality, when you knew that I had something most important to tell you."

"Well, I am all attention, M. Duplay."

"Call me Citizen," said Duplay, pluming himself.

"Well, I listen to you, citizen."

"As you know, I went to the club last night."

"Yes"

"There I met M. Chanderlos de Laclos."

"Citizen Laclos, you mean, I suppose?"

"I stand corrected All men are now equal. Well, I met Citizen Laclos, and told him all that you had related

to me concerning the journey of the King to Paris. Do
you know what he asked me? He asked me to take you
to the Palais Royal, in order that you may give your ver-
sion of the affair to the Duc d'Orleans."

" I?"

"Yes, thou! In the meantime, you had better dress
yourself."

"Do I go this morning, then?"

"Between nine and ten o'clock."

"What time is it now?"

"Half-past eight."

"You know, I suppose, that my only costume is that
of a National Guard?"

"It is the costume of patriots."

"But still, when one goes near princes! Does my coat
want brushing?"

"Leave that to Catherine. You occupy yourself with
putting on a clean shirt, if you have any. I will see that
your clothes and boots are brushed. If you have not any
clean linen, I can lend you some."

"Thank you; I have all that I require in my bag."

"Dress, then; don't waste time."

And Maitre Duplay, Republican though he was, enchant-
ed to conduct me before a prince, took my coat, hat, trousers and boots, down stairs for Catherine to brush.

At nine o'clock exactly, I was ready.

We went along the Rue St. Honoré to the Rue de
Valois, and, arm-in-arm, entered the Palais Royal by the
gate which opens into that street.

Maitre Duplay gave his name. *Citizen* Laclos had, no
doubt, given previous orders, for we were immediately
admitted.

Arrived at the first floor, no sooner had Duplay given
his name, than they sent at once for M. Chanderlos de
Laclos.

M. Chanderlos de Laclos rushed up.

"Is this the young fellow?" asked he.

"Himself," replied M. Duplay.

"Let him come into the presence of his Highness."

He conducted me along a straight corridor into a bou-
doir, which led into a bedroom, the open door of which
allowed me to see that the bed was unmade. The open

windows, with the closed jalousies, gave access to a most refreshing breeze.

His Royal Highness, clothed in a dressing-gown, made of cashmere, with a cap to match, was sipping tea—a new fashion imported from England; every one knows that his Highness was thoroughly English—with a charming dame of twenty-nine or thirty years of age, clothed in an elegant morning dress, and who was, as I afterward learnt, Madame Buffon.

M. le Duc d'Orleans, afterwards so celebrated under the name of Philip Egalité, was a man of from forty-four to forty-five years of age; a fat, full figure, red complexion, with a good carriage, but the head a little too large—who, on account of a quarrel with the Queen, had been cruelly and unjustly treated by the court of inquiry into the naval engagement at Ouessant, where he had comported himself most bravely.

The result of this, on his side, was a most bitter hatred of the Queen.

He received me with a nod of the head; Madame de Buffon regarded me with curiosity. I was far from being elegant, but I possessed great propriety of manner. Without being handsome, I was at an age when youth supplies the want of beauty. I was tall, well-made, with an open expression of countenance, and a well-knit frame. The loyalty of my heart beamed upon my face. In short, I made the same impression upon the Duc d'Orleans and Madame de Buffon as I had upon the King, the Queen, and Madame Elizabeth—that of being a well-looking lad

" You come from Varennes, my friend? " said the Duke.

" Yes, monseigneur," replied I.

" And you saw all that passed at the grocer's—what do you call him? "

" Sauce, monseigneur."

" So it is. And you also saw what took place on the road? "

" Monseigneur, I have not lost sight of the royal family since their arrest."

" Aha! There is a lady, a thorough Royalist. She wishes to know all that has happened to her good King and dear Queen. Will you be kind enough to give her a history of it? "

I commenced the account. When I mentioned Drouet, the Duke interrupted me to ask particulars about him. When I mentioned M. Dampierre, he made another interruption. He made another when I mentioned Barnave, Pétion, and Latour-Maubourg, in fact, he wished to know even the minutest particulars.

Before I had finished, "Go and find Chartres," he said to M. de Laclos.

M. de Laclos went out; I continued my recital.

It was nearly brought to an end, when the door opened, and gave entrance to a handsome young man, whom I had already seen at the Jacobin Club on the occasion of my first visit to Paris.

The young Prince bowed respectfully to his father, gallantly kissed Madame Buffon's hand, threw a scrutinizing glance on me, and seemed to bend his whole attention on what was passing.

"I regret not having summoned you before, Chartres," said the Duke. "Here is a young man who came to tell us an extremely interesting history of the journey from Varennes. He knew M. Drouet well—knew also the unhappy Comte de Dampierre. He has seen the commissioners sent by the National Assembly. He has seen all, in fact; and all he has seen, he has retained; and I am sure you would have felt great pleasure in listening to his recital."

"But," said the Duc de Chartres, "perhaps this young gentleman will have the kindness——" Then, stopping, and looking at his father. "Better still," continued he; "just as M. Laclos told me that you wished to see me, I was going to breakfast."

The Duc d'Orleans appeared to understand, and nodded his head imperceptibly. M. le Duc de Chartres did the same, pointing to me.

"Will you do me the favor to breakfast with me?—and, during the meal, you can relate the whole affair."

I addressed myself to M. Laclos.

"'Tis for me," said I to him, "to thank his Highness for the great honor which he has conferred upon me; but it is for you to explain to him that I have left in the entrance-hall some one who awaits me; but that will not prevent me from giving Monseigneur," continued I, turning to Duc d'Orleans, "the recital which I have just given you."

"But," said the Duc de Chartres, smiling, "it will prevent you from accepting my breakfast."

"Monseigneur," said I, "I am apprenticed to M. Duplay, your carpenter. It was he who had the goodness to tell M. Laclos that I should have the honor of being received this morning by the Prince, your father It would be but a bad return, I think, for his kindness were I to leave him waiting in the antechamber—he who is my master,—whilst I had the honor of breakfasting with you. Excuse me," said I, laughing. "I am a savage from the forest of Argonne; but, in all cases, I know Monseigneur to be sufficiently just and good to make him my judge in this case, and I promise faithfully to comply with his decree."

"But, sir," said Madame de Buffon, "do you know that, for a savage——From what forest said you?"

"The Forest of Argonne."

"You express yourself well. One would think that all your life you had been talking to princes."

"I have not all my life spoken to princes, but princes have often done me the honor to speak to me."

"Truly! Who were they?"

"M. le Prince de Condé and M. le Duc d'Enghien. They used to hunt in the Forest of Argonne, and M. d'Enghien was in the habit of taking me with him."

"Well, nothing can astonish me, after this!" cried Madame de Buffon.

"Did you see my cousin just before his departure?" asked the Duc de Chartres.

"I am probably the last Frenchman to whom he paid the honor of shaking his hand."

"Well, then, you must accept my offer, and breakfast with me."

"That is my affair," said the Duc. "Dear lady, methinks I heard you say that you have some carpentry work to be done in your apartments. I, for my part, have several orders to give Duplay. Let him be brought up, M. Laclos: we will give him our commands ourselves. Let him pass through the *salle-à-manger*, and there he can drink a health to the nation, in a glass of wine, with these young gentlemen."

Thus was the affair arranged.

I told the Duc de Chartres, while breakfasting with him,

all that related to our hunting expeditions in the Forest of Argonne, to my education, the death of Père Deschaumes, my sojourn at Varennes, the arrest of the King, and the return to Paris.

"You are only half-armed, my dear M René," said the Duc de Chartres, when leaving me "My cousin of Enghien gave you a gun : allow me to present you with a pair of pistols"

He then took down a pair from a trophy—they were of Versailles manufacture—and insisted on my accepting them, as they matched my gun in pattern.

When I say insisted, perhaps I exaggerated a little, as nothing could give me greater pleasure than to accept his present.

As for Duplay, he received an order of the value of 5,000 francs, and drank with the Duc de Chartres to the health of the nation, so that he returned home in the best of spirits, rejoiced to have combined, in his morning's visit, pleasure and profit.

CHAPTER XXXIX.

TOUCHING THE PRINCESS LAMBALLE.

It will easily be imagined that the event of which I am treating was the subject of conversation for fifteen days in the house of Duplay in which I was apprentice, in the place of Dumont.

Félicien, seeing that I entertained for Mdlle Cornelie and Mdlle. Estelle only such affection as every well-educated man ought to have for women, drew in his nails and teeth, and became as good a comrade towards me as it was possible for him to be.

Still the revolution marched on with gigantic strides ; the flight to Varennes having given it a terrible impetus

On the 27th and 28th June, the Assembly promulgated the following decrees :—

"The gard du corps is disbanded.

" The King will be given a guard. under the command of the commander of the Parisian National Guard, to contribute to his safety and well being.

" The Queen will have a private guard of her own.

" Upon the events of the 21st of June, the Assembly will nominate three commissioners, selected from their whole body, to receive the declaration of the King and Queen.

" The sanction, the acceptance of the King, and all his legislative and executive functions, are suspended.

" The ministers are authorized, each in his own department, and on his own responsibility, to assume the executive power."

The three commissioners were MM. Touche, Dandré, and Dupont.

There was, therefore, as can be readily seen, positive suspension of the functions of royalty.

This private guard of the ·Queen's was a torment to her every day—every hour—every minute.

We have seen Prudhomme astonished that the Queen, having worn-out shoes, should require new ones, and that she should consider it indecent to leave open the doors of her bath and her bed room.

In fact, the National Guard, frightened of the responsibility placed on their shoulders, literally kept the Queen in eyesight, and compelled her to keep open the doors of her bathing and bed-room. Once, the Queen, inspired with a natural feeling of modesty, having drawn the curtains of her bed the man on guard drew them back, for fear that she should escape by the staircase. On another occasion, the King having come to visit her about one in the morning, and having shut the door of the apartment—not of the Queen, but of his wife—the sentinel thrice opened it, saying, " Shut it as often as you like ; I shall open it every time that you shut it ! "

Happily, in this misery, the Queen found a friend. This friend was the Princess de Lamballe whose history is so well known that it is needless for me to touch upon it.

She was, however, through all vicissitudes, a faithful and affectionate friend to the Queen.

About the commencement of 1791, after the death of Mirabeau, the political horizon became so black that the

King and Queen, the Count de Fersen, and Madame Elizabeth, all counselled the Princess to fly to Sardinia Even the Pope, Pius the Sixth himself, insisted that she should visit Rome, to rejoin the friends of the King who having raised in the Assembly the famous storm concerning the right of emigration sustained by Mirabeau, had happily crossed the frontier; but she firmly rejected all such proposals.

The Duc de Penthièvre who loved her as if she were his daughter, and the Duchess of Orleans, who admired her courage, wished by some means to force her to leave France. The Duc persuaded Louis the Sixteenth to write to the Court at Turin, in order that the King of Sardinia, as head of the family, should interpose his influence to compel the Princess to return to his dominions.

Here is the reply of the Princess de Lamballe:—

"SIRE AND RESPECTED COUSIN,—

"I do not remember that any of our illustrious ancestors of the House of Savoy, before or after the great Charles Emmanuel, of illustrious memory, ever disgraced themselves by an act of treachery. I should do so were I to quit the Court of France at this critical juncture. You will excuse my refusing your truly royal invitation The shedding of blood, and the madness of the States, alike command that one and all should unite their efforts for the preservation of the King and Queen and the royal family of France. It is impossible to shake my resolution. I have determined, once and for all, never to abandon, at a moment when they are forsaken by their oldest servants, those who have none to look to but me

"In happier days, your Majesty can count on my obedience; but to-day, as the Court of France is open to the persecutions of its most atrocious enemies, I beg humbly the right of following my own instincts of right. At the most brilliant epoch of the reign of Marie Antoinette, I felt the warmth of royal favor, and can I now abandon her? To do so, sire, would be to set the seal of eternal infamy not only on my brow, but on those of all my relations; and I fear that more than all other torments."

It was then that the Queen employed a *ruse* to get her to quit France.

She had been sent once before on a mission from the Queen to England ; and the inherent grace of the family of Savoy—the same which made the Duchess of Burgundy so powerful over Louis XIV—enabled her to obtain from the King and Queen of England a promise never to forsake the King and Queen of France.

The moment to recall that promise to the English Court had arrived. The Queen desired the Princess de Lamballe to set out for London, and continue the negotiations already so happily commenced. She therefore left Paris, and reached England, stopping at Calais, at the famous "Hotel Dessein," immortalized by Sterne in his "Sentimental Journey."

It was whilst in London that the Princess learnt the flight to Varennes, the return of the royal family, and their imprisonment in the Tuileries. She sent a young English girl, in whom she had the utmost confidence, to Paris.

This messenger appeared close to the Queen. She had come in the name of the Princess, to learn the exact situation in which the family were placed.

The Queen sent her a letter, and a ring, enclosing a lock of her hair, as white as if her years numbered eighty.

On the ring was inscribed, " Whitened by sorrow."

I give, underneath, an exact copy of the letter :—

" MY VERY DEAR FRIEND,—

"The King is about to accept the Constitution. In a short time, he will be solemnly proclaimed. A few days since, I held a secret consultation in your apartment, with some of our most trusty friends, among whom were Alexandre Lameth, Duport, Barnave, Montmarni, Bertrand de Malville. These two last combated against the counsel of those of the Ministry, and others, who advised the King to accept the Constitution immediately, and without restrictions ; but they formed too feeble a minority for me to decide, as they wished to pray the King to pay heed to their opinion. All the others seemed to think that the contrary measure would re-establish tranquillity, weaken the party of the Jacobins, our enemies, and enlarge greatly the number of our partizans in the nation. Your absence compelled me to call Elizabeth to our aid, to clear the Pavilion of Flora of spies. She did not acquit herself very well.

Poor Elizabeth! you cannot expect much cunning or circumspection in a woman so little accustomed to the intrigues of a Court, and to the dangers which surrounded us. They try to persuade us that we are in no danger. Would that it were so, and that I could again open my arms and heart freely, to receive my best friend! Although these are the most ardent aspirations of my heart, nevertheless, my dear, my very dear Lamballe, pay heed to nothing but your own inspirations. Some people say that they see the future brilliant as the sun at mid-day. For my part, I confess, it seems covered with clouds. I cannot see future events with all the security that I could wish. The King, Elizabeth, myself,—in fact, all the family—wish much to see you; but we should be horrified at the thought of dragging you into the midst of events equally fearful as those you have already witnessed."

"Reflect, then, and act as you think best. If we cannot see you, send us the result of your conferences with the Precipice.* Your young English friend will bring you plenty of letters. Will you have them sent to their respective addresses as quickly as possible, either by her, or in any other way that you may consider more fitting?

"Your affectionate

"MARIE ANTOINETTE."

On receiving this letter, the Princess left London, where she was in safety, and, without the slightest hesitation, returned to the Tuileries, to take her place by the side of the Queen.

But whilst Madame de Lamballe was at London, great events were taking place in Paris. The letter which we have quoted, although undated, is virtually dated, through the fact that the Queen speaks of the King's accepting the Constitution; and it was on the 3rd of September only that a deputation from the National Assembly presented the Act of the Constitution for the acceptance of the King.

Let us now retrace our steps a little, and throw a glance at that terrible day, the 17th of July—day of the Champs de Mars — day of the red flag, which in 1848, furnished to M. de Lamartine, one of his most wonderful oratorical efforts.

* A name the Queen gave to Pitt.

CHAPTER XL.

THE TIDE RISES.

THE Queen was right in not viewing events in the same light as those who surrounded her.

Firstly, the struggle was between the Assembly and the Court. The Assembly won the day.

Then it was between the Constitutionals and the Aristocrats. The Constitutionals won the day. Now it was to be between the Constitutionals and the Republicans.

It is true that the Republicans had only just begun to appear, but in their first birth they formed this terrible principle—*No more monarchy!*

You will remember that the commissioners had been appointed by the Assembly to examine Louis XVI.

These three declared, in the name of their seven committees, that they had found no reason to put Louis XVI on his trial.

The Assembly took the opinion of the commissioners, but the Jacobin Club refused its sanction to the Assembly. The Assembly had then above it a high chamber, which could annihilate its decisions with its veto.

In order to understand the situation and the events about to take place, it is necessary to say that at this juncture there were opposed to each other, three distinct parties.

The Royalists who wished the King absolute—that is to say, without the Constitution; the Constitutionals, who wished the King with a Constitution; and the Republicans, who wished neither King nor Constitution, but a republic.

The Assembly, as we have said, voted that there was no necessity to put the King on trial.

But, through concession to the public feeling, it had voted two measures—one preventive, the other repressive.

This was the repressive measure.

"That Bouillé, and all servants, officers, couriers, and accomplices in the flight, should be prosecuted."

This was the preventive measure :—

"That if a king breaks his oath, or attacks, or does not

defend, his people, he shall be cast from his throne, become a simple citizen, and be tried for the offences committed previous to his degradation "

The repressive measure was one of those timid ones proper to a decayed Assembly, which feels that its power is crumbling away.

During some days, or, rather, nights, the Jacobin sitting became stormy.

During the sitting. in which the true culprit—that is to say, the King—was left alone, in order to arrest and punish the minor offenders—that is to say. Bouillé. Fersen, the gardes du corps, and Madame de Tourzel.—M. Robespierre asked in vain to have the report distributed, and the discussion adjourned

As it was known in advance that the discussion would be stormy, Robespierre went to the club He had been accused, at the Assembly of republicanism. and—mark this well,—on the 13th of July 1791. Robespierre did not disdain to again avow himself a Republican

On that evening, we all went to the Jacobins; M. Duplay and myself in the superior hall. and the three women and Félicién in the inferior where a society was held, called the Society of the Two Sexes.

During my absence from Paris. Robespierre had acquired a great popularity. to which he had succeeded by degrees. He had still the same voice. though. perhaps, he spoke a little stronger than the last time that I had heard him ; and I fancied that I noted a marked progress in his intonation, but still the same spinning-out of his facts.

He had just finished his discourse. when a great disturbance was heard It was the Cordeliers' Club, which, in the persons of Danton and Legendre, had made an irruption among the Jacobins

They were neither vague nor lengthy in their demands.

Danton, in an outburst of none thunder, demanded how the Society dared to take upon itself to pronounce reformed opinions before the nation had done so ? Legendre directly attacked the King — called to reason the societies who, working in an underground manner. undermined the decisions of the Assembly, and terminated in saying, " What I say is for the good of the Assembly itself."

There was almost a menace expressed in these last words.

14

Keeping calm and cold during Robespierre's speech, M. de Laclos, the intendant of the Duc d'Orleans, applauded vehemently Danton and Legendre.

The Constitutionals of the Assembly got up, and went out.

Danton and Laclos conferred together an instant in a whisper; then a voice was heard, crying, " Open the doors for the public deputies ! "

The doors opened, and there entered the fraternal Society of the Halles, and the Society of the Two Sexes, which held its meetings in the Lower Hall. They carried addresses against the Assembly, or, rather, against the monarchy.

Preoccupied with Danton and Legendre, I lost a part of the thread of what passed at the tribune. A young surgeon read a letter, which had been written in the Palais Royal in the presence of three hundred persons. A bishop threw himself into his arms, and urged him to oppose the deputies. Robespierre looked on with his sardonic smile; Danton, Legendre, and Laclos with a hateful grin.

Robespierre saw not what was going on on the other side of Paris, but probably Danton knew; and that was what he was recounting in a whisper to Laclos, and what Laclos was listening to with such attention.

On the other side of Paris was a club—a fraternal society,—in the midst of which rested a young man, who was secretary to the club, in oblivion. This young man one day emerged from his obscurity. to raise around him a gigantic storm, after which he again subsided into mediocrity. The name of this young man was Callieu.

What was Callieu doing in this fraternal society ? Almost nothing. He prepared an address against the Assembly, signed " THE PEOPLE ! "

On the day before that evening—how I came to forget to mention it, I cannot think,—the 12th of July, there was a great disturbance in Paris. All hats were waving in a burst of enthusiasm

On Sunday, the 10th, the body of Voltaire ought to have been removed to the Pantheon, but the weather was unpropitious; and there was no fête in Paris, on account of the rain The removal of Voltaire's corse was therefore postponed till the morrow.

The triumphal procession entered by the barrier of

Charenton; and accompanied by an immense crowd, drawn by horses presented by the Queen, the bier crossed Paris, and stopped at the house where the author of the "Philosophic Dictionary" had died.

There they sang choruses to his glory. The Calas family, led by Madame de Vilette, laid down crowns on the sarcophagus, before the temple of Flora, which was closed, on the pretence of the absence of Madame de Lamballe.

On the 12th, Voltaire entered the Pantheon. On the 13th, in the morning, they played a sacred drama, with a grand chorus and orchestra, in Notre Dame. It was entitled, "Le Prise de la Bastille."

In the evening, Danton and Legendre came to the Jacobins, and turned out the Constitutionals; whilst at the club on the other side of Paris they were signing an address against the Assembly.

On the 14th, the anniversary of the taking of the Bastille, when a drama was performed on the subject, the Bishop of Paris performed mass at the altar of the country in the midst of the rain.

Each day now brought an event. On the evening of the 15th, the Assembly voted not only that the King should be brought to judgment, but that his offices should be suspended until he agreed to *swear to the Constitution.*

The Constitutionals carried it.

The Assembly knew so well that it had committed an unpopular act, that it demanded to be protected by Lafayette and 5,000 men, without counting the National Guard and the pikes of the Faubourg St. Antoine.

The crowd which could not enter—and their name was legion—took up a position on the other side of the citizen guard, who made a ring round the Riding Hall.

The moment the vote became known to the crowd, they yelled "Treason!" and re-entered Paris by its three great arteries, the Boulevards, the Rue St. Honoré, and the street which is now known by that name. They then began to shut the theatres and the houses of play and pleasure, and in consequence of the disturbance, the police themselves closed two or three theatres.

Little work was done in these days of ebullition. M. Duplay sent me to see what was going on at the Assembly; I returned to announce to him the triumph of the King.

"Good!" said he.   "Let us get over supper quickly, and then off to the Jacobins.   There will be a disturbance there this evening."

M. Duplay was right.

Robespierre was in the tribune.   He attacked, in the midst of vociferous plaudits, the vote of the Assembly. When he had finished, M. Laclos took his place.   You must not forget that Laclos was the intendant of the Duc d'Orleans.   He demanded that a bulletin should be issued, proclaiming the forfeiture.

"There will be," said he, "ten million signatures."

"Yes, yes!" cried the spectators, with one voice.   "Ten, fifteen, twenty millions!   The women and children, even, shall be compelled to sign!"

A powerful voice shook the nation.   It was Danton's. For some days the Cordeliers had fraternized with the Jacobins, and Danton walked with Robespierre.

"Only," said Danton, in a low voice, "let us have no women.   They are generally Royalists.   They would vote for the deposal of a King only in order to raise up another."

Saying these words, he stared fixedly at the author of "Liaisons Dangereuses."   Not a smile nor a frown ruffled the habitually stern features of Laclos.

Perceiving the silence kept by the Duke of Orleans' man, he added, "And more, I prefer an address to the adopted societies to a public one."

Laclos said nothing, but appeared as if listening to something outside the building.

All at once, a large mass of people entered the club. They were what were called the Bucks of the Palais Royal, dragging with them about fifty young women of questionable character.

"Ah, ah!" murmured Danton.   "'Tis a planned affair!"

All the newly-arrived mixed with the Jacobins, crying, "The forfeiture—the forfeiture!"

Laclos ascended the tribune.

"You see," said he, "'tis the people—the people who desire the forfeiture.   A petition is necessary, of which I approve."

All this immense crowd, who probably had the word, cried with one voice, "The petition—the petition!"

Then, with uproarious enthusiasm, the petition was voted. It was agreed that the next day, at eleven o'clock, the Jacobins should meet and hear the reading of it, after which it would be brought to the Champs de Mars, where it was to be signed by the populace, and thence forwarded to the adopted societies.

During this tumult, M. Duplay had taken hold of my arm, and drew me sharply on one side. He then pointed me out a woman standing outside one of the tribunes, who appeared to be taking the greatest possible interest in what was passing.

Look at that woman," said he ; " it is the Citizen Roland Platrière—a good patriot."

CHAPTER XLI.

CONCERNING THE BILL OF FORFEITURE.

MADAME ROLAND was very far from having assumed at that period the important position that she afterwards held. As yet she had never fretted and fumed her hour upon the political stage. In fact, she was not yet a minister. I did not pay more attention to her than one commonly pays to a woman. She appeared to be about thirty years of age, of fresh complexion—heat of the blood, if one may say so. Her mouth was large, but filled with irreproachable teeth ; her hands were large and muscular, but well-shaped, her nose was *retroussé ;* her figure was good—small waist and well-filled hips, but, on the whole, having a decidedly voluptuous tendency. Thus was Madame Roland, in the evening of the 15th of July, 1791.

Just as I was observing her, I heard some one call M. Duplay.

Duplay turned round. It was M. Laclos who called him. He held a pen in his hand, and had a sheet of paper on his table. M. Brissot was sitting beside him

" My dear Duplay," said he, " I was about to write the petition for which all are going to vote, but my writing is too much like that of the secretary of the Duc d'Orleans.

There is nothing wrong in the matter, I assure you.   Here is M. Brissot, a member of the National Assembly, and he would not be likely to work against his colleagues.   We must have some one whose handwriting is unknown.   Your young man can write, I suppose?"

"Rather, I should say," replied M. Duplay; "he is a scholar."

"Well," said Laclos, mildly, "be kind enough to call him hither, and tell him what we require.   You will dictate, Brissot, will you not?"

Feeling sure that the conversation concerned me, I approached.

They told me what was required.   It would give me an active participation in what was going on, so I was quite willing.

M. Brissot dictated.

As it was not permitted to make a copy of the petition, I can only give it from memory.   It was well and strongly worded; it had, metamorphically speaking, two heads; the one reproached the Assembly with timidity, and the other accused them of having not dared to usurp the King's so-called prerogative, and asserted, at the same time, that the King's supposed deprivation of his regal rights by the Assembly was, in reality, a sham.

As I was writing these words, Brissot still dictating, Laclos arousing himself, placed his hand on Brissot's arm, and said, "Citizen Brissot, I doubt whether the friends of the Constitution, who compose the greater number of our club, will sign, unless you make a slight alteration in the words, but which will not alter the meaning."

"What alteration?" demanded Brissot.

"Were I in your place, I would insert, after '*his original dignity*,' these words, '*by constitutional means*.'"

Brissot reflected a moment, and then, with a shrug of his shoulders he said, "I see no objection."

Then he continued dictating to me.

"*By constitutional means*."

I turned round to see whether Robespierre and Danton would not make some objection to our employment; but both had gone, and, in fact, the hall was all but empty, so that the petition was dictated to space.

The two editors remarked that the members had retired because they felt their presence to be useless, and knew that the petition would be read to them on the following morning, but soon an emissary arrived, who spoke in an undertone to M. de Laclos. During this time I again read the petition, and then I understood the ponderous significance of the five words which had been so aptly added by the well-known author of "Liasons Dangereuses."

The constitutional means by which they could replace the King, was by placing on the throne the Dauphin, governed by a regency, but the brothers of the King, the Comte d'Artois and the Comte de Provence, being out of France, the Regent's office belonged, of right, to the Duc d Orleans, who would thus take the same place by the throne of Louis XVI as his ancestor had by the throne of his predecessor, Louis XV. I asked myself why it was that Brissot never thought of that, though I did. But I said to myself that perhaps he would not be angry at being hidden behind the word *constitutional,* as he knew that the petition was his own work.

At this moment, the fears of M de Laclos appeared to be realized. The emissary who had whispered in his ear, had come to tell him that the constitutional Royalists of the Jacobins, and those of the National Assembly, were going to rejoin the Feuillants, and thus separate themselves from the pure Jacobin—that is to say, the Republican.

The two heads of the emigration movement were Duport and Lameth.

Their intention was to form a new club, composed of friends of the Constitution—an aristocratic assembly where none were admitted but by a pass-card, and where they received none but electors, who then stayed with the veritable Jacobins—none, with the exception of six or seven demagogue deputies and the *canaille* who followed in the steps of the Duc d Orleans, and who formed the entire club.

"What is to be done?" asked Brissot. "They wish to have the Assembly to themselves."

"Good!" said Laclos: "but what does it matter as long as we have the people on our side? Let us proceed."

Brissot continued his dictation, in which, however, Laclos no longer took part.

On the morrow, Saturday, M. Duplay and myself did not

fail to be at the Jacobin club, where were assembled scarce-
ty thirty persons.

They waited an hour; and at twelve there were assembled, perhaps, forty. The petition was read and applauded.
All paid attention to the phrase introduced by M. Laclos,
and it was decided that the petition should be taken in its
present form to the Champ de Mars, there to be signed on
the altar of the country.

A deputation was organized to carry the petition. M.
Duplay had work to do at the Palais Royal He advised
me to follow the delegates, and then return to report to him
what had passed.

We arrived at the Champ de Mars. As the report had
spread about that the petition would be taken there, thousands of people had asssembled.

The altar of the country was surmounted with an immense picture, representing the apotheosis of Voltaire.

The delegates mounted almost to the top of the altar, and
commenced the reading ; but they saw a group approaching,
whom they recognized as members of the Cordeliers. They
were received with acclamation, and, on their behalf, the
reading was again commenced.

All went well till the phrase introduced by M. Laclos,
" *By all constitutional means.*"

" Pardon," said a voice ; " would you mind reading that
passage again ? "

The reader continued, " *By all constitutional means.*"

" Stop ! " cried the same voice.

A man then approached.

" Citizen," said he, " my name is Bonneville. I am
editor of *The Mouth of Iron.* The people are deceived."

" Yes, yes, yes ! " cried the Cordeliers.

" How deceive the people ? " said the delegate charged
with the reading of the petition.

" I say, for the second time, that the people are deceived ! " cried Bonneville. " *By all constitutional means,*"
signifies " *by a regency.*" And what is a regency ? The
royalty of D'Orleans in the place of the royalty of Louis
XVI."

" In the place of the royalty of Capet ! " cried a voice
that I recognised as having heard before.

" How Capet ? " said a Jacobin.

"Without doubt," replied the same mocking voice. "Since the nobles no longer have titles—since M Mirabeau called himself only Riquetti—since M de Lafayette called himself only M. Moltier—the King Louis XVI can call himself only Capet."

"Take care," said a Jacobin; "France is not yet ripe for a republic."

"If she is not ripe for a republic," cried Camille Desmoulins—for that was the man to whom the voice I recognised belonged—"how is it that she is rotten for monarchy?"

"To the vote—to the vote!" all cried.

They voted, and, with almost perfect unanimity, declared that the obnoxious phrase should be cut out. Then, in the enthusiasm which followed this vote, they all swore neither to recognise Louis XVI nor any other King.

On the morrow, Sunday, it was arranged that the people, forewarned by notice posted on the walls, should go to sign the petition on the altar.

"Still, citizen, we lack one thing."

"What is that?" asked Camille Desmoulins.

"It is to have the law on our side"

"We have it; since the Assembly have suspended the King, we have deposed him."

"We must get from the Hotel de Ville an authorization to hold the meeting to-morrow."

All started for the Hotel de Ville. They had but to keep on the quays; but the distance was rather a lengthy one; but as the refusal of the Mayor might spoil all, and as I wished to give a report to M. Duplay, I went with the others to the Hotel de Ville.

M. Bailly was not there; he was at the Place Vendome, watching the proceedings of the Assembly; but they found his substitute, told him of the matter, found him not unwilling, and demanded a written authorization. He said he did not see the necessity—a verbal permission being quite sufficient, that the people were always legal, exercising only their right of petition.

I returned to M Duplay's, telling him that the petition would be signed to-morrow, and that the signature would be approved of by Bailly, or, at least, by his substitute.

We were ignorant of what was going on in the Assembly.

The Assembly had leant the decision taken by the Cordeliers and the Jacobins. It would not do to allow the people to take this supremacy upon itself. They appealed to Bailly and the municipal council.

At ten o'clock, Bailly and his council decided that on the morrow, Sunday, 17th July, the decree of the Assembly, bearing " that the suppression of executive power should last until the Constitutional Act had been presented to, and accepted by, the King," should be fixed at eight o'clock punctually, and that proclamation of the decree should be with sound of trumpet proclaimed by the huissiers of the city.

Therefore, whoever did not recognise an act proceeding from the National Assembly—that is to say, the people's representatives—should be rebels to the law, and should be treated as such.

CHAPTER XLII.

WHAT TOOK PLACE BETWEEN THE HAIRDRESSER AND THE INVALID.

WE had for neighbor, in the Rue St. Honore, two doors lower down than our own, a hair-dresser, named Léger. This hair-dresser, like all his *confrères*, was a staunch Royalist. No doubt the reader would ask the reason why hairdressers were all Royalists.

That is easily explained.

The hair-dressers' was one of the corporations that had suffered the most in the Revolution. Those under Louis XV, and even under Louis XVI—who had invented such fantastic head-dresses, worn by the ladies of the nobility for more than half a century—were a body of men not to be despised.

Hair-dressers of this period had a select circle of their own, and many privileges, which they would not surrender, even on the night of the 4th of August.

Not only could they mix in the society of the larger circles, but had the *entrées* to the more select boudoirs of the noblesse, and also carried the sword, as was customary with gentlemen.

It is true that this sword, at most times, was of no more use than a harlequin's wand, being but a mere toy. Of some, the blades were simply wood, others having no blade at all, the handle being attached to the scabbard.

But for some time past things went from bad to worse with this celebrated corporation of hair-dressers. Their society was gradually sinking into oblivion, to them worse than death, and Talma had just struck the last blow even to the head-dressing of men, by his creation of the character of *Litus*, which had caused his name to be given to the fashion of wearing the hair cut short.

The most desperate enemies of the new government— that is to say, the revolutionary government—was, therefore, the hair-dressers.

That was not all. By frequenting the mansions of the aristocracy—by holding so often between their hands, for more than an hour at a time, the heads of the handsomest ladies of the Court—by chatting with the several coxcombs whose hair they were in the habit of dressing—by serving their noble clients in the character of messengers of love— by becoming the *confidantes* of the passions of their employers—the hair-dressers had become libertines, for the advantage of their pockets.

Now, on Saturday evening, as I have already stated, at the very moment when the municipality issued the decree against the petitioners, our neighbor Léger came and asked M. Duplay to lend him a centre-bit.

Notwithstanding the difference of opinion which separated these two neighbors, the centre bit was at once lent, without a single question.

An Invalid awaited him at the door, to whom he handed it, at the same time exchanging with him some few words, and each one went his own way.

The following was their projected scheme for the next day :—

At this period, when the women commenced to take such an active part in the revolution, many beautiful patriots intended accompanying their brothers, husbands, and lovers to sign the petition on the altar of the country. Thanks to the centre-bit lent by Maitre Duplay, our libertine hairdresser would be enabled to bore a hole in the platform of the altar, under the shelter of which, if he could not see the lovely features of the charming patriotic women, he could, at least, perceive the interesting proceedings of the people.

Not wishing to enjoy this pleasure alone, the Citizen Léger invited an old Invalid to share it with him. The Invalid accepted the invitation; but like a cautious man, knowing that they could not feed themselves with their eyes, proposed that, in addition to the centre-bit, they should take with them eatables and a barrel of water. This last step was agreed to by Léger. Accordingly, on the morning of Sunday, the 19th, half an hour before the light set in, our two gallants might be seen scaling the altar of the country, with their centre-bit and their provisions. Upon gaining the platform, they gently lifted one of the planks, introduced themselves beneath, replaced the plank, and then commenced their work.

Unfortunately for our two curious friends, the fête attracted none but themselves. From day-break, the Champ de Mars commenced to get animated The "merchands" of cakes and lemonade, hoping that the patriotism would hunger and thirst those who signed the document, commenced arriving from all quarters. Tired of walking about, one of these women ascended the altar, for the purpose of looking at the picture of the triumph of Voltaire. While reading the oath of Brutus, of which she understood nothing, she felt an instrument piercing the sole of her shoe. She immediately cried out for help, and declared there were malefactors underneath the altar; upon which a young man went in search of the guard of Gros Caillou. The guard, fancying the affair was not worth while troubling himself about, refused to stir.

In the absence of the soldiers, he called the passing workmen. These, more sensible to the cries of distress than the guard, came with their tools. They set to work, without delay, to open the altar, and there they found Léger and his companion, in a pretended sleep. They were not long, however, bringing them to consciousness, when they were commanded to explain the cause of their presence there, and to state if their intentions were justifiable, and they were forced to own the truth.

At that moment, a curious individual dropped himself
under the altar, to see what it was like, and there found
the barrel of water. Mistaking this for powder, he rushed
forth, crying, with all his might, that the two prisoners had
intended blowing up the altar, as well as those who would
find themselves thereon. The hair-dresser and Invalid cried
loudly that it was water, and not powder, and that, by
breaking the barrel, they would arrive at the truth, but
the truth was too simple. They thought it more natural
to strangle the two unfortunate men, or decapitate them,
and promenade their heads on the top of a pike.

At this stage of the proceedings, the bailiffs of the municipality arrived, and proclaimed the arrest of the Mayor.
They then proceeded towards the Roule, but were overtaken
at the top of Rue St Honoré by the crowd carrying the
heads of the two supposed assassins on the top of their
pikes. I fancied that I could recognise one of these as that
of a neighbor, it turned out to be that of the poor hair-
dresser, who came the preceding night to borrow the
centre-bit from M. Duplay. I could scarcely believe my
eyes. What crime could they possibly be guilty of? I
called M Duplay. There must have been a strange accent
in my voice, for, with the exception of my grandmother,
who was always occupied reading and re-reading her volume
of the "Arabian Nights," the whole family rushed towards
me, the women shrieked with terror, but one was beginning to get accustomed to these sorts of spectacles, and, by
degrees, they risked looking.

Every one recognised Léger.

What had he done?

We inquired. They were two great criminals, who had
intended blowing up the altar of the country, and those
who might be on it.

Others said they were two National Guards, who were
beheaded by the people for attempting to enforce the execution of the law.

The noise spread in the Assembly. Duport, who, with
Charles Lameth. separated himself from the Republican
Jacobins, was then President. He was not backward in
accusing his late colleagues of the crime.

"Gentlemen," said he, to the Assembly, "Two good
citizens have just perished on the Champ de Mars for hav-

ing said to a deluded mass that they must not break the laws of their country—they were hanged on the spot."

"'Tis true!" cried Regnault de St Jean d'Angely. "I confirm that news; they were two National Guards. Gentlemen, I demand martial law. It is the duty of this Assembly, gentlemen, to pronounce all persons attempting to exort the people to resist, either by personal acts, or by collective or individual writings, guilty of treachery to the nation."

This was just what the Assembly desired, composed, as it was, principally of Royalists and Constitutionalists, and in which the Republicans—that is to say, those who upheld the petition, and, consequently, wished for the dethronement of the King—were to be found in a very small number.

It was therefore decreed that the President of the Assembly, and the Mayor of Paris, should inquire into the real state of affairs, in order to take rigorous measures if events passed as were reported.

They did not give themselves the trouble to inquire into the truth, but took the measures. Robespierre then left the Assembly without saying a word, rushed to the Club of the Jacobins, to announce to them the news.

At the club he found nearly thirty persons; they all tumultuously voted the withdrawal of the petition, and Lanterre was despatched to the Champ de Mars to take possession of it.

Such was the state of affairs when M. Duplay returned from the Jacobins, and asked where were his wife and daughters.

He was told they were gone with Félicién to the Champ de Mars to see the petition signed.

"Not an instant is to be lost!" cried M. Duplay. "If the petition is not withdrawn in time, there will most certainly be a row, perhaps firearms used! Quick!—let us on to the Champ de Mars!"

We left the house to the care of Catherine and the old grandmother and set off in haste for the Porte St. Honoré.

CHAPTER XLIII.

THE RED FLAG.

Upon our arrival, the Champ de Mars presented an aspect of the most profound tranquillity.

A strong detachment of troops, with two or three pieces of cannon, which had been stationed there in consequence of the assassination which had taken place in the morning, seeing that nothing extraordinary took place, gradually withdrew, leaving the place to three or four hundred inoffensive strollers, and a small group of men, to whom no one paid the slightest attention, but which, like many small clouds, contained a terrific tempest.

This group seemed to have as leaders two strange-looking individuals. One of these creatures, whose name was Verrières, was a fantastic-looking hunchback. He had not been seen since the 5th and 6th of October, when he had made himself conspicuous at Versailles. He reappeared, however, on the night before our present date.

The other was from the department of Auvergne, and called Fournier, the American, because he had been overseer of a negro plantation in St Domingo.

He held in his hand a firelock.

The miserable creatures who were listening to the harangue of these two men were a sort of human larva, arising none knew from where.

On entering the Champ de Mars we threw a glance around, to see if we could recognise, in the midst of these three or four hundred strollers, the four persons we came in search of. At that moment, it was all the easier to do so, as every one was following Lanterie to the altar of the country. We followed as the rest. Lanterre announced to the patriots, with a voice which suited admirably these sort of proceedings, that the petition placed there the preceding night could not be signed, as, at the moment this petition was written it was supposed that the Assembly had not yet decided the fate of the King, but that since then, they had recognised his innocence and inviolability in the sitting of the night before. The Jacobins, he continued, intended occupying themselves with the forming a

new petition, which they would, ere long, present for signature.

This declaration was received with murmurs.

"Why should we await the presentation of a petition
already formed? Don't we know, as well as Messieurs
Brissot, Laclos, and Robespierre, what we want?" said an
enormous man, of about forty years of age, a young and
beautiful woman leaning on his arm. "We can also
write," added he, with a smile; "and I might even say
that we commence to think"

"No one hinders you, Citizen Robert," said Lanterre,
who was, probably, not annoyed at the interruption. "You,
and, above all, the Citizen Keralio, whose dear little arm
you have the extreme felicity of squeezing within your
own, are more capable of success than any one else. In
the meantime, I take possession of the one made by the
Society."

So saying, Lanterre placed in his pocket the petition
written by me, dictated by Brissot, amended by Laclos, and
definitely corrected by Benneville and Camille Desmoulins.

"With all this, I neither see my wife nor my daughters," exclaimed M. Duplay.

"I have an idea," replied I, "that, having required
some refreshments, she went to some *café* with Félicien."

"We require pen, ink, and paper," said the citizen
whom Lanterre had called Robert, "which we will find at
the first stationer's."

"Would you wish me to go and fetch it for you?" said
a red-headed individual, with a strong German accent.

"But," said a strange voice, "do you think you can
spare time to go such a distance? How would it be, in the
meantime, if the Queen required your services?"

"The Queen!—the Queen!" demanded the people from
all sides, and at the same time fixing their eyes on the man
with the red hair

"Yes Why, the Citizen Weder is the *valet-de-chambre*
of the Queen, and has come here, probably, to see what
was going on, so that he might be enabled to carry it to her
Majesty. If I make a mistake, and you are not the Citizen
Weder, say what your name is."

"My name is Chaumette, a medical student, of No. 9,
Rue Mazarine. Let every one do as I have done, and

make known his name, then we shall be acquainted with
who are our friends and who are our enemies."

"Yes, yes, let every one say who he is," said a man of
about eight-and-twenty, whose black beard seemed to have
added to the sternness of his features. "My name is
Brune, a typographical worker; and, if futurity could be
seen into," he might have added, "a future Marshal of
France."

"And if you want a printer for your petition, here am I,
Momoro, the printer of liberty!"

"And I, Hébert, journalist, Rue Mirabeau."

Then succeeded such tumultuous uproar of men shrieking their names with all their force, that one could scarcely
distinguish those of Renouard, Lagarde, Moreau, Henriot,
Laschereau, and David.

When this tempestuous noise ceased, the man named
Weder had disappeared.

"M. Robert," said I to him who had offered to frame the
text of the petition, "I have some business in yonder *café*,
where I fancy I can distinguish some of my friends, whence
I will proceed to the nearest stationer's. and bring you
back everything that is necessary for writing purposes."
Then I added to M. Duplay, "Follow me with your eyes,
sir; and if, as I believe, those are the ladies we are in
search of, I will make you a sign with my pocket-
handkerchief."

As I had fancied, it was Madame Duplay and her
daughters. I told them where I had left M. Duplay, and
asked them to go and meet him at the altar of the country.
I then proceeded to the stationer's, and bought two or three
sheets of paper, knowing very well that if even there was
only one sheet required for the petition itself, there would
be one hundred or one hundred and fifty signatures. I
also bought a bottle of ink and a packet of pens already
cut

When returning, I met with M. Duplay and his family.
This gentleman, fearing some serious disorder, was taking
his family home by the nearest road—that is to say, by the
Invalides. Before separating with him, through, I promised
that if anything grave took place, I would return with a
full account to the house.

15

I now hastened to the altar, where I was impatiently awaited.

I have already mentioned the names of Robert and Mademoiselle Keralio. Notwithstanding how well posted we are at the present moment in the history of the Revolution, very few persons are acquainted with the very prominent part taken by these two persons in the proceedings of that terrible day, the 17th of July, which killed with the one blow the absolute royalty, which it ought to have raised from its low position, and the constitutional royalty, which it ought to have upheld, and which, directed against the Jacobins, whom it ought to have extinguished, gave them, on the contrary, an additional strength.

Robert, as I have said, was an enormous man, of forty or forty-five years of age. Being a member of the Club of the Cordeliers, he vainly searched with his eyes some of his colleagues of reputation. Either by accident, or otherwise, he did not succeed in finding a single one of these. On the Saturday evening, Danton was obliged to join a meeting in the wood of Vincennes, and thence he went on to Fontenoy, where his father-in-law was a street vender of lemonade. Legendre had left about the same time, with Camille Desmoulins, and Féron. A meeting had been arranged at Fontenoy, by Danton, and all four dined there together.

A great responsibility was, therefore, about to be placed on the shoulders of Robert; he would be obliged to represent alone, or nearly so, the entire Club of the Cordeliers. We must, however, agree that he accepted his position bravely. The Club of the Jacobins was totally out of the question, since Lanterre, in the name of the Society, had come and withdrawn the petition.

As to the wife of Robert, Mademoiselle Keralio was a young lady—very gay, lively, talented. She was a Breton, and daughter of a Chevalier de St. Louis, called Guniement de Keralio. As inspector of the military colleges of France, he had, on paying a visit to the college at Brienne, given a favorable account of a young Corsican, named Bonaparte—he who afterwards became the Great Napoleon.

His calling not being sufficient for the support of his family, he made translations, and wrote for several journals, among others for the *Mercure*, and *Journal des Savants*.

His daughter assisted him to the best of her powers. At eighteen years of age, she wrote a novel, called "Adelaide;" then the "History of Elizabeth," a long and serious work; afterwards she married Robert, a great friend of Camille Desmoulins, and an enemy of Lafayette, who had written a book entitled, "Republicanism adapted to France." Not less patriotic than her husband, Madame Robert had come with him to add her signature to the petition, declaring that France neither recognised Louis XVI nor any other King, and seeing that it had been withdrawn, she was the first to advise her husband to draw up another.

I had no sooner arrived on the spot with my pens, ink, and paper, than she snatched them from my hands with such gracious vivacity, that I could really say nothing, but thank her. She then handed a pen to her husband, who was not very clever at composition.

"Write, write," said she, "what I dictate."

Then, amidst thunders of applause, and while consulting some with her eyes, and others with words and signs, she set to work to dictate, clearly, and with much eloquence, a petition for the dethronement of the King, which was at the same time a violent charge against royalty.

The affair was done, and well done, in less than three-quarters of an hour.

Robert, who had written the petition, signed it first and passed the pen to his neighbor.

Every one wished for the pen. I had a packet, which I distributed; and as it would take too long for them to sign one after the other, so dense had the mass become, the idea struck me to distribute the three extra sheets of paper, each of which could contain two hundred signatures.

No doubt, the assembly had heard from Weder what was going on on the Champ de Mars. The situation was grave; for if the people broke the decrees of the Assembly, it would cease being the first power of the State.

There was not a moment to be lost. The meeting would have to be dissolved, and the petition destroyed at all risks; the more so, as every instant the mob was becoming more and more numerous; not from the side of Paris, where it was made known to all, that, by proceeding to the Champ de Mars, they would be guilty of an act of rebellion, but from the village of D'Yssy, Vaugirard, Sevres, St. Cloud, and Boulogne, where they were foretold of the reunion, and had not heard of any counter-petition. They flocked to it, as to a fête.

The intentions were good, although nothing was easier than to accuse them of being bad. The Assembly—duped either by mistake, or profiting by the occasion—sent a message to the Mayor, announcing that a band of fifty thousand robbers were congregated in the Champ de Mars, and were about to march upon the Salle du Manège.

They called to their protection a military body, and gave the order to Bailly to disperse the brigands by force. Bailly, who was not aware of the goings on, and who should, before all other things, obey the orders of the Assembly, forewarned Lafayette, and sounded the alarm.

In these times, the paid guard, strongly addicted to aristocratic—or, rather, Lafayettish—principles, for it was nearly entirely composed of the conquerors of the Bastille, were always the first to answer such a call.

This body, perfectly armed and perfectly commanded, were exasperated at the injuries they received from the Democratic journals, and particularly the *Friend of the People*, of Marat, in which he called them the spies of Lafayette; and one one day demanded their noses to be cut off, another day their ears, and even hinted at finishing with them altogether with the assistance of the guillotine.

They applauded vociferously, when suddenly the red flag was seen to float from the balcony of the Hotel de Ville, which was a signal to all the loyal citizens of the town of their help, and never did they require help more than on this occasion.

In the midst of these cries, the Mayor, who was pale as the day on which he marched to the scaffold, descended the Place de Grève, and placed himself at the head of a column of the National Guard. Lafayette, at the head of another column, followed the left bank of the Seine, while Bailly took the right bank.

The red flag was unhooked, and followed the column, headed by the Mayor.

CHAPTER XLIV.

THE MASSACRE OF THE CHAMP DE MARS.

WE thought but little of the danger we were running at the Champ de Mars, and knew nothing whatever of what was going on at the Hotel de Ville. The crowd was nothing more than an ordinary Sunday crowd No weapons whatever were to be seen, save the sabres hanging to the belts of some stray National Guards, who might be taking a walk with their wives and children. Madame Roland says, in her "Memoirs," that she remained there till ten o'clock.

The only extraordinary proceeding that took place was that on the altar.

They continued to sign the petition with a vigor that promised twelve or fifteen hundred signatures before nightfall. Generally the person signing cried out, "Vive la nation! Down with royalty!" threw his cap up in the air, and ceded the place to another.

Two contrary currents were established on the north, south, and east sides of the altar of the country, between the persons ascending and the persons descending. The height of the altar was immense—that it is to say, about one hundred feet. At about four o'clock in the afternoon, it presented the aspect of an enormous hive, swarming with bees.

At a few minutes past four o'clock, we heard the drums, but paid little attention to them, the affair of the hairdresser and Invalid having for some time escaped the memory of every one. In Paris, one soon forgets the events which are of but little interest to remember. There was simply a movement of curiosity on the altar, where two thousand people were seated, and on the ground of the Champ de Mars, where some ten to twelve thousand were walking.

These drums were those of a battalion of the advanced guard of the Faubourg St. Antoine This battalion was totally misinformed of what was taking place in the Champ de Mars. They had received an order from Bailly and Lafayette to fire in case of any resistance being made, but only in case of resistance.

Before entering the Champ de Mars, the command was given to halt, and load their guns. They thought they would have to face some fifty thousand brigands, determined on bloodshed and pillage.

They found, on the contrary, an inoffensive population amusing itself.

The battalion halted a second time; but, as they did not find what they were in search of, they put their guns in clusters, and sent a few unarmed grenadiers to see what was passing on the altar of the country. These came back, saying that they were signing a petition in the greatest possible order, and without the slightest noise.

The people walking in the Champ de Mars did not, on their side, pay the slightest attention to the arrival of the military from the Faubourg St. Antoine.

But about the same time, the drums of Gros Caillon and the Cours la Reine were heard calling to arms.

From Gros Caillon it was Lafayette, and from Cours la Reine, Bailly, who arrived with the National and paid Guards.

Lafayette sent, in advance, an aide-de-camp and a hundred armed men, to find out what was really passing in the Champ de Mars. But from the group, which I have already mentioned as having been commanded by Verriéres and Fournier, a gun-shot was seen to proceed, which wounded the aid-de-camp of Lafayette.

The advance guard returned to Lafayette, and the aide-de-camp, bleeding, made his report on the manner in which he was received.

To him, wounded as he was on his entry into the Champs, all the inoffensive strollers appeared to be brigands.

Lafayette placed himself at the head of the three thousand men he commanded, and marched on the Champ de Mars.

He found Fournier, Verriéres, and those they led, busily engaged in raising a barricade. He marched straight up to the barricade, and destroyed it. From under a cart, Fournier, the American, fired through one of the wheels on Lafayette.

The gun missed fire.

Fournier, the American, was taken, and charged with revolt and homicide.

The National Guard would have shot him on the spot, had not Lafayette torn him from their hands, and rendered him his liberty.

The most curious of all was, that this bloody day was caused by these two bloodthirsty men, Lafayette and Bailly.

The battalion from the Faubourg St. Antoine and Marias entered the Champ at the same time as Lafayette, and ranged themselves behind the altar, in front of the Military College.

Lafayette, fearing that these might sympathise with the people, sent a detachment of the National Guard to join them.

At this moment the promenaders, and those who were signing the petition on the altar, preoccupied, but not alarmed, at the sort of collision which had taken place between the National Guard and the defenders of the barricade, saw, advancing by the Bridge of Bois (to-day the Bridge of Jéna) another body of the army, headed by the Mayor, and over the heads of which floated the red flag.

This red flag informed us that martial law was proclaimed.

Against whom?

It could not be against those who were guilty of no wrong, and who were simply walking by right of the petition accorded to every citizen.

In the midst of the troop following the Mayor were to be distinguished a company of dragoons. The dragoons were well known to be an aristocratic regiment, being used to firing on the people. Also a band of hair-dressers, armed to the teeth, with their hair dressed à l'aile de pigeon, and clad in the height of fashion. Their clothes were of silks and satin, and of every color in the rainbow.

They came, no doubt, to avenge the death of that unfortunate poor fellow, Léger.

The group which had opposed the entrance of Lafayette had gone and reformed themselves a little further off. They were joined by all the blackguards of the quarter.

At the moment when, after a roll of drums, M. Bailly commenced his declaration, a shower of stones fell around

him. A gun was fired behind him at the same time, and
wounded a dragoon.

Bailly gave the order to fire a round of blank cartridge
in the air. The order was executed. This inoffensive discharge injured no one, but had the effect of making Lafayette think that it was real.

The promenaders nearly all rushed towards the altar of
the country, fancying that they, as simple spectators, could
not be fired upon without there having first been a sum-
mony to disperse.

At this moment, the Champ de Mars was invaded by cavalry.

The promenaders vainly search for an issue to re-enter
Paris.

At all sides, nothing but troubles present themselves to
our view; at the Military College, at Gros Caillon, at the
entrance to the wood.

Almost immediately the paid guards made an offensive
movement towards the altar. Abandoning the hostile
group, which continued to shower stones on their heads,
they dashed themselves distractedly and furiously against
the altar; and, without an attack, without provocation or resistance, fired on this mass of brothers—this living pyramid,
this human beehive, of which two-thirds were composed of
defenceless women and children.

The hurricane of fire fell on this disarmed throng, who
only replied by heart-rending cries of agony. The three
faces of the altar were covered with the dead and wounded
bodies of the unfortunate victims.

From the height of the pyramid where I found myself—
between Robert and his wife,—I perceived that the artillery
were about to make fire on the people with the cannon, at
the risk of firing on the cavaliers and paid guard, when
Lafayette perceiving the movement, dug the spurs into his
horse, and galloped to the mouth of the cannon, where he
placed himself.

The first cry of Madame Robert was—"'Tis on the petitioners they would fire! Let us save the petition!" Then
addressing herself to me, she said, " Help me, monsieur—
help me !"

It was no longer a question of signing; every one pre-
cipitated himself by the only side of the altar which had

not been fired upon—that is to say, the side facing the
Military College, and which was protected by the battalions
of the Faubourg St. Antoine and Marais. Both the petition and the sheets, covered with signatures, were seen to
fly before the wind.

Madame Robert took possession of the petition, whilst
her husband and I collected about a hundred sheets of signatures.

We then descended by the west side of the altar.

Around us, seven or eight persons had been killed or
wounded.

A hundred and fifty, at least, fell before this first discharge.

In descending this immense staircase, I lost Robert and
his wife. The National Guards of the Faubourg St. Antoine and Marais cried, "Come with us—we will defend
you!"

I rushed to their sides; the dragoons set out in pursuit
of us; but the battalion of the Marais opened their ranks
to us, and prepared to receive them with the bayonet. An
aide-de-camp came up, and ordered this battalion to march
forward, and make a junction with the other troops. The
aide-de-camp was killed. None obeyed this order but the
paid guards.

The battalion, or rather, the two battalions, of National
Guards, formed themselves into two columns, sent out scouts,
so as to protect any fugitives who might come and ask for
shelter in their ranks, and marched from the Champ de
Mars, leaving this horrible butchery to be completed without their assistance.

CHAPTER XLV.

ROBESPIERRE PAYS A VISIT TO M. DUPLAY.

I HAD no sooner quitted this frightful scene of bloodshed,
than, thanking my saviors, I sprang forward towards the
river, in order to cross it by boat, or, if there was a necessity, to swim it.

The affair seemed to me grave. There must have been some treachery on foot, of which, in my mind the Jacobins ought to be instructed.

There happened to be, in a boat anchored to the river's bank, a man fishing, who did not disturb himself, notwithstanding the thundering of the cannon.

Nothing ever disturbs a man fishing. To untie the rope, jump into the boat, and take possession of the oars, was but the work of a few moments. I had nearly half-way crossed the river before he recovered from his astonishment.

At length, he demanded what I meant by this violence, both to himself and to his boat? I showed him a paper, and said, "An order from General Lafayette." That was sufficient.

I jumped out on the right bank, leaving the boat, with its owner, to regain the left.

Once on solid ground, I took to my heels, and by Cours la Reine, and the Porte St. Honoré, I set out for M. Duplay's house as fast as my legs could carry me.

From Cours la Reine to the Church of the Assomption, in front of which M. Duplay lived, I found the streets greatly agitated and full of people.

The red flag, the Mayor, the dragoons, and the paid guard were seen to pass; then, again, they had heard the terrible discharge of musketry; so that seeing me come from the Champ de Mars, running, the perspiration dropping off me, and all covered with blood, every one inquired of me the whole way along,—"What is the matter?"

I had but one reply to make, and that while I was running.

"The dragoons and the paid guard are slaughtering the people!"

I found M. Duplay at his door, surrounded by a group of neighbors and acquaintances. I related to him all that had taken place.

"Oh, ho!" said he; "the Jacobins must be informed of this. Quick!—let us run to the club!"

About fifty members awaited the news with impatience. They had, as yet, heard nothing. I was the first messenger of the mournful intelligence.

They said that M. Robespierre must at once be informed, and a messenger was despatched to the Assembly to fetch him.

The Jacobins knew one fact, and that was, that all the blame would be left on their shoulders. It was they who had taken the initiative in the affair of the petition. The ·Constitutionals, who had separated from them, in order to form the new clubs Feuillants, washed their hands of this popular movement in opposition to the decree of the Assembly.

They thanked M. Duplay and myself, and refused to recognise any petition tending to the dethronement of the King. Everything was circulated in the name of the Assembly, and the society swore anew fidelity to the Constitution and submission to the decrees of the Assembly.

After what had presented itself to my view the preceding days, and after what I had written at the dictation of Citizen Brissot, I found this submission too prompt. There was at the bottom of it all an abandonment of the rights of the people, and a cowardice which disgusted me.

I left the club, and returned pensively to the house.

A half an hour or so after, might be heard a great disturbance towards the Place Louis XV.

It was the paid guard, who were re-entering Paris by the Rue St. Honoré, to have an occasion to make a demonstration against the Jacobins.

One had hardly the time to form palisades.

The paid guard collected themselves before the Convent, demanding powder to blow the gate and demolish the den of the Republicans. They were laughed at, they were applauded; they were hissed. The street was full of people, looking at one another, ready to come to blows.

It was plain to be seen that one of those misunderstandings had taken place which places the gun to one's shoulder without one's knowing upon whom to fire.

All at once, I could perceive, in the Rue Luxembourg, a man gliding down the street, with an evident desire to pass unnoticed.

I pulled my master's coat, and whispered to him, "The Citizen Robespierre."

It was indeed none other but he, who had been sent to the Assembly, and who had arrived there just in time to have the door shut on his nose.

It was evident that if he was recognised by the paid guard, he would run the risk of being shot.

He was at this moment recognised by a group of persons, and cheered. No doubt, they were Jacobins.

He quickened his pace, descending the street, to gain speedily the Faubourg St. Honoré.

At the Rue de Luxembourg, several cries were raised of "Vive Robespierre!"

He turned pale, and hesitated whether to take the Luxembourg or continue his road. He continued.

"Vive Robespierre!" again cried a man. "And since it is absolutely necessary to have a King, why not have him?"

Robespierre thought himself lost. He looked on all sides for shelter.

Duplay rushed towards him.

"At my house—at my house, citizen!" said he. "My name is Duplay! I am master carpenter, and a good citizen!"

"Yes, yes—at our house!" said Madame Duplay and Mademoiselle Cornélie.

And all three—the man and the two women—surrounded Robespierre, who, without the slightest resistance, allowed himself to be led into the alley.

I entered last, and locked the door.

The retreat was effected so prudently, that hardly a soul had perceived the manœuvre.

Those that did see him said nothing, so that no noise was made at the door.

Robespierre was extremely pale. He sat down, or rather fell, on the first chair that came in his way. Mademoiselle Cornélie wiped his forehead with her pocket handkerchief, while Madame Duplay brought him a glass of fresh water.

I placed the glass to his lips, but his hand shook so, that he made the glass chink against his teeth.

However he drank, looked around him, tried to smile, and said, "I see that I am with friends."

"Say, rather, with admirers—with devoted admirers!" replied M. Duplay.

"Oh, yes!" replied the three women.

"Oh, if I had known it," said M. Duplay, "I would not have allowed you to present yourself at the National Assembly."

"How so?" said Robespierre.

"Yes; it was Réné,"—M. Duplay pointed me out,—"it was Réné, a good young man, a staunch patriot, and a friend of M Drouet de St. Menehould, who, you know, arrested the King; it was Réné who came and announced the massacre on the Champ de Mars We have but one bond to the Jacobins, and, as I belong to the club——"

"Ah, I now recognise you," said Robespierre.

"Then it was decided to go and fetch you"

"And I arrived just in time to see the gates shut. Not wishing to return home, at the bottom of the Marais, I was going to get a little shelter at the house of Pétion, who lives in the Faubourg St. Honoré. You came across me on my road, and brought me here I ask permission to remain here all night Surrounded by the spies of Lafayette, and satellites of Bailly, the life of an honest man runs great danger. I do not fear death, but my ambition is to die in a way useful to my country."

I assisted at this scene without the slightest emotion. It seemed to me a great honor to address this great man

"Then," said he, "you are the friend of the Citizen Drouet?"

"He cared for me like a father," said I. "The little I know I owe to him and to Rousseau"

"Ah, young man, you have Rousseau?"

"I know him by heart."

"Good master—great master! I, also, was his scholar, and I hope to do him credit one of these days."

Duplay and his wife listened with their mouths open, nearly on their knees

For some time, Duplay seemed as if he wished to ask a question. His wife and he had exchanged two or three significant glances.

"Would the Citizen Robespierre do us the honor of supping with us?"

"I would not trouble you so much," said Robespierre. "And then, again, my sister would be anxious."

"But you were going to sup with the Citizen Pétion."

"Yes; but from Pétion's I could have let my sister know."

"Very well; she can be informed from here as well."

"Have you any person certain?"

"There is me, citizen," said I.

" Would you have that kindness ? "

" I will be only too happy to render this service to M. Duplay."

" Then have the goodness to give me pen, ink, and paper."

The two young girls brought him the pen and paper.

He wrote, in a small hand, the following :—

" MY SISTER,—
        " Don't be uneasy.   I am in safety.
                            " Your brother,
                                    " MAXIMILIAN."

He then sealed his letter, and wrote the address in a bold hand, which reminded me greatly of his character,—

> *To Mdlle. Charlotte de Robespierre.*
> *No. 7 Rue Saintange*
> *At the Marais.*

I took the letter, and went on my mission.

CHAPTER XLVI.

INSTALLATION.

I HAVE already said that nature had gifted me with strong legs, and it was in days like the present that I appreciated the gift.

As yet, I knew not sufficient of Paris to be enabled to extricate myself from the labyrinth of streets which joined the Rue St. Honoré, and which stretched from the Rue Aubry le Boucher to the Rue Boucherat, so that I spent six or seven minutes in making the necessary inquiries, and at last arrived.

I saw a sombre house in a sombre street.   It was No. 7. I mounted a dark-looking staircase, and arrived at the second floor.

Three doors opened on the landing : one of them bore an inscription :—

"Le Citoyen Maximilian de Robespierre, et Deputé à l'Assemblée Nationale."

I knocked.

I heard footsteps approaching the door, and then stop cautiously.

"Is it you, Maximilian?" asked a voice, in which could be discerned traces of emotion.

"No, mademoiselle," I replied; "but I bring news of him."

The door was quickly opened.

"Nothing has happened to him?" asked a stately female of about forty years.

"Here are a few words to reassure you," I replied.

I then handed her the letter.

It was too dark for her to be enabled to read it in the passage on the landing.

Mademoiselle de Robespierre re-entered the apartment, inviting me to follow her.

I entered a sort of dining-room, opening on a study and bedroom.

All was cold, cheerless, and almost unfurnished. If not actually miserable, it was far below mediocrity.

Mademoiselle Robespierre read her brother's letter.

"When my brother thinks it needless to tell me where he is, he has his reasons. You have seen him, sir?"

"I have just left him, mademoiselle."

"Nothing has happened to him?"

"Nothing."

"Give him my congratulations, sir, and thank for me those people who have been hospitable to him. I would that, after the long walk you have had, I could offer you refreshment; but my brother is so sober, and has such few wants, that we have naught but water in the house."

At this moment, the tramp of footsteps was heard in the corridor. A woman showed herself at the door of the dining-room, and, dimly, a man could be perceived behind her.

Despite the semi-darkness, I recognised the female, and could not resist crying out, "Madame Roland!"

Mademoiselle Robespierre repeated, in an accent of astonishment, "Madame Roland!"

"Yes, I, myself, mademoiselle, and my husband, who,

hearing that Robespierre has been threatened by his enemies, are come to offer him a shelter in our little house at the corner of the Rue Guenegaud."

" I thank you in my brother's name, madame," replied Mademoiselle Charlotte, with dignity. " He has already found the asylum which you so nobly offer him, and which I know not myself. Here is the gentleman who brought the news," continued she, pointing me out to Madame Roland.

" That proves, mademoiselle," said, in his turn, the Citizen Roland, " that other citizens are more favored than we ; " and remarking that he was unwilling to intrude longer on her privacy, he bowed, and departed with his wife.

As my errand was fulfilled, I followed them, and returned in close conversation with them. Madame Roland was at the Jacobin Club when the paid guard made an irruption among them.

The terror was such among the few members of the society present, that one of them, anxious to escape, escaladed the gallery set aside for women. Madame Roland made him ashamed of himself, and compelled him to descend the way that he had come.

They asked me about Robespierre. I told them that I was not authorized to inform them of his place of shelter, but only could assure them that he was in a place of safety among people who would die for him.

Madame Roland asked me to tell Robespierre that they would bring him to trial—that is to say, accuse him that evening at the Feuillants. In that certainty, she and her husband were going to M. Buzal, to pray him to defend his colleague.

We separated at the top of the Pont Neuf—M. Roland and Madame to go down the Rue du Roule. I to follow the Rue St. Honoré.

It was quite night when I arrived at Duplay's. Félicién had rejoined the family during my absence ; they were at table, and he regarded askance the new arrival, who took the place of honor between Madame Duplay and Mademoiselle Cornélie. I told M. Robespierre all about the fulfilment of my message, and reported to him his sister's reply.

I told him also that M. and Madame Roland had paid a visit to his house.

Here he interrupted, and repeated after me,—"Citizen Roland! Citizeness Roland!"

He appeared so astonished at the visit, that he was some time asking me the cause.

I took my place at the table.

"Monsieur," said Robespierre, after a moment's silence, with his habitual politeness, "does it please you to serve me to the end?"

"Not only will it be an honor, and a pleasure," replied I, "but a duty."

"Well," said he, "this time you have only a few steps to go, and I shall not have to write a letter. Go to the Rue St Anne; on the left hand side, in going up the street, by the Boulevards, you will see the Hotel de Berry; there you will inquire for a young man named St. Just. He lives on the fourth floor, in a room overlooking the court. If he be at home, tell him that I want him. My kind host, I hope, will allow me to receive him here. At present, this young man is of no account, but one day he will lead us all. If he be not at home, well; you leave your name and the address of this house, where I have found such good friends, and such noble protectors, and under the address you write, 'Urgent for the sake of the public safety.' Whenever he returns, he will come straight here, you may be sure."

I wished to leave the table, but, placing his hand on my shoulder, he said, "Finish your supper. I am not in so great a hurry, and we have all the night before us."

Five minutes after, I was proceeding up the Rue St. Anne.

The Hotel de Berry led out of the Rue Neuve des Petits-champs and the Rue Neuve St. Augustin.

I asked for Citizen St. Just.

The conciérge threw his eyes over the keys hung on the wall, and saw that of St. Just was not there.

"No. 19, fourth story, at the bottom of the corridor."

I mounted a dark staircase, and found the indicated corridor, and in that corridor, No. 19.

I knocked; a powerful voice said, "Come in!"

I turned the key in the lock, and saw a young man in

16

his shirt-sleeves, working by an open window at the correction of proofs.

He was so absorbed in his work, that I approached and touched him before he turned round.

The book, the proofs of which he was correcting, was, I could see, entitled, " Mespasse temps ou le Voirvel organe."

The preoccupation of the young poet was caused by the desire to find a rhyme.

The rhyme found, he turned to me.

" Pardon," said he ; " what want you ? "

" Citizen St. Just," replied I, " I come on behalf of Citizen Robespierre."

" You ? "

" Yes.   He desires your presence immediately."

" Where ? "

" If you are not prepared, I will leave you the address; but if you are, I will conduct you thither."

" Is he at the Rue Saintange ? "

" No; he is close by here—in the Rue St. Honoré."

" At the Jacobins ? "

" There are no longer Jacobins.   The club is dead."

" Who dared do it ? "

" The paid guard, who, an hour before, dared do another thing."

" What was the other thing ? "

" Fire on the people at the Champ de Mars—slay, perchance, six or seven hundred persons ! "

St Just shouted with rage.

" What ! you a patriot—the friend of M. Robespierre,— and not know better than that what takes place in Paris ? " said I.

" I promised my publisher to have those proofs corrected by Thursday; and in order to accomplish this I told the servant not to disturb me for anything.   He brought my breakfast in my chamber, and here is my dinner already served.   I have not had time to eat.   I knew last night from the Jacobins they must withdraw the petition ; and I doubted not that, the petition withdrawn, there might be a disturbance at the Champ de Mars.   But let us not lose a moment.   Since Robespierre requires me, I am at his orders."

The young man put on a white waistcoat, irreproachable

in its cleanliness, a gray coat; a sword and dagger he hung at his side, then took his hat, and said but the words, "Show the way!"

I went in front, and he followed.

CHAPTER XLVII.

A BREAK.

HERE comes a break in my personal adventures during the course of the great struggle for liberty throughout France. I leading the way, and St. Just following, we went down the Rue St Anne, and had almost reached the Rue Neuve des Augustins, when the powerful voice of St. Just (one that was soon to be heard by the Nation, which was to hush at his first word) addressed me.

"Citizen!"

"Citizen St Just?"

" Give me the address whither we are going!" he said.

"Why, I am leading you! Do you mistrust me?"

His face flushed.

"I mistrust no man," he replied.

"Then why do you ask for the address?"

"By way of precaution."

"What need is there of precaution?"

"Was not the Citizen Robespierre in danger not an hour since, by being in the streets?"

"Yes."

"Then the Citizen St. Just is equally in danger of a bullet from the barrel of a paid guard."

"I shall not desert you."

"But——"

"Yes, citizen."

"What if you are killed?" St. Just replied calmly. "I should not know whither you came."

"True," I replied; and he taking out his tablets, wrote upon them, from my dictation, the address of the Citizen Duplay.

In this act may be seen an example of that forethought

and preparation ,which gave St. Just a position to which otherwise he never would have attained.

"Good!" he said, having carefully taken down every particular. "Go forward."

How necessary was his precaution, the next few minutes showed.

We had only reached the end of the Rue St. Anne, when a sudden rush of people along the Rue Neuve des Augustins warned us that danger was at hand.

I turned and looked at St. Just.

Without regarding me, while apparently his sight was on the alert on all sides, he repeated his direction, "Go forward."

Suddenly, shots were heard, and, in a few moments, the street surged with people, who poured out from the houses and joined those who were speeding down the street, running by their sides and asking what the commotion meant. So far, very few of the citizens were aware of the massacres that had taken place upon the altar of the country.

Paris, in fact, was that day, for the first time, wholly shadowed by the red flag—which was not to be furled again until a reign of terror, never equalled in the history of the world, was to be followed by the inauguration of Napoleon's splendor.

We were proceeding as rapidly as possible past the current of excited people, when, unquestionably, a deadly fire opened from a small turning on the left.

Suddenly, I turned to the left, to see who had struck me; for I felt that a blow had been aimed at my shoulder which had nearly sent me off my feet.

As I turned, no man faced me, and I was wondering where the blow came from; when, as suddenly and unexpectedly as I received the blow, I felt sick and weak.

It was a woman who screamed, "Blood!"

She pointed to the ground.

As though looking through a mist, I followed the direction of her pointing finger.

There was blood upon the ground.

All this had passed in a space not longer than six moments.

"Citizen" said the voice of St. Just, "you are wounded; the ball, however, was meant for me."

The last words sounded faintly in my ears, and I thought that he, too, was hurt.

"And you, citizen—are you wounded?"

"No," he replied, in a still fainter voice, as it appeared to me; but it was my senses forsaking me.

"Citizens," I heard him say, "if I fall, you will find an address in my pocket, which is the home of this lad."

That was all I heard. Suddenly, the earth appeared to slip from under me, and there was an end of my consciousness.

When next I knew myself, I awoke to life with the feeling of a beating red-hot hammer upon my left shoulder; I appeared to be struggling out of a state of fearful horror. When this cleared off, and I knew myself to be once more alive, once more Citizen Réné Besson, I was in a little room, which I soon learnt was an apartment belonging to Citizen Duplay; and, at my side, reading a book, was Citizeness Cornelie Duplay, who had constituted herself my nurse.

And inasmuch as this history is not so much one of myself as of the Revolution, and of my part in it, I will only briefly recount the events of the next few weeks—of the next few months, in relation to myself.

It appeared that I had been wounded in the shoulder, not dangerously; but the loss of blood was very great, and I was weak as a little child. I could not raise my hand even to my head, while I had scarcely voice sufficient with which to thank my kind nurse for the offices she performed about me.

For weeks I lay upon that narrow bed, my constitution, and the temperate life I had hitherto led, fighting well in, my favor. I could tell through chapters how gradually the memory of Sophie Gerbaut faded from my mind, and of how Cornelie Duplay took her place in my heart.

But I said nothing of my love; and when, weak, but quite safe, I sat once more at Citizen Duplay's hospitable table, I still kept my passion to myself.

Released, however, as I was, from my bed, I was still a prisoner in the house, which I did not quit for a couple more months.

Meanwhile the Revolution was progressing.

The sight of the altar of the country, after the flight of the people from its steps, was terrible. It is said that the great mass of the dead lying bleeding upon that mighty structure was composed of women and children.

As the National Guard marched back to the city, after this massacre of many hundreds—a massacre which would have been multiplied by ten, had not Lafayette thrown himself before the cannon—they were greeted with low cries of "Murder!" "Murder!" "Vengeance!"

That day utterly parted the people from the thought of royalty. Paris was now ready to spill blood, for massacre would now take the name of vengeance. In many a street in the common parts of Paris were to be found the surviving relatives of those who had been slain. These were naturally prompted by a spirit of revenge—by a determination to pay blood with blood.

Nothing could wash out this hate—no words uttered by the weak and vacillating King could now stem the torrent of hate. Louis XVI and Marie Antoinette were already condemned to death in the hearts of the people. Nothing could save them.

The people were now ripe for rage, and therefore the terrible Danton gained power. The total reverse of Robespierre, they were to rise to power together. Robespierre was feeble, small, thin, and excessively temperate. Habitually, he ate little, drank water, and used perfumes when he was not surrounded by flowers; for he was as passionate an admirer of flowers as Mirabeau himself. Danton, on the other hand, was a huge monster—athletic, rude, coarse. He pleased the worst rabble of the city, because he resembled them. His eloquence was as thunder, and his very phrases were short, clear, and plain, like the words of a general accustomed to command. His very gestures intoxicated the people, who, however, more than by anything, were attracted by his wit, which, coarse, brutal, and often unjust, was never obscure, and always to the point. Men who went to hear his wit, remained to be converted to his ways of thinking.

His one quality was ambition—his one passion, excitement. He was quite devoid of honor, principles, or morality—he was already drunk with the Revolution; but it was a drunkenness which produced madness—not sleep. Moreover, he had the peculiar power of controlling himself even in his most excited moments—times when he would launch a bitter joke in the midst of his denunciations—a joke which should compel his hearers to yell with laughter, while he himself remained perfectly impassive. He laughed contemptuously at all honesty. He despised a man who could pity. In a word, he was a wild beast gifted with speech, but who could no more think beyond himself and his wants or desires, than can the beasts that perish.

The first great act of the people after the massacre upon the altar of the country, was the expression of a desire to honor the remains of Voltaire—the man whose writings, together with those of Rousseau, had actually sown the seed of revolution against that royalty which in Gaul and France had unceasingly mastered the people through two weary thousand years, before the death of Voltaire, in 1778 —thirteen years before the events I am now recording. The power of the Court and the Church still maintained such sway over the minds and hearts of the people, that it was impossible to hope to bury the great man without creating a popular outrage. His nephew, therefore, secretly removed the body from Paris, where Voltaire died, and bore it far away to the Abbey of Seilières, in Champagne, where it found a resting-place

Now it was the National Assembly ordered the removal of Voltaire's remains to the Pantheon, the cathedral of philosophy, where he buried many great men—that building upon the face of which has been carved "France, in gratitude to great men."

"The people owe their freedom to Voltaire!" cried Regnault de St. Jean d'Angély; "for by enlightening them he gave them power. Nations are enthralled by ignorance alone; and when the torch of reason displays to them the ignominy of bearing these chains, they blush to wear them, and they snap them asunder!"

Like a conqueror, seated on his trophies, they placed Voltaire's coffin in the midst of the spot upon which the horrible Bastille had stood, and upon a great heap of stones which had formed part of that stronghold; and thus Voltaire, dead, triumphed over those stones which had gained a victory over him in life, for Voltaire had been a prisoner in the Bastille.

On one of the blocks which formed this second altar of the country they carved this inscription :

"RECEIVE ON THIS SPOT, WHERE DESPOTISM ONCE FET-
TERED THEE, THE HONORS DECREED TO THEE BY THY
COUNTRY."

All Paris poured out to walk in the triumphal procession
which accompanied the quiet ashes to their last resting-place.
The car upon which the coffin lay was harnessed by twelve
horses, four abreast, their manes plaited with golden tassels
and beautiful flowers, the reins being held by men dressed
in ancient Greek costume. On the car was a sort of altar
upon which lay a waxen statue of the philosopher crowned
with laurel. This was placed over the remains.

The money spent upon this pageant was immense;
whence it came, no one has ever learnt. It was almost
miraculous. Meanwhile, the people were living upon a
couple of ounces of bread apiece, and a few miserable vege-
tables. That passion and vengeance could have been kept
alive upon such reducing diet, is the truest evidence of the
justice of the national cause.

The military formed a portion of the procession, while
cannon boomed incessantly during the march. Finally—
and it is the most significant fact of this remarkable pageant
—a *printing-press* was made to take part in the procession.
At this press, agile printers were taking off impressions of
sentences in honor of Voltaire, the printed papers being
cast to the seething multitude fresh printed as they were.

Here and there the red cap—the cap of liberty—might
be seen, surmounting the ominous pike.

Every actor and actress in Paris followed, dressed in the
costumes of the characters of Voltaire's plays. Members of
all the learned bodies followed; a gigantic pyramid was carried along, bearing the titles of all his works; and, finally,
the statue of the demigod himself—a statue of gold—was
borne upon the shoulders of men dressed in Grecian costume, this being followed by a casket of gold, containing a
copy of each of his works.

Troops of singing-girls dressed in white met the quiet
cause of all this demonstration, and showered white flowers
upon the catafalque; hymns to his genius were sung, the
air was sick with perfume, and the city trembled with the
roar of adoration.

Night fell before the procession reached the temple dedi-

cated to the remains of great men, and here Voltaire was
enthroned, for he was King of France in that hour; and
the weak, vacillating, and kindly Louis XVI, away there
in the Tuileries, was crownless, awaiting to pay in his person—he the least odious of his race—for the unceasing
crimes and cruelties of his forefathers.

CHAPTER XLVIII.

THE THREAT IS LOUDER.

THROUGHOUT August, affairs were tending more and
more to dangerous threats The National Assembly were
ostensibly framing a new constitution; but the delegates
proceeded very slowly, except in the matter of contradiction,
at which they were very brisk.

The King's brothers became still further estranged from
him; while the efforts made beyond the frontier, tending to
liberate the royal family from the state of imprisonment in
which they lived, only tended to hasten the growing belief
of the people that by the death of the King, alone could
the nation hope to destroy the chances and the plans of
those Royalists who had escaped from France, and were
blindly endeavoring to serve their own interests by inducing
foreign Courts to declare war against France, and march
upon Paris.

Throughout this period the King gave little expression of
opinion, worked and read incessantly, and bore the threatening aspect of affairs about him and his family with great
patience. He was an estimable man, honest to a degree,
but stupid, hopelessly prejudiced, and apparently without
any capability of experiencing tenderness or sorrow

It was now that Roland, the husband of the celebrated
Madame Roland, rose to eminence. Nothing in himself, he
became notorious through his wife—one of the most beautiful, accomplished, and brilliant, as one of the most unfortunate, the world has yet seen Her husband was much
older than herself—cold, deadly, impassive ; but, on the other
hand, his steady principles were never for one moment
shaken.

She was a republican, heart and soul; and when the people, towards the close of the year 1791, began to believe that the differences between the King and the nation would be amicably settled, she never swerved one moment in maintaining that a republic, and only a republic, could save France from invasion.

General Dumouriez was also rising to power. He was rather a courtier than a soldier, although he was destined to win victories: especially amongst women, he was very successful. He attempted to obtain favor from Madame Roland herself; but that single-hearted lady, true to her ice-cold husband, put down the General's pretensions with calm contempt. He, however, gained much attention from Marie Antoinette, as the man who, amongst those who had acquired the confidence of the people, was the most aristocratic, and who had, therefore, the most sympathy with the falling royal cause. The Queen was right. After gaining several battles for France against the Austrians, he turned his army upon Paris, intending to intimidate the Republicans. The army revolted, and Dumouriez himself had to take refuge in the camp of those very Austrians whom but a short time previously he had conquered. They would have nothing to do with him; and, finally, he fled to England, always open to the refugee, and there he died in obscurity.

This general, therefore, helped to destroy the royal family. At his first interview with the King, he said, " Sire, I devote myself wholly to your service. But a minister of to-day is no longer the minister of yesterday. Without ceasing to be your Majesty's devoted servant, I am the slave of the nation."

The Queen sent for him privately when he had become the idol of the people.

" Sir," said she, " you are all-powerful at this moment; but it is through popular favor, and that soon destroys its idols. I tell you I oppose the changes which are being made in the constitution, so beware!"

" I am confounded," the General replied; " but I am more the servant of my country than of your Majesty. Think of your safety, of the King's, of that of your children! You are surrounded by enemies. If, in the King's interests, you oppose the new constitution made by the Assembly, you will endanger the royal family, and in no way prevent the course of events."

"Sir," the Queen frantically replied, "this state of things cannot last for ever. Beware for *yourself*."

"Madame," said Dumouriez, who *had* accepted the post of Premier of the Ministry, and who, at this time, appears to have very faithfully served the nation—his great fault was his fickleness,—"madame, when I became Prime Minister, I knew that my responsibility was not my greatest danger."

The Queen shrank back. "Do you think me capable of having you assassinated?"

Tears were upon the Queen's face.

"Far be such a fearful thought from me, your Majesty. Your soul is great and noble, and the bravery you have shown on many occasions has for ever made me your Majesty's most devoted slave."

The Queen's anger was appeased in a moment, and she placed her right hand upon the General's arm in token of reconciliation.

Thus it was that this unhappy woman, who had begun life so extravagantly, while the masses were starving, irritated the people, and especially all those who had dealings with her, by the apparent childishness and weakness of her general character. It was felt that no reliance could be placed upon her. Born of the great feudal Austrian family about whom etiquette was so plastered, that only nobles could sit down in the presence of the royal family, and then upon a very low stool, she was brought to France at a very early age, to a Court almost as ridiculous as the one she had left. But while the Austrians had been excited to no feelings of hate against their Emperor, Voltaire, Rousseau, Diderot, had taught the French to look upon royalty as made up of merciless, greedy puppets; and, unfortunately, Marie Antoinette—a pure and noble-hearted woman in herself—had the appearance of totally agreeing with this description.

While the people were starving, her passion for jewels became absorbing; while mothers were begging meals for their little ones, she was taking parts in little comedies at Versailles.

Her memory can scarcely be blamed. She had never

seen the people; and, as a proof that she knew nothing about them and their wants, we hear about her the celebrated anecdote, which helped to send her to the scaffold. Being told the people wanted bread, she replied, "If there is no bread, why do they not eat cake?"

The people never forgave that—she washed those words only partly out with her blood. Did she really mean what she said, or were the words intended for a joke? Did she really think that if there was no bread there must be cake; or did she utter that fatal sentence as a witticism? I venture to think that she was ignorant of the very meaning of starvation; for courtiers treat kings and queens like children. A misfortune this, when the people expect them to be men and women—the condition of things when the Revolution broke out.

Louis XVI was incapable of managing anything but a lock; his wife thought she could govern for him, and she made a sorry mistake.

The King's grandfather, Louis XV, the preceding King, had said, "After me, the deluge." The deluge was upon the royal family, sweeping around them, and was to overwhelm the family."

The popular feeling was far stronger against the Queen than the King.

"See," she said, one day, before Dumouriez and the King, and pointing through a window near her; "a prisoner in this palace, I dare not venture to present myself at a window that overlooks the garden. But yesterday I wished to breathe the air, and went to the window. An artilleryman used the language of a guard-room, and hurled his words at me; held up his sword, and said he should like to see my head on it. I have seen them murdering a priest, and meanwhile, not ten yards away, children and their nurses are playing at ball. What a country, and what people!"

That the Queen incessantly conspired to induce a foreign army to march into France, is very certain.

The King soon mistrusted Dumouriez, who at once offerered to resign his position of Minister. The King at once accepted, and another friend was lost by royalty.

On taking his leave, Dumouriez foretold what was to happen.

"Sire," said he, "you think you are about to save religion. You are destroying it. The priesthood will be killed; your crown will be taken from you; perhaps even the Queen and the royal children——"

Dumouriez could not finish the sentence

"I await—I expect death!" said the King, much moved; "and I pardon my enemies."

He turned away, with quivering lips.

Dumouriez never saw Louis XVI again.

He fled from Paris, and especially from La Belle Liégeoise, who, in her blood-colored dress, was now rising to utter power.

"Build the new parliament," she cried, "on the site of the Bastille, and let every woman give her jewels, that the gold may be coined to pay for the work."

And taking the golden earrings from her ears, the rings from her fingers, she cast them before her hearers.

Her power was so great, that during every sudden outbreak her "nod" condemned any man brought before her, to death; her "Let him go," set him at liberty.

She was mad for years before she was placed in the asylum where she ended her days, twenty years after the death of the King and Queen. Not a Frenchwoman, but born at Liége, she had been brought up respectably; she was even accomplished; but at seventeen she had fallen a victim to the snares of a young French nobleman.

Thus fallen, she threw herself into all shapes of debauchery; and when the Revolution broke out, she came to France, to hunt down and destroy the man who had destroyed her

This she did in the raging time to come, of which I have to tell, and she showed him no mercy.

Neither found she any mercy for herself. The furies of the Revolution—the *tricoteuses*—seized her, stripped her to the skin, and whipped her in public, as an obscene prostitute This act brought into active force the latent madness from which she had been suffering for some time. She was removed to a madhouse, and there she dragged through twenty years of life. In fierce memory of the indignity which had been put upon her, she would never put on any clothing, and so she lived, clutching the bars of her den, screaming, alternately, "Blood!" and "Liberty!"

It took twenty years to enfeeble her constitution, and to wear her life away into the peacefulness of death.

She was the greatest enemy the Queen had. She declared Marie Antoinette as frail as herself; for this demon in woman's shape insanely gloried in her condition. And when she gloried in this statement against the "Austrian"—the most opprobrious name the people could find to cast at the Queen—her hearers applauded loudly.

So the months drifted on, the events of every day darkening the fortunes of the royal family.

And now came the time when the palace was besieged. The King, looking from his window, saw the meeting of a huge crowd without any alarm: he was, by this time, accustomed to sudden crowds.

Again a soldier had led the way for the mob. An artillery officer, instead of obeying orders, and retiring his guns to defend the palace, pointed to its windows, and cried, "The enemy is there!"

Two minutes after, the people had got possession of the Tuleries.

The king—who, whatever his faults, was no coward—rushed forward towards the massive folding-doors, which the populace finding bolted, were breaking open.

As he approached, the panels fell at his feet. He ordered a couple of valets to open these folding-doors.

"What have I to fear," he said, "from my people?"

A ragged man rushed forward, and thrust a stick, pointed with iron, at the King. A grenadier of the guard struck it down with his bayonet. And now the man fell, whether in a fit or not will always remain a question. Certainly. as he rushed forward, he was foaming at the mouth. All that is known farther of him is this—that the mass pressing forward, he was trampled to death.

For a moment, the power of majesty was once more asserted.

He had left the Queen, the royal children, and his noble sister, Madame Elizabeth, in an inner room, and had ordered the door to be closed after him. This had been done.

The king now moved to another room, larger, pretending that there he could speak to a greater number of citizens. Suddenly, hearing a scuffle, the King turned, to find the mob surrounding Madame Elizabeth, who was endeavoring to reach the King's side

"It is the Queen!" screamed several fierce voices. And they were the voices of women

In a moment, they turned upon her.

The abhorred Queen was before them, as they thought. In another moment she would have been killed

"It is Madame Elizabeth!" cried the soldiers.

The mob fell back with reverence Even at that point they could respect Elizabeth, the purity and simplicity of whose life formed the one favorable point in the united lives of the royal family, and one to which the whole mass of the people gave implicit credence.

But she was to die with her family.

"Ah! what have you done?" she cried. "Had they been allowed to take me for the Queen, and have killed me, I had perhaps saved the Queen's life!"

By this time, about twenty of the King's friends stood about him, their swords drawn.

"Put up your swords," said the King; "this multitude's more excited than guilty"

"Where is the Austrian?" now resounded upon all sides.

The question which excited the multitude was against the priesthood, whose members, known to favor royalty, were abhorred by the people. The king had refused to sign an act by virtue of which the priesthood would have been annihilated.

A butcher, named Legendre. cried to the King, "The people are weary of being your plaything and your victim!"

Meanwhile, those who could not gain an entrance to the besieged palace called loudly to those within, "Are they dead? Show us, then, their heads!"

"Let him put it on!" cried the butcher, thrusting a coarse red cap of liberty towards the King on the end of a pike.

The King smiled, and put the symbol of liberty upon his head.

"Long live the King!" now cried some voices.

The people now called upon the King to restore Roland —Madame Roland's husband—to power, from which he had been dismissed.

The King was inflexible.

"This is not the moment for deliberation," said the King.

"Do not be afraid!" whispered a grenadier to Louis.

"My friend," said the King, "does my heart beat rapidly?"

And he placed the man's left hand upon his breast.

The pulsation of the King's heart was perfectly equable.

"If you love the people, drink their health!" cried a man in rags, pushing forward a common bottle.

The King smiled and took the bottle, saying, "To the nation!"

And now the cries of "Long live the King!" were so strong that they floated out upon the crowd waiting to see the King's body cast amongst them; and, instead, they learnt that once more the King had—if only for a time—reconciled himself to his people.

Meanwhile the Queen was undergoing her agony.

Only the conviction that she was more immeasurable hated than the King, prevented her from joining him before the people She feared her presence might exasperate the people beyond all control.

She remained in her bedroom, pressing her two children to her heart.

Suddenly, a beating at the door, and the screams of many fierce women, upon hearing the words, "The Austrian is there!"

But they had to call masculine help before they forced the door.

They found the Queen unprotected, except by her children, whose presence probably saved their mother from assassination.

Only a few ladies were with her, one of whom was that unhappy Princess de Lamballe, who would not remain in England, who returned to France, and who was one of the first to fall a victim to the Reign of Terror.

The Queen was found by the screaming crowd of women standing as I have described, in a bay window, while between her and the mob, a long, heavy table had been placed across the window.

By the Queen stood her daughter—near fourteen years of age.

The Dauphin—then seven years of age, and extremely handsome—was placed upon the table before her.

The men in the crowd were for the greater part silent; the women were implacable—one of these thrust forward a republican red cap, and told the Austrian to put it on Louis's head. This she did.

The child took it for a plaything, and smiled.

And now a pretty, rosy, youthful girl came forward, and using the coarsest possible language, upbraided the Queen savagely.

"Pray what harm have I done you?"

"Me?—perhaps not. But what harm have you not done the nation?"

"Poor child!" the Queen replied. "You but repeat what you have been told. Why should I make the people miserable? Though not born a Frenchwoman, my children are French, and I shall never see my native land again. I was happy when you loved me!"

The girl's head fell.

"I did not know you," she said; "and I see now that you are good!"

And now Santerre—good name for a leader of the people—approached,

"Take the cap off the child!" he cried; "don't you see that he is stifling?"

The crowd was tremendous.

And approaching the Queen he whispered, "You have some awkward friends here. I know of some who would serve you better."

This was the first intimation the Queen really had that there was a party amongst the people actually willing to raise the royal family they had so utterly degraded.

Five hours that torture lasted before the palace was cleared. The King and Queen had also been forced to put the national cockades upon their heads. When once more the royal house was free, the unhappy people could scarcely find strength with which to embrace

Several of the members of the National Assembly wept.

To one, Merlin, the Queen said, "You weep, sir."

"Yes, madame," he replied, gravely; "I weep over the misfortunes of the woman, the wife, and the mother; but, beyond this, my heart is stone. I hate kings and queens."

17

These words were the key-stone to French feeling. Louis XVI and his wife were driven to the block, not as a man and a wife, as father and mother—but as *King* and *Queen*.

CHAPTER XLIX.

THE KING QUITS THE TUILERIES.'

THE National Assembly had ordered the provinces to send 20,000 troops to Paris. With them they brought the revolutionary hymn, the "Marseillaise." It was written and composed by a young artillery-officer, named De Lisle. It was completed at the piano, after a night's bout. He fell asleep over the instrument, and at length awakening, gradually recalled the air and words of a song, the fierceness of which sent more French men and women to the block than did any other motive.

That song drove revolutionary France mad, and took from the royal family all hope of mercy.

The royal family, however, were still at the Palace of the Tuileries; and while they remained there, the semblance of royalty was kept up—albeit, in fact, they were utterly prisoners.

The Queen, early in August, still utterly relied upon Lafayette, who did not disguise his desire to retain the monarchy, under a protectorate—he himself to be the Protector.

"Mistrust Lafayette," had said Mirabeau; but the Queen's faith was strong, and her confidence hastened events.

However, one Gaudet, only twenty years of age, was rising to power amongst the Girondists; and he having intimated that he felt great interest in the royal family, matters were so managed that he had an interview with Marie Antoinette, who, poor lady, took him by the hand, and led him to the little cot in which her child was sleeping.

"Educate him to liberty, madame," said the orator. "It is the one condition of his life."

He kissed the child. Nine months afterwards he was one of those who sent the King and Queen to the scaffold.

The royal family were now prohibited from shutting a door, and so much did they dread poison, that they only pretended to eat of the dishes prepared and set before them, and really subsisted upon cakes, and other food brought to them in the pockets of their attendants, who purchased the eatables at obscure shops.

The Queen made the King wear as a breastplate fifteen-fold silk; but while the poor man complied, he said, "They will not assassinate me, but put me to death like a King, in open daylight."

He never appears to have thought of the possible execution of the Queen herself.

"He is no coward," she said of the King; "but he is calm in the presence of danger. His courage is in his heart, only it does not show itself—he is so timid."

The family now only showed themselves when going to church on Sunday, and then they were assailed with cries of "No King!" Louis said it was as though God himself had turned against him.

One night, a chamber-valet, who slept at the Queen's door, was awakened, to find an assassin, dagger in hand, stealing into the Queen's room.

Murders now became quite common. One D'Epremesnil, who had been a great favorite with the people, showed signs of moderation. Suddenly turned upon by the mob, he was cut down, dragged through the gutters, and was about to be thrown into a common sewer, when he was rescued by a squad of the National Guard. As he lay dying, Pétion, the Mayor of Paris, looked upon him, and fainted. Recovering his senses, the victim said to the Mayor, "And I—I, too, was once the idol of the people! May you meet with a better fate!"

The sound of the soul-stirring "Marseillaise" had maddened Paris. The hourly news of the march of the Prussians upon France fatally intensified that hatred of all who were favorable to royalty—a hatred which was now about utterly to burst all bounds.

An almost complete insurrection was adjourned to August 10.

It was said by the people that Marie Antoinette daily

cursed the people; that she had offered a pistol to the King, and prayed him to destroy himself : that she had vowed, sooner than leave the royal palace, she would be nailed to its walls.

In truth, she was battling with her natural royalty—defending the unemotional King, and endeavoring to take his place without intruding on his prerogative.

Meanwhile, the principal movers in the drama were being thinned by murder. Mandat, the commandant general, suspected of treachery rather than of duty, was shot down before his son's eyes, and his body was cast into the Seine.

On the morning of that terrible 10th of August, Madame Elizabeth, the King's sister, who had been watching through the night, listening to the ringing of that bell which all the Royalists knew was the tocsin of murder,—this pure-hearted Elizabeth called to the Queen.

" Sister," she said, " come and see the sun rise."

And Marie Antoinette looked for the last time upon a sunrise (it was typically blood-red) which she was to see through the palace windows.

To Rœderer, the deputy, was due the first suggestion of that act which was really the King's abdication—that of abandoning the royal palace, and asking hospitality of the Parliament.

" Place yourselves, madame," he said, " in the care of the National Assembly. Your persons will then be as sacred as the constitution."

The constitution itself was to be a thing of the past in a few weeks.

At five in the morning, the Queen had her children dressed and brought to her. The King himself, by his appearance, should have steeped the guard in confidence. He should have appeared in uniform. On the contrary, he appeared in a suit of violet silk—court mourning, in fact, without boots or spurs, in white silk stockings and pumps; while his hair presented an absurd spectacle, for it had not been dressed since the previous day ; and while one side was still rounded and curled, the other was flat and ragged. He looked about smilingly, but with that vagueness in which no reliance can be placed. He was simply a good, stupid, amiable man. He kept apart, all his reign, making locks; he forgot his people, and he was weak enough to suppose his people would forget him.

As for the Queen she was never more royal.

"Take these!" she said, seizing a couple of pistols and forcing them into his hands; "and conquer or die with your friends."

The King however, handed them to a gentleman by his side, saying, "No, if I wore arms, the people might be angry."

A royal progress was made in the court-yard of the Tuileries, even in the palace-garden beyond. At first received with faint applause, the cries of hate soon overwhelmed the King, and it was with difficulty he gained the palace alone.

The tocsin had now been calling to arms through many hours.

Meanwhile, Danton, the man of blood, was maddening the people

"To arms!" he cried. "Do you not hear the call?"

The infuriated people were now upon the palace.

They attempted once more to burst the doors, while the artillerymen refused to fire upon the insurgents.

And now the fatal but inevitable mistake was made.

"Sire," cried Rœderer to the King, "time presses. It is no longer entreaty we use, and only one means is left us. We ask your permission to use violence towards you; and, by force, to place you under the safety of the National Assembly."

The King still did not wish to leave the palace. He turned to the Queen.

"Let us go."

Never again did the royal couple step beneath the roof of that palace. They left it for a barred prison—that barred prison for the scaffold.

The King and the royal family were taken to the Assembly, and put in the reporters' box, amidst the reporters themselves.

There were few members present when the King entered the house, but it soon filled up. The heat was intense, and the King perspired frightfully. This box was supposed to be not in the Assembly, because a grating was placed before it. As the day went on, it was feared the people might break in from behind, and catch the King in this dungeon. It was, therefore, ordered that the grating should be removed; and the workers being unskilful, the King's knowledge in metal-work prevailing, he came forward, and helped at its removal; so that in the event of an attack by the people, whose menaces could be heard, the members of parliament might shelter the royal family by forming a living rampart around them.

This agony lasted fourteen hours; but it did not tell upon the King's heavy nature. At his usual hour, he was hungry, asked for food, and he ate a hearty meal as calmly as though he had passed some hours at lock-making. The Queen, who suffered dreadfully at the sight of this evidence of callousness on the part of the King, ate nothing, but drank a glass or two of iced water with much eagerness.

The people, learning that the King had left the palace, turned upon this building to destroy it—not to sack it. The Revolutionists were greedy for blood—not wealth. "Death to thieves!" was their implacable motto. The Tuileries were chiefly defended by seven hundred Swiss, two hundred badly-armed gentlemen, and one hundred National Guard. At the end of the day, not one-tenth of them remained alive.

The palace was forced. There stood a Swiss on guard, many files of comrades behind him. He had orders not to fire. The people hooked his belt with a pike, dragged him forward, and disarmed him. Another took his place; he, also, was disarmed. Five times was this episode repeated.

A shot was fired—some say, by a Swiss; others, by an insurgent; and this appears to have beeen the signal.

The people turned upon the five disarmed Swiss, and beat them to death. One man of huge stature and strength killed four. The Swiss were now ordered to fire. Many aimed at the huge man, and he fell with many more. In a moment, the hall was strewn with the dead and the dying. From that moment, the Swiss were doomed; though, for a short time, they were victorious; for the people were driven back.

Meanwhile, the rattle of the musketry echoed through the building in which the National Assembly were delibera-ting; and its cause soon became known.

"Long live the nation!" cried the parliamenterians,

glaring at the King, who, unhappy man, now helped on the massacre of his Swiss guards by sending a written order to their commander to cease firing, whatever happened. This was really their death-warrant; for fidelity keeping them near the King's person, fidelity would compel them to obey his last command—for this order was the last Louis XVI ever gave.

Suddenly, shots sounded close at hand. The members thought it was the Swiss guard, about to fire upon and massacre the National Assembly. In truth, it was the National Guard firing upon that division of the Swiss which had accompanied the King to the National Assembly.

"Now," cried the President, "is the time to prove ourselves worthy of the people, and of the position they have given us, by dying at our posts."

It was a false alarm; it was royalty dying.

The people now rallied, broke into the palace, and, maddened by the sight of the dead citizens in the great hall, charged the Swiss, who were serried on the grand staircase.

Upon those stairs they were driven, leaving comrades upon every step. The incline afforded good shooting to the people, who, when they had forced their way to the top of the stairs, had slain every soldier who had faced them. The Swiss guard died bravely to the very last man.

After that it was massacre, not fighting. Wherever a Swiss was found on guard throughout the palace, he was hacked to pieces. Many were thrown alive from the windows to the people below. Some few of these solitary Swiss sentinels showed fight; many threw down their arms, and either faced death unarmed, or uselessly asked for mercy.

Seventeen were found kneeling in the palace chapel. In vain did they show their fire-arms, which, clear and bright, proved they had not fired upon the people. They were foreigners; the news came hourly that all Europe was about to pour upon France, and they were killed before the very altar.

It is said the people had, to stimulate their bloodthirstiness, dissolved gunpowder in the wine and brandy they drank.

Not a Swiss escaped.

The Queen's women remained trembling in the palace.

One man alone defended their door, and fell—generous sentinel!

Danton was the very king of the massacre; and publicly he thanked the people for their day's work.

Meanwhile, calm, patient, implacable, Robespierre—he who was to conquer Danton—waited quietly abiding his time, but always feeling his way.

The Assembly soon learnt the true state of affairs; and, by their orders, a few Swiss were saved, by being hidden in the passages and cellars of the House of Assembly.

And now, the Revolutionists, eager for blood, but not for riches, brought before the National Assembly the spoils of the Tuileries. Sacks upon sacks of gold, plate, precious stones, costly ornaments, and even heaps of letters—even the money found upon the dead Swiss was set out in a separate pile.

The Girondists now felt that the time was come to abandon the throne. Vergniaud drew up an act for the *provisional suspension of royalty*. This was at once passed.

The King's fall was signed. A few hours before, he abandoned his palace. Now, by this Act, the King's authority was revoked; payment of money to royalty was stopped; and the National Assembly declared to hold possession of the persons of the royal family until happier times arrived.

This was virtually dethroning the King, and taking him prisoner.

And how did the King accept this news?

He smiled, and said jocosely, "This is not too constitutional!"

He was the only human being that smiled in that place upon that fatal day—he whose heart should have felt the heaviest weight of grief.

But the people around the building shouted for the King's life.

The people, however, must not be looked upon harshly. They had not stolen; and though many hundreds had been slain by them, they had lost three thousand six hundred men. The Swiss did not die unavenged.

Then the people went back to their work, tired of bloodshed, for a few days.

And the royal family were taken to the prison of the Temple, which three of them quitted only for the scaffold.

CHAPTER L.

THE MASSACRES OF SEPTEMBER.

THE wretched Queen's head and eyelids drooped for a moment as she heard the words which dethroned her husband; then, once again, her head was high and defiant. Together with the misfortune of the Austrian Hapsburg, she inherited their pride and courage. From that hour to the moment of her death, her courage never failed her. She appears to have equally forgiven and despised.

Events now followed with terrible rapidity. The Prussians entered France and the town of Verdun fell into their power. That humiliation brought about the massacres of September. The town council purposed their capitulation Then Colonel Beaupaire, the commandant, opposed it, and refusing to sign the capitulation. he blew out his brains at the council. His body was removed, the capitulation signed, the Prussians marched in, and the daughters of the principal inhabitants, strewed flowers before the foreign troops.

All of those girls—to be excused, by reason of their youth—were, during the Reign of Terror, sent to the guillotine.

Beaupaire's body was carried away by his men, who marched out of Verdun with all the honors of war, and to it was accorded a state funeral, while the heart was placed in the Pantheon.

Every day, Danton was rising into power.

Every day, Robespierre was following him, and marking him down with the vigor of a sleuth hound

It was he who organised the September massacres. On the 28th of August, a grave-digger, who knew the plan of certain catacombs, was awakened at six in the morning by a Government agent, and told to prepare this place. within ten days, for receiving a large number of bodies He was ordered to be silent, on pain of death.

On this same day, organised bands of fierce-looking men, springing no one knew whence, patrolled the streets. The gates of Paris were closed, so that no one could escape, though thousands had fled between the day of the King's first fall and this one, the 28th of August.

Every house was visited. Five thousand persons, suspected of leaning towards royalty, were seized during the following night. Every court-house, convent, prison, was overflowing with prisoners.

Robespierre still remained quiet and watchful—still lived in hiding in the house of good Duplay, the joiner.

On that night, Robespierre went to the apartments of St. Just, in the Rue St. Anne, and found him calmly going to bed.

"Why not?" asked St. Just. "Murder will be done to-night, but I cannot prevent it. And again, those who will die are our enemies. Good night."

He fell asleep. Awaking, hours after, he marked Robespierre, pale, haggard.

"Have you returned?"

"*Returned!*"

"What! have you not slept?"

"Slept!" cried Robespierre; "when the blood of thousands is being shed by hundreds of assassins—when pure or impure blood runs down the streets like water! Oh, no," he continued, with a sardonic smile; "I have not slept—I have watched, like remorse or crime; I have had the weakness not to close my eyes. But *Danton—he has slept!*"

On Sunday (of all days in the week), it being the 2nd of September, at three in the afternoon, the signal for the massacre was given, by one of those strange accidents with which we are all acquainted. Five coaches, filled with prisoners, were passing. These prisoners happened, by chance, to be all priests.

"See the friends of the Prussians!" cried one in the crowd. It was enough. The rage of knowing that the Prussians had conquered Verdun made them mad in a moment.

From that hour until four days were passed, murder was unceasing all over Paris. It was enough to look like a Royalist, and death followed.

Half the priests were killed in the carriages, before they reached the prison gates.

Inside those gates, as inside the gates of all the other ordinary or improvised prisons, sat the revolutionary tribunes, twelve fierce men, who decided rapidly the fate of the prisoner, while they drank and smoked.

They were chiefly in shirt-sleeves. However, here and there might be seen white-handed men, who evidently were the master spirits of those terrible juries, which, in their way, were merciful, for they did not condemn a prisoner to death. If acquitted, the decree was "Set this gentleman at liberty;" if guilty, "To the Force,"—a decree which was a pun, for there was a prison called La Force, while the word " force " may be said to be ' death," therefore, "à la force " conveyed to the prisoner the idea that he was to be conveyed to the prison of La Force. In this belief, when approaching the prison gate, he had no idea death was at hand. The gate opened, and he was delivered to the force of an organised band, who quickly despatched him. Each band of executioners was controlled by a hidden chief. They moved from prison to prison as the revolutionary juries sat, and they did their work with the steadiness of actual business.

The prison massacres began with the Swiss, at the Abbaye. They knew what was coming. They were one hundred and fifty. A young officer led the way. He was very young and beautiful, and the murderers fell back. He folded his arms. The bayonets came nearer. He rushed forward, grasped five or six of the bayonets in his arms, and fell upon their points.

They all died—their commander, one Major Redding being the last. He said he would see his men out. There were not enough wagons to carry the bodies to the catacombs, so they were heaped up until the return of the tumbrils.

Benches were set for women to see these massacres, and they and their children danced round the dead bodies.

At the " Abbey " prison the prisoners were shot down in the chapel, and while two priests, eighty and white-haired, were preparing them for death.

Some anticipated execution by suicide.

One Sombreuil, a prisoner, was condemned to death, and he was loosed to the mob. Bayonets were at his breast, when his daughter, who was waiting in the midst of the murderers, flung herself before him and asked for his life.

The crowd accorded it upon one condition—that she should drink a glass of blood, then flowing from one of the dying.

This she did, and saved him.

Another father and daughter, the Cazottes, left the prison together—he condemned, she free. But the daughter cried that she would die with him. So they spared both lives. So far, the national madness had not destroyed pity for women

The King's first gentleman, one Thierri, being pierced by a pike, cried, "God save the King!" and died, waving his hat as he was transfixed to the woodwork to which he clung.

A deputy of the National Assembly came to one of the prisons, to claim two prisoners; whom obtaining, as he passed from the prison, the murderers, eating as they sat on the bodies of their victims, asked him, "Are you tired of life?"

"No."

"Then see the heart of an aristocrat!"

The speaker tore the heart from the gaping breast of the dead man upon which he was coolly seated.

Yet these murderers refused all recompense. The first bands were men of comparative education; but, not being bred butchers, they soon sickened at the task, and left it to be continued by men of more iron nerves than theirs.

Blood had by this time, drenched nine prisons. From one alone, the tumbrils had removed one hundred and ninety bodies.

Sixty assassins; this was the number to be seen at each prison door, waiting for the blood of the aristocrats.

Meanwhile, one hundred and sixty heads fell upon the scaffold, some being those of women The poor Princess de Lamballe, the Queen's devoted friend, was not one of those saved. She had followed the royal family to the Temple prison, but she was torn from them after a few days. She was a very young widow, passionately loved by her father-in-law, who lived far away in the country. He forwarded 12,000*l.* to save her life, if possible. It was her want of courage, or, perhaps, ability to dissemble, which cost this poor lady her life. On September 3rd, she appeared before the tribunal. She had passed two days continually fainting; and when ordered with feigned brutality, by two National Guards to follow them she asked permission to die where she was. One of them leant down, and whispered, "It is to save you."

Upon coming before the tribunal, the sight of the blood all about deprived her of consciousness. It was long before she comprehended what was required of her.

"Swear the love of liberty and equality, and hatred of kings!"

"I swear the first," she said, "but not the second. It is not in my heart."

One of the judges whispered to her—"Swear everything or you are lost."

She remained silent.

"Well—when you go out, cry 'Long live the nation'!"

She nodded, but upon being led out by two men, one of them a leader in the massacres—one Girard Nicholas—upon sight of the dead bodies, she cried, "Good God! how horrible!"

Nicholas put his hand over her mouth. They had traversed half the street in safety when a drunken barber, trying to strike off her cap with his knife, wounded her in the forehead. The men about believed her condemned, and in a few moments she was dead, her head cut off, and set amongst the glasses on the counter of a wine-shop where they drank to her death. The barber then set the head upon a pole, and carried it in procession to the Temple. There the crowd forced an entrance, and insisted upon shewing the head to the ex-Queen.

The King was called upon to show himself to the people; and though an unknown friend endeavored to prevent Louis from seeing the head, the kind intention was foiled, and the King recognised the features. Marie Antoinette was now demanded, and she presented herself to the people; but the King active for once, saved his wife from the sight of poor Lamballe's head. She only learnt what had happened in the evening.

Three days' murders! At two other prisons, five hundred and seventy-five victims awaited burial. At the end of the three days, the murder of women was common. A beautiful girl, one of the people, having wounded her lover from jealousy, and he being a national soldier, she was burnt alive, under circumstances of peculiar atrocity, suggested by the wretched woman, "La Belle Heleise," whose advancing madness was her excuse. Her own time, when she was to be lashed by her own sex, was fast approaching.

A negro—a huge giant—was especially famous during these three days. He, it is said, killed over two hundred. He gave himself no rest; stopped only to drink wine, and, naked to the waist, was a fearful sight, seen, as he habitually was, with the fair head of a slain woman swinging in his left hand. At last, he himself was slain, but not for two years, during which, where blood flowed, he was ever to be seen. At the end, he said he had revenged himself, not upon the enemies of France, but upon the enemies of his race—*the whites.*

It is said ten thousand fell in those three days and nights.

The murderers began at last to turn upon one another. Especially was this the case with the bands who adopted death by burning.

A weaver—one Laurent—drew up a list of those it was intended to kill, and placed upon it the name of a tradesman, who refused to give him credit. The tradesman, having a friend in a member of the National Assembly, threw himself upon his protection. The name was erased, and Laurent's written above it; and when Laurent pointed to the tradesman at the place of execution, he was himself seized, and cast into the flames.

Meanwhile, the Prussians on the frontier were preparing to advance.

This threat of invasion gave the public sentiment an impetus towards panic, which there was no resisting.

The National Assembly, which was composed, for the greater part, of men of ripe age, was practially abolished by the constitution of a "Convocation," in which the majority of the men of power were under thirty, while amongst them, several were scarcely more than of age.

The King, once in prison, it has been seen how the fact was followed by the fearful massacres of September 2nd, 3rd, and 4th. Scarcely were they complete, than the men in power began to protest against their enormity, and it was endeavored to be shown, with some success, that these wholesale murders were perpetrated by a fierce organization of but comparatively few men, who cast this great shame upon France.

Certainly, the same men were at the doors of the various prisons, while the rough order established amongst them, far more clearly pointed to the operation of a secret society, than to the sudden unorganized rage of a maddened people.

The Convention was really divided into Girondists and Jacobins—the former led by Roland and Vergniaud, their party being distinguished by moderation, the latter, led by Robespierre (now rapidly becoming the leading man in the Revolution), Danton, and the miserable savage, Marat, who even condescended to attract the approbation of the lowest rabble, by wearing rags, as clothes, offensive from very want of cleanliness—a shape of vanity fortunately rarely to be found.

The life or death of the King was really the question of the Convention, it was the test of Royalty or Republican-ism, and no man knew this better than Robespierre. It was by the exercise of this knowledge that he rose to power—to that power, by the exercise of which almost all the men who had formed a portion of the National Assem-bly, who were members of the Convention which super-seded the Assembly, were sent to the scaffold before he himself mounted the fatal ladder

It was evident how things lay when the question of lodging the President of the Convention was mooted. It being proposed that he should lodge in the Tuileries, then called the National Palace, Tallien cried, " Why, out of this chamber, your President is but a plain citizen, there-fore, if he is wanted, let him be sought for in the garrets where, in general, only truth and virtue are to be found."

Danton and Robespierre were now mortal, although con-cealed, enemies. They knew that one must destroy the other—which ?

The theory of a republic was now declared ; it was the first step to the beheading of the King, to whom I will now return

The Temple, to which the royal family had been taken, was an old building, half monastery, half castle, which had once been one of the strong-holds of those monk-soldiers, the Knights Templars. It was composed of a couple of towers, one seventy feet high, the other much smaller, and a large space of ground, surrounded by a comparatively low wall. This enclosure contained many houses, and especially a very fine building, once the palace of the Templars themselves. Many of the windows of the surrounding houses, which formed part of the lowest quarter of Paris, overlooked these grounds, in which there was an avenue of chestnut trees, and a pretty garden.

The towers had not been used for almost hundreds of years, and the contents of their several floors were of the most wretched description The rooms themselves, built round a central staircase, were desolate in the extreme; while the walls being nine feet deep, the windows loopholes, and even these barred, it need not be said that the interior was never wholesomely light

The royal prisoners were taken to the old palatial building upon their arrival, and the poor King at once expressed a sense of relief at the serenity his wife and children now enjoyed, compared with the dangers they ran at the royal palace.

The family supped together, and the King, as usual, ate heartily. The municipals told off to watch the prisoners, stood during the meal, but this slight semblance of respect was soon to disappear

Louis chatted cheerfully as to what their life should be —how he would be his son's school-master—how the garden was large enough for exercise—how they should live, and employ the day. He even inspected the rooms, the beds, the linen; in a word, was once more the man he had always been—a rather quiet spirited, inquisitive, active, dull man.

But this respite lasted only during a few hours. The King had appointed the various bed-rooms, but before the Dauphin could be put to bed in the one set down as his, an order came from the authorities, ordering that the royal family should be lodged in the smaller tower.

They waited until after midnight before their new place of imprisonment was ready, and then themselves carried what was wanting to the tower. The King's servant asking where his master was to be lodged, the municipal officer replied, " Your master has been living under gilded roofs; he will find none here, and learn at the same time how we lodge the murderers of the people."

Madame Elizabeth was lodged in the kitchen, on the ground floor; the so-called Court on the second; the King, Queen, and children, on the floors above. The walls and the floors were bare, except for some obscene pictures on the walls, which the King took down, turning them to the wall.

The King went to bed, and fell asleep. Not so the Queen, who remained awake the whole night.

The next day, adapting himself to even these fallen circumstances, the King ordered the day's plans; and pushing about the room, came upon a small collection of books, chiefly Latin—a discovery which once more brought a smile of pleasure to his face.

Ten days afterwards, 20th August, and when the royal family had retired for the night, the noise of many advancing feet awakened them. The authorities of the prison came armed with orders from Parliament, to deprive the royal family of every attendant who had hitherto followed their fortunes. The agony the Queen experienced upon parting with the Princess de Lamballe was intense.

"From this night," cried Marie Antoinette, "I do date my captivity."

Within a fortnight, as I have related, the poor Princess de Lamballe's head was raised on a pike to the window of the Queen's prison. One Tison's wife was appointed to look after the Queen; while Simon, afterwards celebrated for his cruelty to the Dauphin, and Rocher, a mere brute, were the gaolers-in-chief.

It was Rocher who never passed by the Queen without blowing clouds of tobacco-smoke in her Majesty's face.

The walls of the Temple were ablaze with comments upon the royal family. Here might be read an attack upon Louis's stoutness, there a savage comment upon the Queen. Even the children were not spared. For instance, this sentence was scrawled upon the walls: "What are King's children? Whelps who ought to be strangled before they are old enough to devour the people."

The unfortunate captives at last dreaded to take the air; the guard saluted whenever a municipal passed by, but they reversed arms as the King went by.

At last, they limited the number of steps the royal family might take when exercising.

18

The upper windows of the house overlooking the prison were now the only consolation left to the unhappy royal captives But that comprehensive freemasonary of misery with which we are all somewhat acquainted, the friends of the fallen family, who were still at liberty, took the upper rooms, from which they could see their King and his family. The captives soon learnt, by almost indescribable signs, the windows which were friendly to them. This one would show a white flower; from another, a hand would be waved; and now and again a placard would be raised for a moment.

On the 24th of September, the King, having fallen asleep after dinner, was aroused by a great tumult in the street, below his window.

It was the people declaring the abolition of royalty, and the declaration of a republic.

"My kingdom," he said to the Queen, "has passed away like a dream, and it has not been a happy dream. God gave it me, and the people take it away. I pray that France may be happy."

On the evening of the same day, one of his gaolers asked the King brutally, if he knew that he was living in a republic.

"I have heard it," he replied; "and I have prayed that the republic may deal justly with my country. I have never placed myself between the people and their happiness."

So far, the King had been allowed to wear his sword and his heraldic orders.

"You must know," said his gaoler, "that the republic has suppressed these baubles; so take them off. You are now but a citizen, as we are, and must be as we are; yet, what you want, ask the republic for, and you shall not be denied."

"I thank you," said the King calmly. "I want for nothing"

Very calmly, he continued his interrupted reading.

Amongst the books he read at this time were "The Life and death of Charles I, of England," and the "Decline and Fall of the Roman Empire"

The Convention, however, had not behaved illiberally to the captives. The members assigned twenty thousand

pounds to their use; but very little was really expended in
the direction it was intended to go. The royal family were
wretchedly off for clothes. They had borrowed here and
there, and the Queen herself employed many hours daily
in mending and patching the clothes of the family, which
had been much torn during the day which ended in the
imprisonment of Louis and his family in the Temple.

The English ambassador, in fact, was the chief donor of
the clothes which enabled the royal family to be the pos-
sessors of a mere change of linen.

It is said that the wretched gaolers vied with each other
in making the fallen captives shed tears. That man who
succeeded was envied by his comrades. Well has it been
said that the success of a revolution which was the result of
generations of misgovernment, had fallen heavily upon those
royal personages who had least helped to produce the national hate of royalty, while that victory had of itself driven
the vanquishing people into madness.

But the last degradations had not been put upon the
Bourbons. Soon there came an order from the Convention,
to the effect that the King was to be utterly separated from
his family.

They were now to be debarred that last consolation of
the unfortunate—to suffer together.

The despair which ensued even moved the wretch, Rocher. But the order was imperative, and that night the King
was removed from the small tower, and was imprisoned in
the larger. He was now quite alone.

This occurred before the termination of September; and,
as though to make the desolation still more complete, the
whole family were utterly deprived of the means of writing,
even to each other. Not a scrap of paper was allowed—not
a pencil—not even a fragment of chalk.

The great tower was being repaired. All the accommodation offered to Louis was a bed and a chair, set in heaps
of brick and plaster rubbish, which overspread the floor.

Poor man! nature compelled him to be active; and,
therefore, being deprived of reading and writing materials,
he passed this first excruciating night of his acutest misery
in counting the steps of the sentinel as he passed up and
down in the corridor outside the King's cell.

This night, the King, for the first time, shed tears. His

only companion was a valet, named Cléry, who had been appointed by the municipal authorities when the King's servants were removed. He was a Revolutionist; but his heart was in the right place.

The one fragment of hope to which the king clung on this wretched night was the suggestion made by this valet, that as he had, since his appointment, dressed daily the hair of the ladies of the family, that he should be able to carry messages between them and the King.

Daylight dispelled this hope. It was intimated that Cléry was not to leave the tower—that the isolation of the King from all exterior communication must be complete.

When the man made application to this effect, the answer he scoffingly received was, "Your master will never see even his children again."

"'Tis an outrage upon nature!" urged the King, when he was visited by the authorities. "You murder five hearts in one—you do that, indeed, which is worse than murder!"

The authorities turned their backs upon the King, not deigning to answer him.

All that was brought him as food on that first morning of the separation from his family, was a piece of bread, and a pot of water, into which a lemon had been squeezed.

"They have forgotten we are two," said the King, advancing to Cléry, and breaking the bit of bread in half; "but I do not forget. Take this; the remainder is enough for me."

The servant refused, but the King insisted; and so the valet took it, and wept as he ate. The King also wept. What a picture to contemplate!—a king and a valet eating a fragment of bread between them, and tears falling upon the wretched meal!

The King again asked for news of his family, and a reply not forthcoming, he entreated that he might have some books given him to drive away the hours.

The Queen had passed the night in a series of fainting-fits; but, even at that pass, that far higher spirit than the King's, which had begotten her so much of the popular hate, still supported her. The King, though weeping, could eat half the morsel of bread—she resolutely refused to touch food.

This determination startled the municipals. They were answerable to the Convention for the prisoners. What if the Queen should starve herself to death?

"Well, they shall dine together to-day." said a municipal officer, "and to-morrow the Commune must decide."

The Queen, holding her children in her arms, flung herself upon her knees, and began rapidly praying—so also did Elizabeth.

"I believe," said the brutal Simon, "that these confounded women are even making *me* weep! Bah!" he added, turning to the Queen: "you did not let tears fall when you caused the people to be assassinated, on the 10th of August!"

"I never harmed human being," said the Queen.

The Commune decreed that the family should take their meals together. The members knew somewhat of Marie Antoinette's determination, and they found that, if separated from her husband, she really would die from inanition. It has to be recorded that the re-union of the King and Queen, during the last four months of their lives, was due, not to the pity, but the fear, of their gaolers.

But they only met at meals, and then they were compelled to speak French only, and in a loud voice. The children were never again allowed play about their father. This family was killed by inches. Their hearts were dead before the knife of the guillotine mercifully released them.

Cléry took pity upon them, and, at the risk of his own liberty and life, forwarded, by his wife, who was allowed to come and see him once a week, a line of farewell to this or that friend, from the King and Queen. These adieux, some of which still exist, are written with the stump of a pencil, upon the margins of printed pages, and which were torn from books.

The King's cell was, in a few days, set in something like order; but, with a refinement of cruelty beyond description, the walls were hung with a paper representing the interior life of prisons.

Now quite desolate, this is how the King spent his time. He rose at daybreak, and, kneeling, prayed for a long time. Then, the light quickening, he went to the window, and read the psalms for the day. After this, the King read what books he could obtain—he read many scores during his captivity—and this reading appeared entirely to occupy his mind. At nine, the family met, when he kissed them all on the forehead. After breakfast, he taught his son in various branches of knowledge. The Dauphin, precocious in misery, had by this time tested the dispositions of most of the sentinels; and when one he knew to be less brutal than the majority mounted guard, the poor child ran with the news to his mother, and he was happy for the day.

At two, the family again met, and dined. But the King dared not give way to the fine appetite which never deserted him at any period of his life, for he knew not only that the quantity of food he ate was recorded, and the amount spead over Paris, but that the Queen herself was exceedingly desirous that this weak point in the King's prison-life should not give cause to enable it to be said that the King's appetite in prison was so great that necessarily he must be hardened and callous to a degree.

After dinner, the King and Queen were allowed to remain for a brief time together—nay, they were allowed a pack of cards and a set of chessmen; but they were forbidden to speak in a low tone to each other, and a sentinel always kept the unhappy couple within view.

At four, the King generally fell asleep, when the family remained religiously silent.

At six, the lessons were re-commenced with the Dauphin, and these went on until supper-time, when the Queen herself undressed the Dauphin, who said, in a low tone, the following prayer: "Almighty God, who has created and redeemed me, I love you. Watch the days of my father and my family, and save us from our enemies, and give my mamma, and my aunt, and sister strength to bear all their trouble."

The Dauphin put to bed, the Queen read aloud to the King, her daughter, and Madame Elizabeth.

At nine, the king was conducted back to his prison, where he read until midnight, when he went to bed, and slept until daybreak. He, however, did not retire until he had learnt who was master of the guard for the following day. If the name was one associated with kindness, the King's heart was light, and he fell asleep with utter serenity.

The prison was very damp, and, after a time, the King

fell ill. Cléry watched him, and himself fell ill as Louis became convalescent. This valet, long after all was over, recounted some beautiful particulars of this illness.

The Dauphin would nurse him, and passed day after day in the man's sick-room, while the King himself would often come in the night, bare-footed, and merely in his night-dress, to see how the valet was progressing, or to give him medicine.

It being ordered that more bolts should be placed upon the doors of the tower in which the King was imprisoned, the mason employed to sink the holes in the stone-work into which the bolts were to run, going to a meal, and leaving his work tools upon the ground, the King took up a chisel, and began laboring at the means taken to strengthen his prison. The mason recognised the King at this labor.

" Ah," said he " when you leave this place, you will be able to say you worked at your own prison."

" And how shall I leave it " " asked the King, who suddenly drew his son towards him, and retired to his cell, where he paced up and down a long while.

The watch was intense. Every loaf of bread sent to the royal table was searched and broken, the fruit—the very kernel of a peach, upon one occasion split to find a letter."

A deputation arriving, asked the King whether he lacked anything.

" Yes," he said; " my wife and family want clothes—you see we are in rags."

Meanwhile, the King's cousin, the Duke of Orleans, who had become a Republican under the name of Citizen Philip Equality, uttered no word in favor of his royal cousin languishing in the Temple.

Another misfortune now fell upon the King. It will be remembered how fond the King was of lock-making. His master in the art, one Gamain, had loved the King dearly, but he turned upon the fallen monarch. It appears that prior to quitting the Tuileries, the King, being desirous of hiding certain treasures, and especially certain papers received from abroad, relative to the schemes in progress for helping the King by the invasion of France, he had worked with this blacksmith at the formation of a hiding place in the walls of the palace for the iron box, which contained these papers and valuables.

After the arrest of the King, Gamain fell ill of a slow consuming illness, probably low fever. when gradually he convinced himself that a certain glass of water the King had himself handed the locksmith, while they were both putting the finishing strokes to the hiding place, was poisoned, and that the King's motive was a conviction that the secret of these State papers could only be safe through his, the blacksmith's, death. This man must surely have been overpowered by delirium when such a conviction took possession of him. His illness continuing, the thought of revenge took possession of him; and finally, he denounced the whole affair to the Convention.

This act did more to send the King to the scaffold than any other process executed against Louis XVI. In the first place, the theory of the poison was at once accepted, and it appeared necessarily very feasible to a multitude ignorant of the question of poisons; and, in the second, no proof could be brought against Louis of conspiring with a foreign Power to invade France; an act which was treason —therefore one which, proved, called for the penalty of death.

Gamain led the way to the spot where lay concealed the hidden treasure, and upon papers found in that box Louis XVI was put upon his trial.

The King became accustomed to captivity—found it almost rest—rest which was disturbed only on December 11 (1792), when the noise of an approaching procession drew the attention of the royal family to their windows.

The King learnt that he was to be put upon his trial. Two hours afterwards, he was on his way to the Convention.

To him, the city appeared as though besieged. Every soldier around the royal carriage had had served out to him sixteen cartridges.

The King looked wretched. His razors had been taken from him, and his hair was rough and scrubby about his face. He had grown thin, and his clothes hung miserably about him. But he was quite unmoved.

He took his seat quietly before the Convention.

"Citizens," cried the President, "Louis Capet is at the bar. You are about to give a lesson to kings."

The accusation was then read. It accused him of high treason in calling upon the foreigner to enter France.

He listened quite unmovedly until he was accused of "shedding the blood of the people." He raised his eyes to heaven It was clear he had not anticipated being called a sanguinary prince

At the close of the first day's examination, the King's fatal appetite failed him, and he refused an offer to obtain refreshments; but almost immediately afterwards, seeing a soldier gnawing a piece of bread, he asked for a part, and ate it with relish.

Upon the return-ride to the Temple, he counted the number of streets.

It was the King's sister, Elizabeth—a veritable angel,—who foresaw what was to happen.

"Was the Queen mentioned in the indictment?" she asked.

"No," replied the King.

"Thank heaven!" said the good Princess; "for if the Queen were taken, who, then, should look after these children?"

These very words foretell what the Princess foresaw—that if the Queen's blood was demanded, her own would follow.

CHAPTER LI.

THE KING'S TRIAL PROCEEDED WITH.

THE King had scarcely quitted the Convention upon the occasion of his first appearance there, than he was accorded the privilege of even the commonest prisoner on his trial—that of choosing two counsel for his defence. The King chose two—one named Trouchet; the other, Target. The former willingly accepted the office: the second dreaded to appear as the accomplice of the King; and wrote a cowardly letter, saying, to defend Louis Capet would be to outrage his own principles But this precaution, so far from saving him, marked him out to the terrorists as a man who was a coward, and in his turn, he was drafted to the scaffold, undefended and unlamented.

An old man, and a great one, of a family notorious for
their wisdom and their justice—one Malsherbes, aged
seventy-four, and who had served twice as a Minister during Louis XVI's reign—took the position offered to the
wretched man, Target, and refused by him.

Indeed, he asked for it. The act is well worth admiration. At seventy-four, when most men are weary of life,
this good man asked for a position which he knew was one
which might involve the forfeiture of his own existence.
Said he, " I was twice summoned to the council of him
who was my master at a time when everybody was ambitious of the post, and I owe him this service now that this
office is, in the eyes of most persons, one of danger ; and
had I the means of acquainting him with my wishes, I
should not seek another mode of striving to serve him " (he
was speaking to the President of the Convention) ; " but I
think, seeing the position you hold, that you can most
safely convey to Louis XVI my desire to serve him."

The Convention, violent as were its members, reverenced
this devotion of friendship, and honest Malsherbes was
appointed to the task of defending the fallen King.

" Malsherbes," said a friend to him, as he was leaving
the Convention, "you are the friend of Louis XVI ; how
can you bring him papers in which he will read the expres-
sions of the wrath of the people against him ? "

" The King is not like other men," returned M. de Malsherbes. " He possesses a great mind, and such faith as
raises him above all things."

" You are an honest man," replied the friend. " But if
you were not, what is to prevent you from bringing him
poison, as a weapon, or advising him to commit suicide ? "

Malsherbes hesitated for a moment, and then he replied,
" If the King were of the religion of the philosophers—
were he a Cato or a Brutus—he might kill himself. But
he is pious—he is a Christian—he knows that religion forbids him to lay violent hands upon himself, and he will not
commit suicide."

Malsherbes went daily after this to see the King, to commune with him upon the defence which was to be set up.

But of what avail was any defence ? The question was
not whether or not the King was guilty, but whether or
not his death would be of advantage to the establishment
of the republic.

During these final days of his life, the King was entirely deprived of the consolation of seeing his family. He was now kept completely isolated. However, by the mercy of Cléry, his servant, on the one hand, and that of Turgy, the Queen's attendant, on the other, the desolate couple communicated. A few words were written on a morsel of thin paper, which, being folded, a needle was run through it and it was in this condition concealed in a hank of sewing-thread, which was put in the Queen's work-box by Turgy, who placed the thread, and its answering line, in Cléry's way, who conveyed it to a place where the King would look for it.

Louis XVI never had any doubt that he would be executed. On the other hand, he does not appear, up to the time of his trial, to have assumed for one moment that the Queen would suffer.

Before his sentence was pronounced, he made his will. It is a long document. Here are some of the chief lines in this testament :—" I, Louis XVI of that name, and King of France, confined for four months in the Tower of the Temple, at Paris, by those who were my subjects, and deprived during eleven days of all communication with even my family, and, moreover, implicated in a trial, the outcome of which no man can with certainty foresee—for who can measure the passions of men ?—having no one, save God, as a witness of my thoughts, or to whom I can address myself, do here declare, in His presence, this my last will and testament. I bequeath my soul to God, my creator, and pray that, in all his mercy, he will accept it. I die in the faith of the Church, and bow to its laws. I pray the good Lord to forgive me as I have forgiven. I have striven hard to remember some of my sins, and to abominate them. I bow before God. I beg all that I have accidentally injured—for by my will I never hurt human being—to forgive me the harm they may believe I have caused them.

" I pray all men of charity to add their prayers to mine. I pardon, from the bottom of my heart, all those who are my enemies, without that I have given them cause to be other than my friends ; and I ask God to pardon them also, for they know not what they do. I also pray pardon for those whose zeal in my cause has done me so much harm. I recommend to God my wife and children, my sister, my aunts and brothers, and all those belonging to me through blood, or by any other way   I pray heaven to look pityingly upon my wife, and children, and sister, all of whom have too long suffered with me, and to strengthen them if they lose me, so long as they shall remain in this world.   To my wife I recommend my children, whom she has never ceased to love ; and I pray my wife to teach her children to look upon the pomps and vanities of this world—if they should be so unfortunate as to suffer them—only as dangerous and vanished possessions, and to turn their thoughts to eternity. And I pray my sister to be gentle as ever to my children, should they have the misfortune to lose her."

This is the first time, in sooth, the King betrays the least intimation of his fears that his blood will not suffice to appeased the national rage.   And even here it may be doubted whether Louis does not rather refer to natural than violent death, for the Princess Elizabeth was younger than the Queen.   It will be seen that, even at this pass, and solemn moment, the King has not the least thought that the Princess herself will be despatched below the knife of the guillotine.

The King's will continued ·—

" I pray my wife to pardon me all she has suffered, and will suffer, on my account, and all the sorrow I may have caused her in my life, as she may be certain I forgive her if she can possibly suppose that she has ever caused me a grief.

" I pray my children, after their love to God, which is above all, to love one another, and to live in peace ; to be grateful and obedient to their mother ; and in memory of me, I pray them to look upon my sister as their second mother.

" I pray my son, should he be so luckless as to become King, to forget the troubles I shall have passed through, and to forgive the people, who know not what they do, that which they will accomplish.   Let him not forget that he was born for the happiness of his subjects ; that he can only reign safely by upholding the laws ; and that he can only do this while his power lasts.   Once let him lose power, and he becomes more injurious than ever he was useful ; and, above all, let him remember the load of debt I owe to the children of the men who have already fallen in defending my cause."

[These words are obviously the result of Louis's study of the history of England, of the stigma that rests upon the memory of Charles II. through persistently ignoring the just claims of the children of the men who had died in the cause of his beheaded father, Charles I.]

The King concludes his will by recommending Cléry to the Convention, and asking that the sword, purse, jewels, and other ornaments taken from him may be given to that person after the writer shall be dead.

He signed the will "Louis," as though he still reigned.

This will is sublime in its simplicity; its Christianity, pity, regret, and massive setting aside his life as past away, are all very beautiful points, while the belief that his death would compensate all, and that the country would not visit his faults upon the heads of his family, shows still an amount of faith in his people which is truly touching.

Upon the defence being read, the King found it opened with an appeal to the people, and a description of the wretched condition of the royal family. The two counsel and the King, who were the only people who heard this defence read, and which had been put into form by the reader, Desèze, were all moved at the beauty of the language.

But the King was inflexible.

"All that must be struck out," he said.

And he insisted—for was he not a dying man? The wishes of the dying are obeyed.

After the reading of the defence, the King being left alone with Malsherbes, he was tormented by the thought that he could not compensate his counsel for their labors.

"Desèze and Trouchet," he said, "owe me nothing. They gave me their time, exertions, and, perhaps, their lives, and I cannot pay them. Even if I leave a legacy, it will not be paid. Again, what could pay such work as theirs?"

"Sire, you have the power of repaying them."

"How?"

"Take them, for one mere moment, to your heart."

So, next day, when the two gentlemen came, he held open his arms, and pressed these brave men, one after the the other, to his heart.

This was all that he had to bestow—a royal accolate, the peaceful kiss of a dying man.

At this second examination, they gave the King a suit of

clothing, in which he looked at worst passable. But another shape of indignity was put upon him: he was kept waiting in a cold waiting-room during a whole hour.

The King was advised not to shave, that the savagery of his gaolers in even depriving him of so common a necessary as a razor should move his judges. But the King refused to avail himself of this theatrical effect. He was rather fitted to fall with dignity into the repose of death, than to war, fight, battle for life.

Louis XVI forgave the men who were to condemn him before they tried him; but his very pardon became his most perfect revenge in the eyes of posterity.

The King's counsel spoke logically, but with no power of words. Having finished, Louis XVI, who had followed his advocate as though rather interested for this gentleman than for himself, rose and uttered these words:—

"You have now heard the grounds of my defence, and I shall not repeat them. In speaking to you for the first, and perhaps the last, time, I declare that I can accuse myself of nothing; that my advocate has spoken the truth, and nothing but the truth. I never feared that all I did should be make public, but I grieve that you accuse me of spilling the blood of the people. And that the misfortunes of the 10th of August are attributed to me. I had thought that the numerous evidences of love for my people which I have shown would have placed me above such an accusation. This is not the case, and I must bear with what has happened. I declare that I exposed my life to save the shedding of one drop of the blood of my people."

He turned, and left the chamber.

"Let him be judged!" cried Bazere.

"'Tis time the nation learns if she is right in wishing to be free, and if this is a crime!"

"I ask," cried Languinais, "that the sentence be declared by a ballot of all France!"

"To prison with Languinais!" cried many voices.

"You are too openly a Royalist," cried Thuriot.

"Why," cried another, "he wills to try us, and make Louis himself judge"

"And I say," replied Languinais, fearlessly, "that you constitute yourselves accusers, judges, jury, and executioners. Let the people declare themselves! Let there be liberty of speech, to declare whether the King shall live or die."

"Down with him!" cried a voice.

"You shall hear me," cried Languinais.

"Put him upon his trial! place him in the dock, and let him instantly be tried!"

"To prison with him!"

Silence was at last restored; but when Languinais sat down, he knew he was a condemned man—he knew nothing could save him.

Meanwhile, in an antechamber, where the murmurs of his judges were audible, the King's counsel were endeavoring to cheer him with a little hope. The people had demonstrated with somewhat of kindly feeling in favor of the King at various theatres.

On his return to the Temple, the King having nothing of value with which he could partially repay his counsel, took off his laced cravat and gave it to Desèze.

On the 1st of January, after the French fashion of wishing friends a happy new year, Cléry approached his master's bed and offered him best wishes for the continuance of his life.

The King put his hands together and prayed, for he remembered that this was the day in the year when his thousand courtiers flocked to his palace to congratulate him.

Rising, he sent to ask if his daughter was better (for the Princess was ill), and to wish the Queen *a happy new year.*

From the first to the 16th of January, he was kept immured in the great tower of the Temple, perfectly isolated No one was allowed to see him, not even one of his family. The fallen King passed his time reading the history of England, especially the volumes of the life and execution of Charles I—history which appeared to fascinate him.

Meanwhile, the members of the Convention were daily disputing the question of the King's life or death.

St. Just now rose to the surface. Unpityingly he cried, "If the King is innocent, the people are guilty. You have declared martial law against the tyrants of the whole world, and spare your own. The Revolution only begins where the tyrant ends "

Another cried, "If with this, my hand, I alone could strangle all tyrants, I would not hesitate to rid the world of them."

But the rising party in the house lived by favor of the eager revolutionists, whom they dared not oppose. With them it was necessary that the King should die.

Another, upon another day, cried, " We have lost three hours this day talking of a thing they call a King. Are we, then, revolutionists? No; we are vile slaves."

Camille Desmoulins stuttered, " Let him be killed, with this word on his brow—' Tiaitor !' and this on his back— ' King !' "

Another cried, " Henceforth, let murderers and thieves be buried in the royal vaults !"

At length the Convention agreed to the plan of every member of the Convention voting upon these three questions :—

1. Is Louis guilty?

2 Shall the decision of the Convention be submitted to the ratification of the people.

3. What shall be the sentence?

To the first question, nearly seven hundred as against about a dozen, voted " Yes."

On the second, two hundred and eighty voices voted for the appeal to the people; four hundred and twenty-three against it.

It was now (January 16) that Danton first betrayed his insatiable thirst for blood

" I thought," cried he, " we were assembled for other purposes than those of the drama."

" 'Tis a question of liberty !" cried several voices.

" Question of liberty ? " cried Danton. " 'Tis a question of a comedy—that taking off the head of a tyrant with the axe of a King! I demand that we do not separate before we have pronounced sentence upon Louis ! His accomplices have fallen without delay, therefore let him fall at once !"

Everything declared in favor of Louis's death by this same January 16. On this day itself, a poor fellow named Louvain, who had been one at the taking of the Bastille, venturing to say that the republic ought to be established without the death of Louis XVI, a friend and companion near him plunged his sword into his breast.

In the evening, a book-pedlar, suspected of royalism, leaving a public reading-room, was accused by the people of distributing pamphlets in favor of the King's cause. He was assassinated with thirty dagger-thrusts.

Upon this day the soldiery swept over Paris, brandishing their swords, singing patriotic songs, and looking eagerly for the least signs of opponents.

In a certain church in Paris, the hearts of past-away kings were kept in silver vases. These were seized and broken open, and the contents cast into the common sewer.

At the Hall of the Convention a fearful scene was progressing—the voting upon the sentence. It is night-time, and the hurriedly raised black hangings suggest more an execution than a place of justice. The Convention is held in an old monastery—dark, drear, and wretched. A few scattered lanterns make the darkness visible, and throw a pale light upon the faces of passers-by. At the two principal entrances are cannon, the attendant artillerymen with the continuously lighted fuse in hand. The cannon is there rather to be turned upon the members of the Convention than to intimidate the people.

"*Its death—or thine!*"

These were the words each Conventionist heard as he passed into the Hall—words uttered in whispers, but which shook the hearers as though they were thunder.

Persons who knew the various members were present, who received them and commented upon their opinions. As Danton, Marat, Robespierre and Camille Desmoulins passed, the ranks showed all the signs of respect. Others were threatened. Languinais passed through a forest of thrusting pikes to reach the voting table.

The Hall itself was very dark, the benches being filled with young and beautiful women of the people class. Before them were a number of butchers, reeking from their slaughter-houses.

Fifteen hours had the deputies sat—few remained. Of those present, some were in little groups—others had fallen asleep.

The first votes left everything in uncertainty. *Death* and *Exile* were voted alternately.

Verginaud, the leader of the Girondists, who had sworn to save the King's life, whose vote would control that of all the Girondists, voted "*Death!*"

The King was doomed, because the Jacobins were all certain to vote "Death" to a man.

19

Robespierre started, and Danton said, in a low, scoffing voice, " These are your orators ! "

The last man but one called to vote was the King's cousin, the Duc d'Orleans, Philip Equality. It was thought the ties of nature and of blood would compel him to vote for exile.

He said these words :—

" My thoughts being fixed wholly upon duty, convinced that whoever shall now or hereafter attempt to establish monarchy in this land is worthy death—I vote *death !* "

This man, this monster to his own blood, had in early youth been so abject a coward, that, during a naval engagement between the French and English, he had gone down into the cock-pit, whence no one could induce him to remove until the action was over. The cowardice of his youth was well supplemented by his voting the King's death.

Even Robespierre condemned him. Returning to Duplay's house in the evening, he said, " The miserable man ! He was expected to listen to the pleadings of his own heart, and vote exile ; but he would not, or dared not. The nation despises him henceforth ! "

The monstrous act did not save him from the Reign of Terror. He died on the scaffold—the most guilty wretch who there ended life.

Followed the man Orleans, a deputy, lying on a handbed. He was dying, and he voted *death !*

A herald arrived from the King of Spain, interceding for the King's life.

Danton rose to speak, without the Speaker's permission.

" Thou art not yet King, Danton ! " cried a voice.

" I am astounded at Spain's insolence ! " cried Danton. " I desire that war against Spain be immediately declared ! "

The intercession damaged, rather than benefited, the royal cause.

The scrutiny of the votes now commenced.

Three hundred and thirty-four voted for exile or imprisonment.

Three hundred and eighty-seven voted for death. Thus *death* was in a majority of fifty-three ; but, by subtracting from this number the forty-six voices which had also voted a suspension of the execution of death, the majority in favor of *immediate death* was *seven!*

The Girondists, who did not wish for the King's death, had voted his execution, and thereby favored their enemies, the Jacobins, whose thirst for death was unquenchable.

On the morning of the 19th January, Louis, who had been by this time restored to his family, saw Malsherbes approaching him. The old man fell on his knees.

"I see," said the King; "Death!"

———————————————

CHAPTER LII.

NEAR THE BLOCK.

THE King, learning that he was to die at once, became a man almost heroic.

With calm curiosity, and as though making inquiries concerning the affairs of another man, and not of his own, he learnt the particulars of the voting; and he made special inquiries concerning the votes of various members of the Convention.

"Pétion and Manuel," he said,—"I am sure they did not vote my death?"

No answer returned.

"And my cousin, the Duc d'Orleans,—how voted he?"

Malsherbes bowed his head.

The King now exhibited the first signs of pain—of agony.

"That vote affects me more than all the rest."

This was as the words of Cæsar, falling, "And *you*, too, Brutus?"

Here a posse of authorities arrived, to announce his sentence to the King, with all the pomp and display of circumstance.

The King stood up, his head erect, his eyes upon his judges, and he listened to his fate—*death within twenty-four hours*—with the intrepidity of a brave man. One look towards heaven, as he heard the words which curtailed his life, and then he was once more facing his enemies.

The communication read, the King advanced, and, taking it, put the document very calmly into a little portfolio.

"Sir," he said to the officiating minister of the Convention and speaking half royally, half supplicatingly, "I request you to deliver this letter to the Convention."

The secretary hesitated to take the paper.

"I will read it to you," said the King; and he commenced. "I demand from the Convention three days, in which to prepare my soul for God, I require freely to see the priest, whom I am about to name, and that he be protected while extending to me the charity of his holy office. I demand to be freed from the shameful watchfulness which has surrounded me now for many days past. I ask, during these my last moments, leave to see my family when I will, and without witnesses. And I pray most earnestly that the Convention will at once take into consideration the fate of my family; and that they may, after my death, at once be allowed to go whither they will. I recommend to the love of the nation all persons who in any way have claims on me. These are, many of them, old men, and women, and children. Many of them must be in want."

These words show that even at this point the King had not the least thought of the popular vengeance going beyond himself, and falling on the Queen. He cannot comprehend that they will kill women and children—his faith in loyalty and manhood is too strong to admit of any such suspicion in his breast. The faults of Louis, those rather of apathy than action, were many; but he was a brave and loyal gentleman, who certainly could not comprehend cowardice.

The name of the minister for whose holy office the King asked, and which was written upon the separate piece of paper, was Abbé Edgeworth de Fermont—a gentleman descended from a good Irish family.

The secretary took the two papers; whereupon the King bowed, as though dismissing his ministers at Court, thereby intimating his desire to be left alone.

The minister retired.

When they were gone, the King walked up and down his prison with a firm, steady step. Suddenly he looked up—his fatal appetite, that scourge of the Bourbons, was upon him—and asked for his dinner.

It was served without a knife—a spoon replacing that utensil He was far more indignant at these precautions than at hearing his death-warrant read.

"Do they think me such a coward," he cried, "as to deprive my enemies of my life? Do they think if a knife is given me to feed with, I shall save the guillotine the trouble of destroying me? Poor creatures! I am accused of public crimes—I have committed no crimes; and, therefore, why should I so much fear death as to anticipate its terrors. I die innocent, and therefore, fearlessly. I would that my blood might atone for France, and that thereby the troubles I foresee coming be averted."

At six o'clock, Garat, the reader of the sentence, and Santerre, had an interview with the King, to bring the answer of the Convention to his commands.

The Convention had decided that no farther time should be given to the King. A few members had shown some sentiment of mercy. The reply was the exhibition of half a dozen sabres on the part of the fiercer deputies, who declared that if these men who pleaded for the concession of the King's request were not silent living, they should be mute dead.

These courageous men, however, fought the good fight of pity through five hours.

A majority of thirty-four refused all delay.

One man, Kersaint, protested with a reckless nobleness of courage, which has placed him in the rank of great heroes.

He gave in this written protest:—

"CITIZENS,—

"It is impossible for me any longer to support the disgrace of sitting in the Convention with blood-thirsty men, when their opinion, aided by terror, prevails over that of good men. If the love of my country has forced me to endure the misfortune of being one in a body of men amongst whom there is a section who applaud the murders of September, I will at least defend my memory from the charge of having been their accomplice. I have but the present moment in which to do this act; to-morrow it will be too late."

The Convention was angered, not confounded, by this

language. The Minister of Justice was charged to inform the Citizen Louis that he could see the priest whom he had named, and that he could see his family without any interference by his gaolers,—but that on the morrow he must die.

The King accepted the decision without a murmur; for he did not so much battle for those days' longer life, as ask for a few hours' pause between life and eternity.

He asked Malsherbes to seek the priest.

" 'Tis a strange request to make to one of the school of philosophers," he said, with a smile; " but I have always preserved my faith as a curb on my power as a King. As a consolation in mine adversity, I have proved it in the depths of my prison; and if ever you should be sentenced to a death similar to mine, I trust you may find the same solace in your last moments."

The Abbé Edgeworth and the ex-King were old and fast friends. The priest did not hesitate a moment, and at once hastened to the prison, albeit he knew that the probability was that he would never be free again.

Abbot Edgeworth was taken from his obscure lodging, in the first place, to the Convention, where many of the members made a demonstration in admiration of his courage; for, by this time, to be a priest was to be in danger of death.

With the fall of the King's head, the utter Reign of Terror was to commence.

Garat, while in his carriage, conveying the Abbot to the Temple, broke out into admiration of the King.

"Great heavens!" he cried, "with what a terrible mission am I not charged! What a man is this Louis XVI—what resignation he shows, and what courage! No mere human strength could give such force; in this there is something of the supernatural."

The priest remained silent; he hesitated to betray himself.

Not a word more was said up to the moment when the carriage stopped at the Temple.

The Abbé remarked that the first room through which they passed was filled with armed men. Thence they passed to a larger apartment, which the Abbé saw had been a chapel; but the signs of religion had been swept away—the altar was broken in pieces.

Here the Abbé was searched for weapons by a number of rough men, while the minister passed up into the King's cell.

When the Abbé followed him, the old man fell at the King's feet, and burst into tears, with which the King mingled his own.

" Pardon me," said Louis, raising him, " this is indeed weakness ! I have so long lived amongst my enemies, that I have grown to think little of their hatred, and my heart has grown hard and callous. But the sight of an old friend restores to me that tenderness which I thought was long since dead, and I weep in spite of my will to be unmoved."

Then, taking the priest by the hand, he drew him into the little turret which served him for a studio. In this room, all that was to be found consisted of a couple of chairs, a small earthenware stove, a few books, and an ivory crucifix.

" I have," said he to the Abbé, " arrived at that moment in my life when I must earnestly seek to make my peace with heaven, so that I may humbly hope to pass from a weary life to one of peace and quietude."

With these words, he produced his will, and read it over twice to the Abbé, electing him as his judge in this final act of life. He feared that, in the very act of pardoning his enemies, he might accuse them, and he was specially desirous that any appearance of this nature should be avoided.

His voice only faltered when he spoke of the Queen, his sister, and his children. He lived now only in the love he had for his family; apart from them, he had resigned all thoughts of life.

A calm conversation ensued. The King inquired after many old friends; speaking, not with the air of a man who is vanishing into death, but with the appearance of a man who, after absence, asks eagerly for those he loved and left behind.

Hour after hour passed away, and still the Abbé waited for the King to give an intimation that he wished to pray with the minister.

At seven, he was to have his last interview with his family ; and as this moment approached, he appeared to dread it far more than the thought of the scaffold.

He was unwilling that so great an agony as this parting must necessarily be, should trouble the calmness of his death, which, obviously, he looked upon in the light of a sacrifice.

The Queen and princesses had the news by this time, for the street criers bawled the fact of the next day's execution of the King under the very windows of the Temple tower. All hope was dead; and the only sentiment which swayed them was this: would the King be prevented from taking a last good-bye—would he be prevented from kissing them, and blessing them, before he went forth to die?

One last word—one last kiss!—this was now the boundary of the wishes of the once brilliant Marie Antoinette, one of the proudest princesses, and, as a wife, one of the greatest martyrs, the world has yet seen.

At last the members of his family were told that they were to see the King prior to his execution. And this was their joy in the midst of a desolation from which their only relief was death itself.

The poor creatures prepared for this interview hours before it could take place. They asked incessantly of their gaoler if it was time for the King's arrival, and bore patiently with the rough, rude answer only too frequently bestowed upon them.

The King himself, though apparently more calm, was equally agitated. He had never experienced but one affection—that for his wife; but one friendship—his sister's; but one joy—his children. The cares of the throne may have hidden much of these qualities, but never extinguished them; and, in his adversity, they had flowed back in the shape of a wealth of consolation

Nevertheless, the King's calmness, almost callousness, appears amazing in its contemplation. Re-entering the ordinary room, or cell, in which he passed his imprisoned days, he began to set in order to receive the Queen.

"Bring some water, and a glass."

Cléry pointed to a caraffe standing on the table.

"No," said the King; "it is iced; and I fear, if the Queen drinks it, that it may disagree with her."

The door, at last, was thrown open, and the Queen, leading her son, threw herself into his arms, and was about to lead him to her chamber.

"No, no," whispered the King; "I may only see you here."

Madame Elizabeth followed, leading the Princess Royal.

Cléry closed the door upon the family; and, for the first and last time since their return to Paris from Varennes, they were *unwatched*. The King was almost dead, and dead men can do no harm, even to revolutionary authorities.

The King gently forced his wife to sit on his right, while his sister he placed on his left; and, as he sat down between them, they put each an arm about his neck, and laid their heads above the heart which, in a few hours, was to cease beating. The Dauphin was on his father's knee, while the little daughter's head lay in her father's lap.

It is said that for more than half-an-hour not a word was spoken, but the sudden bursts of grief, and especially the Queen's frantic, terrific screams, were heard not only throughout the prison, but positively in many of the streets adjacent to the gaol.

Yet nature is very good, and enables us to bear our trials by the force of physical weakness. But soon, indeed, the miserable family, their eyes exhausted of tears, were able to talk in low whispers, to console each other, and to give each other many agonized last embraces. This dread agony lasted through an hour and a half. The ex-royal family had been together two hours.

Of those five unhappy people, only the little Princess, aged seven or eight, lived to tell in after years, what happened at that interview. They confided to each other what they had thought about during their separation; repeated promises over and over again to forget and forgive all their enemies, should either of them ever come to power; and, finally, sublime prayers, offered by the King, to the effect that he trusted his death might cause the nation the loss of not one drop of blood. The directions he gave his son (so soon to follow him into the grave) were not royal, but, better, they were Christian.

Those who listened—miserable creatures—heard only a low, sweet murmur.

At last the King rose.

The moment had arrived.

The Queen threw herself at the King's feet, and entreated him to allow her and her children to remain with him all night. This request, in mercy, he would not grant;

but warded off the request by gently intimating that he must have some hours' tranquillity, in which to gain strength to die fittingly.

He, however, promised his family that they should see him at eight in the morning.

"Why not at seven?" asked the Queen.

"Very well—at seven," he replied.

"You promise?" cried the women and children.

He then led them to the door—they uttering louder cries as he did so.

"Adieu, adieu!" he cried, in a voice equally yearning after passing-away love, and an expression of hope in the future.

The poor little Princess here fell inanimate at her father's feet. The attention the Queen now gave the child ameliorated the agony of that parting.

The King availed himself of the heart-rending event to turn away. He closed the door, and the agony of royalty was ended.

"Ah!" he cried, entering the turret, where the Abbé Edgeworth was awaiting him, "what a scene! Alas! why do I love so deeply—why am I so deeply loved?"

He paused for a few moments; then he added, "But I have done with to-day—let me prepare for eternity."

At this point Cléry appeared, and asked the King to take some refreshment. Louis refused at first; but even at that ghastly pass his appetite asserted itself, and he ate and drank during five minutes—only bread and wine; and this he did standing, after the manner of a traveller hurrying on a journey.

The priest now asked the King if he would like early in the morning to communicate.

The King turned, and a last look of pleasure shone upon his face. He was essentially a religious man, but he had despaired of being permitted to take the communion, for the Convention, amongst other things, had abolished the theory and practice of the Lord's Supper.

The Abbé therefore sought the commissaries on duty, and asked for the necessary articles, without which, according to the Roman Church, the ceremony of the communion cannot be effected.

The gaol authorities were excessively confused. On the

one hand, they were ashamed to refuse this consolation to a dying man; on the other, the constitution of the country then held that this belief in transubstantiation, or the passage of the bread and wine into the actual body and blood of Christ at their raising, was a superstition

"And if we give you permission," cried one of the leading men, "how do we know you will not cheat the scaffold of his blood by poisoning him with the holy wafer? It is well known to us that certain kings have been poisoned in the holy wafer, given to them as the very blood of the Redeemer."

"I can set that doubt at rest," said the Abbé. "You can yourselves supply me with both bread and wine."

The hope of "communicating" elevated the dying King almost to ecstasy. He fell upon his knees, and until far into the night recited the simple, almost innocent, sins of which he had been guilty. A very innocent and simple-hearted man, the list could not have been formidable.

Then he lay down, and fell asleep, as calmly as a little child—as though that final night was to be succeeded by a long and peaceful morrow.

CHAPTER LIII.

THE SACRIFICE OF BLOOD.

THE Abbé, meanwhile, prayed unceasingly in an outer chamber, and separated only from the King's by a wooden partition.

He and Cléry, the recently-appointed but faithful attendant on the King, heard the condemned man's breath regular and peaceful, uninterrupted by cries or restlessness. His heart beat regularly, with no more fear than is experienced by clockwork which has nearly run down, and is about to stop.

At five, it was necessary to awaken the King.

"Has it struck five?" he inquired, of Cléry.

"Not yet, by the town clock," the man replied "but several bells have sounded the hour."

"I have slept heartily," remarked the King; 'I suppose because, yesterday, I was very much fatigued."

Cléry now lighted the fire, and helped his dying master to dress.

The King "communicated," the altar being raised in the room in which he usually sat.

He took the substantiated, or, rather, consecrated, bread, with awful gravity, but with utter calmness.

While the priest was disrobing, the King retired to the little turret; and here, being joined by Cléry, the good servant knelt, and requested the King's blessing.

Louis XVI raised his hand, and desired him to convey that blessing, through himself, to all who loved their King, and especially to those of his gaolers who had shown to the royal family anything like pity or kindness.

Then, leading the valet to the window, he gave him, so that those watching through the glass of the doors should not see the act, a seal, which he had detached from his watch, a small parcel, taken from his bosom, and the wedding-ring with which, at their royal marriage, the Queen had pledged her faith to him. This ring he took from the hand upon which he had worn it since placed there at his marriage.

"When I am dead," he said. "you will give this seal to my son, and this ring to the Queen. Tell her that I give it up with great pain, and only because I do not will that it should share in the profanity to which, of course, my body will be subjected. And this little parcel has in it locks of the hair of all my family. Give it, also, to my lady. Say to the Queen, and to my most dear children, and to my sister, that though I promised to see them this morning, I meant to spare them the grief of another bitter separation. It costs me more than I can describe, to go without kissing them again!"

Here he wept, for the last time in his life, it being one of the very few occasions when he was moved to tears.

"I give to you," he added, in a sweet, low, suppressed voice,—"I give to you my last farewell, to take to those I love!"

Cléry retired, weeping, though his tears were an evidence against him which might cost him his life.

A moment passed, and the King. leaving the little room, asked one of the gaolers for a pair of scissors.

" What for, citizen ? "

" I wish the Citizen Cléry to cut off my hair; it is the only legacy I have to leave my family '

" 'Tis well," said the gaoler

And Cléry performed this ghastly office.

Cléry, turning to the commissaries, said, " And now, citizens, I beg that I may be allowed to accompany the Citizen Louis Capet "—he dared not call him King, to do so would have termined his own life—" to the scaffold I seek permission to perform this last office, and that it may not be left to the executioner "

" Bah ! The executioner is good enough for *him !* " cried one of the more influential commissaries.

The King turned away.

The Abbé, following him some moments afterwards, found the King calmly warming himself near the stove, and evidently contemplating his approaching end with a certain calm joy which was to be envied by very many of those who had condemned him.

" Good heavens ! " he cried, " how glad I am that while on the throne, I maintained my faith in the Eternal ! What now would be my sufferings, if I had not steadfast hope in the world to come ! Oh, yes ; above there is a Judge of courage, who cannot be influenced or threatened —who will judge me honestly, and accord to me that justice which has been denied me in this world "

The winter day now broke, and light struggled between the bars and planks which combined to shut out light from the loyal prisoners, one of whom was now destined soon to be free.

The roll of the drum, on one side or the other far and near, now was heard, hurried steps passed ; the click of arms could be distinguished ; and soon horses, heavily mounted, were heard beating along the street.

A heavier sound—cannon, and strongly-built tumbrils or wagons were heard, taking up their position in the court-yard of the prison, and about its entrance

The King, true to the last to his marvellous character— which his friends describe, as one not to be swayed by pas-sion, which his enemies analyzed to be one of callousness and incapability of feeling, not only with regard to others, but even for himself—the King commented on these sounds, not as though they affected him and his life, but as though they were an agreeable puzzle he was putting together.

" 'Tis probably the National Guard assembling," he said, in a half curious voice, to the still praying Abbé, when the first roll of the drum swept through the cold morning air.

A few moments passed, and the trampling of horses' hoofs at the foot of the tower attracted his attention. Then followed the voices of officers, giving military directions.

"They are come," he said.

He spoke without impatience or fear, after the manner of a friend quietly waiting for a friend, and at last hearing the amicable step upon the stair.

And now the King's last torture—not his execution, for that was in mercy extended to him—commenced.

Through two long hours was this poor man tortured by a refinement of cruelty for which there can be found no extenuation, to which no parallel can be discovered.

Through these two hours came frequent summonses at the door. Upon each occasion the King rose, ready. Upon each occasion some poor, petty excuse was made. He himself (the King) opened the door, answered the wretch and coward who tortured him, bowed civilly when he learnt his presence was not required, and closing the door, waited until a fresh summons beat upon his heart.

Ah, posterity cannot forgive those acts! Long must the question remain unsettled whether or not Louis XVI was rightfully put to death. Possibly he but paid the debt his ancestors had incurred. Millions had died of starvation. Taxes annihilated industry through generations previous to the uprising of the people. Even salt was weighted with a tax which caused it to be sold at an enormous rate —thirty pence a pound. Finally, Louis may have been guilty, as a man who was false to his oaths to keep the land of France free of enemies, of calling foreign help to France. It must be felt that when his throne was sinking from beneath him, other kings, in the interests of thrones, being desirous of maintaining Louis upon his, would willingly offer that foreign aid which it is felt Louis had been more than humanly self-denying in refusing. He fell a sacrifice to the errors of the two Louises who had preceded him on the throne—a blood compensation for the waste, luxury, and sensuality of half a dozen generations of French nobles.

The measure of the people's misery being full, they rose, and rose successfully. Their mistake—one which ultimately suffocated all the good it was intended they should effect —took the shape of success, intoxicating itself with victory.

Give a lesson to kings not to exceed their duty—yes! All France knew that the English Revolution, which sent Charles I to the block, had resulted in a social condition in England which offered an example for France to follow.

But having once passed upon a man the dignity of approaching death ; having thrown round him the darkness of the coming tomb—to crush his heart—to humiliate him —to embitter his last moments—to play with his life as a cat with a poor, palpitating mouse—to try to resuscitate the desire to live—to seek to change the calmness of resignation back into the whirlpool of despair—these are not the acts of men, but demons.

Yet let not these acts be set down to the people. In times of trouble, all the scum boils to the surface, and it is the surface we see, not the clarified water below it. Few, very few men completed the murders of September ; seven-eighths of all France knew nothing about these wholesale murders until they were achieved

But the miserable attempt to torture the King's last hour upon earth failed utterly—he was beyond attack. His soul had already passed away.

At nine o'clock there was a tumultuous noise upon the staircase, and now there was a summons at the door. It was thrown open

As far as the King's eyes could stretch were armed men —all gazing towards Louis.

Santerre appeared, attended by twelve municipals, and ten gendarmes, all of whom fell into two lines in the apartment.

The King turned to the little turret door, and with his hand upon it, looked towards Santerre.

In this final moment all the reserve and imperiousness of a prince returned to Louis XVI.

"You are come for me," he said. "Await me—and for a mere moment."

He paused, closed the door, and knelt at the minister's feet.

"It is finished," he said. "Bless me, and let me go."

A moment, and he rose, came out, placed himself smilingly between the double row of armed men. In his hand was a paper. It was his will. Addressing himself to the man who appeared to be the chief of the squad, he said, "I pray you to give this letter to the Queen."

The Republicans started, and the act reminded the King of the error he had committed.

"To my wife," he said, correcting himself, to please the Republican ears.

"It's no affair of mine," replied the man addressed, and in savage tones. "I'm not here to carry messages to your wife, but to take you to the scaffold."

This unhappy creature, one Jacques Roux, had actually been a priest, who had thrown off the cassock and joined the revolutionary army.

"True," said the King, his head falling.

But the name of a man in those ranks was to be made illustrious amongst pitying and tender-hearted men. The King, looking up, glanced rapidly along the two lines of faces to find one pitying look. His eyes rested upon one Gobeau, a man with a frightful name, but possessed of a far better heart.

"I pray you give this paper to my wife."

Gobeau hesitated, and looked from the King to his comrades, from his comrades back to Louis.

"You may read it—if you will. 'Tis but my wishes, which I trust the Commune may read."

The man Gobeau asked the consent of his comrades, and then took the paper.

The morning was very cold, and to complete the resemblance between the fates of the two beheaded Kings, Charles I of England, and Louis XVI of France, exactly as Charles's valet put a cloak round his master, so that he should not appear to tremble at the scaffold, so Cléry, knowing nothing of the parallel, put a cloak about his master.

Both kings were beheaded towards the end of January.

"I do not require a cloak," he said. "Give me my hat."

As he took it, he shook the faithful Cléry's hand. Then, turning to Santerre, and looking him full in the face, he said, " I am ready.'

Santerre and his troop rather followed than escorted him.

The King passed down the staircase slowly, and without any signs of tremor. Now, it is in descending a staircase that a man, convulsed by agitation, is almost sure to stumble.

The King did not make one false step.

Reaching the foot of the steps, the King encountered one Mathey.

"Citizen Mathey," said Louis, "you offended me very cruelly last night, and I replied angrily. For the sake of this hour, pray pardon me."

Mathey, instead of replying, pretended to turn his head away, and not see the King. However, it is only just to say, in some extenuation of the brutality of most of those to whom the King addressed himself during the last hour of his existence, that death was now so quickly dealt to any man whose words could be twisted into an expression of even pity for fallen loyalty, that it was only at the risk of exposing life that a man could be humane in an answer to any question addressed to him by any one of the royal family.

The King was now crossing the court-yard. He had achieved half the distance before his heart failed him; and, turning yearningly, he looked towards the tower within which the Queen was confined. A moment, and his face was towards the people glaring in at the gate. Once more he looked, as he passed out of the court-yard; then he, death, and eternity were alone!

A carriage awaited him, an armed man standing each side the door. One of these men entered the carriage, and took a front seat; the King followed, and took the place of honor—the right, facing the horses. The Abbé Edgeworth followed, and sat beside Louis. The second gendarme now entered, and slammed and fastened the door, and the carriage was at once started.

Sixty drums lead the way, incessantly sounding, and a mass of armed men surrounded the victim.

The reign of terror had begun, in truth. A Governmental order had been issued, forbidding any citizen to show

20

himself at a window; and the infraction of such an order
was, in itself, probably a condemnation to death.   The
citizens were also forbidden to cross any of the streets upon
the line of march.

A strange effect was this procession.

The morning was lowering, cold, dead, and damp; and
the noisy sixty drums, purposely used to drown any cry
that might be raised, led the way for a hurried, half-
disciplined, half-armed horde of armed men ; in their midst,
a carriage, half-filled with two such as those who formed
the escort.

And this procession marched through a double row of
steel—of pikes and bayonets, held by silent men.   At dis-
tances were squads of the regulars, armed and prepared as
for an action in the field.

A strange sight!   Thousands of armed men—soldiers
with cannon and musket, prepared against a numerous foe ;
a swiftly passing crowd of men, armed to the teeth, jealously guarding a carriage half-filled with two such as they
themselves were,—all against—what ?

Sixty drums beating to drown—utter silence !   Two
hundred thousand men, to keep order amongst—space !
Armed men—and that was all !

On the line, not a human being to be seen beyond the
serried lines of armed men.   Not a woman's form for the
eye to rest on—every window blind, every street passed, a
desert.   Paris was a city of the dead.   Even the market-
places were silent, and not even the voice of a child was to
be heard.

Cannon gaped at every street corner, the artillerymen
holding lighted matches ; in a word, on all sides were to be
seen evidences of preparations to meet a formidable enemy
—on not one was the shadow of an enemy to be seen.

The King could scarcely be perceived though the forest
of steel in which he was lost.   He wore a brown coat and
a white waistcoat.   His hair was raised up already for the
executioner's hands.

So great was the noise created by the drums, that he
could not hear what the Abbé Edgeworth said, or even
what he himself said to that self-devoted gentleman.

Therefore he took the minister's breviary, and opened it
at those particular pslams which he had learnt in his cap-

tivity, suited to his situation. These he began to recite while the priest prayed beside him

It is said the expression of the two men-at-arms were those of astonishment and admiration.

All these warlike preparations were met by the opposition of seven or eight opponents.

The procession moved from the Temple up to the boulevards, the line of which was kept by the procession, until it reached the place of execution, on that spot which is now the Place de la Concorde. At that point on the line of march which now lies between the Portes St Denis and St. Martin, occurred the one sign of any opposition to the tragedy which was about to be completed.

There was a sudden stir; and, suddenly, seven or eight young men, sword in hand, rushed from the Rue Beauregard, dashed forward through the line of armed men, and even reached the carriage, they crying, "Help, help, those who would save the King!"

The leader of these frantically-daring young men was one Baron de Batz, a man of extremely adventurous tendencies. Chiefly by his means, three thousand young men had combined to effect this diversion in the King's favor, and they were to respond to the call to arms led by Batz.

The three thousand made no reply; the seven or eight devoted men stood alone in the midst of nearly a quarter of a million of armed enemies.

But some mercy was shown them, for those about them did not massacre the youths,—they were all very young. They even escaped into a side street; but here they were fallen upon by a squad of gendarmes, rapidly told off for that purpose; and being caught sword-in-hand, they were shot down, and left where they fell.

CHAPTER LIV.

EXECUTION OF LOUIS XVI.

As the Place de la Revolution, the place of execution, came in view, a ray of sunshine fell upon the guillotine—

one of those coincidences which the superstitious and the wonder-loving remember and treasure up.

This open space was filled with a hundred thousand of the lowest rabble; soldiers thick about the scaffold; and high above the people stood a something, the woodwork of which was painted a blood-color.

This was the *guillotine!*

The guillotine had only just been introduced. It had been invented in Italy, and imported into France by a humane doctor, named Guillotin, whose name was cruelly taken and applied to the machine, an " e " being added to make it feminine—for, according to the custom of most men in most times, a something terrible and merciless is always feminine. If the women had the naming, perhaps the other gender would as frequently be applied to things of terror.

The guillotine was essentially a humane invention. Previous to its introduction, the condemned man knelt down and placed his head on a block. A headsman then with an axe endeavored to sever the head from the body. The least swaying on his part, and instead of death, a wound was the result. Often an executioner, unnerved by the failure of his first blow, would hack and chop many times before the victim ceased to show signs of life, and before the head was off the body.

The guillotine exactly fell in with the views of the equallist Republicans, for they objected to the executioner, because it was a disgrace to a man to be an executioner. On the other hand, the guillotine, consisting of a heavy, razor-like knife, which worked in grooves, and fell upon a neck irrevocably placed below the knife, the head was separated at a blow, in a moment, and death achieved with the least possible cruelty.

But if the guillotine was merciful—and of this there can be no doubt—on the other hand—it may be questioned if so many people would have been condemned to death during the Reign of Terror if the old slow mode of decapitation had remained.

By a singular fatality the head of Guillotin himself was taken off by the very instrument he had introduced from Italy into France.

All the vagabondage of Paris was present at this execution. The trees bent under the masses of people who had climbed into them. There was not breathing room, while, by connivance of the most bloodthirsty of the revolutionary leaders, the spaces immediately round the scaffold were occupied by the men who had effected the massacre of September

These men were there to applaud.

But when the carriage containing the King drew up before the scaffold, the mob was silent—even the September men, for a little time, held their peace.

The King perceiving the carriage stop, looked up, and said to the Abbé, " We have arrived, I think."

The minister replied by a gesture.

One of the three brothers Sanson, the three executioners of Paris, opened the door.

The gendarmes got out, whereupon the King, closing the door, and placing his hand upon the minister, he said authoritatively to those who were pressing forward, " Gentlemen, I recommend this gentleman to your care. Be brave enough to save him from insult after I am dead. I charge you to save him !"

No one replied.

" I charge you to save him !"

One of them, more sinister than the rest, replied.

" Yes, yes," he said; " be at peace—we will save him, and let us hear no more about it "

Louis now stepped from the carriage.

Three executioners' attendants came forward, and wished to undress him at the foot of the scaffold.

He waved them back, took off his coat, cravat, and turned down his shirt.

The executioners again approached him.

" What do you seek to do ?" he asked, angrily.

" Bind you !" they said, seizing his hands.

" Bind *me !*" the King cried, all the passion of centuries of petted and idolized royal blood rising in the veins which were now in a few moments to be empty. " Never !—I will not permit it. Do your work, but you shall not bind me—do not even dream of such a thing ! "

This man, the descendant of hundreds of kings, could not, even after recommending his soul to God, uncrown himself. The Convention might call him a citizen—but he had, as all kings must, lived in the belief of that half-divinity which is still in some places supposed to surround a king.

The executioners had their duty to do. Here was a man to be guillotined. Men who were guillotined had to be bound. Then they must bind their man.

They again approached.

A veritable struggle was about to commence at the foot of the scaffold.

The King saved himself from himself in time. He remembered the dignity of his death, and he looked towards the Abbé.

"Sire," said the man of religion, "compare yourself to One far greater than yourself, who was bound with cords, and who will soon welcome you as a brother"

The King looked to heaven, appeased, but the royal pride still lingered.

"Truly, only the Divine example enables me to bear this disgrace."

It is probable this final demonstration, in his very extremity, of his superiority to touch from common hands, helped to harden the nation against the life of the widow. On the other hand, it proved the first occasion on which he showed the least sign of impatience with his tormentors.

"Do as you will," he said. "I will drink the cup to the dregs."

Supported by the help of the aged minister, he ascended the steps of the scaffold, and, it must be admitted, with signs of physical fear—the first he had yet shown. Possibly this condition of body was chiefly brought about by the actual physical resistance he had made at the foot of the ladder. But upon coming to the level, all his natural calmness or courage, whichever it was, came to his aid; and, stepping quickly forward across the platform without help, he contemplated the means of his death.

Suddenly, he turned, and faced the people, and used the royal gesture of his life. It was quite natural—a habit of his life—and testified to no violent defiance of his position, and of those who placed him where he stood.

The drummers mechanically obeyed.

"People," he said, in a voice which was heard afar off, even in the very confines of the square,—"People, I die innocent of all the crimes of which I am declared guilty. I forgive those who send me to death, and I pray God that the blood you are about to shed may not fall upon France"

The crowd trembled—murmured

He was about to speak again, when the officer of the troop gave orders to the drums to beat and the King's voice was drowned

He had said enough Nothing could add to the majesty of those few words. The agony was spared him of learning who the man was that gave the order which drowned his last words. It was the Count d'Oyat, a natural son of Louis XV, and therefore by blood, if not by marriage, the King's uncle—Louis XVI being the grandson of Louis XV.

What a fate! His cousin voted for his death, and the last words he uttered were drowned by the command of his uncle

The condemned man turned slowly away. As they fastened him to the plank, he cast one look upon the praying minister, and the next moment the plank was sinking forward, carrying down Louis of France, his face towards the earth.

Another moment—the time for the passage of the heavy blade—and Louis of France was dead!

CHAPTER LV.

WHAT FOLLOWS.

I saw Louis XVI die.

"Go," said Robespierre, "see liberty declared, and a King proved to be no more than a man."

I stood amongst those at the foot of the scaffold.

I will say no more than this—Louis died bravely, and like a man. And I think the people were sorry. Of course they had more to regret before the Reign of Terror was over.

Robespierre changed nothing in his mode of life after he came to Duplay's. He drank water, he lived very temperately and frugally, was always master of himself By the way, another of Duplay's daughters coming home, Maximilian actually fell in love with her, in a grave, calm way; and it was agreed that, when liberty was completely obtained, and France was at peace, that they should be married, live in a cottage, and hide away from the world.

I had frequently been at the Temple during the incarceration of the King, and often saw various members of the unhappy family. I am desirous that my hearers should believe that the men who surrounded the Capets in their imprisonment, were no more good examples of the revolutionary masses than I am an angel. A few hundred ferocious men rose to the surface of the Revolution, and disgraced it. At heart, its adherents sought to make France happy, and the people richer.

But let me return to the course of events.

*   *   *   *   *   *

There is very little known of what the widowed Queen did or said during the night before the execution, and upon that morning itself, beyond the fact that she passed from prayer to insensibility continuously. The entire family seem to have been conscious, from the first, that the separation with the King, on the eve of the execution, was final —that his promise to see them in the morning was a pious fraud.

As the morning progressed, after she knew by the lessening noise of the drums that he was on the way to execution, her great anxiety appeared to be to ascertain the exact moment when he died, so that from praying for him. she might entreat his soul to pray and plead for her and his children.

The loud cries of "Long Live the Republic," and the rumbling return of the cannon, were the first evidences she received that all was over.

She appears from that time to have passed into a state of half-unconscious moroseness—a condition which is one of the mercies of nature, and which only ended in her life

She knew, she said, that he would die like a man, and that was her consolation, when, with a cruelty beyond measure, she was refused any information concerning his last moments.

Cléry, the valet, now, apart from her family, the dearest being to her in all the world, as the man who had been with the King during his last days,—Cléry was now a prisoner, and remained one during a whole month, during which time he had not the faintest approach to an opportunity to give the queen the King's last words, or place in her keeping the hair and ring with which the King had entrusted him.

About these relics there is a strange but of tender history. One Toulan concealed under the most frantic demonstrations of Republicanism, a sacrificial devotion to the royal family. He feared these relics would be wilfully destroyed by some drunken, ruthless hand; and pretending that he would not allow the chance of their being delivered to the Queen, he insisted on their being placed under the keeping of the chief officers of the Commune.

The Queen asked very humbly permission to wear mourning for the King, and this was granted, on condition of extreme parsimony and meanness.

There was a special debate, in order to obtain the Dauphin a few shirts.

The more merciful men of the Revolution fully expected that the death of the King would be followed by the liberation of the Queen, her children, and the Princess Elizabeth. This hope being held out to the Princess Elizabeth, she carried the grateful news to the Queen, who heard it, without interest, and returned an answer almost stupid to this good news. Either she knew that a nation who had not spared her husband would not spare her, who had always been the least liked of the two, or she did not care to live. Probably the latter surmise is the nearer correct.

Her only expression of resolution took place when she was requested for her health's sake to walk in the garden of the prison. She resolutely refused. She said she could not pass the door of the King's prison—could not put her feet upon the stairs down which he had marched to death. It was only at the end of six weeks—at the close of February —that she consented, for the sake of the children, who never left her side, to walk on the platform at the top of the tower. Here, between the battlements of the parapet, she could be seen from the neighboring houses, and this tending to create pity, it was ordered that the spaces between the battlements should be filled up with boards—an order which pleased the Queen, for it shut out from her sight a city which, to her, appeared a mere charnel-house. This intended petty cruelty—which was a relief—took place towards the end of March.

The King had now been dead ten weeks, and Marie Antoinette had yet to live six cruel months.

Her bodily health was breaking, but she had no knowledge of this fact. Her heart was dead. She was simply decaying. For whole nights she would lie awake, never complaining, never showing signs of weariness.

Her life had passed into *waiting.* She was weary almost of the love of her children. Upon the face, and in her step, walk, in every gesture, and at rest, at last, or awake, the woman appeared to be pleading, "Good Lord, how long shall this endure ? "

She was now more closely watched. The Princess Elizabeth, at peace, become essentially a religious woman, contrived to obtain intelligence of what was happening One Hue—once valet to the King when in prosperity—conveyed messages through the friendly Toulan into the prison. These messages were put in the pipe of a portable fireplace, and found by the Princess Elizabeth, who replied in letters written with sympathetic ink, so that only those who knew how to treat them could read their contents.

These letters contained minutes of all that was doing in Europe in the royal cause. Many promising lines thus came to the prison. The Queen heard them read, said a vacant word or two, and sank back into her usual condition of partial lethargy.

She only came back to life when she heard the voices of either of her children. Then she lived. When they were silent, she was dead, though her heart still beat.

CHAPTER LVI.

THE REIGN OF TERROR.

The remains of Louis XVI were conveyed in a cart to the graveyard, flung into a hole, and lime cast upon the remains, that the bones might never be found, in order to be exalted into relics

Paris was silent—except for the voices of the more excited of the Revolutionists, who overrun the city, announcing the death of the tyrant, and proclaiming the advent of liberty.

The body of the people did not respond to this enthusiasm—they did not confound punishment with victory. The body of the King was not cold before the people began asking themselves whether or not a righteous act had been committed. The King's death left this problem to be discussed by the nation. Many years have elapsed as I write, and the problem is still discussed—had the people a right to kill Louis XVI?

The result of the King's death upon the more moderate Republicans, and upon those who had agreed to the new constitution, but were Royalists at heart, were in some cases terrible. To many, this execution appeared a sacrilege, which must bring down upon the people who had committed it one of those vengeances in which heaven demands for the spilt blood of one just man the blood of an entire people.

Men died of grief when they learnt the awful facts, and many more went mad.

Women cast themselves in panic from housetops, others from the bridges into the River Seine.

Sisters, wives, and mothers of the Conventionalists, who had condemned lovers to death, shrank from them as from lepers.

One of the principal judges at the trial, Michael Lepelletier, was almost immediately stabbed in an eating-house by one Paris, a hot-headed Royalist, who escaped only for a short time. Tracked, he shot himself; and upon the body was found a paper bearing these words:—

"I alone did the deed—let no other man be suspected. I did not mean to kill the wretch, Lepelletier, but he came in my way. I was waiting for the parricide D'Orleans, of whom I hoped to rid the world. All Frenchmen have become cowards."

Three days after, Lepelletier was publicly buried, after the antique Greek mode, and thousands were squandered upon this pomp.

Meanwhile the nations were rising against France, although about this time the Prussians had been worsted by the French on the eastern frontiers.

In England, the horror produced was great; and one Chauvelin having returned from London to Paris, declaring to the Convention that the English masses were ready to rise and massacre the King (George III) in his palace, the French ambassador at London was ordered to leave England within twenty-four hours.

The Convention thereupon declared war against Holland and England.

Catharine II, of Russia, revoked the treaty of 1786, by which the French were more favored in Russia, than other foreigners; and ordered all the French in Russia to return to France, who would not swear that they abhorred revolutionary sentiments. This Empress joined the coalition against France.

The Convention had already declared war against Spain.

And now, England, Prussia, Austria, Russia, and Spain were all at war with France—which was at war with itself.

Even Sweden had declared against the Republic. Not a friendly national face looked upon France beyond the boundaries.

In mercy to what was now to happen to France, let it be said that. cast upon her own resources, the armies of other people advancing upon her by land, and by sea, despairing of help from the United States, which had not yet recovered the blood spilt in obtaining her independence, France was panic-stricken at the fear of civil war, and rashly sought, by the most unpardonable acts, to exterminate this probability by the extermination of all those who were suspected of favoring Royalism.

The leader of blood amongst the Conventionists, immediately after the execution of Louis XVI, took the hideous form of Marat. Dirty, mean, fetid, disgusting in look and action, he endeared himself to the most foul amongst the lowest by these attributes. But, like Robespierre, who was a very fop in appearance and action, he accepted no public money, and lived most obscurely in three or four garret-like rooms, most meanly furnished. This man was the idol of the commonest people, who saluted him almost as though a God : and he must have had some occult power of attraction, for a woman really beautiful devoted her life and honor to this creature. Nor was he without the sentiment of self-sacrifice ; for, though dying, though every violent speech he made, which was always prefaced by the cry "*Blood!*" brought him nearer to the grave, he never hesitated to exert himself, and quitted his bed or his bath, in which he passed the greater part of his time, to go down to the Convention, and denounce men on the most frivolous pretences.

The moderate party in the Convention—the Girondists —who in theory desired to save the King, and in practice condemned him to death, were by this time in danger. They were in the way of the fiercer party, led by Marat, Danton, and Robespierre, who were to eclipse both; and these Girondists were already in the hands of their opponents, condemned to follow the King to the scaffold.

It was in such language as the following that Marat, who gained a poor living as the editor of a very fierce paper, spoke, in his *Friend of the People:*

"I pray my readers pardon me to-day if I speak of myself; not because I am vain, or a fool, or because I wish to serve the people, and, therefore, must justify myself in their sight, for I am accused of being a monster, greedy of blood—a tiger, longing for gore!

"Born with a sensitive heart, carefully nurtured, at twenty-one, I was pure, and had long since given myself up to knowledge.

"My mother gave much in charity, and all she gave passed through my hands. At eight, I could not endure cruelty, and the sight of it enraged me to madness.

"As a child I was weak, and never did I know the joys of childhood. I was so loved, that I was never punished but once, when eleven, and then unjustly. I sprang from the window of the room in which I was confined, and found liberty in the streets, where, even now, only liberty is to be found."

He concluded this article :—

"Restored to health, I only thought how I could be useful to the cause of freedom. And yet they accuse me of having sold myself,—I, who could amass millions by merely selling my silence,—I, who am in poverty and want!"

Strange enough, like Robespierre, Marat firmly believed he was an instrument in the hands of God. "The Revolution," he would say, "is the Gospel, and I am its apostle."

But all the raving in the world could not hide the fact that France had suddenly become poor. To be rich, was to run the risk of being accused of being an aristocrat. And as all gold and silver was in the hands of the rich, and these were flying from France, the land was actually being drained of specie.

Paper money was issued—a currency which the people mistrusted, as the people always mistrust the unusual; and the Girondists were popularly accused of causing the disappearance of the precious metals.

The walls of popular hate were closing round that score of devoted men.

The aspect of the land was horrible. People feared to go about in anything but rags, dreading to be supposed rich, and therefore only fit to die; land remained uncultivated, for its owners had fled; and the half-destroyed, empty houses of the nobility began falling into ruins. Not a carriage was to be seen, nor a jewel, nor any sign of luxury. All was abject, wretched, debased. The bakers' shops were almost like prisons (to this day, bakers' shops in Paris are often barred); and the only prodigality was that of wine, the many years store of which flowed in terrible abundance. It was cheaper than bread, and steeled the heart to pity. Commerce had ceased, and not a sail beyond that of a French fishing-smack was to be seen in the French waters.

Marat now advocated the pillage of every store-house in the land, and the hanging of some of the owners in their own gateways, as an example to the rest.

And now that which was most feared occurred—civil war. La Vendée, in the north-west of France—the Brittany of to-day—rose almost to a man, and defied the republic.

Spain now began to pour her soldiers upon the south, while Austrians and Prussians were gaining victory after victory in the north and east.

So north, south, east, and west, enemies' faces were turned upon France, while England was preparing to sweep her navy around the whole of the coasts of the now devoted land.

The Convention commanded that a black flag should float from the towers of the Cathedral of Notre Dame de Paris.

The theatres were closed.

Only one cry was heard in the streets—"To arms—to arms!"

Danton and Robespierre now quarrelled One Legendre undertook to reconcile them, and they met without previous warning. Danton, a bull-dog in ferocity, and with the bull-dog's generosity advanced, and held out his hand. Robespierre, with the silent stealth of the tiger, which waits and pounces, affected not to see it, ate his dinner in silence, and went away, after the utterance of a few words, which were the first that openly indicated his intention of betraying Danton.

Danton was beginning to repent. His remorse was natural. He had lost his wife, whose death had been accelerated by terror. Unable to endure his loneliness, he sought another wife; her parents rejected him with loathing But, after a little, they pitied his misery and gave their daughter to this strangely compounded man.

Danton now contemplated what was done after Napoleon had reigned and lived, after Louis XVIII had reigned and died, after Charles X had been driven from the French throne —the giving of a King to France, not belonging directly to the hated Bourbons, but to the younger branch, the Orleanists, the leader of whom, Philip Equality, had voted Louis XVI's death. He was never crowned, he died on the scaffold His son, Louis Philippe, ultimately became King of France

Philip Equality refused the proposal

Meanwhile, the convention was becoming a mere field of battle. On one particular night, the two sides clash — a poniard is drawn, a pistol is clapped to a breast, and murder is nearly done. It is felt that one party must be swept away, or nothing will be done The moderate party, the Girondists, twenty-two in all, are to-night nearer the scaffold by a long journey than they were in the morning.

Marat is declared a traitor by two hundred and twenty voices, against ninety-two Marat defies the vote, throws himself into the arms of the people, and is borne home in triumph.

The people rise in his favor.

On the 24th of April (the Queen has been waiting death during three months) Marat is strong enough to appear and defy Parliament. He commands them to declare him innocent of treason. This defiance is carried to the thousands of armed men waiting the issue outside the House of Assembly. A cannon-like roar from the people declare their will—and he is pronounced innocent.

The people place him on a plank, the throne of the people, and bear him through the streets, after crowning him with flowers.

" It is you, the people," he cries, "who crown themselves upon my head. I am the King of Poverty. May every head, which would rear itself above the level of the people soon fall, when I cry ' Kill ! ' "

A few days, and, in his arrogance, he says to his brother Conventionists, " I hold you as a little water in the palm of this hand; and as readily as I spill it, so I can spill the blood of all of you ! "

By this time, Philip Equality, for what he had been—a Duke—had become hated of the people. Strangely enough, he who had been so cowardly as a youth, now, when his life was threatened, became brave. When he was arrested, he was perfectly calm ; when separated from the elder of his two sons, he was perfectly resigned. He had turned from his family to serve the people, and he now wore their chains.

The people now demanded the deaths of all the leaders of the more moderate Conventionists.

" Death to the twenty-two ! "

The people had slain a King—therefore they began to demand the lives of those who sought, as Republicans, to govern the stricken land.

CHAPTER LVII.

WHOLESALE MASSACRE.

THE twenty-two deputies were already condemned by the will of the ensanguined mob.

On the eve of the last day in May (1793), of those twenty-two, only one, the leader, Vergniaud, slept in his own home. The others feared an assassination, and sought the aid of friends

A vote being carried against the moderates, the victors proposed to walk with the people through the city, which was illuminated. The Girondists, as a measure of precaution, joined in the procession.

While the procession was progressing, that now organized band, the Revolutionary Committee, sent to arrest Madame Roland's husband.

That evening, Roland, who does not show well in this business, fled into hiding. Madame Roland then determined to go down to the Convention and upbraid it. So far, the French had not begun to behead women. Starting from her home, she was surprised to find the city had been suddenly illuminated. Making her way to the Convention, she found it closed. And she learnt that the moderate party were overthrown, and that they would soon be headless

She returned home, to await her fate. She did not seek to fly. Roland, poor man, remained in concealment—only, after a time, to be ashamed of his cowardice, and to commit suicide.

She prepared to send away her daughter to trusted friends, made up a packet of clothing to take with her to prison, and waited. At midnight, they came beating at her door, and she had to be awakened; for no fear of death deprived her of that balm of life—sleep.

"How much you are beloved!" said the leader of the sectionaries, seeing the eagerness with which the young daughter kissed her mother.

"Because I love," she replied, proudly.

Reaching the carriage waiting for her, she was asked if she would have the window closed.

"No," she replied; "I have done no harm, and I can face my enemies."

"You are braver than many men waiting the decree of justice."

"If in France there were justice, *I* should not be seated with *you*. I shall go to the scaffold as fearlessly as I go to prison. I despise life."

21

Marat now became supreme. "Rise, sovereign people!" he cried; "no man dare oppose you."

There was never given a more fearful impetus to murder than these words.

What it pleased men to call a Committee of Public Safety was now organized, and its operation was the killing of every human being who could by any means be made to appear not utterly to sympathise with the seething mob.

The Convention existed, but its power was completely at an end. Its votes were laughed at. Queen Guillotine was the one power left in France.

Every day the foreign arms directed against France obtained successes. Meanwhile, the land was like a vessel without a rudder. No man was strong enough to control the mob. Indeed, it was only when Napoleon Bonaparte rose, that internal peace was established. It is not to be wondered at that he came to be looked up to as a demi-god.

Twenty thousand Royalist volunteers were now in arms against Marat, in one department of France alone.

Marat was at this time King of Paris. Robespierre was waiting. Danton was threatening and trembling at the same time. Another week, and the foul Marat would have conquered both, and been proclaimed, by the voice of the streets, President of the Republic.

But his hideous career was to be arrested by the feeble hand of a girl—Charlotte Corday.

Just before the commencement of the Reign of Terror in France, there might have been seen in a quiet corner of a quiet old street in Caen (that city in Normandy so much mixed up with the early history of English), a quiet old house, called the Grand Manor—a house around a court-yard, in the centre of which was a mossy fountain. Near this fountain, through the sunny hours, might frequently be seen a very beautiful girl, the niece of an aged woman, who was the maiden's aunt. This was Charlotte Corday. Fair of skin, and grey of eye, her hair was what had not inaptly been termed gilded-black. In other words, it was black hair, golden-tipped, with golden hues veining it. She was always dressed plainly, in brown cloth, and her voice was sweet and lingering. No man has ever breathed a word against her character.

By a peculiar course of study—which it is needless to

analyze—she had brought herself to that condition of mind when the sufferer experiences the belief that a self-sacrifice of some nature must be made, in order to appease an inexplicable, unknown longing to do some good—a something which is supposed to be good—in the world.

She was essentially a Republican; but gradually, slowly, the conviction enchained her, that Marat was its monster, and that he must die. Her resolve appears to have been hastened by the departure of her lover, who joined the Caen volunteers. This gentleman, one Franquelin, was, it is said, accused by Marat as a conspirator against the republic, and assassinated by villains hired for that purpose. He did not die on the spot, as it was at first reported, but returned home after Charlotte Corday's execution His last words were an entreaty to his mother to bury with him Charlotte's portrait, and all the letters she had ever written to him

Supplemental to the latter motive, Charlotte Corday believed Marat was ruining all France. Here she believed truly

She obtained a letter to one of the Conventionists No one had the slightest idea of her intentions. She retained a sweet, soft gaiety, which was quite natural to her, and which accompanied this lady to the scaffold. An anecdote is very characteristic of her life. Just before she started for Paris, passing a *café*, outside of which some men were card-playing, she said, "Cards! Do you know your country is dying?"

Taking a sheet of drawing-paper one morning, she said, "Aunt, I am going to sketch the hay-makers—kiss me"

Going out, she met a child, of whom she was very fond. "Here, Robert," she said, giving him the drawing-paper; "kiss me, and be a good boy. You will never see me again."

She chattered in the coach most of the way to Paris. One young man fell in love with her, and asked to apply to her friends She mirthfully repulsed him, and told him to wait, at least for some days.

It was now July. On the eleventh of that month, Charlotte Corday reached Paris. At five in the afternoon she retired to rest in a public-house, and slept until next day, when she presented her letter at the house of the conventionist, Duperret. When she saw him, she vaguely en-

treated him to flee from Paris.   " After to-morrow evening,"
she said, " it will be too late."

Duperret spoke of her as a beautiful girl, slightly de-
ranged.

Her great desire was to remain unknown by name in
connection with the death of Marat. With this view, she
determined to kill him before the people, so that she might
at once be torn to pieces, and her mutilated face be beyond
recognition. But she learnt that Marat was so ill that he
could not appear in public again. He still issued, daily,
stronger and more defiant demands for men's lives. It was
said he remained at home from fear of assassination. Charlotte Corday resolved to seek him in his home.

She wrote this letter :—

" I have just arrived from Caen. Your patriotism allows
me to be presumptive enough to hope that you will hear
privately what I have to say concerning events in that city.
I shall present myself at your door about one o'clock.   I
pray you for the good of all France—receive me ! "

She went to his house, and was refused admittance. She
wrote another letter :—

" I cannot believe that it was you yourself refused me admission : you are too good a patriot. I repeat, I have important news to tell you; that I have just arrived from the
north, and I have secrets to disclose. I am persecuted.
Will *you*, then, not aid me ? "

At seven the next morning she dressed herself very carefully. She wore a white dress, with a silk scarf crossed over
the breast and knotted behind—a white Normandy cap,
bound with a green ribbon—her hair falling over her shoulders. Her face was bright, fresh-colored, her countenance
smiling.

Thus she presented herself at the house occupied by
Marat, who happened to be in his bath, which he used, not
for its cleanly offices, but because it reduced the bodily
inflammation which had now become habitual to him.

The house, which bore all the aspects of that poverty in
which Marat was really plunged, was jealously guarded.

But what men could suspect a beautiful girl, clothed in brilliant white, her face flushing with youth and beauty?

Charlotte Corday stepped from her coach, and approached the house. She reached the outer door of the apartments in which Marat lived, and there her entrance was jealously opposed by Albertine, Marat's mistress, and a female friend.

Marat, hearing the altercation, and associating the pleading voice with the letters he had received, imperatively ordered the applicant to be admitted.

Now mark what occurred. The woman Albertine, offended, walked away, her friend followed her, and Charlotte Corday was alone with Marat.

The room was dark, close, and smelt abominably. He was wrapped in a dirty sheet, and sitting in a bath, across which was a rough piece of wood which he made his desk, for he passed hours in the water. He was writing when Charlotte Corday entered. He had finished this sentence:—"I demand that every man in France who has the blood of the Bourbons in his veins, however little, shall be put upon his trial, and his wife and children also."

She approached this human monster, her eyes downcast. He spoke to her imperiously—"What is the state of Normandy?"

"Certain deputies have taken refuge in Caen."

"Their names?"

She gave certain names, and he wrote them down.

"Good!" he said; "before another week is past, they shall be guillotined."

At this moment she raised the dagger she took from the breast of her dress, and plunged it down into his bosom.

"Help, my dear, help!" he cried, and fell back dead.

Albertine, the woman, and a man named Basse rushed forward in time to see his last-drawn breath. By this time the water was like that crimson stream Marat was forever demanding. He was bathed in it himself now.

She did not attempt to escape. She drew out the dagger, let it fall, and took two or three steps to the window. The man Basse caught up a chair and beat her down, whereupon the woman, Albertine, trampled upon her.

The news spread in an incalculably short space of time, and the seething people called up into the air, "Throw her out to us, we are waiting."

Soldiers rushed in, forming a hedge of steel about Charlotte Corday, and beat back the blaspheming crowd.

Charlotte showed no fear, crossed her hands ready for the cords, and her first words were "Poor woman!" in reference to Albertine, who was rending the air with her cries.

She said afterwards she had not asked herself the question, "Could this man be loved?"

"Poor people!" she said to those who endeavored to tear her to pieces; "you desire my death, whilst you owe me an altar for having freed you from a monster! Oh, throw me to the people," she said to the soldiers; "as they regret him, they are fit to be my executioners!"

She was not cast among the people—at least, she died in peace. She boasted of her act, and declared herself a martyr.

Paris turned pale at the news. The panic reaching the Convention, business was arrested. One Henriot, the Commandant-General of the National Guard, entered. "Tremble!" he cried. "Marat has been assassinated by a girl, who boasts of her deed! Tremble! Such a fate threatens all! Mistrust green ribbons, and let us swear to avenge the death of this great man."

Charlotte Corday, accused of murder, stood beautiful and smiling in the midst of accusers, all of whom wore fierce looks of hate and rage.

She was fearless until she reached the street, when the blaze of shouts so terrified this young country girl, that she fainted. Restored to consciousness, (they had bound her weak hands), she cried, "Alas! do I still live?"

Then quite consistently, she thanked her guardians for saving her from the crowd.

She never for one moment looked upon her act as a crime. When interrogated at her trial, she adhered to this statement—"I saw civil war enveloping France. I considered Marat its chief cause, and to save my country I sacrificed myself, and slew him."

That her virtue was attacked at her trial, is a condition of things which clearly proves how deeply dyed in prejudice by this time had become the revolutionary tribunals.

One Chabot under pretence of suspecting a concealed paper, tore off her breast kerchief. She leaped back at the outrage, the string of her dress broke, and her fair chest was exposed to the gaze of a number of savage men. Her hands were corded, so that she could not save herself from degradation; and her virtue gave of itself h i best proof, for she crouched down to hide her disarranged dress. Entreating them to untie her hands, they complied; and turning her back to the wall, she rapidly completed her toilette Where the cords had been, the flesh was marked with great blue bands; and very meekly she asked to be allowed to put on her long gloves before the knots were again tied. Upon her dress, after her death, was found pinned a long address to France, in which she entreated all men to destroy the Jacobins, and save France.

She was condemned to die the following morning. An artist, during her trial, having been remarked by her drawing her face, she requested he might complete it, and the painter was introduced to her cell One man endeavored to save her by maintaining she was insane. In this shape of pity, he nearly lost his own head.

She wrote of Marat finally —"Pardon me, oh men! The name of Marat dishonors your race. He was a beast of prey seeking to devour France by war and hate. I thank Heaven that by birth he was no Frenchman."

She was pained by the accusation made by Chabot, the wretch who had torn away her neckerchief, who declared she had been his mistress, far more than by the thought of approaching death. "Chabot," she wrote, "is a mere madman. I never even dreamed of this man. He need not be feared—he has not intellect enough to be dangerous."

In the same paper she said, "All Parisians are such good citizens, they cannot comprehend how a useless woman, whose longest term of life would be good for nothing, can calmly sacrifice herself for her country. To-morrow, at twelve, *I shall have lived !* "

Again she said, " 'Tis crime gives the shame—it is not the block." This is the verse of the great French poet Corneille, who was her ancestor.

Tried at eight in the morning, and knowing she should die at mid-day, she said, upon leaving the prison, " Madame Richard, pray let my breakfast be ready upon my return, or we shall not have time to take it together."

At her trial, it being maintained that the nature of the blow which killed Marat had been that of one accomplished

in the use of the dagger, she cried, "Miserable wretch—
he takes me for an assassin!"

The counsel for her defence urged that she only pleaded
that in killing Marat she was doing a public good.

The jury directly found her guilty, and ordered her property to be confiscated.

"Sir," she said to her defender, "you have done well.
But I cannot pay you, for you have heard how my property
has been seized. However, I do you this honor; I pray
that you will pay the few pieces of silver I owe to the
prison people—they ought to be paid."

Going back to her prison, where the painter finished her
portrait, she conversed about painting.

A knock at the cell-door, and the executioner entered,
carrying scissors with which to cut away her hair, and the
red garments worn by the condemned on their way to execution.

"Sir," she said to the painter, "I can only offer you a
lock of hair."

And taking the gaoler's scissors, she cut a lock of the
wonderful hair.

A priest coming, she said, "I thank those who have
been kind enough to send you, but I do not require your
services. The blood I have spilt, and my own, which I am
about to shed, are the only sacrifices I can offer the Eternal."

The executioner now cut off her hair, and flung over her
head the red garment.

"This," she said, "is the toilette of death, arranged by
somewhat rude hands, but it leads to immortality."

As she stepped upon the cart, such as carried all those
condemned to death to the place of execution, a violent
storm burst over Paris. Women danced about the death-
cart, uttering imprecations; hers was the only calm face to
be seen. Strangely enough, the rain wetting the red flan-
nel—her only covering to the waist—it clung to her skin,
and betrayed her to be exquisitely formed, especially as her
hands were so tied behind her that she was forced to hold
herself upright.

As she neared the scaffold, the sun appeared, and the
gold threads in her hair shone out magnificently.

The leaders of the rebellion, Danton, Robespierre,

Camille Desmoulins, standing at a window, saw her pass. She had preserved them from Marat, but, at the same time, she had shown how a tyrant could be slain. She saved their lives by her act; but she taught, also, how they might be taken.

One Adam Lux, a German, was hopelessly stricken by love as she passed along. He followed to the scaffold's feet, asking to die with her.

Reaching the scaffold, she turned pale, and, for one moment, shrank, but the next, recovering herself, ascended the steps as rapidly as her long red dress and pinioned arms would allow.

When the executioner pulled down her dress, that her neck might be bare, she was for the last time outraged while living. She placed herself upon the plank, and, the next moment, her head fell.

Legros, a miserable scaffold-dog, took up the head by the remaining hair, and struck at the cheeks. It is said the skin grew scarlet, as though the modesty of Charlotte Corday outlasted her life.

Did her face change color? Some hold that the head has consciousness and power after being severed from the body, and that it can see and hear. Nay, it was urged during the Revolution that the passion of the heads remained, because the interior of the wicker baskets in which the heads were carried away were often found to be gnawed, as though the teeth of the heads gnashed after separation from the body. For my part, I believe that this gnawing was effected by rats, which at that time, even more than now, overran Paris.

Such was the death of Marat—of his murderer, whom we cannot praise. But who can blame her? Assuredly her death was necessary to purge her of assassination, to some extent.

Adam Lux, wild with love, published a defence of Charlotte Corday. He was seized, and, three days afterwards, died by the very knife which destroyed her life.

Chénier, the patriotic poet, sang her heroism. He was soon arrested, and therefore beheaded.

But what good had Charlotte Corday done?

She had strengthened the love of the people for desperate measures; she had made a martyr of their most foul leader. She gave a dignity to those who advocated the scaffold. The liberal twenty-two knew that this last act annihilated them.

CHAPTER LVIII.

MARIE ANTOINETTE.

THE Convention ordained the *worship* of Marat, and cast his corse to the people as an idol.

He was called Cæsar, and his funeral was modelled upon the historical narrative of that given by Rome to the great Julius

The body was carried by torchlight to the garden of the house in which he made his most inflammatory speeches; and there he was buried under trees heavily laden with countless brilliantly-illuminated paper lamps.

His head was placed in an urn, and hung in the centre of the Convention. His memory was decreed an altar, and at its foot his admirers appropriately called for blood.

The enemy was now approaching on all sides, and thousands more Royalists were in array.

Meanwhile Danton was sinking in estimation, Robespierre rising, for Robespierre was a patient man.

Danton, dazzled with his new wife, wished to live the life of a small country gentleman. It was too late.

Robespierre was breaking in health, but his temperance would stand him in good stead of health for a long while. His motto was " Wait."

The Committee of Public Safety was meanwhile reaping a rich harvest of death.

Money was no longer to be seen.

Bread was rare.

People were dying of starvation (especially the old) in every street.

The more cruel of the Conventionists carried by acclamation these decrees—the true legal inauguration of the Reign of Terror:

" Six thousand soldiers and twelve hundred artillerymen

to do blindly the bidding of the Committee of Public Safety.

"All men who have been in the Government occupation during the late King's life, to quit Paris.

"The delivery of the Revolutionary Tribunal of the Moderate Conventionists.

"The right to search any house at any hour of the night.

"The transportation beyond the seas of every common woman in the land

"Finally, the payment of workmen who should leave their shops to follow up the public service."

By these measures the mob were not only encouraged to take life, but paid to do it. Nothing could save such a system resulting, if long continued. in national death!

By the way, *Sunday* was chosen as the best day for working these mob committees

This was followed by Merlin's decree. which provided for the arrest (without proof) of any suspected person, and of all those who not working, were enabled to live in a better condition than one of penury. This was an attack upon all people who had hidden money. In fact, starvation had by this time become the only mode of avoiding the guillotine

Prisons were not large enough to contain prisoners, and all the confiscated churches were converted into gaols. Death was decreed for almost every act of life—certainly for every act of pity.

A hundred men, less two, were beheaded in sixty days in Paris alone.

The Queen was too noble a victim to escape.

The Convention suddenly ordered her trial, and commanded her separation from the two children.

Now all the lethargy which has possessed her since the King's death departs, and she becomes as a lioness fighting for her young.

By this time, all the beauty of Marie Antoinette had vanished, and there remained a very broken old woman, aged about a little more than thirty, with very scanty white hair, falling in patches from an almost bald head. The body, as the soul, had shrunken—a skeleton remained, covered with mere skin.

This was the Queen, who leapt into life when her dulled hearing comprehended that she was to be separated from her children. They had but the mercy only to remove the son.

The boy clung to his mother, who lost all dignity, dug her nails into the child's flesh, and called upon the men to kill them both.

For two hours this lasted, and then she became a woman again—a mother; and dressing him to look as smart as possible, she gave him up with her own hands to his gaoler, Simon, who took him at once to the room where the child was destined to die. For two days and nights the child lay upon the floor, taking neither food nor drink.

The Queen never took her son in her arms. He was to outlive her but a little time, and then die of sheer ill-usage and neglect.

The Queen, however, still had her husband's sister and her daughter with her. The only consolation they had, was ascending to the platform of their tower, to catch a glimpse of the boy on the platform of the other tower.

Simon's work it was to deprave the body and soul of the wretched child. He forced him to drink strong wine, and made him answer to the name of "Wolf." He beat him if he wept, encouraged him to every possible disgusting act, and compelled him to sing obscene songs, while he (his master) smoked and drank.

Once, he nearly destroyed one of the poor Prince's eyes; at another, he raised a poker against him. Sometimes he was kind; and, upon one occasion, he said, "Capet, if the soldiers come and deliver you, what will you do?"

"Forgive you," said the child.

The man Simon actually wept, but he cried immediately afterwards, "There's some of the blood of the lion in the whelp."

In the middle of the night of the 2nd of August, the Queen was awakened, and told she was to be removed *alone*, to another prison.

In vain the women threw themselves at the feet of the men. They had but their duty to do.

The Queen was compelled to dress before them, while they ransacked the room, and seized every little object the Queen still retained. The miserable creatures left her a handkerchief.

And now, exactly as Louis XVI had told his children to

forgive their enemies, so now desolate Marie Antoinette told her daughter, in her last words to the poor child, to forgive those who parted them.

"I give my children to you, sister Be a second mother to them."

For precisely as Louis appears to have had no conception of the monstrosity of putting a woman to death, so the Queen, in leaving the Temple, appears not to have supposed for one moment that the Princess Elizabeth would be claimed by the scaffold,—she who had led the life of a true woman, who had nursed and helped the people, and never joined in the frivolities of the Court

The Queen was taken to the prison of the Conciergerie, which is composed of the dungeons below high water mark, to be found amongst the foundations of the Palace of Justice.

To a wretched cell, having in one corner a straw bed, and by the light of one candle, was the ex-Queen taken.

A woman desirous of death in the dungeon of a stronghold, and yet they only believed her safe when two soldiers, swords drawn, stood at the outer door watching, with orders not to lose sight of the Widow Capet, even when asleep

Madam Richard, that good woman who tended Charlotte Corday in her last moments, was the Queen's most humane gaoler She found something like furniture for the cell, procured wholesome food for the captive, and often brought a low-whispered message from the royal prisoners still in the Temple

A little while, and the dampness of the cell rotted the Queen's only dresses—two very common ones; and her under-clothing becoming in tatters, she was half naked.

CHAPTER LIX.

MARIE ANTOINETTE FINDS PEACE AT LAST.

MARIE ANTOINETTE in her last prison, however, was not without pitying friends. The fierce communists ordered that she should drink the water of the Seine, drawn as it

flowed past her prison-walls; but an honest couple, named
Bault, obtained the posts of chief gaolers at the Conciergerie, in the full aim of assuaging the Queen's wretchedness.
Instead of Seine water, the poor prisoner found daily in
her cell refreshing draughts of water drawn from that well
at Versailles which was the Queen's chief cellar. She was
a great water drinker.

Madame Bault, to affect harshness, never entered the
Princess's cell, asserting that to do so was to be contamin-
ated. The royal trade-people of former days—especially
the fruit-women—brought little offerings secretly; and so
it came about that the Queen, in her last prison and days,
ate such pure, simple meals as those which had been her
favorite food in the old days—a piece of melon, a handful
of figs, a little bread and a glass of water from her favorite
well.

The two gowns which the Queen possessed—one white,
the other black,—and which she wore alternately, soon fell
to pieces in the damp prison. Her underclothing was
always damp when put on, and often her shoes would be
completely wet; for between her and the river there was
only the part protection of a wall.

Human nature demands some work. Not allowed writing
or sewing materials (Bault's daughter mended the Queen's
tatters, and gave away the little fragments which she cut
away in the process as relics of the poor lady), with a pin
she scratched her thoughts upon the driest portion of the
walls of her prison. After her death many of these sentences were copied by one of the commissioners. They
were mostly German and Italian verses bearing reference
to her fate, and little Latin verses from the Psalms. No
French did she use, for she had been brought into the land
where that language was spoken to be cast into prison, and
to suffer death. The drier walls were covered with these
mute appeals.

Some idea may be gained of the cruelty exercised
towards the desolate prisoner, when she, asking for a lighter
coverlet, and Bault forwarding the request to a high authority, the latter received this reply.—

"Take care! Another sign of sympathy such as that,
and you will visit the guillotine before she does!"

Another shape of industry did the poor Queen find. She

wished to leave her daughter a memento of her last days, and she had nothing to give; so she converted a couple of bone toothpicks into knitting needles, pulled some worsted shreds from the heavy old coverlet which they refused to replace with a lighter, and knitted a—garter. This she dropped near the friendly Bault, who, with the heart of a father, understanding the poor little bit of workmanship, let fall his handkerchief, and so possessed himself of the little treasure. After her death the tribute reached the young Princess for whom it was worked—truly a message from the grave.

A few days before her trial, an order, possessed by something of mercy, arrived, by force of which she was relieved from the continuous state of the guard set to watch her. By this relief, she was enabled to kneel, from which act she had been warned throughout her confinement.

On October 13th, Fouquier-Tinville notified to Marie Antoinette the fact of her having been indicted for high treason.

She listened to the reading of the indictment as though to a death-warrant—the shape, in fact, it really took.

As a matter of form, she chose two counsel for her defence—men who had secretly sought the appointment, and who, afterwards, of course, paid for their pity with their lives.

On the 14th, at noon, she made as elegant a toilette as she could—hid the rags and the patchiness of her white hair as much as possible, and went up the stone stairs of her dungeon to the judgment-hall above her prison. The passages were full of people, who reviled her as she passed along. She bore her head well up, but she could not change the fallen mouth, the pinched nose, tarnished eyes, and shrunken, weakened body. But the black circles round those eyes artificially increased their failing brilliancy, and they fired glances of scorn and fearlessness at her gibing enemies. She had never possessed the humble, religious feeling and sweet patience which distinguished Louis. A perfectly pure woman, at heart, she was somewhat of a Voltairean; she despised death, and feared no power. We are as we are made; so, in her final trial, she met the scowls of the people, chiefly of women, face to face. Some authorities say that one girl uttered a cry of pity as

the Queen passed—she was strangled. These unsexed
wretches had undertaken to accompany the Queen to the
scaffold with every possible indignity.

And she stands before her—judges.

"What is your name?"

"I am called Marie Antoinette, of Lorraine, in Austria,"
she replies, in a low, musical voice.

"Your condition?"

"Widow of Louis, formerly King of the French."

"Your age?"

"Thirty-seven."

Fouquier-Tinville now read the indictment. It was the
summing up of all her declared crimes of high birth, condition, and rank. She was quite guilty of all these things.
The chief accusations were merely echoes of all that had
been whispered of her in the foulest places. She was
accused of prodigality, licentiousness, and treason to
France.

She showed no sign of emotion, beyond an unheeded
movement of the fingers over the bar of a chair, as though
they were recalling some half-forgotten music

She answered all questions quite patiently, showed sorrow
only when reference was made to the Princess de Lamballe,
and only lost her quietude when one Hébert was called.
It is to be hoped this man was mad. At all events, he
spoke to the Queen's acts while in the Temple; declared
that she was depraved and debauched, and that she had
even corrupted her own son, "that she might poison his
body and his soul, and so reign in his name over the ruin
of his understanding.

This man was mad—there can be no doubt upon the
point. he even included saintly Madame Elizabeth in this
frantic idiotic accusation.

Heaven be thanked, those present turned upon him, and
cried "Shame!" The Queen herself shrank, raising her
hand as though to guard her from the wretch.

But one juryman was nearly as bad as Hébert.

"Why does not the accused answer?" this foul wretch
asked

"I do not answer," she said—and once again, it is said,
she looked radiantly beautiful in her momentary indignation—"because these are accusations to which nature refuses
a reply."

She turned to the women, with whom the court was crowded.

"I appeal from him to all mothers present."

To the honor of these women be it said, they cried Hébert down—and so he passes out of this history.

The Queen met questions having reference to the King with equal calmness. It being alleged that she endeavored to obtain ascendancy over him through his mental weakness, she replied, "I never knew that character of him. I was but his wife, and it was my duty and my pleasure to yield to his will."

By not one word, tending to save herself, did she injure the memory of her husband.

One line in the trial is enough to show what a mockery it was.

The Public Prosecutor cried, "All France bears witness against this woman!"

For form's sake, the jury deliberated an hour. She was recalled to hear her sentence, but the cheering and screaming of the people told her its terrors before the judge spoke —*death!*

Nine months since the King died, and now there was an end to her weary waiting

Asked if she had anything to say why the sentence of death should not be carried out, she respected herself in her very silence, and turned away, as though quite prepared for execution.

It was now five in the morning, and her last day was come. At half-past five she was permitted to write a letter to the King's sister, Madame Elizabeth. This lady never saw it. The document was found long afterwards amongst the papers of one Couthon.

"I write to you, my sister," she begins, "for the last time. I have been condemned, not to an ignominious death—that only awaits criminals—but to go and rejoin your brother. Innocent as he, I hope to show such firmness as the King's in his last moments. I grieve bitterly at leaving my poor children. You know that I lived but for them and you—you who, in your love, have sacrificed all for us. I learnt, at my trial, that you are separated from my little girl. In what a position I leave you! I

22 .

dare not write to her; they would not give her my letter, and, indeed, I do not know that you will receive this."

Some words of this final letter are inexpressibly touching. " Let my son never forget his father's last words. *Let him never seek to avenge our deaths !* "

She then goes on to apologize for the child's possible conduct to her, after the influence over him necessarily obtained by Simon, his tutor, and meekly she urges that he is so young he is incapable of knowing what he does.

" Think of me always," she says, in conclusion. " Good heaven, and my children ! How heart-rending it is to leave them for ever—for ever ! "

This letter being finished, she kissed each page lovingly, and folded it.

So far, the Republic had not entirely declared against high heaven, and priests were still recognised by those who had subscribed to the articles of the Revolution, and one of these men was offered to Marie Antoinette to aid her in her last moments. She refused to see him. The Convention (still sitting) insisted upon one of these officials accompanying her to the scaffold. There was no devotion amongst them. All hesitated, for all feared that the Queen would be torn to pieces on her way to the scaffold.

One proffered his help.

" Thank you," said the Queen ; " I have no need of your services, though I am a great sinner. But I am about to receive a great sacrament."

" Martyrdom," said the priest, in a low voice ; and he bowed and retired.

She prayed alone.

However, she had been secretly informed that at a certain house on her way to execution a minister would be stationed, who would give her absolution as she passed in the cart.

She dressed herself in the white gown, put a white cap on, bound with a black ribbon—and so came before the people.

Then she drew back—her queendom still remained. She had not thought the people so fallen that she should be taken to the scaffold in the common cart. The King had been taken to death at least in such a vehicle as he had been accustomed to.

Alas! When Louis died all pity had expired; with her death, all France was to gasp with thirst for blood

She mounted the cart—her hands having been bound behind her, and in the midst of a raging crowd. The cart swayed, and she could scarcely keep her seat on the plank.

She grew red and pale by turns, as she was dragged through the mob. The patience and pity exhibited by the King she could not imitate. Her lips were bitter each moment; but she never took her dry, hot eyes from the raging people.

Suddenly, her head falls humbly, and, her hands being tied, she makes the sign of the cross by three motions of the head.

Her pride had passed with that unseen blessing from the house on her way to execution. When the Palace of the Tuileries came in view—the place where she had spent nearly half her life—tears fell down her face.

A few turns of the wheels, and she was at the foot of the scaffold.

Reaching the place, accidentally she trod upon one of the executioners' feet.

"Pardon me," she said, in a sweet, courtly voice.

She knelt for an instant, rose, stretched her neck towards the distant towers of the Temple, and cried, " Good-bye, my children! I am going to your father "

She did not, like her husband, speed to Heaven. It was rather that she fled from earth.

The executioner was trembling more than his victim, so that she suffered a long agony of a few moments after she was upon the plank.

The assistant executioner took his brother's place.

The head fell. It was taken up and carried around the scaffold.

" *Long live the Republic!* " saluted this brave display.

The Revolution thought itself avenged—it was befouled.

She came a foreigner—and they killed her.

Thus she died. Frivolous in prosperity, she died with intrepidity. Her misfortune was her mistrust of the people in her early days—her catastrophe, that all the sin and wickedness of the Court was laid to her account.

Called upon to fill a throne, those who called her gave her not even a tomb—for you may read in a parish register, " *For the coffin of the Widow Capet, six shillings!* "

With her life, France threw away all Christian mercy. Crimson swept over the breadth and length of the land.

<hr />

CHAPTER LX.

THE TWENTY-TWO.

THE twenty-two had literally been under the control of the police, though not arrested, since May 31st. But as events progressed, their destruction became almost necessary to the safety of those members of the Convention, who, obtaining power wholly through the will of the more violent, could only retain it by a perfect recognition of the will of those who had given them the victory.

The twenty-two were therefore seized, and placed in a building coverted from a convent into a prison, and here they made full preparations to die.

To this day, the walls of this place may be seen covered with mementoes of the prison-days of the victims of the Revolution. They are chiefly short verses, written in blood, the purple hues of which many of the inscriptions still retain.

A few days after the Queen's day of peace arrived, their trial commenced.

Of what were they accused?

Really, nothing; but they were in the way, and a threatening division of the masses insisted upon their death.

After four days' mockery of justice, the twenty-two were declared guilty of having conspired against the unity and indivisibility of the republic, and the whole were condemned to die.

A cry of horror burst from the condemned, for many of them could not believe that innocent men could be sent to the scaffold.

Valasé, one of the youngest, slipped from his seat to the floor.

"What, Valasé! art losing courage now?" cried his friend Brissot, upholding him.

"No; I am dying!" returned Valasé; and his fingers

quivered about the handle of the poniard with which he had taken his own life.

Silent horror for a moment prevailed; the Girondists blushed and bowed their heads before their dead companion, who had given them an example of fearlessness in meeting death.

Only one, named Boileau, showed cowardice. He cast his hat into the air and screamed, "I don't belong to these men! I am a Jacobin!"

But instead of pity he only gained contempt.

And now a cry was heard; it came from Camille Desmoulins: "Let me fly," he cried; "it is my book which has killed them!"

But the crowd seized Desmoulins, and forced him to remain.

The twenty-two came down from the high seats upon which they had heard their trial and sentence, and for a moment stood round the dead body of their friend, who had shown them how to die. Almost simultaneously they raised their hands and cried, "Innocent! Long live the republic!"

Then they cast all the money they had with them amongst the crowding, storming people, who greedily seized it. This was done, not to excite the mob to revolt, but with the thought that, their death at hand, they had no farther need of wealth.

There was something strangely classic and Roman-like in their death. They left the hall singing loudly the celebrated hymn, the "Marseillaise;" and in reference to their death, they sang with amazing power the celebrated two lines,

> "March on, march on! O children of the land,
> The day, the hour of glory, is at hand!"

This terrible hymn they were still singing as they entered their prison. It was now late in the evening, and they were to suffer on the following morning.

The tribunal had decreed that the yet warm corpse of Valasé should be carried back to prison, conveyed in the same cart with his accomplices to the scaffold, and interred with their bodies. The only sentence, perhaps, which punished the dead.

Four men-at-arms carried the body upon a litter, and thus the procession reached the prison.

The twenty-two were to pass the night in the same room, the corpse in one corner. The twenty-one—even Boileau, who repented of his momentary cowardice—came, one by one, and kissed the dead man's hand, then covered his face, saying, "To-morrow, brother!"

One Bailleul, a Girondist and a Conventionist, but who had escaped the proscription, yet had not left Paris, had promised that, after the trial, he would prepare and send to the prison, either a triumphant or a funereal supper, according to the sentence.

The promise was kept. Upon the oaken table, stretching the length of their dungeon was set out a supper, royal in its magnificence. Every luxury to be obtained, every delicate wine with a name, filled those portions of the table not covered by a wealth of flowers and great clusters of brilliantly burning wax candles.

To one Abbé Lambert, who lived fifty years after that night, we owe all we have learnt concerning that final meal. This minister was waiting to offer consolation to the condemned as they passed to the scaffold.

The supper lasted from midnight until the dawn of day —at the end of October, about half-past five. It was the feast of their marriage with death. No sign was given of their approaching end. All ate with sobriety, but with appetite; and it was only when the fruit and wine alone remained on the table that the conversation became excited and powerful.

Many, especially the younger men, who did not leave families behind them, were very gay and witty. They had done no great wrong, and were sacrificed to duty, therefore they met death with cheerful faces.

With solemn break of day, the conversation became graver.

Brissot cried, "now that we, the honest men amongst those who govern, are about to die, what will become of the republic? How much blood will it require to wash away the memory of ours?"

"Friends," cried Vergniaud, "we have killed the tree by over-pruning it. It was aged—Robespierre cuts it down. Will he be more fortunate than ourselves? No;

the land of France is now too weak for honest growth. The people play with laws as children with toys; they are too weak to govern themselves, and they will return to their kings as children to their toys, after they are tired of having thrown them away. We thought ourselves at Rome; we were in Paris. But, in dying let us leave to the whole of France—the strength of hope. Some day—some great day—she will be able to govern herself."

At ten o'clock the executioners arrived to prepare the victims for the scaffold. Gensonné, picking up a lock of the black, brilliant hair cut from his head, gave it to Abbé Lambert, and begged him to carry it to his wife. "Tell her," he said, "it is all I can send, and that I die thinking of her."

Vergniaud drew his watch from his pocket, scratched his initials and the date in it with a pin, and sent it by the hands of one of the executioners' assistants to a young girl whom he loved deeply, and whom it is said he intended to marry.

Every one sent a something to some one or more in memory of himself, and it is pleasant to be able to state that every message and remembrance were faithfully delivered.

When the last lock of hair had fallen, the victims were marshalled, and they were led out to the carts waiting to receive them.

They sang the "Marseillaise" to the scaffold—they sang it when they reached it, the song growing fainter and fainter as each head fell; and the hymn only ceased, as the last head fell—that of their leader, Vergniaud.

The dead body of their friend was carried with them.

Such was the end of the founders of the French republic.

With them the brightness, beauty, youth, wit, frankness of the Convention passed away, and their places were filled by sullen, threatening men.

CHAPTER LXI.

THE RED FLAG.

THE first to fall was the Duc of Orleans (father of Louis Philippe, King of the French), He had done nothing against the interests of the republic, but his birth was a crime, and his death was decided on.

The Prince and his sons were at table when the fatal indictment arrived.

"So much the better," said he. "This must end one way or the other. Kiss me, children. And I wonder of what they accuse me?" he said, opening the paper. "The scoundrels!" he added; "they accuse me of nothing. Come, boys, eat; for this summons is indeed good news."

He was taken to Paris, where, at this time, no man of mark, being put upon his trial, escaped the guillotine.

The one plausible accusation brought against Orleans must have compressed his heart.

"Did you not vote the King's death in the hope of succeeding to his throne?"

"No; I obeyed my heart and my conscience."

He heard his sentence calmly, despite the fact of his cowardice in his early years; and he replied sarcastically to his judges, "Since you were determined to condemn me, you should have found better pretexts than you have; for, as it is, you will deceive no man into believing that you think me guilty. I am in the way. And you too," he said, turning to a once Marquis d'Autonelle, an old friend, —"you to condemn me! Finally," he continued, "since I am to die, I demand not to be left in gaol a whole night, but to be at once taken to the block."

This desire was not complied with. Returning to the gaol, his rage was terrible.

The Abbé Lambert approached and said, "Citizen Equality, will you accept my assistance, or, at least, the offer of my condolence?"

"Who are you?"

"The Vicar-General of the Bishop of Paris. If you will not accept my religious help, can I be of any service to you after your death? Have you messages to send?"

"No; I can die without help, and like a good citizen."

He went to the place of execution at three, accompanied by three others.

Reaching the scaffold, he looked at the knife calmly; and the executioner offering to remove his boots, he said, "You will do it more easily afterwards."

He was dressed very beautifully for his death, and he died without fear. He had followed the Revolution blindly —had thrown away fortune, name, reputation, in its cause, and it destroyed him simply because he had belonged to royalty.

Terror was rapidly reddening all the land.

The guillotine was not quick enough, and squads of soldiers shot down the condemned.

Such sentences as the following, were accepted as truths :—

"The time is come when the prophecy shall be fulfilled. The wealthy shall be despoiled, and the poor shall be enriched.

"If the people want bread, let them profit by the sight of their misery, to seize on the possessions of the wealthy.

"Do you seek a word which furnishes all you need?— die, or cause others to die."

The great Terror began at Lyons.

"The great day of vengance has arrived," cried one Cholier. "Five hundred men amongst us deserve to share the fate of the tyrant. I will give you the list—be it your part to strike !"

He then seized a crucifix, dashed it upon the ground, and trampled upon it.

Here is another theory which was applauded :—

"Any man can be an executioner—it is the guillotine which really takes life"

This Cholier, who had trampled upon the crucifix, clung to it when condemned to the death he was always seeking for others. The knife was blunt, and five times it was raised before the head fell. "Quick—quick !" the wretch cried, when it was raised for the fifth time.

Some time after, when the Terror was rising to its height, Cholier was looked upon as a martyr; his body was burnt, and the ashes placed in an urn, were carried triumphantly through the streets, and placed upon an altar of patriotism raised to him.

The altar in question was soon thrown down.

But only after the Terror ended.

With Cholier's after-death triumph, the "moderates" began to fall. Ten of the municipals of Lyons (the place of Cholier's exploits) were beheaded in one day, and a mine was exploded which destroyed the finest parts of the city.

Lyons was almost annihilated At a cost of half a million of money (English), houses worth twelve millions were destroyed. Why? France was mad. So hurriedly was this destruction effected, that hundreds of the workmen themselves were buried in the ruins.

Life, however, was cheap.

Rags only were to be seen—a decent dress was equivalent to condemnation. The city was dead but for the thunder of fallen houses, the roar of cannon and the rattle of musketry mowing down suspected people, and the shrill cry of the ragged as they marked another head fall beneath the guillotine knife. It was now looked upon as a distinction, and reserved only for important people.

An entire generation was destroyed in Lyons alone. Great houses were unowned—for their owners were dead. Castles, churches, factories, work-shops, were closed, for their heads had all passed under the guillotine.

Starvation increased, for the land lay a-dying.

The guillotine was getting old and worn-out at Lyons.

One morning, sixty-four are marched out to death. They are bound, and ranged in a line before an open trench. Three pieces of cannon, loaded with bullets, sweep the ranks. Not half are touched. "Forward!" is the word given to the dragoons, who hack and shoot down the victims. This lasts two whole hours.

Nine hundred and thirty executioners, in the shape of an entire regiment, were to send their victims, marshalled in a row, into eternity at the same moment. At the order "Fire!" four bullets struck at the life of the victims, all of whom are tied to a rope stretched from tree to tree.

Strange—when the smoke arose, only half were found dead. The rest remained either wounded or untouched. The unscathed stared in horror; the wounded screamed to be despatched.

The soldiers could not fire again. Some of the prisoners had freed themselves, and were escaping. The dragoons were ordered forward to cut them down. The victims were killed piece-meal. One man, a mayor of his town, reached the river, but there his bleeding hand betrayed him, and he was cast into the river.

The soldiers protested against the use to which they were put. The massacres lasted until night-fall. Yet when the grave-diggers came next morning, some hearts still beat. The sextons put the martyrs out of their misery at once by blows on the head with their pickaxes.

"We are purging the land," wrote Collet d'Herbois to the Convention.

Every day twenty-two were regularly shot. By this time, the fear of life rendered death sweet. Girls, men, children, prayed that they might be shot with their parents. Sometimes they permitted this, and little boys and girls were shot, holding their father's hands.

Women who were seen to shed tears at executions, were shot.

Mourning was prohibited under pain of death.

One lad of fourteen, says, "Quick—quick! You have killed papa! I want to overtake him!"

One De Rochefort* was accompanied by a son to the butchering-ground, whither he went with three relatives. The men fell—the boy, aged fifteen, remained standing.

The executioner hesitated—the people murmured.

"God save the King!" cried De Rochefort.

A moment—a report—he fell, shattered to death.

A lovely girl, fourteen, is brought before the judge for refusing to wear the national cockade.

"Why do you refuse to wear it?" asks the judge.

"Because you do!" replies the child.

Her beauty, rather than justice, pleading for her, a sign was made that a wreath should be put in her hair, the emblem of liberation.

She cast it upon the ground. She died.

A man came to the Hall of Justice.

"You have slain my father, my brothers, my wife—kill me. My religion forbids me to destroy myself. In mercy, kill me."

In mercy—they killed him.

* Grandfather of the Henri de Rochefort who writes the *Lanterne.*

A woman, who had fought bravely in the earlier and fairer time of the Revolution, was carried to the scaffold, though about to become a mother. She did not fear death —she pleaded for the other life.

She was laughed at—hooted—and so died.

A girl of seventeen, and much resembling Charlotte Corday, was accused of having served as an artillerist in the trenches of the forces opposed to the national forces.

" What is your name ? "

" Mary ; the name of the mother of the God for whom I am about to die."

" Your age ? "

" Seventeen ; the age of Charlotte Corday."

" How !—at seventeen, fight against your country ? "

" I fought to save it."

" Citizen—we, your judges, admire your courage. What would you do with your life if we gave it you ? "

" Use it to kill you ! "

She ascended the scaffold, alarmed at the crowd of people —fearless of death. She refused the executioner's help— cried twice, " God save the King ! "—and lay down to die.

After her death, the executioner found amongst her clothes a note written in blood. It was from her lover, who had been shot some days before.

The lovers were only separated by a few days. Their history touched the people, but the people of that day did not know how to pardon.

These awful executions were at last arrested, not because the victims were exhausted, but because the soldiers threw down their arms and positively refused any longer to play the shameful parts of executioners.

Napoleon Bonaparte, the tyrant-liberator of the oppressed republic, now rose to his first distinction.

The English were in possession of Toulon. Admiral Hood was preparing to flood France with English red-coats.

Within a week Bonaparte had compelled the English to retire, but not before they had destroyed the arsenal and the whole of the French navy.

On the beach, fifteen thousand refugees from various parts of France sought to get away to the combined English and Spanish fleets.

A storm arose in the midst of this destruction. Seven

thousand were rescued from the vengeance of the Republican arms; eight thousand perished

These refugees were chiefly carried to Leghorn, where their descendants still reside.

The Convention ordered that Toulon should be razed to the ground for having submitted to the English

This frantic order, however, was not carried out.

Napoleon was now Emperor of Toulon. Already he disobeyed orders, and rose daily to power.

Marat had risen over the Girondists and Liberals, Danton over him; Robespierre was to destroy Danton, but Napoleon was to set his foot upon them all, and command, until, in his turn, in 1815, he was to succumb.

CHAPTER LXII.

THE BLOOD OF WOMEN.

MADAME ROLAND who had now been imprisoned through five long months, was the next celebrated victim demanded by the people. She had conquered her weariness by writing her life.

At one time, she sought to avoid death by poison; but the memory of her child prevailed, and she lived on to the end.

When the Girondists fell, she knew all hope of life for herself was at an end. She was then removed to the prison whence Marie Antoinette went to the scaffold—nay, she was imprisoned in the adjoining cell; and here she passed her days, watching the fragment of sky she could see through the bars of her prison, or admiring the little bunches of flowers the gaoler's good-hearted wife sent to her dungeon almost daily.

She was tried for being the wife of Roland, and the friend of the Girondists. She was proud of the accusation, declared herself to be so, and she heard her condemnation to death with a calm bearing and a smiling face.

"I thank you," she said, "that you think me worthy to share the fate of great and good men."

That same day she was placed in the last of a number of carts, her only companion being an old man. Her beauty was more than radiant, seated so near trembling age.

She wore a white dress, and her long black hair streamed down her back.

Near the scaffold had been erected a colossal statue of Liberty. When she ascended the scaffold, she bowed to the statue, and cried, " Oh Liberty, how much crime is committed in your name!"

But she had shown her woman's tenderness at the foot of the scaffold. She said to her companion, " Go first, that you may not see me die. Let me save you that pain."

She died quite fearlessly.

The next day, some peasants, driving home their flocks, found the dead body of a man, a sword-stick blade through his heart. The position of the remains proved suicide, effected by putting the sword-handle against a tree, when the sufferer flung himself upon the point. A paper found upon the dead man contained these words : —

"Whoever thou art that findest these remains, respect them as those of a virtuous man. After my wife's death, I will not remain another day upon this earth, so stained with crimes."

This was Madame Roland's husband.

Very different from this honest woman's death was that of Madame Dubarry, mistress of Louis XV. Her crime was the concealment of a treasure. As a King's favorite, she had amassed enormous wealth. Strangely enough, it was a favorite of her own—a negro boy she had adopted — that denounced her. She was condemned, and she went shrieking to the scaffold—the only instance of this kind amongst all the women who died during the Reign of Terror.

Her beauty was her crime.

" Life!" she cried. " Life for repentance—for devotion to the Republic! All my treasures for a little life!"

The knife only cut short these ignoble cries.

The next thing done was the abolition of the name of the days of the weeks and months of the year, because they were idolatrous.

Finally, the Catholic faith was abolished, the church bells were cast into money, the worship of the Goddess of Reason, was proclaimed. The proclamation was carried into effect at the Cathedral. An actress, one Mdlle. Maillard, beautiful, talented, and a favorite of the late Queen's, was compelled to play the part of the goddess.

She was borne into the church (the only one now open in all Paris) upon a kind of litter, covered with oak branches, and followed by girls dressed in white, singing jubilant songs. About the altar were the opera choristers and others. The actress was now placed upon the altar, and she was worshipped by those present. The Bishop had been compelled to appear, and he sat motionless with fear, tears of shame coursing down his face.

The burial places of the Kings were now invaded. The remains of a thousand years of kings were torn from the vaults of St. Denis, and cast into the country ditches. Nothing was spared—anything which suggested royalty, was destroyed.

Meanwhile, Carrier, at Nantes, surpassed in outrage all that had gone before him. It was charitable to suppose he was sheer mad.

Men, women, children, and especially priests, were shot down by Carrier's orders. He said trial was useless. His rivals had abandoned the guillotine for the butchery of the soldier's lead. Carrier improved upon this. He said he hated blood, so he positively sank hundreds, thousands of accused, in huge barges. They were carried down to the bottom, and there to this day they remain.

Carrier was the deputy sent by the Convention, of which Robespierre was now King.

These massacres lasted months. Some complaints were sent to Paris. Carrier seized two hundred of the principal merchants of the place, cast them into prison, tortured them, and then drowned the men.

At last, his madness becoming apparent, he was recalled. Robespierre did not demand his punishment; and this omission of justice was one of the accusations brought against Robespierre at *his* trial.

A woman began the attack upon Robespierre. She was Rose Lacombe, beautiful, eloquent, revolutionary; but pitying and hating blood. She was seized with love for a young prisoner, tried to save him, failed, and she devoted herself to Robespierre's death.

Robespierre, to retain his popularity, determined to sacrifice Danton, Camille Desmoulins, and others. They fell—all of them.

As these victims, on their way to execution, passed Duplay's house, the shutters of which were closed, the crowd burst into a roar of applause. Robespierre watching, trembled.

A very short span, and his time was to come.

Hérault de Séchelles was the first to alight from the cart. He turned to embrace Danton, when the executioner pulled him away.

"Brute!" said Danton; "but you cannot prevent our lips touching in the basket."

Camille Desmoulins was the last but one of the four. He was quite resigned. He looked at the knife, then turning to the people, he said, "Look on at the end of the first apostle of liberty! He who murders me will not survive me long!"

"Send this lock of hair to my mother," he said to the executioner.

They were his last words.

Danton ascended last. He never looked more haughty and defiant. For one moment he broke down. "Wife!" he screamed.

Then he added, "Come, come, Danton; no weakness. Executioner, show my head to the people; it is worth looking at!"

The executioner caught the head as it was falling, and carried it round the scaffold.

The mob applauded. Such is the end of favorites.

Eight thousand people were awaiting death in the prisons of Paris alone, within a month of Danton's death.

Robespierre was delicate and decent in his power and supreme cruelty, but he capped all his compeers. Men and women were not shot or drowned in Paris, but the guillotine worked unceasingly.

Certain children had, in 1791, taken part in receiving the Prussian General at Verdun. They were all brought to Paris, and guillotined.

The nuns of Montmartre were carried, abbess, young girls, and old women, all to the scaffold—for praying! As the Girondists sang their hymns, so these poor women sang theirs. The last death ended the last note of this hymn.

It was thus Robespierre—now alone of all those with whom he first came into power—and his statellites maintained their power.

One, and only one, grown-up scion of royalty remained —Madame Elizabeth

It was then more than a year since the King died. She and the Princess remained together—deprived even of cards, because of the kings and queens in the pack.

As for the Dauphin, he was confined in a room the bed of which he never left His bread was thrown to him. No one ever spoke to him, and his clothes had not been changed for nearly twelve months. His window would not open He was allowed no books, paper, or playthings; in a word, he was brutalized at six years of age His limbs stiffened, and he became an idiot, in which state he died.

The aunt and sister could hear nothing about the child. They were treated tolerably well, but during Lent they were only given fat meat to eat. This their consciences would not allow them to touch, and for forty days they only ate bread.

The summons came suddenly at night-time. The little Princess, the only one of the five prisoners of the Temple who survived the Reign of Terror, wept, clung to her aunt —but lost her.

Her defence was very simple :—"I am tried because I am the King's sister. You call him a tyrant Had he been, you would not have been where you are; I not be where I am!"

The people demanded her life, and they obtained it.

The very women who generally yelled around the carts were dumb, as this serene, angelic woman was carried through the streets. She died so peacefully, that many envied her.

23

CHAPTER LXIII.

ROBESPIERRE FALLS.

ATHEISM was now preached openly.

Robespierre pronounced in favor of an unknown deity, and in so magnificent a speech, that it may be said he gave back religion to France.

But his time had come.

What was his crime in the eyes of his accusers? Unpopularity.

One night he is addressing the Convention, when the uproar is so incessant, that in endeavoring to make himself heard, his voice fails him.

The people were already looking towards Napoleon—the man of the sword, not of the tongue.

Robespierre fell back upon silence, but he was always to be seen at his place at the Convention. Hour after hour, friends became enemies.

He knew he was condemned, but he waited.

Here is the final scene :—

Robespierre and his friends, St. Just, Couthon, and Lebas, seated in a room by themselves, hear the jingle of approaching soldiers. Lebas takes one of a couple of pistols, and presents it—" Robespierre, let us die."

"No; I await the executioner," says Robespierre, and the other two murmur in assent.

The sounds come nearer.

A report—and Lebas falls. He has shot himself through the heart.

The soldier-insurgents swarm into the room.

"Down with the tyrant! Where is he?"

These were the cries Robespierre heard.

He did not quail.

"Which is the man?" asks a soldier of Leonard Bourdon, who did not face his fallen enemy.

He pointed the questioner's pistol at Robespierre, and he said, "That is the man."

The report was heard, and the next moment Robespierre's head fell upon the proclamation he was signing at the instant.

The ball had entered the left side of the face, and carried away part of the cheek and several teeth.

Couthon tried to rise, and fell to the ground.

St. Just sat calmly glancing from his fallen friend to his enemies.

The procession to the Convention was horrible enough. It was now daybreak.

First was carried Robespierre, on a litter, his face tied up in a handkerchief; then came his brother, insensible, in the arms of two men; then followed the dead body of Lebas, over which they had thrown a table-cover.

Couthon, who had rolled in the mud, followed; and the procession was closed by St. Just, walking bare-headed.

"The recreant Robespierre is here!" said the President of the Convention, a man just chosen. "Shall he be brought in?"

"No, no!" cried the Conventionists. "The corpse of a tyrant can carry nothing but contagion along with it. To the scaffold!"

Robespierre was put aside in a room, and hundreds of people pushed in to assure themselves the tyrant was dead.

He heard and saw all; but could not speak.

At three, he and his friends were tried. At six, they were being conveyed in carts to execution.

There was no lack of people to see Robespierre die; women dressed as for a ball, believing that with Robespierre the Reign of Terror was at an end.

Children huddled around the carts—orphans of his victims—crying, "Kill him! kill him!"

His procession to the scaffold was a line of loud-spoken imprecations.

He never spoke or uttered a cry, except when the bandage was taken from his face; then a scream, heard many hundred yards away, burst from him.

His head fell—he and the Terror ended together.

France fell into the hands of Napoleon.

* * * * *

My tale is done. I have said very little about myself— I, René Besson, found in my old age by Alexander Dumas, seated in the sunlight. I married Estelle Duplay (the furies broke into the house of Duplay, the day after

Robespierre's death, and killed his poor wife), and found peace and happiness. One last word! I have never regretted saving Sophie Gerbaut, and the Viscount de Malmv, from the Terror. That I did. I am now an old man. My very last words are these. The Revolution was terrible, but it did the world more good in the long run than the world has yet found out.

RENE BESSON.

THE END.

BEST COOK BOOKS PUBLISHED.

Mrs. Goodfellow's Cookery as it Should Be,................. .....Cloth, $1 75
Petersons' New Cook Book,...................................... .....Cloth, 1 75
Miss Leslie's New Cookery Book,................................. .. Cloth, 1 75
Widdifield's New Cook Book, ...Cloth, 1 75
The National Cook Book. By a Practical Housewife,...... ...Cloth, 1 75
The Family Save-All. By author of " National Cook Book," Cloth, 1 75
Mrs. Hale's Receipts for the Million,............................ Cloth, 1 75
Miss Leslie's New Receipts for Cooking,...... .... Cloth, 1 75
Mrs. Hale's New Cook Book,........................ .. .. Cloth, 1 75
Francatelli's Celebrated French, Italian, German, and English
   Cook Book. The Modern Cook. With Sixty-two illustrations.
   Complete in six hundred large octavo pages,... ....Cloth, 5 00

WORKS BY THE VERY BEST AUTHORS.

The following books are each issued in one large duodecimo volume, in paper cover, at $1.00 each, or each one is bound in cloth, at $1.75 each.

✗ The Initials. A Love Story. By Baroness Tautphœus,.... .. .. 1 50
✗ Family Pride. By author of " Pique," " Family Secrets,' etc. 1 50
✗ Self-Sacrifice. By author of " Margaret Maitland," etc 1 50
✗ The Woman in Black. A Companion to the "Woman in White," ... 1 50
A Woman's Thoughts about Women. By Miss Muloch,........ ...... 1 50
✗ Flirtations in Fashionable Life. By Catharine Sinclair, ... 1 50
Rose Douglas. A Companion to " Family Pride," and "Self Sacrifice," 1 50
✗ False Pride, or, Two Ways to Matrimony. A Charming Book,...... 1 50
✗ Family Secrets. A Companion to " Family Pride," and "Pique,"... 1 50
The Morrisons. By Mrs. Margaret Hosmer,............................ 1 50
Beppo. The Conscript. By T. A. Trollope, author of " Gemma,".. 1 50
Gemma. An Italian Story. By T. A. Trollope, author of " Beppo," 1 50
Marietta. By T. A. Trollope, author of " Gemma,"........ .. .. 1 50
My Son's Wife. By author of " Caste," " Mr. Arle," etc 1 50
✗ The Rich Husband. By author of " George Geith,"...... .... 1 50
Harem Life in Egypt and Constantinople By Emmeline Lott 1,50
The Rector's Wife ; or, the Valley of a Hundred Fires.. .... 1 50
Woodburn Grange. A Novel. By William Howitt,.. .... 1 50
Country Quarters. By the Countess of Blessington,.... .... 1 50
✗ Out of the Depths. The Story of a "Woman's Life,"...... .... 1 50
The Coquette; or, the Life and Letters of Eliza Wharton.. ... . 1 50
The Pride of Life. A Story of the Heart. By Lady Jane Scott ... 1 50
✗ The Lost Beauty. By a Noted Lady of the Spanish Court,.. .... 1 50
Saratoga. An Indian Tale of Frontier Life. A true Story of 1787, 1 50
Married at Last. A Love Story. By Annie Thomas, ... 1 50
✗ The Quaker Soldier. A Revolutionary Romance. By Judge Jones, ... 1 50
The Man of the World. An Autobiography. By William North,.... 1 50
The Queen's Favorite ; or, The Price of a Crown. A Love Story,... 1 50
Self Love: or, The Afternoon of Single and Married Life,......... .. 1 50
✗ Cora Belmont: or, The Sincere Lover. . A True Story of the Heart,. 1 50
The Lover's Trials ; or Days before 1776 By Mrs. Mary A. Denison, 1 50
✗ High Life in Washington. A Life Picture. By Mrs. N. P Lasselle, 1 50
The Beautiful Widow; or, Lodore. By Mrs Percy B Shelley,...... 1 50
✗ Love and Money. By J B. Jones, author of the " Rival Belles,". . 1 50
The Matchmaker. A Story of High Life. By Beatrice Reynolds,.. 1 50
The Brother's Secret; or, the Count De Mara. By William Godwin, 1 50
The Lost Love. By Mrs. Oliphant, author of " Margaret Maitland," 1 50
The Roman Traitor. By Henry William Herbert. A Roman Story, 1 50
   The above books are each in paper cover, or in cloth, price $1 75 each.

WORKS BY THE VERY BEST AUTHORS.

The following books are each issued in one large duodecimo volume in paper cover, at $1 50 each, or each one is bound in cloth, at $1 75 each.

The Dead Secret. By Wilkie Collins, author of " The Crossed Path," 1 50
Memoirs of Vidocq, the French Detective. His Life and Adventures, 1 50
The Crossed Path, or Basil. By Wilkie Collins,...... .... 1 50
Indiana. A Love Story. By George Sand, author of " Consuelo," 1 50
The Belle of Washington. With her Portrait. By Mrs. N. P. Lisselle, 1 50
The Bohemians of London. By Edward M. Whitty,. 1 50
The Rival Belles; or, Life in Washington. By J. B. Jones, . .. 1 50
The Devoted Bride. A Story of the Heart. By St. George Tucker, 1 50
Love and Duty. By Mrs. Hubback, author of " May and December," 1 50
Wild Sports and Adventures in Africa. By Major W. C. Harris, 1 50
Courtship and Matrimony. By Robert Morris. With a Portrait,.... 1 50
The Jealous Husband. By Annette Marie Maillard, ... 1 50
The Refugee. By Herman Melville, author of " Omoo," " Typee," 1 50
The Life, Writings, Lectures, and Marriages of Fanny Fern, .. 1 50
The Life and Lectures of Lola Montez, with her portrait, on steel, . 1 50
Will Southern Scenes. By author of " Wild Western Scenes,". 1 50
Career Lyle, or, the Autobiography of an Actress. By Louise Reeder. 1 50
Coal, Coal Oil, and all other Minerals in the Earth. By Eli Bowen, 1 50
The Cabin and Parlor. By J. Thornton Randolph. Illustrated, . 1 50
Jealousy. By George Sand, author of " Consuelo," " Indiana," etc 1 50
The Little Beauty. A Love Story. By Mrs. Grey 1 50
The Adopted Heir. A Love Story. By Miss Pardoe. 1 50
Secession, Coercion, and Civil War. By J. B. Jones,. 1 50
The Count of Monte Cristo. By Alexander Dumas. Illustrated, . 1 50
Camille; or, the Fate of a Coquette. By Alexander Dumas,. 1 50
Six Nights with the Washingtonians. By T. S. Arthur. ... 1 50
Lizzie Glenn; or, the Trials of a Seamstress. By T. S. Arthur. . 1 50
Lady Maud; or, the Wonder of Kingswood Chase. By Pierce Egan, 1 50
Wilfred Montressor, or, High Life in New York. Illustrated . 1 50
The Old Stone Mansion. By C. J. Peterson author " Kate Aylesford," 1 50
Kate Aylesford. By Chas. J. Peterson, author " Old Stone Mansion,' 1 50
Lorrimer Littlegood, by author " Harry Coverdale's Courtship,' 1 50
The Red Court Farm. By Mrs. Henry Wood, author of " East Lynne." 1 50
Mildred Arkell. By Mrs. Henry Wood, author of " Red Court Farm," 1 50
The Earl's Secret. A Love Story. By Miss Pardoe. 1 50
The Adopted Heir. By Miss Pardoe, author of " The Earl's Secret," 1 50
Lord Montague's Page. By G. P. R. James, ... 1 50
The Cavalier. By G. P. R. James, author of " Lord Montague's Page," 1 50
Cousin Harry. By Mrs. Grey, author of " The Gambler's Wife," etc. 1 50
The Conscript. A Tale of War. By Alexander Dumas, ... 1 50
The Tower of London. By W. Harrison Ainsworth. Illustrated, . 1 50
Shoulder Straps. By Henry Morford, author of " Days of Shoddy," 1 50
Days of Shoddy. By Henry Morford, author of " Shoulder Straps," 1 50
The Coward. By Henry Morford, author of " Days of Shoddy,". .. 1 50
  The above books are each in paper cover, or in cloth, price $1 75 each.

The Wandering Jew. By Eugene Sue. Full of Illustrations, ... 1 50
Mysteries of Paris; and its Sequel, Gerolstein. By Eugene Sue. 1 50
Martin, the Foundling. By Eugene Sue. Full of Illustrations,.... 1 50
Ten Thousand a Year. By Samuel C. Warren. With Illustrations, 1 50
Washington and His Generals. By George Lippard 1 50
The Quaker City, or, the Monks of Monk Hall. By George Lippard, 1 50
Blanche of Brandywine. By George Lippard, ... 1 50
Paul Ardenheim, the Monk of Wissahickon. By George Lippard 1 50
  The above books are each in paper cover, or in cloth, price $2.00 each.

NEW AND GOOD BOOKS BY BEST AUTHORS.

The Last Athenian. From the Swedish of Victor Rydberg. Highly recommended by Fredrika Bremer. Paper $1.50, or in cloth,...... $2 00
Comstock's Elocution and Reader. Enlarged. By Andrew Comstock and Philip Lawrence. With 236 Illustrations. Half morocco,......2 00
Comstock's Colored Chart. Every School should have a copy of it... 5 00
Across the Atlantic. Letters from France, Switzerland Germany, Italy, and England. By C. H. Haeseler, M.D. Bound in cloth,... 2 00
Colonel John W. Forney's Letters from Europe. Bound in cloth,. 1 75
The Ladies' Guide to True Politeness and Perfect Manners. By Miss Leslie Every lady should have it. Cloth, full gilt back ... 1 75
The Ladies' Complete Guide to Needlework and Embroidery. With 113 illustrations. By Miss Lambert. Cloth, full gilt back,. 1 75
The Ladies' Work Table Book. With 27 illustrations. Cloth, gilt,. 1 50
The Story of Elizabeth. By Miss Thackeray, paper $1.00, or cloth,... 1 50
Life and Adventures of Don Quixote and his Squire Sancho Panza, complete in one large volume, paper cover, for $1 00, or in cloth, 1 50
The Laws and Practice of Game of Euchre. By a Professor. Cloth, 1 00
Whitefriars; or, The Days of Charles the Second. Illustrated,........1 00

HUMOROUS ILLUSTRATED WORKS.

Each one full of Illustrations, by Felix O. C. Darley, and bound in Cloth.

Major Jones' Courtship and Travels. With 21 Illustrations,........ 1 75
Major Jones' Scenes in Georgia. With 16 Illustrations, ... 1 75
Simon Suggs' Adventures and Travels. With 17 Illustrations 1 75
Swamp Doctor's Adventures in the South-West. 14 Illustrations,... 1 75
Col. Thorpe's Scenes in Arkansaw. With 16 Illustrations, ... 1 75
The Big Bear's Adventures and Travels. With 18 Illustrations........ 1 75
High Life in New York, by Jonathan Slick. With Illustrations, ... 1 75
Judge Haliburton's Yankee Stories. Illustrated, ... 1 75
Harry Coverdale's Courtship and Marriage. Illustrated,... . ... 1 75
Piney Wood's Tavern, or, Sam Slick in Texas Illustrated, ... 1 75
Sam Slick, the Clockmaker. By Judge Haliburton Illustrated,. 1 75
Humors of Falconbridge. By J. F. Kelley. With Illustrations 1 75
Modern Chivalry. By Judge Breckenridge. Two vols, each. 1 75
Neal's Charcoal Sketches. By Joseph C. Neal. 21 Illustrations,... 2 50

ALEXANDER DUMAS' WORKS.

Count of Monte Cristo,..........	1 50	Memoirs of a Physician..........	1 00
The Iron Mask,.	1 00	Queen's Necklace, ...	1 00
Louise La Valliere,....	1 00	Six Years Later, ...	1 00
Adventures of a Marquis, ...	1 00	Countess of Charney,........ . .	1 00
Diana of Meridor, ...	1 00	Andree de Taverney, ...	1 00
The Three Guardsmen,..........	75	The Chevalier,..	1 00
Twenty Years After, ...	75	Forty five Guardsmen, ...	75
Bragelonne......	75	The Iron Hand	75
The Conscript. A Tale of War,	1 50	Camille, "The Camelia Lady,"	1 50

The above are each in paper cover, or in cloth, price $1 75 each.

Edmond Dantes,....	75	Man with Five Wives, ...	75
Felina de Chambure,.	75	Twin Lieutenants, ...	75
The Horrors of Paris, ...	75	Annette, Lady of the Pearls,...	50
The Fallen Angel,...	75	Mohicans of Paris,..	50
Sketches in France,.	75	The Marriage Verdict,..	50
Isabel of Bavaria,....	75	The Corsican Brothers,..... .	50
Count of Moret,......... 50	George,... . 50	Buried Alive,.. ..	25

☞ Books sent, postage paid, on receipt of the Retail Price, by
T. B Peterson & Brothers, Philadelphia Pa

CHARLES DICKENS' WORKS.

☞ GREAT REDUCTION IN THEIR PRICES. ☜

PEOPLE'S DUODECIMO EDITION. ILLUSTRATED.

Reduced in price from $2.50 to $1 50 a volume

This edition is printed on fine paper, from large, clear type, leaded, that all can read, containing One Hundred and Eighty Illustrations on tinted paper, and each book is complete in one large duodecimo volume.

Our Mutual Friend,	. .Cloth, $1 50	Little Dorrit,	.. ..	Cloth, $1 50
Pickwick Papers,	.... Cloth, 1 50	Dombey and Son,	. .	Cloth, 1 50
Nicholas Nickleby,	Cloth, 1 50	Christmas Stories,...	.	Cloth, 1 50
Great Expectations,	. Cloth, 1 50	Sketches by "Boz,"	..	Cloth, 1 50
David Copperfield,	. Cloth, 1.50	Barnaby Rudge,..	.	Cloth, 1 50
Oliver Twist, ...	. .Cloth, 1.50	Martin Chuzzlewit,		Cloth, 1 50
Bleak House,	. .Cloth, 1 50	Old Curiosity Shop,	...	Cloth, 1 50
A Tale of Two Cities,	. Cloth, 1 50	Dickens' New Stories	.	Cloth, 1 50
American Notes; and The Uncommercial Traveler,......... .				Cloth, 1 50
Hunted Down; and other Reprinted Pieces,.		....		Cloth, 1 50
The Holly-Tree Inn; and other Stories, ...		....		Cloth, 1 50

Price of a set, in Black cloth, in nineteen volumes...	.	.. .	$28 00
" " Full sheep, Library style,..	.....	. . . .	38 00
" " Half calf, sprinkled edges,	.	..	47 00
" " Half calf, marbled edges,	.	. . .	53 00
" " Half calf, antique,..	. ..	... .	57 00
" " Half calf, full gilt backs, etc , ...		.. ..	57.00

ILLUSTRATED DUODECIMO EDITION.

Reduced in price from $2 00 to $1 50 a volume.

This edition is printed on the finest paper, from large, clear type, leaded, Long Primer in size, that all can read, the whole containing near Six Hundred full page Illustrations, printed on tinted paper from designs by Cruikshank, Phiz, Browne, Maclise, McLenan, and other artists. The following books are each contained in two volumes.

Our Mutual Friend,	Cloth, $3 00	Bleak House,..	Cloth, $3 00
Pickwick Papers,	Cloth, 3 00	Sketches by "Boz," .	Cloth, 3 00
Tale of Two Cities,	Cloth, 3 00	Barnaby Rudge, ..	Cloth, 3 00
Nicholas Nickleby	Cloth, 3 00	Martin Chuzzlewit, .	Cloth, 3 00
David Copperfield,	Cloth, 3 00	Old Curiosity Shop, ...	Cloth, 3 00
Oliver Twist,	......Cloth, 3 00	Little Dorrit	Cloth, 3 00
Christmas Stories,	. .Cloth, 3 00	Dombey and Son, . ..	Cloth, 3 00

The following are each complete in one volume, and are reduced in price from $2 50 to $1 50 a volume.

Great Expectations,	Cloth $1 50	Dickens' New Stories,.	Cloth, $1 50
American Notes, and The Uncommercial Traveler,		.. .	Cloth, 1 50
Hunted Down, and other Reprinted Pieces,		..	Cloth, 1 50
The Holly Tree Inn, and other Stories,		. .	Cloth, 1 50

...ice of a set, in thirty-three volumes, bound in cloth,	..		$49 00
" " Full sheep, Library style, .	. ..	.	66 00
" " Half calf antique,	. . ..	..	90 00
" " Half calf, full gilt backs, etc ,	. .	.	99 00

☞ books sent, postage paid, on receipt of the Retail Price, by
T. B. Peterson & Brothers, Philadelphia, Pa.

CHARLES DICKENS' WORKS.

ILLUSTRATED OCTAVO EDITION.

Reduced in price from $2 50 to $2.00 a volume.

This edition is printed from large type, double column, octavo page, each book being complete in one volume, the whole containing near Six Hundred Illustrations, by Cruikshank, Phiz, Browne, Maclise, and other artists.

Our Mutual Friend,......Cloth, $2 00	David Copperfield,... ...Cloth, $2 00
Pickwick Papers, ...Cloth, 2 00	Barnaby Rudge,.. .. ..Cloth, 2.00
Nicholas Nickleby, ...Cloth, 2 00	Martin Chuzzlewit, ... Cloth, 2 00
Great Expectations, ...Cloth, 2 00	Old Curiosity Shop, ...Cloth, 2.00
Lamplighter's Story, ...Cloth, 2.00	Christmas Stories...... ..Cloth, 2 00
Oliver Twist, ...Cloth, 2 00	Dickens' New Stories,...Cloth, 2.00
Bleak House, ...Cloth, 2 00	A Tale of Two Cities,....Cloth, 2.00
Little Dorrit,... .. ..Cloth, 2 00	American Notes and
Dombey and Son, ...Cloth, 2 00	Pic-Nic Papers,.... .. Cloth, 2 00
Sketches by "Boz,". ..Cloth, 2.00	

Price of a set, in Black cloth, in eighteen volumes,.. . .....$36 00
"   "   Full sheep, Library style,.... .... 45 00
"   "   Half calf, sprinkled edges, ... 55 00
"   "   Half calf, marbled edges, ... 62 00
"   "   Half calf, antique, ... 70 00
"   "   Half calf, full gilt backs, etc , ... 70.00

"NEW NATIONAL EDITION" OF DICKENS' WORKS.

This is the cheapest complete edition of the works of Charles Dickens, "Boz," published in the world, being contained in *seven large octavo volumes*, with a portrait of Charles Dickens, and other illustrations, the whole making nearly *six thousand very large double columned pages*, in large, clear type, and handsomely printed on fine white paper, and bound in the strongest and most substantial manner.

Price of a set, in Black cloth, in seven volumes,.. .. .. $20.00
"   "   Full sheep, Library style, ... 25 00
"   "   Half calf, antique,. 30 00
"   "   Half calf, full gilt back, etc., ... 30.00

CHEAP SALMON PAPER COVER EDITION.

Each book being complete in one large octavo volume.

Pickwick Papers..	35	Christmas Stories,..	25
Nicholas Nickleby, ...	35	The Haunted House, ...	25
Dombey and Son, ...	35	Uncommercial Traveler,..........	25
David Copperfield,..........	25	A House to Let, ...	25
Martin Chuzzlewit, ...	35	Perils of English Prisoners,.....	25
Old Curiosity Shop,......	25	Wreck of the Golden Mary, .	25
Oliver Twist..	25	Tom Tiddler's Ground,...	25
American Notes, ...	25	Our Mutual Friend, ...	35
Great Expectations,........	25	Bleak House, ...	35
Hard Times, ...	25	Little Dorrit, ...	35
A Tale of Two Cities,..	25	Joseph Grimaldi,.........	50
Somebody's Luggage,.............	25	The Pic-Nic Papers, ...	50
Message from the Sea,...	25	No Thoroughfare...	10
Barnaby Rudge,.....	25	Hunted Down, ...	25
Sketches by "Boz,"......	25	The Holly-Tree Inn,.......... . .	25
Mrs. Lirriper's Lodgings and Mrs. Lirriper's Legacy.			25
Mugby Junction and Dr. Marigold's Prescriptions, ...			25

☞ Books sent, postage paid, on receipt of the Retail Price, by

CHARLES LEVER'S BEST WORKS.

Charles O'Malley, ... 75 | Knight of Gwynne, ... 75
Harry Lorrequer,................. 75 | Arthur O'Leary, ... 75
Jack Hinton, ... 75 | Con Cregan, ... 75
Tom Burke of Ours,.............. 75 | Davenport Dunn,................. 75

Above are each in paper, or finer edition in cloth, price $2 00 each.

Horace Templeton,............... 75 | Kate O'Donoghue,.......... 75

MADAME GEORGE SAND'S WORKS.

Consuelo,. . ... 75 | Fanchon, the Cricket, paper, .. 1 00
Countess of Rudolstadt,.... .... 75 | Do.   do   cloth, 1 50
First and True Love, ... 75 | Indiana, a Love Story, paper, 1 50
The Corsair,......... .... 50 | Do   do.   cloth, . 1 75
Jealousy,   paper, ... 1 50 | Consuelo and Rudolstadt, both
Do.   cloth,... .. .. 1 75 | in one volume, cloth, ... 2 00

WILKIE COLLINS' BEST WORKS.

The Crossed Path, or Basil,... 1 50 | The Dead Secret. 12mo 1 50

The above are each in paper cover, or in cloth, price $1.75 each.

· Hide and Seek,........ ... . 75 | Mad Monkton,...... 50
After Dark......... . ... .. 75 | Sights a-Foot,.. 50
The Dead Secret. 8vo .... 75 | The Stolen Mask, ... 25
Above in cloth at $1.00 each. | The Yellow Mask, ... 25
The Queen's Revenge, ... 75 | Sister Rose, ... 25

MISS PARDOE'S WORKS.

Confessions of a Pretty Woman, 75 | Rival Beauties, ... 75
The Wife's Trials, ... 75 | Romance of the Harem, . .   75
The Jealous Wife,. 50

The five above books are also bound in one volume, cloth, for $4 00.

The Adopted Heir. One volume, paper, $1 50, or in cloth. $1 75
The Earl's Secret. One volume, paper, $1 50, or in cloth, ... 1 75

MRS. HENRY WOOD'S BOOKS.

Red Court Farm,...... .... 1 50 | Lord Oakburn's Daughters; or,
Ester's Folly.... .. .. 1 50 | the Earl's Heirs,.. . ... 1 50
St. Martin's Eve,.................. 1 50 | Squire Trevlyn's Heir , or,
Mildred Arkell. .... 1 50 | Trevlyn Hold. 1 50
Shadow of Ashlydyat, ... 1 50 | The Castle's Heir, or, Lady
Oswald Cray,..... .. .. 1 50 | Adelaide's Oath,.......... ...... 1 50
Verner's Pride,. 1 50

Above are each in paper cover, or each one in cloth, for $1 75 each.

The Mystery,..... ... . 75 | A Life's Secret,.. 50

Above are each in paper cover, or each one in cloth, for $1.00 each.

The Channings, ... 1 00 | Aurora Floyd. 75

Above are each in paper cover, or each one in cloth, for $1 50 each.

Oakville College,. .. .. 50 | Better for Worse, ... 75
The Runaway Match,. ... . 50 | Foggy Night at Offord. 25
The Lost Will, ... 50 | The Lawyer's Secret, ... 25
The Haunted Tower,. .... 50 | William Allan 25
The Lost Bank Note,......... .. . 75 | A Light and a Dark Christmas, 25

GEORGE W. M. REYNOLDS' WORKS.

Mysteries of Court of London,..	1 00	Mary Price, ...	1 00
Rose Foster. Sequel to it,.....	1 50	Eustace Quentin,...................	1 00
Caroline of Brunswick,..........	1 00	Joseph Wilmot,..................	1 00
Venetia Trelawney,......	1 00	Banker's Daughter,..............	1 00
Lord Saxondale,..........	1 00	Kenneth, ...	1 00
Count Christoval, ...	1 00	The Rye-House Plot,............	1 00
Rosa Lambert, ...	1 00	The Necromancer, ...	1 00

The above are each in paper cover, or in cloth, price $1.75 each.

The Opera Dancer,.................	75	The Soldier's Wife,..............	75
Child of Waterloo, ...	75	May Middleton, ...	75
Robert Bruce,.	75	Duke of Marchmont,............	75
Discarded Queen,..................	75	Massacre of Glencoe,............	75
The Gipsy Chief........	75	Queen Joanna, Court Naples,	75
Mary Stuart, Queen of Scots,...	75	Pickwick Abroad,...........	75
Wallace, the Hero of Scotland,	1 00	Parricide,......	75
Isabella Vincent,................	75	The Ruined Gamester, ...	50
Vivian Bertram,..................	75	Ciprina; or, the Secrets of a	
Countess of Lascelles, ...	75	Picture Gallery, ...	50
Loves of the Harem,.	75	Life in Paris, ...	50
Ellen Percy, ...	75	Countess and the Page,..........	50
Agnes Evelyn,..................	75	Edgar Montrose,.................	50

WAVERLEY NOVELS. BY SIR WALTER SCOTT.
CHEAPEST EDITION IN THE WORLD.

Ivanhoe,.	20	The Betrothed,......................	20
Rob Roy, ...	20	Peveril of the Peak,............	20
Guy Mannering, ...	20	Quentin Durward,.	20
The Antiquary......	20	Red Gauntlet,...................	20
Old Mortality	20	The Talisman,..	20
Heart of Mid Lothian,......	20	Woodstock, ...	20
Bride of Lammermoor,..........	20	Highland Widow, etc,......	20
Waverley.	20	The Fair Maid of Perth, ...	20
St. Ronan's Well, ...	20	Anne of Geierstein, ...	20
Kenilworth,.......	20	Count Robert of Paris,..........	20
The Pirate,.........................	20	The Black Dwarf and Legend	
The Monastery, ...	20	of Montrose,...	20
The Abbot,.......	20	Castle Dangerous, and Sur-	
The Fortunes of Nigel,..........	20	geon's Daughter, ...	20

Above edition is the cheapest in the world, and is complete in twenty-six volumes, price Twenty cents each, or Five Dollars for the complete set.

A finer edition is also published of each of the above, complete in twenty six volumes, price Fifty cents each, or Ten Dollars for the complete set.

Moredun. A Tale of 1210, ...	50	Scott's Poetical Works, ...	5 00
Tales of a Grandfather, ...	25	Life of Scott, cloth,.	2 50

"NEW NATIONAL EDITION" OF "WAVERLEY NOVELS."

This edition of the Waverley Novels is contained in *five large octavo volumes* with a portrait of Sir Walter Scott, making *four thousand very large double columned pages*, in good type, and handsomely printed on the finest of white paper, and bound in the strongest and most substantial manner.

Price of a set, in Black cloth, in five volumes,......		$15 00
" " Full sheep, Library style,..........		17 50
" " Half calf, antique, or Half calf, gilt,.......... ...		25 00

The Complete Prose and Poetical Works of Sir Walter Scott, are also published in ten volumes, bound in half calf, for... . ...$60 00

☞ Books sent postage paid on receipt of the Retail Price, by

HUMOROUS AMERICAN WORKS.

Beautifully Illustrated by Felix O. C. Darley.

Major Jones' Courtship,.........	75	Drama in Pokerville...	75
Major Jones' Travels, ...	75	The Quorndon Hounds, ...	75
Simon Suggs' Adventures and		My Shooting Box, ...	75
Travels, ...	75	Warwick Woodlands,....	75
Major Jones' Chronicles of		The Deer Stalkers, ...	75
Pineville, ...	75	Peter Ploddy...	75
Polly Peablossom's Wedding,..	75	Adventures of Captain Farrago,	75
Mysteries of the Backwoods,...	75	Major O Regan's Adventures,.	75
Widow Rugby's Husband, ...	75	Sol. Smith's Theatrical Appren-	
Big Bear of Arkansas.	75	tice-ship.. .	75
Western Scenes, or, Life on		Sol. Smith's Theatrical Jour	
the Prairie,......	75	ney-Work. .. .	75
Streaks of Squatter Life. . .	75	The Quarter Race in Kentucky,	75
Pickings from the Picayune,. .	75	Aunt Patty's Scrap Bag. ..	75
Stray Subjects, Arrested and		Percival Mayberry's Adven-	
Bound Over,....	75	tures and Travels,. ...	75
Louisiana Swamp Doctor, ...	75	Sam Slick's Yankee Yarns and	
Charcoal Sketches, ...	75	Yankee Letters,. . ..	75
Misfortunes of Peter Faber. ...	75	Adventures of Fudge Fumble,	75
Yankee among the Mermaids,..	75	American Joe Miller, ...	50
New Orleans Sketch Book,. ...	75	Following the Drum, ...	50

D'ISRAELI'S WORKS.

Henrietta Temple, ...	50	Young Duke,...	50
Vivian Grey,.....	75	Miriam Alroy, ...	50
Venetia,.........	50	Contarina Fleming, ...	50

FRANK FAIRLEGH'S WORKS.

Frank Fairlegh,..	75	Harry Racket Scapegrace,.....	75
Lewis Arundel.....	75	Tom Racquet,..	75

Finer editions of above are also issued in cloth, at $1 75 each.

Harry Coverdale's Courtship, 1 50 | Lorrimer Littlegood, ... 1 50

The above are each in paper cover, or in cloth, price $1 75 each.

C. J. PETERSON'S WORKS.

The Old Stone Mansion,.. . 1 50 | Kate Aylesford. 1 50

The above are each in paper cover, or in cloth, price $1 75 each.

Cruising in the Last War, ...	75	Grace Dudley ; or, Arnold at	
Valley Farm, ...	25	Saratoga, ...	50

JAMES A. MAITLAND'S WORKS.

The Old Patroon,. 1 50		Diary of an Old Doctor,........ 1 50	
The Watchman,.................. 1 50		Sartaroe,.. . . .. 1 50	
The Wanderer,.... . ... 1 50		The Three Cousins,. 1 50	
The Lawyer's Story, ... 1 50			

The above are each in paper cover, or in cloth, price $1 75 each.

WILLIAM H. MAXWELL'S WORKS.

Wild Sports of the West, ...	75	Brian O'Lynn,....................	75
Stories of Waterloo,.....	75		

☞ Books sent, postage paid, on receipt of the Retail Price, by
T. B. Peterson & Brothers, Philadelphia, Pa.

WILLIAM HARRISON AINSWORTH'S WORKS.

Life of Jack Sheppard, ...	50	Tower of London,............... ..	1 50
Life of Guy Fawkes, ...	75	Miser's Daughter, ...	1 00
Above in 1 vol , cloth, $1.75.		Above in cloth $1.75 each.	
Court of the Stuarts,.....	75	Life of Grace O'Malley,....	50
Windsor Castle.........	75	Life of Henry Thomas, ...	25
The Star Chamber,......	75	Desperadoes of the New World,	25
Old St Paul's,.......	75	Life of Ninon De L'Enclos,....	25
Court of Queen Anne,..	50	Life of Arthur Spring, ...	25
Life of Dick Turpin,..	50	Life of Mrs. Whipple and Jes-	
Life of Davy Crockett,...........	50	see Strang, ...	25

G. P. R. JAMES'S BEST BOOKS.

Lord Montague's Page,.........	1 50	The Cavalier, ...	1 50

The above are each in paper cover, or in cloth, price $1 75 each.

The Man in Black,.......... . .	75	Arrah Neil.	75
Mary of Burgundy, ...	75	Eva St. Clair, ...	50

DOW'S PATENT SERMONS.

Dow's Patent Sermons, 1st Series, $1.00; cloth,.	1 50	Dow's Patent Sermons, 3d Series, $1.00; cloth,.......... 1 50
Dow's Patent Sermons, 2d Series, $1.00; cloth,..........	1 50	Dow's Patent Sermons, 4th Series, $1.00; cloth,.......... 1 50

SAMUEL C. WARREN'S BEST BOOKS.

Ten Thousand a Year,...paper,	1 50	Diary of a Medical Student,..	75
Do. do. cloth,	2 00		

Q. K. PHILANDER DOESTICKS' WORKS.

Doesticks' Letters,...........	1 50	The Elephant Club, ...	1 50
Plu-Ri-Bus-Tah,..................	1 50	Witches of New York, ...	1 50

The above are each in paper cover, or in cloth, price $1.75 each.

GREEN'S WORKS ON GAMBLING.

Gambling Exposed, ...	1 50	The Reformed Gambler,.........	1 50
The Gambler's Life, ...	1 50	Secret Band of Brothers.	1 50

Above are each in paper cover, or each one in cloth, for $1 75 each.

MISS ELLEN PICKERING'S WORKS.

The Grumbler,..	75	Who Shall be Heir?.	38
Marrying for Money, ...	75	The Squire,........	38
Poor Cousin, ...	50	Ellen Wareham,..................	38
Kate Walsingham, ...	50	Nan Darrel,.............. ...	38
Orphan Niece,..	50		

CAPTAIN MARRYATT'S WORKS.

Jacob Faithful,...	50	Newton Forster, ...	50
Japhet in Search of a Father,..	50	King's Own	50
Phantom Ship......................	50	Pirate and Three Cutters,......	50
Midshipman Easy,.....	50	Peter Simple,..................	50
Pacha of Many Tales,....	50	Perceval Keene,..................	50
Frank Mildmay, Naval Officer,	50	Poor Jack.	50
Snarleyow,.............	50	Sea King,.........................	50

☞ Books sent, postage paid, on receipt of the Retail Price, by

EUGENE SUE'S GREAT WORKS.

Wandering Jew, ... 1 50 | First Love, ... 50
Mysteries of Paris,.. . . 1 50 | Woman's Love, .. . 50
Martin, the Foundling, . .. 1 50 | Female Bluebeard, . 50
Above in cloth at $2 00 each. | Man-of-War's-Man, . 50
Life and Adventures of Raoul De Surville,. 25

MRS. GREY'S WORKS.

Cousin Harry, ... 1 50 | The Little Beauty,..... ... . 1 50
The above are each in paper cover, or in cloth, price $1 75 each.

Gipsy's Daughter, . . 50 | Young Prima Donna, ... 50
Old Dower House, ... 50 | Hyacinthe, ... 25
Belle of the Family, . .. 50 | Alice Seymour.. . 25
Duke and Cousin,.. . . 50 | Mary Seaham. . . 75
The Little Wife, ... 50 | Passion and Principle, ... 75
Lena Cameron, ... 50 | The Flirt. 75
Sybil Lennard . .. 50 | Good Society, . 75
Manœuvring Mother .. . . 50 | Lion-Hearted, ... 75
Baronet's Daughters, ... 50 |

J. F. SMITH'S WORKS.

The Usurer's Victim, or, | Adelaide Waldegrave; or, the
Thomas Balscombe.... .. ... 75 | Trials of a Governess,. 75

REVOLUTIONARY TALES.

The Brigand. . ... 50 | Old Put: or, Days of 1776, ... 50
Ralph Runnion, . . . 50 | Legends of Mexico. 50
Seven Brothers of Wyoming.. 50 | Grace Dudley. 50
The Rebel Bride, ... 50 | The Guerilla Chief, . .. 75
The Flying Artillerist. . 50 | The Quaker Soldier, paper, .. 1 50
Wau-nan-gee, ... 50 | do. do. cloth, . . 1 75

EMERSON BENNETT'S WORKS.

The Border Rover, ... 1 50 | Bride of the Wilderness,. . 1 50
Clara Moreland. . .. . . 1 50 | Ellen Norbury, ... 1 50
Viola, or Adventures in the | The Forged Will, ... 1 50
Far South-West, ... 1 50 | Kate Clarendon, ... 1 50
The above are each in paper cover, or in cloth, price $1 75 each.

The Heiress of Belletonte, and | Pioneer's Daughter and the
Walde-Warren,.. ... . 75 | Unknown Countess. 75

T. S. ARTHUR'S HOUSEHOLD NOVELS.

The Lost Bride, ... 50 | The Divorced Wife.. . 50
The Two Brides .. .. 50 | Pride and Prudence 50
Love in a Cottage, ... 50 | Agnes, or the Possessed. 50
Love in High Life, ... 50 | Lucy Sandford . . . 50
Year after Marriage, .. . 50 | The Banker's Wife. . . 50
The Lady at Home, . . . 50 | The Two Merchants, . . 50
Cecelia Howard, ... 50 | Trial and Triumph, . 50
Orphan Children,.. . ... 50 | The Iron Rule, ... 50
Debtor's Daughter,.. . .... 50 | Insubordination or the Shoe-
May Moreton. .. . 50 | maker's Daughters, ... 50

Six Nights with the Washingtonians With nine original Illustrations By Cruikshank. One volume, cloth $1 75 or in paper $1 50
Lizzy Glenn; or, the Trials of a Seamstress. Cloth $1 75, or paper, 1.50

EXCITING SEA TALES.

Adventures of Ben Brace, ..	75	Gallant Tom, ...	50
Jack Adams, the Mutineer, ..	75	Harry Helm.........	50
Jack Ariel's Adventures,. ...	75	Harry Tempest, ...	50
Petrel, or, Life on the Ocean,.	75	Rebel and Rover,....	50
Life of Paul Periwinkle,. ..	75	Man-of-War's-Man,.'	50
Life of Tom Bowling,.......	75	Dark Shades of City Life,......	25
Percy Effingham,....	75	The Rats of the Seine,..	25
Cruising in the Last War,......	75	Charles Ransford,............ . .	25
Red King,......................	50	The Iron Cross,.............	25
The Corsair	'0	The River Pirates, ...	25
The Doomed Ship, ...	50	The Pirate's Son,..............	25
The Three Pirates,.	50	Jacob Faithful,.....................	50
The Flying Dutchman, ...	50	Phantom Ship,....................	50
The Flying Yankee,...........	50	Midshipman Easy, ...	50
The Yankee Middy, ...	50	Pacha of Many Tales,...	50
The Gold Seekers, ...	50	Naval Officer, ...	50
The King's Cruisers..	50	Snarleyow, ...	50
Life of Alexander Tardy,....... ·	50	Newton Forster,..	50
Red Wing, ...	50	King's Own, ...	50
Yankee Jack, ...	50	Japhet, ...	50
Yankees in Japan, ...	50	Pirate and Three Cutters,.......	50
Morgan, the Buccaneer,.........	50	Peter Simple, ...	50
Jack Junk, ...	50	Percival Keene, ...	50
Davis, the Pirate, ...	50	Poor Jack, ...	50
Valdez, the Pirate,........	50	Sea King, ...	50

GEORGE LIPPARD'S GREAT BOOKS.

The Quaker City,......	1 50	The Empire City, ...	75
Paul Ardenheim, ...	1 50	Memoirs of a Preacher,....	75
Blanche of Brandywine, ...	1 50	The Nazarene, ...	75
Washington and his Generals;		Washington and his Men, ..	75
or, Legends of the American		Legends of Mexico, ...	50
Revolution.......................	1 50	The Entranced, ...	25
Mysteries of Florence.	1 00	The Robbers, ...	25
Above in cloth at $2.00 each.		The Bank Director's Son,......	25

MILITARY NOVELS. BY BEST AUTHORS.

With Illuminated Military Covers, in five Colors.

Charles O'Malley, ...	75	The Three Guardsmen, ...	75
Jack Hinton, the Guardsman,	75	Twenty Years After, ...	75
The Knight of Gwynne, ...	75	Bragelonne, Son of Athos, ...	75
Harry Lorrequer	75	Forty-five Guardsmen, ...	75
Tom Burke of Ours,.......... . .	75	Tom Bowling's Adventures, ..	75
Arthur O Leary, ...	75	Life of Robert Bruce, .. .	75
Con Cregan,...	75	The Gipsy Chief,.......	75
Kate O'Donoghue, ...	75	Massacre of Glencoe,......	75
Horace Templeton,.	75	Life of Guy Fawkes, ...	75
Davenport Dunn, ...	75	Child of Waterloo..	75
Jack Adams' Adventures, . .	75	Adventures of Ben Brace,......	75
Valentine Vox............... .	75	Life of Jack Ariel,...	75
Twin Lieutenants, ...	75	Wallace, the Hero of Scotland,	1 00
Stories of Waterloo,...	75	Following the Drum,.	50
The Soldier's Wife,..	75	The Conscript, a Tale of War.	
Guerilla Chief,........	75	By Alexander Dumas, ...	1 50

Books sent, postage paid, on receipt of the Retail Price, by
T. B. Peterson & Brothers, Philadelphia, Pa.

GUSTAVE AIMARD'S WORKS.

The White Scalper,	50	Trapper's Daughter,	75
The Freebooters,	50	The Tiger Slayer,	75
The Prairie Flower,	75	The Gold Seekers,	75
The Indian Scout,	75	The Rebel Chief,	75
The Trail Hunter,	75	The Smuggler Chief,	75
The Indian Chief,	75	The Border Rifles,	75
The Red Track,	75	Pirates of the Prairies,	75

LANGUAGES WITHOUT A MASTER.

French without a Master,	40	German without a Master,	40
Spanish without a Master,	40	Italian without a Master,	40
Latin without a Master,	40		

The above five works on the French, German, Spanish, Latin, and Italian Languages, whereby any one or all of these Languages can be learned by any one without a Teacher, with the aid of this book, by A H Monteith, Esq., is also published in finer style, in one volume, bound, price, $1.75.

HARRY COCKTON'S WORKS.

Sylvester Sound,	75	The Sisters,	75
Valentine Vox, in paper,	75	The Steward,	75
do. finer edition, cloth,	2 00	Percy Effingham,	75

WAR NOVELS. BY HENRY MORFORD.

Shoulder-Straps,	1 50	The Days of Shoddy. A History of the late War,	1 50
The Coward,	1 50		

Above are each in paper cover, or each one in cloth, for $1.75 each.

LIVES OF HIGHWAYMEN.

Life of John A. Murrel,	50	Life of Davy Crockett,	50
Life of Joseph T Hare,	50	Life of Sybil Grey,	50
Life of Col Monroe Edwards,	50	Life of Jonathan Wild,	25
Life of Jack Sheppard,	50	Life of Henry Thomas,	25
Life of Jack Rann,	50	Life of Arthur Spring,	25
Life of Dick Turpin,	50	Life of Jack Ketch,	25
Life of Helen Jewett,	50	Life of Ninon De L'Enclos,	25
Desperadoes of the New World,	50	Lives of the Felons,	25
Mysteries of New Orleans,	50	Life of Mrs Whipple,	25
The Robber's Wife,	50	Life of Biddy Woodland,	25
Obi, or, Three Fingered Jack,	50	Life of Mother Brownrigg,	25
Kit Clayton,	50	Dick Parker, the Pirate,	25
Life of Tom Waters,	50	Life of Mary Bateman,	25
Nat Blake,	50	Life of Captain Blood,	25
Bill Horton,	50	Capt. Blood and the Beagles,	25
Galloping Gus,	50	Sixteen Stringed Jack's Fight	
Life & Trial of Antoine Probst,	50	for Life,	25
Ned Hastings,	50	Highwayman's Avenger,	25
Eveleen Wilson,	50	Life of Raoul De Surville,	25
Diary of a Pawnbroker,	50	Life of Rody the Rover,	25
Silver and Pewter,	50	Life of Galloping Dick,	25
Sweeney Todd,	50	Life of Guy Fawkes,	75
Life of Grace O'Malley,	50	Life and Adventures of Vidocq,	1 50

MILITARY AND ARMY BOOKS.

Ellsworth's Zouave Drill,	25	U S Light Infantry Drill,	25
U S Government Infantry & Rifle Tactics,	25	The Soldier's Companion,	25
		The Soldier's Guide,	25

Books sent postage paid on Receipt of the Retail Price by

WORKS AT 75 CENTS. BY BEST AUTHORS.

Hans Breitman's Party. With other Ballads New and Enlarged
  Edition, printed on Tinted paper. By Charles G. Leland,........ ... 75
Webster and Hayne's Speeches in Reply to Colonel Foote,............. 75
The Brigand; or, the Demon of the North. By Victor Hugo,......... 75
Roanoke, or, Where is Utopia? By C. H. Wiley. Illustrated, ... 75

Banditti of the Prairie,..........	75	Flirtations in America............	75
Tom Racquet,......................	75	The Coquette,......	75
Red Indians of Newfoundland,	75	Thackeray's Irish Sketch Book,	75
Salathiel, by Croly, ...	75	Whitehall,.....................	75
Corinne; or, Italy,.	75	The Beautiful Nun,.............	75
Ned Musgrave	75	Mysteries of Three Cities,......	75
Aristocracy, ...	75	Genevra. By Miss Fairfield,..	75
Inquisition in Spain, ...	75	New Hope; or, the Rescue,.....	75
Elsie's Married Life,.............	75	Crock of Gold. By Tupper,...	75
Leyton Hall. By Mark Lemon,	75	Twins and Heart. By Tupper,	75

WORKS AT 50 CENTS. BY BEST AUTHORS.

The Woman in Red. A Companion to the "Woman in Black,"...... 50
Twelve Months of Matrimony. By Emelie F. Carlen.... 50

Leah, or the Forsaken, ...	50	The Admiral's Daughter, ...	50
The Greatest Plague of Life,...	50	The American Joe Miller,......	50
Clifford and the Actress, ...	50	Ella Stratford,..	50
Two Lovers, ...	50	Josephine, by Grace Aguilar,..	50
Ryan's Mysteries of Marriage,	50	The Fortune Hunter, ...	50
The Orphans and Caleb Field,.	50	The Orphan Sisters,............	50
Moreton Hall,........	50	Robert Oaklands; or, the Out-	
Bell Brandon, ...	50	cast Orphan,..	50
Sybil Grey,..	50	Abednego, the Money Lender,.	50
Female Life in New York,......	50	Jenny Ambrose,.........	50
Agnes Grey, ...	50	Father Tom and the Pope, in	
Diary of a Physician,...........	50	cloth gilt, 75 cents, or paper,	50
The Emigrant Squire, ...	50	The Romish Confessional	50
The Monk, by Lewis, ...	50	Victims of Amusements, ...	50
The Beautiful French Girl, ..	50	Violet, ...	50
Father Clement, paper, ...	50	Alieford, a Family History, . .	50
do. do. cloth,..	75	General Scott's $5 Portrait....	1 00
Miser's Heir, paper, ...	50	Henry Clay's $5 Portrait,......	1 00
do. do cloth,.............	75	Tangarua, a Poem,.....	1 00

WORKS AT 25 CENTS. BY BEST AUTHORS.

Aunt Margaret's Trouble, ...	25	The Mysteries of Bedlam,. ...	25
The Woman in Grey,.	25	The Nobleman's Daughter,,	25
The Deformed, ...	25	Madison's Exposition of Odd	
Two Prima Donnas,..	25	Fellowship, ...	25
The Mysterious Marriage, ...	25	Ghost Stories. Illustrated, ...	25
Jack Downing's Letters, ...	25	Ladies' Science of Etiquette,...	25
The Mysteries of a Convent, ..	25	The Abbey of Innismoyle,......	25
Rose Warrington, ...	25	Gliddon's Ancient Egypt	25
The Iron Cross, ...	25	Philip in Search of a Wife,.....	25
Charles Ransford, ...	25	Rifle Shots, ...	25

THE SHAKSPEARE NOVELS.

The Secret Passion, ...	1 00	Shakspeare and his Friends,... 1 00
The Youth of Shakspeare,......	1 00	

  The three above Books are also published complete in one large octavo
volume, bound in cloth. Price Four Dollars.

PETERSONS' ILLUMINATED STORIES.

Each Book being in an "ILLUMINATED COVER," in five colors, full of Illustrations. This is the most saleable series of 25 cent books ever printed.

Rebel and Rover,	25	Ninon De L'Enclos' Life,	25
First Love	25	The Iron Cross,	25
The Two Merchant,	25	Buddy Woodhull the Beautiful	
A Year After Marriage,	25	Haymaker,	25
Love in High Life,	25	The River Pirates,	25
The Divorced Wife,	25	Dark Shades of City Life,	25
The Debtor's Daughter,	25	The Rats of the Seine,	25
The Lily at Home,	25	Mysteries of Bedlam,	25
Mary Moreton,	25	Charles Ransford,	25
The Two Brides,	25	Mysteries of a Convent,	25
Dick Parker,	25	The Mysterious Marriage,	25
Jack Ketch,	25	Capt Blood, the Highwayman,	25
Mother Browning,	25	Capt Blood and the Beagles,	25
Galloping Dick,	25	Highwayman's Avenger,	25
Mary Bateman,	25	Rody the Rover's Adventures,	25
Rinaldo Surville	25	Sixteen Stringed Jack's Fight	
Life of Harry Thomas,	25	for Life,	25
Mrs Whipple & Jesse Strang's		Ghost Stories. Illustrated,	25
Adventures,	25	Arthur Spring.	25
Jonathan Wild's Adventures,	25	The Valley Farm,	25

USEFUL BOOKS FOR ALL.

Lady's and Gentleman's Science of Etiquette. By Count D'Orsay and Countess de Caldabrella, with their portraits,	50
Ladies' One Thousand and Ten Things Worth Knowing.	50
Knowlson's Complete Farrier and Horse Doctor,	25
Knowlson's Complete Cow and Cattle Doctor,	25
The Complete Kitchen and Fruit Gardener.	25
The Complete Florist and Flower Gardener,	25
Arthur's Receipts for Preserving Fruits, etc,	12

LIVES OF GENERALS AND OTHER NOTED MEN.

Moore's Life of Hon Schuyler Colfax By Rev. A Y. Moore, of South Bend With a Fine Steel Portrait. One vol. cloth. Price .	1 50
The Lives of Grant and Colfax. With life-like portraits of each, and other engravings Cloth, $1.00 , or in paper cover,	75
Illustrated Life, Speeches, Martyrdom and Funeral of President Abraham Lincoln. Cloth, $1.75 ; or in paper cover,	1 50
Life and Services of General Sheridan. Cloth, $1 00 , or in paper,	75
Life, Battles, Reports, and Public Services of General George B. McClellan Price in paper 50 cents, or in cloth	75
Life and Public Services of General George G. Meade, the Hero of Gettysburg.	25
Life and Public Services of General Benjamin F. Butler, the Hero of New Orleans,	25
Life of President Andrew Johnson. Cloth, $1 00 ; or in paper.	75
The Impeachment and Trial of Andrew Johnson, cheap paper cover edition, price 50 cents, or a finer edition, bound in cloth, price	1 50
Trial of the Assassins and Conspirators for the murder of President Abraham Lincoln Cloth, $1 50 ; or cheap edition in paper cover,	50
Lives of Horatio Seymour and Francis P Blair, Jr Complete in one duodecimo volume. Price 50 cents in paper, or in cloth,	75
Life of Archbishop Hughes, first Archbishop of New York,	25

☞ Books sent, postage paid, on receipt of the Retail Price by

LIEBIG'S WORKS ON CHEMISTRY.

Agricultural Chemistry,..........	25	Liebig's celebrated Letters on	
Animal Chemistry,..............	25	the Potato Disease,...........	25

Liebig's Complete Works on Chemistry, is also issued in one large octavo volume, bound in cloth. Price Two Dollars.

SIR E. L. BULWER'S NOVELS.

The Roue, ...	50	The Courtier, ...	25
The Oxonians,.................	50	Falkland,.	25

DR. HOLLICK'S WORKS.

Dr. Hollick's great work on the Anatomy and Physiology of the Human Figure, with colored dissected plates of the Human Figure, 1 25
Dr. Hollick's Family Physician, a Pocket Guide for Everybody,..... 25

GEORGE FRANCIS TRAIN'S SPEECHES.

Union Speeches. In 2 vols., each	25	Downfall of England,...........	10
Speech to the Fenians,.	25	Slavery and Emancipation,.....	10

REV. CHAS. WADSWORTH'S SERMONS.

America's Mission,.......	25	A Thanksgiving Sermon,.......	15
Thankfulness and Character,...	25	Politics in Religion,........	12
Henry Ward Beecher on War and Emancipation, ...			15
Rev. William T. Brantley's Union Sermon,.......			15

EXPOSITIONS OF SECRET ORDERS, ETC.

Odd Fellowship Exposed,.......	13	Dr. Berg's Answer to Arch-	
Sons of Malta Exposed, ...	13	bishop Hughes, ...	13
Life of Rev. John N. Maffit,...	13	Dr. Berg on the Jesuits,.........	13

RIDDELL'S MODEL ARCHITECT.

Architectural Designs of Model Country Residences. By John Riddell, Practical Architect. Illustrated with twenty-two full page Front Elevations, colored, with forty-four Plates of Ground Plans, including the First and Second Stories, with plans of the stories, full specifications of all the articles used, and estimate of price. Price Fifteen Dollars a copy.

GOOD BOOKS FOR EVERYBODY.

Southern Life, or, Inside Views of Slavery,............. .... 1 00
The Rich Men of Philadelphia, Income Tax List of Residents,...... 1 00
Childbirth. Its pains lessened and its perils obviated. Showing that the pains of childbirth may be mitigated, if not entirely prevented, 1 00
Peterson's Complete Coin Book, containing fac-similes of all the Coins in the World, with the U. S. Mint value of each coin......... 1 00
New Card of Stamp Duties, approved by the last Acts of Congress,...... 15
Political Lyrics. New Hampshire and Nebraska. Illustrated....... 12

CHRISTY & WHITE'S SONG BOOKS.

Christy & Wood's Song Book,.	10	Serenader's Song Book,...	10
Melodeon Song Book,...........	10	Budworth's Songs.....	10
Plantation Melodies.	10	Christy and White's Complete	
Ethiopian Song Book, ...	10	Ethiopian Melodies. Cloth,	1 00

CURVED-POINT STEEL PENS.

The Slip Pen,	-	-	-	per dozen .25, per gross,	$2.50
The Barrel Pen,	-	-	-	per " .50, "	5 00
Magnum Bonum Pen,	-	-	-	per " .75, "	8.00

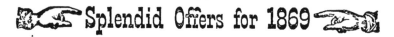

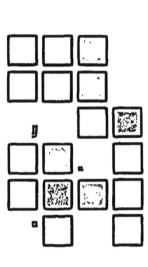

Lightning Source UK Ltd.
Milton Keynes UK
UKHW020634170822
407432UK00006B/884